Writing section by Amanda Jeffries

Straightforward

Advanced **Student's Book**

MACMILLAN

CONTENTS

	Reading & Listening	Speaking	Writing	
			Student's Book	Workbook
1A	R Three extracts on change	Discussing the effects of change	An autobiography p126	Writing an autobiography: time expressions, describing your family, verb-noun collocations
1B	L Radio programme about starting at a new job	Discussing the first day at a new job		
1C	R *Growing up on television*	Discussing different ages		
1D	L The quarterlife crisis	Roleplay: life changes **Did you know?** Age UK		
2A	R Three articles on improving memory	Discussing ways to improve memory		Writing a biography: phrases in apposition, future in the past, time phrases, writing a biography of a famous person
2B	L Interview with Dominic O'Brien	Performing and discussing a memory technique		
2C	R *The rise of the bicycle*	Ranking and discussing methods of transport		
2D	L Dialogue about museums	Roleplay: presenting and discussing proposals for a new national museum **Did you know?** Trafalger Square statues		
3A	R *Enough*	Discussing 'enoughness'	An article p128	Writing a website article: writing definitions, making a deduction, describing cause & effect
3B	L Radio programme about a recycling initiative	Comparing and contrasting photos showing rubbish **Did you know?** PlasTax		
3C	R *Me and my big mouth*	Roleplay: Sonya Thomas interview		
3D	L Radio programme about the island of Nauru	Discussing island life		
4A	R Three blogs	Describing and discussing complaint situations		Writing a blog: narrative expressions, explaining consequences in the past, writing a blog about an embarrassing incident
4B	L Interview about problems with the voice	Discussing how to protect your voice		
4C	R *Treated by the King's Speech therapist*	Ranking performance activities		
4D	L How to write speeches	Making a speech **Did you know?** Queen's Speech & State of the Union Address		
5A	R *Ingvar Kamprad: leader of the flatpack*	Talking about internationally-known entrepreneurs	A work email p130	Writing a work email: formal and informal style, making arrangements, making requests
5B	L Interview with Paddy Radcliffe	Making a product pitch to investors		
5C	R *A woman's work is never done*	Roleplay: deciding on a housework rota		
5D	L Five people talk about the Sex Discrimination Act	**Did you know?** Women in the Anglican Communion		
6A	R *There's more than one way to stay in shape*	Ranking leisure activities		Writing an email to a friend: invitations & responses, writing an email of invitation to a social event
6B	L The history of healthcare products	Discussing health problems		
6C	R *Natasha's Story*	Discussing international adoptions		
6D	L Interview about a babysitting agency	Choosing the best alternatives in babysitting situations **Did you know?** Attitudes to children in the UK		

	Reading & Listening	Speaking	Writing Student's Book	Workbook
7A	**R** *A new broom*	Discussing misbehaviour at school	A narrative p132	Writing a narrative: using narrative tenses, linking events, describing emotion
7B	**L** Dialogue about rudeness	Discussing good and bad behaviour Selecting posters for a national campaign		
7C	**R** *A missing person*	Ranking and comparing books		
7D	**L** Radio news reports	Discussing law breaking **Did you know?** Canadian Mounties		
8A	**R** Mr Hilditch & Robert and Lizzie	Describing people's personality and appearance		Writing a description: the five senses, participle phrases, writing a description of a visit
8B	**L** Dialogue about birth order	Discussing quotations about sisterhood **Did you know?** Famous American siblings		
8C	**R** *End of a friendship*	Discussing relationships		
8D	**L** Six people talk about being single	Discussing compatibility		
9A	**R** *The city of tomorrow*	Submitting and presenting a plan for a new town	A letter of complaint p134	Writing a letter of complaint: explaining the results of problems, articles
9B	**L** Radio programme about squatting	Roleplay: viewing a property **Did you know?** Listed buildings in the UK		
9C	**R** *A happy marriage*	Selecting holiday activities		
9D	**L** Dialogue about experimental travel	Ranking travel options		
10A	**R** *The poet in the sky*	Discussing endurance races		Writing a letter of thanks: expressions of thanks, explaining why you are grateful, writing a letter of thanks
10B	**L** Six people talk about success	Discussing views about success		
10C	**R** A true story about flying in storm clouds	Discussing problematic situations **Did you know?** Tornados		
10D	**L** A stabbing incident	Ordering and describing a picture story		
11A	**R** *I wandered lonely as a cloud*	Romanticism **Did you know?** Romanticism	An essay p136	Writing an essay (1): expressing a viewpoint, arguing against a viewpoint
11B	**L** Interview with Will Ramsay	Selecting artworks for buildings		
11C	**R** *The quietest place on Earth*	Describing the thoughts of people in photos		
11D	**L** Six people talk about music in different situations	Roleplay: neighbours discuss music problem		
12A	**L** Twelve scientific explanations	Discussing science questions **Did you know?** Science in schools		Writing an essay (2): result clauses, writing an essay
12B	**R** An extract from a science fiction story	Submitting and presenting a project for a competition		
12C	**L** Radio discussion about technology in sport	Debating technology in the home		
12D		Ranking and selecting photos **Did you know?** Revision quiz		

1A | All change

VOCABULARY & SPEAKING: change

1 Work in pairs. Discuss the questions.

- Which of these do you know how to change?
  - a nappy • a tyre • a light bulb • a plug
- Which, if any, of these would you like to change? Why or why not?
  - your name • your image • your lifestyle
- What changes, if any, would you make to the following? Why?
  - your home • your school or workplace

2 Complete the sentences with the correct form of a verb in the box.

adapt   alter   convert   shift
switch   transfer   transform   vary

1 I have no idea what the current rate is for _____ my country's **currency into** sterling.
2 I need to _____ my **diet** more – I always eat the same things.
3 I often channel-hop when I watch TV, _____ between **channels** to see what's on.
4 I don't _____ **easily to new situations**.
5 I get my mother to _____ my **clothes** if they don't fit properly.
6 The internet has **radically** _____ my **life**.
7 I cannot understand why such vast sums of money are involved when a **football player** _____ **from one club to another.**
8 I think the focus of language lessons should _____ **away from** grammar and **towards** more vocabulary learning.

3 Work in pairs. Discuss the sentences in exercise 2. How true are they for you?

READING

1 Read the extracts A–C and answer the questions.

1 What type of change or changes does each extract illustrate?
2 Where might you expect to find each extract? Give reasons for your opinions.

2 Match the highlighted words and expressions in the extracts to the definitions 1–9. The verbs appear below in the infinitive form.

1 waste
2 not happen as planned
3 focus on
4 save for later use
5 be independent of
6 combine
7 be unable to deal with
8 come to appear in
9 involved in a difficult situation

3 Read the extracts again and answer the questions.

Extract A
1 In what way do the protagonists of *The Romanov Bride* differ?
2 What, according to the extract, are the author's strengths?

Extract B
1 Why does Tom consider he and Lou were irresponsible?
2 Why did he decide to become a stay-at-home father?

Extract C
1 What explanation does the writer suggest for the comment about snow?
2 What aspect of climate change 'might come as a surprise' and why should it be surprising?

4 Work in pairs. Discuss the questions.

- What major changes have taken place recently in your country? Have these changes been for the better or for the worse?
- What are the advantages and disadvantages of being a stay-at-home parent? Would/Do you enjoy being one? Why or why not?
- How worried are you by climate change? What do you do on a personal level to help combat it?

SPEAKING

1 Work in small groups. Discuss what the effects might be if the following changes were to occur in your country. Would they be positive or negative changes?

- The average temperature increases by 5°C all year round.
- The third most important political party wins a majority at the general election.
- The official retirement age is increased by five years.
- All primary and secondary school lessons have to be taught in English.
- The government introduces a four-day working week.
- The minimum age for driving a car is increased by three years.

2 Which changes would you like to see introduced either regionally, nationally or globally?
How might such changes benefit your region/country/the world?

A At the turn of the century, Russia finds itself embroiled in a growing class battle. The long-standing rule of the elite Romanov dynasty is challenged by the common people, those whose lives are marked by poverty, illness, and unemployment. Once a peaceful demonstration goes horribly awry, rebellion takes hold of the country, turning hopes of change and communication into calls for violent protest and retribution. Swept away by the political current, Elisavyeta, a beautiful Romanov Grand Duchess, and Pavel, a worker turned rebel leader, see their lives drastically altered by the events that surround them.

Based on the true story of the life and death of Grand Duchess Elisavyeta Fyodorovna, Robert Alexander's *The Romanov Bride* is a gripping and emotional journey through one of the most turbulent times in Russian history. Alexander fuses a talent for quick-paced, clear-eyed prose with an uncanny ability to understand the mind of the worker as well as the aristocrat. Alternating between Elisavyeta's and Pavel's competing yet complementary perspectives, he presents an honest view of the revolutionary experience from both sides of the social divide. Although they are worlds apart, Elisavyeta and Pavel have more in common than they realize; both love their country and their countrymen, are committed to their beliefs, and – most importantly – have lost the love of their lives.

B And Tom's habits didn't change when, in 1998, he met his wife, Lou. 'Together we were earning around £100,000 and yet it just got frittered away in cabs and restaurants.' This, now, is a source of immense regret. 'We could so easily have put a bit aside, but we were just irresponsible.' Then, in 2002, he was made redundant. Bliss, their baby daughter, was three weeks old. 'It was a strange time,' he recalls, 'on the one hand panic, but also this amazing feeling of a new future.' After fourteen years in advertising, Tom was ready for a different challenge. 'Towards the end of my time in advertising, I became really interested in the idea of making something, packaging it and sending it off to market.' He also wanted to be his own boss.

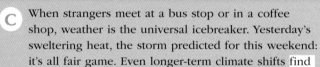

The plan was for Lou to work full-time until Tom established himself as a freelance advertising consultant, which would give him time to plan his own business. But he soon discovered there was no work. It was Bliss who dictated what happened next.

'She was about six months old and going to a nursery two or three mornings a week while I went for job interviews. It was just heart-rending,' he remembers. After a few months, he couldn't handle it any more. 'We thought, right, one of us will look after her. And it looked like it was going to be me.' Tom began his new life, as a stay-at-home father.

C When strangers meet at a bus stop or in a coffee shop, weather is the universal icebreaker. Yesterday's sweltering heat, the storm predicted for this weekend: it's all fair game. Even longer-term climate shifts find their way into chitchat. 'It used to snow harder when I was a kid' is a classic example – and one explicable in part by the fact that any amount of snow looks more impressive from a child's height.

Today, however, such clichés have an edge to them, because we know that humans play a role in determining the course of climate. When we hear about Arctic tundra melting or a devastating hurricane, we're now forced to consider the fingerprints of humanity – and that's going well beyond small talk. Indeed, climate change is as much a divider as weather has traditionally been a unifier. Weather has always seemed to transcend politics, but human-induced climate change is wedded to politics: it's an outgrowth of countless decisions made by local, regional and national governments, as well as individuals and corporations. Sadly, it's also become a polarized subject, linked to other issues so frequently that it often serves as shorthand for one's entire world view.

It might come as a surprise, then, how much of the basic science behind global climate change is rock-solid and accepted by virtually all parties. Most of the debate among experts these days revolves around interpretation. Just how warm will Earth get?

1B | First day

SPEAKING

1 Work in small groups. Talk about how you might feel and what your main concerns would be on your first day in each of these situations:

- in a new school
- in a new job
- in a new house
- on holiday in a foreign city
- on a diet

2 Discuss the following questions.

- How did you feel on your first day in this class? Why?

LISTENING

1 You are going to listen to part of a university radio interview about starting a new job. Before you complete the sentences in exercise 2, try to predict the type of information which will be required in each sentence.

1 possibly an adjective or maybe the person's profession

2 🔘 **1.1** Listen and complete the sentences with up to three words.

1 Jim Redman used to be _____.
2 Jim mentions the importance of getting a good _____ before your first day at work.
3 He says you should ensure you are not remembered for _____ on your first day.
4 He recommends practising the _____ beforehand.
5 As at the interview stage, Jim suggests you should _____ on the first day.
6 Taking notes is a good idea, especially of _____.
7 Jim advises trying to be _____ with all co-workers.
8 Jim agrees with the presenter that you should avoid _____.
9 His key word for those starting a new job is _____.
10 In case of doubt, Jim suggests phoning the company to find out their _____.

SPEECH FEATURE: approximation

In conversation we tend to use approximating expressions rather than speak in precise terms.

1 Complete these approximating expressions from the recording with the words in the box.

> about   up   so   something   very

1 And with ____ **like** 350,000 graduates leaving university this year, competition for jobs is intense.
2 **It's coming** ____ **to** a quarter to nine.
3 Familiarize yourself with the route ____ **a week** beforehand.
4 Hold yourself back a little for the first **month or** ____.
5 It's ____ **nearly** ten to nine.

> Here are some more approximating expressions:
> *It cost me three pound fifty **something**.*
> *It took **around** two weeks or **something like that**.*
> *There were **just under** / **over** / **roughly** / **upwards of** / **somewhere in the region of** / **some** two thousand people there.*
> *I've been here for twenty **odd** years.*
> *We'll leave at six**ish** / seven thirty**ish**.*

2 Express the phrases using two different approximating expressions.

53 people: *just over 50 people, 50 or so people*

1 19 days
2 5.56pm
3 £21.24
4 5 hours 11 minutes
5 233 kilometres
6 7,241 light years away

3 Work in pairs. Tell each other about yourselves using approximating expressions for numbers, ages, lengths of time, money and so on. You could talk about the items in the box.

studies   work   English   family
interests   hopes and ambitions   other

I've been working as an accountant for something like five years now. There are some 40 or so people working in the company, but there are only about five of us in my department.

GRAMMAR: simple & continuous verb forms

1 Name the tenses in bold in the following sentences from the recording.

1 We've just **been talking** about successful interview techniques.
2 What advice can you give those students who **have received** that much-coveted job offer and **are looking forward** to starting work?
3 The move from an academic environment to the world of work **represents** a huge change.
4 Well, when I **was talking** about interview techniques earlier, I **mentioned** the need to ask questions.
5 The impression you make on the first day **will have** a lasting effect.
6 At 9 o'clock we'**ll be handing over** to Rob Benton for an hour of jazz music.

2 Explain why the simple or continuous form is used in each of the sentences in exercise 1. When you have finished, check your ideas in the grammar box on the right.

3 Choose the correct alternative to complete the texts. In some cases both alternatives may be possible.

1 As you *know / are knowing*, I *have / 'm having* a party on Saturday to celebrate my 21st birthday. I've *hired / been hiring* a hall and my brother's rock group has *agreed / been agreeing* to play. Do you think you *'ll come / 'll be coming*?
2 My son Mark *is / is being* so uncooperative at the moment. We *aren't / aren't being* sure if it's just because he *grows / is growing* up and he *wants / is wanting* to test us or whether perhaps he *feels / is feeling* jealous of his baby sister.
3 My sister Annie *lives / is living* abroad and yesterday morning she *was taken / was being taken* to hospital. It *appears / is appearing* she *fell / was falling* and *broke / was breaking* her wrist while she *had / was having* a shower. I've *phoned / been phoning* the hospital all morning but they *don't answer / aren't answering*. I *think / am thinking* I've *phoned / been phoning* about seven or eight times.

4 Note down one example for each of the following, then compare and discuss each one with your partner.

- a problem in your country or local area which is getting worse
- something you have recently started or stopped doing
- something you have been doing for a long time
- the place you went to on your most recent holiday
- what you were doing this time last Sunday
- what you will or might be doing this time next Sunday

Continuous forms can be used to:
- describe actions in progress at a specific time which is either stated or understood.
  *He **was cooking** his dinner when I phoned.*
- talk about an activity that has recently stopped.
  *It looks as though it'**s been raining** here.*
- emphasize repetition, duration or the temporary nature of an event.
  *I've **been trying** to speak to him for weeks.*
  *She's only **working** there this month.*
- talk and ask about arrangements or plans.
  *I'm **playing** tennis with Paul tomorrow.*
  ***Will** you **be going** into town later?*
- describe change and development.
  *The weather's **changing** – it's **getting** cold again.*

Simple forms can be used to:
- describe single or habitual actions, or repeated actions with a stated frequency or number.
  *I often **went** to France as a child.*
  *You've **told** me that three times today!*
- describe states.
  *I **think** I **know** what she **wants** for Christmas.*

Some state verbs can be used in the continuous form, but with a change in meaning.
  *The situation **appears** to be improving.*
  (= seems)
  *Janet Burns **is** currently **appearing** in The Seagull at the Connaught Theatre.*
  (= is performing)

Some others can be used in either simple or continuous form with no change in meaning.
  *I **feel**/'m **feeling** terrible. My back really **aches**/is really **aching**.*

The continuous form of the verb *to be* can be used to describe temporary behaviour.
  *You're **being** very naughty!*

❯ SEE LANGUAGE REFERENCE PAGE 14

1c | Growing up

Vocabulary & speaking: age

1 Put the phrases in the box in chronological order.

> a twentysomething   a senior citizen   a toddler
> a preteen   a newborn   a 30-year-old   a teenager
> a middle-aged man/woman

2 Say approximately how old the following people are.

1 She recently came of age.
2 He's just turned 30.
3 She's on the wrong side of 40.
4 He's having a midlife crisis.
5 She's coming up to retirement.
6 He's getting on for 70.

3 Using the language from exercises 1 and 2, say how old you think the people in the photos A–E are.

4 Work in pairs. Take turns to talk about the ages represented in the photos A–E. Do not mention the ages; your partner will try to guess them. Talk about:

- the advantages and disadvantages of being this age.
- the main concerns of people at this age.
- what people normally hope to achieve by this age.

Reading

1 Read the title and introduction of the article. What areas of a person's life might be covered in a series such as this?

2 Read the whole article and answer the question.

- Which of the areas you discussed in exercise 1 are mentioned?

3 Read the article again and choose the correct words to complete the sentences.

1 The writer suggests that the participants' experiences have influenced *their decisions / how they feel about their lives / viewers' opinions of them.*
2 The writer says that Neil's *past is reflected in his face / work is poorly paid / physical health is better now.*
3 Andrew has the impression that his life *is not as successful as it could have been / has been very uneventful / was carefully planned for him.*
4 The writer says that Tony's background *highlights the unfairness of the class system / has been no obstacle to success / was severely deprived.*
5 Tony is a *lawyer / jockey / taxi driver.*
6 We learn that some of the participants are *American / less than enthusiastic about appearing in the series / unlikely to contribute to future programmes.*

4 Work in pairs. Discuss the questions.

- How have you and your life changed in the last seven years?
- Would you be interested in appearing in a documentary series like *7-Up*? Why or why not?

Grammar: reference & substitution

1 What do the highlighted words in the article refer to?

2 Complete the sentences with the words in the box.

> that   those   there   so   not   nor
> one   ones   do   does   ~~did~~

Sure. I'll pick you up at the same time as I _did_ last week.

1 Yes, we have got some striped _____, but I think a plain _____ would suit you better.
2 I didn't enjoy it and _____ did Lara.
3 I know. _____'s why she resigned.
4 I never watch it but my wife _____.
5 Of course I _____. We go _____ on holiday every year.
6 Yes, go on. If _____, she might start to worry.
7 I certainly hope _____. I don't know what I'll do if he says 'no'.
8 Yes, and the sports facilities are better than _____ of the other schools in the area.

3 Write the preceding line of dialogue for each sentence in exercise 2.

A: *Can you give me a lift tomorrow?*
B: *Sure. I'll pick you up at the same time as I did last week.*

4 Work in pairs. Take turns to read out in random order the sentences you have written in exercise 3. Reply to your partner's sentences using the appropriate responses from exercise 2.

> Use *this, that, these, those* before nouns or on their own to **refer back** to previously stated ideas.
> > *... and told them she was pregnant. They were delighted at **this news** and ...*
> > *... in the 1890s. In **those days** there were no fridges ...*
> > *He had failed the exam. **This** came as no surprise ...*
>
> Use the following to **substitute** and avoid repetition of previously-used words and clauses: *then, there, one(s), so, not, neither, nor, do, does, did.*
> > *'I'm not sleeping as well as I **did** on holiday.' (= slept)*
> > *'Is it raining?' 'I think **so**.' (= it is raining)*
> > *I don't eat meat and **neither does** Elisa.*
> > *(= Elisa doesn't eat meat either)*
>
> ❯ See Language Reference page 14

growing UP on television

A

B

In 1964 Granada Television made a documentary entitled *7-Up*, featuring fourteen seven-year-olds 'from startlingly different backgrounds', sharing their thoughts, describing their feelings and
5 **revealing their hopes and dreams for the future. Since then the programme makers have charted the lives of these individuals, broadcasting updates on their progress every seven years. David Taylor watched *49-Up*, with the participants now well into**
10 **middle age.**

What strikes one about the 7-Uppers who still appear in the programme is that most, if not all of them, seem at last to have found happiness. The university professor, the teacher, the librarian, the barrister, the builder and the taxi driver
15 have all had their ups and downs, yet in spite, or perhaps because of this, they appear more content with their lives than ever before, able to reflect on their experiences and better appreciate what they have achieved. For some, the process has taken a long time: 'Now is the first time that
20 I actually feel happy in my own skin,' admits a calm and composed Susie, who at 21 was visibly ill-at-ease in front of the cameras.

Even Neil, who at 28 feared for his sanity, agrees that he now has 'a stronger sense of purpose'. Of all those appearing
25 in the series, Neil surely underwent the most dramatic changes, and his story represents all that is unpredictable in life. The angelic features of the seven-year-old who was going to be an astronaut and if not, a coach driver, are now rough and weathered, bearing testimony to the time he spent on
30 the road, homeless and wandering around the west coast of Scotland. He is still without a full-time job but his political work as a member of a local district council keeps him occupied and enables him to supplement the income he receives from state benefits.

35 Whilst for some participants, things did not turn out quite as they would have hoped, for others life held fewer surprises. 'It was as if my life was mapped out for me,' says Andrew, who at seven years old already knew the schools he would attend, the university he would study
40 at and the profession he would follow – that of a lawyer. Andrew came from a privileged background, and although

he acknowledges that the world for younger people nowadays is much more competitive and less
45 predictable than before, his children will undoubtedly benefit from the private education his earnings have enabled him to provide for them.

And then there's Tony, the working-class lad from the
50 East End of London. One of the programme's original aims was to expose Britain's rigid class system, but Tony is evidence that humble beginnings need not prevent one from getting on in life. His route to financial wellbeing was not the academic one that Andrew followed, but like the
55 lawyer, he was always clear about what he wanted to do: he left school at fifteen, trained to be a jockey, and knew that if that didn't work out, he would drive a London cab – which he does to this day. And like Andrew, he and his wife have bought a second home: not a converted barn
60 in the English countryside, but a house in Spain, where he hopes to set up a sports bar in the near future.

The success of the *7-Up* series in America shows that the programme is perhaps more about universal truths than local class concerns, dealing with issues that all classes
65 have to deal with such as work, relationships and families. For a number of the participants, however, it is an intrusion into their privacy. They are uncomfortable about having their lives held up to such close scrutiny, and the producer Michael
70 Apted has to work hard every seven years to persuade them to come back on the programme.

And most do: of the original fourteen 7-Uppers, twelve
75 chose to appear in this latest instalment. One can only hope that they will come back for the next one, as their contributions provide
80 a fascinating record of the human condition. 'It's like *Big Brother*,' says John, the barrister. 'It is actually real-life TV with the added bonus that you can
85 see people grow old, lose their hair, get fat.'

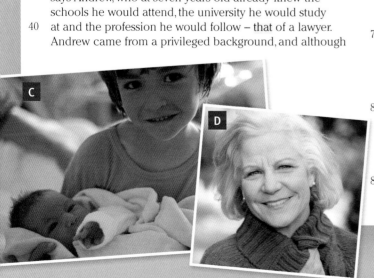

C

D

E

1D | The quarterlife crisis

LISTENING

1 Work in pairs. Compare the two photos in A, B and C. Describe the decisions we have to make and responsibilities we have to assume when we make the change from childhood to adulthood.

2 Read the magazine extract and discuss the questions.

> We've all heard of the **midlife crisis** – those feelings of worry, doubt or dissatisfaction that some people experience when they reach middle age and reflect on what they have, or have not, achieved in their lives. But for some time now, people have also been talking about the **quarterlife crisis**, which affects many young people between the ages of eighteen and 35.

- What do you think the quarterlife crisis consists of?
- What feelings might young people experience and why?

Check your ideas on page 138.

A
B
C

3 🔊 **1.2–1.6** Listen to the speakers 1–5 talking about the quarterlife crisis and decide whether they would (✓) or would not (✗) agree that twentysomethings have good reason to complain about their situation.

4 🔊 **1.2–1.6** Listen again and match one of the statements a–h to the speakers 1–5. Three of the statements are not required.

a I share my problems online with people in a similar situation.
b Many twentysomethings are envious of their friends.
c Young people are too demanding.
d My expectations have not been met.
e The problems are not specific to twentysomethings.
f Life used to be more straightforward.
g Teenagers have an easier life than twentysomethings.
h Having a range of options makes life interesting.

5 Work in pairs. Discuss the questions.

- Do you sympathize with those who claim to be suffering a quarterlife crisis? Why or why not?
- In what ways is life easier or more difficult for young people now compared to previous generations?
- Do you prefer to have your life 'all mapped out' or does uncertainty 'add a bit of spice to life'? Give reasons.

VOCABULARY: noun suffixes

1a From which adjectives are the nouns 1–5 from the recording formed?

stability – stable

1 insecurity
2 responsibility
3 reality
4 maturity
5 uncertainty

b From which verbs are the nouns in the box from the recording formed?

decisions   dissatisfaction   expectations   realization

2a Use the suffixes in the box to form nouns from the groups of verbs 1–4.

-ence	-ment	-al	-ure

1	bury	deny	survive
2	disappoint	achieve	involve
3	fail	depart	proceed
4	exist	occur	obey

b Use the suffixes in the box to form nouns from the groups of adjectives 1–4.

-ence	-ness	-cy	-ity

1	sincere	flexible	generous
2	sad	tired	serious
3	pregnant	fluent	accurate
4	absent	patient	intelligent

3a Complete the text with the correct noun form of the words in brackets.

'I look back on my _childhood_ (child) with great (1) _____ (fond). I had more (2) _____ (free) to do what I wanted then, and in my childish (3) _____ (innocent) I had fewer (4) _____ (inhibit) and more self-(5) _____ (confident). Although age supposedly brings with it greater (6) _____ (wise), there's a lot of (7) _____ (true) in the maxim, (8) '_____ (ignorant) is bliss'. I had no cares in the world and used to do everything with such (9) _____ (enthuse); now the only thing I look forward to is my (10) _____ (retire).'

b Do you share the feelings of the speaker in exercise 3a?

Speaking

1 Read the five paragraphs on page 139. Have you ever been in any similar situations yourself?

2 Work in pairs, A and B. Each of you should choose a different situation on page 139 and make a list of all the ways in which you might benefit from such a move.

3 Now consider your partner's situation and think about why this move would not be a good one. Make a list of the disadvantages and problems it might bring, both to your partner and any other people mentioned, and think of alternative solutions.

4 Roleplay the following dialogue, using your notes from exercises 2 and 3.

A: Explain why you want to go ahead with your decision.
B: Try to dissuade your partner from going ahead with his/her decision.

Now change roles and have the second dialogue.

5 What do you think would really be the best course of action in each case?

6 Work in pairs. Discuss the questions.

- What is the biggest decision you have made in your life so far?
- What difficulties did you face?
- What were the consequences?

Did you know?

1 Work in pairs. Read about *Age UK* and discuss the questions.

Age UK is one of a number of charities representing the interests of older people in the UK. It aims to ensure that they are valued by society, become integrated and feel fulfilled, and concentrates its efforts on combating poverty and neglect, reducing isolation, defeating ageism and promoting quality in the care of older people.

The charity offers help and advice on a number of issues including health, home safety, money and care. It also regularly runs campaigns aimed, for example, at fighting age discrimination, stopping psychological and physical abuse, or organizing donations to prevent deaths from cold-related illnesses in winter.

In addition, *Age UK* works overseas and in partnership with the charity *HelpAge International*. Around one-quarter of its expenditure goes towards improving the lives of disadvantaged older people in the developing world.

- Are there any similar charities in your country?
- To what extent are older people valued, respected and integrated into society?
- How, if at all, has the situation changed in recent years?

GRAMMAR

Simple & continuous verb forms

1 Continuous forms are used to:

- describe actions which were, are or will be in progress at a specific time, which is either stated or understood.
  *When I last met him, he **was** still **looking** for a job.*
  *I'm **having** a really hard time at work at the moment.*
  *Don't call me at 1.30. I'll **be having** my lunch then.*

- describe an activity that has recently stopped.
  *We've just **been playing** tennis.*

- suggest that a situation or action is temporary or incomplete.
  *My flat's **being decorated** so I'm **staying** at my mum's.*
  *I've **been writing** my thesis – I've almost finished.*

- emphasize duration, using *for* or *since*.
  *She'd **been waiting** for him for over an hour.*
  *I've **been sitting** here since three o'clock.*

- refer to repeated actions. *Always, forever, continually* are used with present and past continuous to show that the speaker finds the repetition annoying or curious.
  *I've **been taking** that herbal remedy you recommended.*
  *You're **forever forgetting** your keys!*
  *She **was always climbing** trees as a child.*

- describe change and development.
  *Simon's **growing up** – he's **getting taller** and taller.*

- talk about future arrangements.
  *I'm **meeting** Sally at three tomorrow.*

2 Simple forms are used to describe:

- single completed actions.
  *I've **written** my thesis. I **submitted** it yesterday.*

- habitual actions.
  *I often **went** fishing as a boy but I rarely **go** now.*

- repeated actions where the frequency or number is stated.
  *I **phoned** the bank twice yesterday, and I've **made** another three calls today.*

- timetabled or scheduled events in the future.
  *My train **leaves** at six thirty tomorrow morning.*

- states. State verbs include *appear, believe, know, like, own, prefer, remember, seem, understand, want.*
  *I **understand** why you **like** it, but I **don't want** one.*

  Some state verbs can be used in the continuous form, but with a change in meaning, eg *appear, expect, fit, have, see, smell, think.*
  *I'm **seeing** Alan on Friday.* (see = meet)
  *Sorry, I **don't see** what you mean.* (see = understand)

  The continuous form of the state verb *be* can be used to describe temporary behaviour.
  *You're **not being** very helpful. In fact, I think you're **being** very rude.*

When describing feelings, the verbs *feel, hurt* and *ache* can be used in the simple or continuous form with no difference in meaning.
  *I **feel**/'m **feeling** tired and my neck **hurts**/'s **hurting**.*

However, with some time adverbials the simple form must be used:
  *I **feel** tired all the time.*
  *My neck **hurts** when I turn my head.*

Reference

This, that, these and *those* can be used as determiners before nouns to refer back to previously-mentioned people, things or ideas.
  *… but he would have the opportunity to travel. It was for **this** reason that he accepted the job.*
  *… fish, reptiles and amphibians. **These** creatures are all cold-blooded, unlike birds and mammals, which …*

They can also be used on their own as pronouns. *This* is more common than *that* in writing.
  *… so they decided to hold another meeting. **This** took place the following February and …*
  *'No, you can't have any sweets.' 'Oh, **that's** not fair!'*

The pronouns *that* and *those* often occur in sentences which include a comparison.
  *Its **sense of hearing** is far more acute than **that** of most other birds.*
  *The most successful **students** tend to be **those** who keep good vocabulary records.*

Notice in these two examples how *that* and *those* avoid repetition of the nouns to which they refer (*sense of hearing* and *students*). The same is true of other pronouns.
  ***The woman** was clearly angry with **her son**. **She** told **him** to apologize immediately for his rudeness.*

Substitution

Like pronouns, a number of other words can be used to substitute and avoid repetition of previously-used words and clauses.

- Auxiliary verbs *do, does, did* in place of a verb.
  *Susie didn't come to the show but her husband **did**.*

- *So/Neither/Nor* + auxiliary verb + subject.
  *She doesn't like it and **neither/nor do I**.*
  *His firm's had a good year and **so has ours**.*

- *So/Not* in place of a *that* clause.
  *'Is John going tonight?' 'I don't think **so**. I hope **not**.'*
  (= *I don't think <u>that John is going tonight</u>. I hope <u>that John isn't going tonight</u>.*)

- *If so/Not* in place of a conditional clause.
  *Are you unemployed? **If so**, we've got work for you.*
  ***If not**, would you like to earn some extra cash?*

- *One/Ones* for countable nouns.
  'How many sweets have you got?'
  'Four – two blue **ones,** *a green* **one**
  and the **one** *that's in my mouth.'*
- *Then/There* for a time or place.
  'How do you know he was at the
  disco last night?' 'Because I saw
  him **there then.'**

WORD LIST

Change

change a nappy	/ˌtʃeɪndʒ ə ˈnæpi/
change a light bulb	/ˌtʃeɪndʒ ə ˈlaɪtˌbʌlb/
change a plug	/ˌtʃeɪndʒ ə plʌg/
change a tyre	/ˌtʃeɪndʒ ə ˈtaɪə(r)/
adapt *v* **	/əˈdæpt/
alter *v* **	/ˈɔːltə(r)/
convert *v* **	/kənˈvɜː(r)t/
shift (away) from/towards *v*	/ʃɪft (əˈweɪ) frəm/təˈwɔː(r)dz/
switch *v* ***	/swɪtʃ/
transfer *v* ***	/ˈtrænsfɜː(r)/
transform *v* **	/trænsˈfɔː(r)m/
vary *v* ***	/ˈveəri/

Age

come of age *v*	/ˌkʌm əv ˈeɪdʒ/
come up to retirement	/ˌkʌm ʌp tə rɪˈtaɪə(r)mənt/
get on for (+ *age*) *v*	/ˌget ˈɒn fə(r)/
midlife crisis *n C*	/ˌmɪdlaɪf ˈkraɪsɪs/
newborn *n C*	/ˈnjuːˌbɔː(r)n/
on the wrong side	/ɒn ðə ˈrɒŋ ˌsaɪd/
preteen *n C*	/ˈpriːˌtiːn/
senior citizen *n C*	/ˌsiːniə(r) ˈsɪtɪz(ə)n/
toddler *n C* *	/ˈtɒdlə(r)/
turn (+ *age*) *v*	/tɜː(r)n/
twenty something *n C*	/ˌtwentiˈsʌmθɪŋ/

Noun suffixes

accurate *adj* **	/ˈækjʊrət/
accuracy *n U* **	/ˈækjʊrəsi/
bury *v* **	/ˈberi/
burial *n C* *	/ˈberiəl/
certain *adj* ***	/ˈsɜː(r)t(ə)n/
certainty *n U* **	/ˈsɜː(r)t(ə)nti/
child *n C* ***	/tʃaɪld/
childhood *n U* **	/ˈtʃaɪldˌhʊd/
consult *v* **	/kənˈsʌlt/
consultant *n C* **	/kənˈsʌltənt/
decide *v* ***	/dɪˈsaɪd/
decision *n C* ***	/dɪˈsɪʒ(ə)n/
employ *v* ***	/ɪmˈplɔɪ/

employee *n C* ***	/ɪmˈplɔɪiː, ˌemplɔɪˈiː/
enthuse *v*	/ɪnˈθjuːz/
enthusiasm *n U* **	/ɪnˈθjuːziˌæzəm/
expect *v* ***	/ɪkˈspekt/
novel *n C* ***	/ˈnɒv(ə)l/
novelist *n C* *	/ˈnɒvəlɪst/
obey *v* **	/əˈbeɪ/
obedience *n U*	/əˈbiːdiəns/
occur *v* ***	/əˈkɜː(r)/
occurrence *n C* **	/əˈkʌrəns/
proceed *v* ***	/prəˈsiːd/
procedure *n C* ***	/prəˈsiːdʒə(r)/
research *n U* ***	/rɪˈsɜː(r)tʃ, ˈriːsɜː(r)tʃ/
researcher *n C*	/rɪˈsɜː(r)tʃə(r), ˈriːsɜː(r)tʃə(r)/
spectate *v*	/spekˈteɪt/
spectator *n C* *	/spekˈteɪtə(r)/
stable *adj* **	/ˈsteɪb(ə)l/
stability *n U* **	/stəˈbɪləti/
tired *adj* ***	/ˈtaɪə(r)d/
tiredness *n U*	/ˈtaɪə(r)dnəs/
true *adj* ***	/truː/
truth *n U* ***	/truːθ/
wise *adj* **	/waɪz/

Other words & phrases

add a bit of spice to life	/ˌæd ə bɪt əv ˈspaɪs tə laɪf/
ageism *n U*	/ˈeɪdʒɪz(ə)m/
alienate *v*	/ˈeɪliəneɪt/
angelic *adj*	/ænˈdʒelɪk/
avoid (sth) like the plague	/əˈvɔɪd laɪk ðə ˈpleɪg/
barn *n C* **	/bɑː(r)n/
bear testimony to	/ˌbeə(r) ˈtestɪməni tʊ, tə/
chitchat *n U*	/ˈtʃɪtˌtʃæt/
cocooned *adj*	/kəˈkuːnd/
come as a surprise	/ˌkʌm æz ə sə(r)ˈpraɪz/
composed *adj*	/kəmˈpəʊzd/
cool *adj* ***	/kuːl/
crack jokes	/ˌkræk ˈdʒəʊks/
devastating *adj* *	/ˈdevəsteɪtɪŋ/
do a dummy run	/duː ə ˈdʌmi ˌrʌn/
embroiled in *adj*	/ɪmˈbrɔɪld ˌɪn/
expectations ***	/ˌekspekˈteɪʃ(ə)nz/
find one's way into *v*	/ˌfaɪnd wʌnz weɪ ˈɪntʊ/
fritter (sth) away *v*	/ˌfrɪtə(r) əˈweɪ/
fulfilled *adj*	/fʊlˈfɪld/
fuse *v* *	/fjuːz/
go awry *v*	/ˌgəʊ əˈraɪ/
grasp *v* **	/grɑːsp/
gripping *adj*	/ˈgrɪpɪŋ/
handheld *n C*	/ˈhændˌheld/
handle *v* ***	/ˈhænd(ə)l/
harsh *adj* **	/hɑː(r)ʃ/

have one's ups and downs	/həv wʌnz ˈʌps ən ˌdaʊnz/
heart-rending *adj*	/ˈhɑː(r)t ˌrendɪŋ/
hold (sth) up to close scrutiny	/həʊld ʌp tə ˌkləʊs ˈskruːtɪni/
human-induced *adj*	/ˌhjuːmən ɪnˈdʒuːst/
humble beginnings *n pl*	/ˌhʌmb(ə)l bɪˈgɪnɪŋz/
icebreaker *n C*	/ˈaɪsˌbreɪkə(r)/
ill-at-ease *adj*	/ˌɪl ət ˈiːz/
in a similar vein	/ɪn ə ˈsɪmɪlə(r) ˌveɪn/
in short supply	/ɪn ˌʃɔː(r)t səˈplaɪ/
intrusion *n C* *	/ɪnˈtruːʒ(ə)n/
jot (sth) down *v*	/ˌdʒɒt ˈdaʊn/
live up to expectations	/ˌlɪv ˈʌp tʊ ˌekspekˈteɪʃ(ə)nz/
long-standing *v*	/ˌlɒŋ ˈstændɪŋ/
map (sth) out *v*	/ˌmæp ˈaʊt/
meet expectations	/ˈmiːt ˌekspekˈteɪʃ(ə)nz/
overwhelming *adj* *	/ˌəʊvə(r)ˈwelmɪŋ/
pointer *n C*	/ˈpɔɪntə(r)/
put (sth) aside *v*	/ˌpʊt əˈsaɪd/
quarterlife crisis	/ˌkwɔː(r)tə(r)laɪf ˈkraɪsɪs/
quick-paced *adj*	/ˈkwɪkˌpeɪst/
revolve around *v*	/rɪˈvɒlv əˌraʊnd/
self-restraint *n U*	/ˌself rɪˈstreɪnt/
serve as shorthand for	/ˌsɜː(r)v əz ˈʃɔː(r)tˌhænd fɔː(r)/
settle down *v*	/ˌset(ə)l ˈdaʊn/
startlingly *adv*	/ˈstɑː(r)t(ə)lɪŋli/
stick with *v*	/ˈstɪk ˌwɪð/
sweltering *adj*	/ˈswelt(ə)rɪŋ/
take out a mortgage	/ˌteɪk aʊt ə ˈmɔː(r)gɪdʒ/
transcend *v*	/trænˈsend/
transition *n C* **	/trænˈzɪʃ(ə)n/
tread water	/ˌtred ˈwɔːtə(r)/
turbulent *adj*	/ˈtɜː(r)bjʊlənt/

2A | Memory

VOCABULARY: memory & memories

1 Make the following statements true for you. Choose the relevant alternative in bold where necessary.

1 I have a *good / poor* memory for names and faces.
2 I **keep forgetting** _____.
3 I *know / used to know* the poem '_____' by heart.
4 I **have** *vivid / only vague* **memories of** the family holidays I went on as a young child.
5 I have *fond / painful / bittersweet* **memories of** my schooldays.
6 The *song / piece of music* '_____' **brings back memories of** _____.

Work in pairs. Discuss your sentences.

READING

1 Read the texts A–C, which describe different methods for improving memory. Which methods do you find most and least appealing? Tell your partner, giving reasons for your opinions.

2 Read the texts again and decide whether the following are stated (✓) or not stated (✗).

Text A
1 Most people cannot remember facts and figures.
2 You can train your memory to learn whole conversations.
3 The writer has not always had such a good memory.

Text B
4 Memory-enhancing drugs will not cause significant damage to our overall health.
5 Coffee will one day cease to be used as a stimulant.
6 Mental cosmetics would place greater demands on people to perform well.

Text C
7 Exams make you hungry.
8 Alzheimer's disease is caused by a failure to eat the right foods.
9 Drinking water increases the size of the brain, enabling it to store more information.

3 Work in small groups. Discuss the question.

• What techniques do you use for committing information to memory?

GRAMMAR: gerunds & infinitives

Use the **full infinitive** (with *to*):
• to express purpose.
  *I drink water at work **to improve** my concentration.*
• after certain adjectives, eg *easy, surprised, likely.*
• after certain verbs, eg *agree, hope, refuse.* (1)
• after certain nouns, eg *ability, decision, effort.* (2)

Use the **bare infinitive** (without *to*):
• after modal verbs. (3)
• after these verbs: **help, make, let, had better.* (4)
  **The infinitive with *to* is also possible after *help.*

Use the **gerund**:
• as the subject of a sentence or clause. (5)
  ***Drinking** water at work improves my concentration.*
• after prepositions. (6)
• after certain verbs, eg *appreciate, consider, deny.*
• after *have difficulty* (*in*), *it's no use, it's (not) worth, can't help.*

Some verbs can be followed by either the gerund or infinitive:
• with no change in meaning, eg *begin, continue.*
• with a change in meaning, eg *forget, go on, regret.*

❯ SEE LANGUAGE REFERENCE PAGE 24

1 Match each of the highlighted verbs in text A to one of the uses 1–6 in the grammar box.

2 Complete the sentences with the correct form of the verb in brackets.

1 I can't help _____ (*wonder*) why they decided to buy that awful house.
2 I must remember _____ (*get*) some stamps.
3 I didn't get round to _____ (*phone*) John yesterday – I was just too busy.
4 He gave up teaching and went on _____ (*become*) a best-selling author.
5 We appreciate your _____ (*agree*) to come at such short notice.
6 I regret _____ (*inform*) you that your application has been unsuccessful.
7 She suddenly stopped _____ (*laugh*) and began _____ (*cry*) instead.
8 I keep _____ (*forget*) _____ (*buy*) some stamps.

3 Complete the sentences with an appropriate verb form so that they are true for you.

1 I **have no intention of** _____
2 I wish I **had the power** _____
3 I often **have difficulty** _____
4 I really should **make more effort** _____
5 My _____ (*family member*) **has a tendency** _____
6 I (don't) **regret my decision** _____

4 Work in pairs. Discuss your sentences.

A NEVER FORGET FACTS & FIGURES

Have you ever struggled to remember a fact or figure? Perhaps it was a famous date in history. Or maybe it was a song that hit number one, the name of a chemical compound or the capital of Sweden. Whatever it was, that particular fact or figure has buried itself deep within the vault of your memory
10 and you just can't seem to retrieve it.

My advice is, don't put up with having an average memory. Improving your memory is a skill. If you master some basic techniques, remembering facts and figures can become a stimulating mental exercise – not
15 to mention a chance to show off in conversation! Plus, a good memory for facts and figures can help you to sail through exams. People think that because I can remember so many facts and figures I must have a photographic memory. This isn't the case. There was
20 a time when I struggled to remember seven or eight digits in a row, let alone 20 or 30 – and now I'm the eight-times winner of the World Memory Championships. I didn't just wake up one morning with the ability to remember. I simply
25 studied the techniques for making my mind more supple and put them into practice. Here, I reveal these
30 methods, sharing with you my specially devised exercises that will help you never forget facts and figures.

never forget
facts & figures
dominic o'brien
eight times world memory champion

C FOOD FOR THOUGHT

Increasingly, it is recognized that diet plays a vital role in exam performance. According to senior nutrition consultant Lorraine Perretta, the brain needs fuel just like any other organ. 'Without the correct diet, it cannot give its peak performance,' she
10 says. 'Eating the right foods can dramatically improve learning, concentration and memory.'

Patrick Holford, author of *Optimum Nutrition for the Mind*, points out that the brain uses a quarter of all the carbohydrates you eat under normal conditions, rising to around 40 per cent at
15 times of intense concentration. 'During an exam, your legs don't need the energy as you are sitting down. Your brain uses it all and that's why you are starving at the end of an exam. You would train your body for a physical exam, so why not do the same for a mental test?'

20 In order for the brain cells to communicate effectively with each other they need neurotransmitters, the messengers that carry information. Acetylcholine (ACh) is the neurotransmitter responsible for memory, and studies have found that people with Alzheimer's may have less of it. Foods rich in the vitamin complex
25 needed to make ACh include egg yolks, peanuts, liver, broccoli, fish and cheese.

Drinking water is also important. The brain is 70 per cent water, and when it is dehydrated it works more slowly. This is particularly true of memory; a dehydrated brain releases the stress hormone
30 cortisol, which adversely affects the brain's ability to store information. Too much coffee will also slow down the thinking process and make you feel foggy.

B Drugs to boost brain power will become 'as common as coffee'

Powerful stimulants that improve memory, intellectual agility or other aspects of mental performance will almost certainly be developed over the next 20 years. They will have few side effects, little or no addictive properties and could be used for boosting exam performance, making
5 **better business decisions or even eliminating bad memories.**

'In a world that is increasingly non-stop and competitive, the individual's use of such substances may move from the fringe to the norm, with cognition enhancers used as coffee is today,' says the Foresight report of the government's Office of Science and Technology. 'Cognition enhancers are likely to be developed to
10 treat people who need to improve attention, memory or wakefulness and to help people forget, sleep more efficiently and be less impulsive.'

Drugs that help people to forget disturbing experiences raise the prospect of a future portrayed in films such as *Eternal Sunshine of the Spotless Mind*, where characters are able to forget painful relationships.
15 But the possibility raises disturbing practical, ethical and social issues. 'It is possible that such an advance could usher in a new era of drug use without addiction,' says the report. 'If we ever find ourselves in a society that embraced cognition enhancers, "mental cosmetics" could become accepted and raise expectations about the performance and behaviour of individuals and groups.'

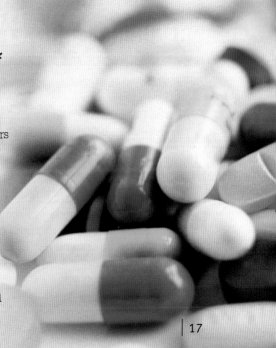

VOCABULARY: playing cards

1 Work in pairs. Use the words in the box to help you name the playing cards in the photo.

the ten of diamonds

hearts	clubs	diamonds	spades
jack	queen	king	ace	joker

2 Complete the text with the words in the box. Write the correct form of the verbs.

Nouns:	face	hand	odds	pack	suits
Verbs:	bet	count	deal	draw	shuffle

LISTENING

1 Close your book and see how many of the playing cards pictured on this page you can remember.

2 You are going to hear an interview with Dominic O'Brien, memory expert and eight-times winner of the World Memory Championships.

BASIC RULES OF **BLACKJACK**

The object of the game is to achieve a total that is greater than that of the dealer and which does not exceed 21. The game is played with a standard (1) _____, or deck of 52 cards. The four (2) _____ – hearts, clubs, diamonds and spades – have no relevance in blackjack and jokers are not used. Cards from 2 to 10 are worth their (3) _____ value (eg the 5 is worth five points), the jack, queen and king (4) _____ as 10 and the ace is worth either 11 or 1.

Players are (5) _____ first one card, then another, both face up. Each player then decides whether to (6) _____ further cards from the deck. The dealer, whose first card is face down, is the last to complete his or her (7) _____. Because cards are not (8) _____ between each game, more experienced players keep track of those that have already been played, in order to calculate the probability or (9) _____ of the next card having a high or low value. 'Card counting', as it is called, is particularly useful in helping professional gamblers decide how much money to (10) _____.

🔊 **1.7** Listen to Part 1 of the recording and complete the notes with a number.

World Memory Championships

– started in 1991; 10 events over (1) _____ days

Memorizing tasks	Time to memorize
A number with approx. (2) _____ digits	one hour; 90 mins. to recall
Packs of playing cards – about (3) _____ packs	one hour (4) _____ mins.
100 fictitious historic dates	
Spoken number: (5) _____ digits	1 digit per second
One deck of cards (fastest time)	Dominic's personal best: (6) _____ seconds
Typical age range of contestants: (7) _____ to 35.	
The Guinness Book of Records (8) _____ individual cards	12 hours to memorize; (9) _____ hours to recall
Errors made: (10) _____ Max. no. of errors allowed: 0.5 per cent (= 14)	

Which of the tasks and achievements you heard about in Part 1 impress you most?

3 🔊 **1.8** Listen to Part 2 and answer the questions.

1 What three techniques does Dominic use to memorize information?
2a Which of the playing cards on page 18 does he associate with each of the following?

Bill Gates   Kylie Minogue   James Bond

b Where in the house does he place these three people and what are they each doing there?
3 What were the findings of the brain study carried out on Dominic and other top memorizers?

4 🔊 **1.9** Listen to Part 3 and decide whether the statements are true (T) or false (F). Correct the false statements.

1 Before going into a casino Dominic spent six months studying the game of blackjack.
2 During that time, he dealt out 1,000 hands to himself.
3 As a result of his success in a casino, he decided to become a professional gambler.
4 In the United States he was banned from thirteen casinos, but made winnings of 10,000 dollars.
5 At school he was an A-grade student.
6 He began training his memory when he was thirteen.

SPEAKING

1 Work in two groups, A and B. You are going to use Dominic O'Brien's techniques to memorize a sequence of eight cards.

Group A: Turn to page 140.
Group B: Turn to page 147.

2 Work with a student from the other group. Turn to your partner's page and listen as he/she …

1 names his/her cards in their correct order.
2 tells you the story of the journey which helped him/her remember the cards in sequence.

3 Work in pairs. Discuss the questions.

• When might the journey method be useful for memorizing items in a set order?
• Would you use this method? Why or why not?

PRONUNCIATION: chunking

1 🔊 **1.10** Listen to the following extract from the listening. Notice how Dominic makes a slight pause in between each group of words or 'chunk' of speech. Chunking helps the listener make sense of what the speaker is saying, just as punctuation helps the reader make sense of what the writer has written.

… it's the use of association/so if I say 'key'/ you think of 'door'/'rabbit'/you think of 'carrot'/that's association/the second one is the use of location/I use journeys/familiar journeys/a journey round my house/a journey round a golf course/to store information/ to keep the sequence going/and the most important ingredient is the use of imagination/something that we all possess/ erm, and that combination works very well …

2 Practise reading the audioscript in exercise 1 aloud, pausing slightly after each chunk.

3 🔊 **1.11** Turn to audioscript 1.11 on page 156. Chunk the script, marking each division with a line (/). Then listen to the recording to compare your ideas.

2c | Bicycle history

SPEAKING

1 Work in groups of three. Each choose a different photo above, then each argue the case that your method of transport has had the most positive impact on our lives today.

2 Are your real views the same as or different from those you expressed in exercise 1?

READING

1 Work in pairs. Discuss the question.

• Why do you think the following comments were made about the effect of the bicycle in the late 19th century?

[The bicycle] revolutionized day-to-day life, especially for the middle and working classes.
'Bicycling,' declared the American suffragist Susan Anthony in 1896, 'has done more to emancipate women than anything else in the world.'

2 Read the article and compare your ideas.

3 Read the article again and match the titles a–h to the paragraph headings 1–8.

a   When did the bicycle cross the Channel?
b   What were the very earliest forms of bicycle?
c   How did that go down?
d   What is the link between the two?
e   What other side effects did the bicycle have?
f   What's so special about the bicycle?
g   But what effect did it have on women's lives?
h   When did it become less of a health hazard?

4 Work in small groups. Each of you should make your own choice for the greatest technological innovation since 1800. Write a sentence using the following words:

_____ *has done more to* _____ *than anything else in the world.*

Explain your choice to the group, justifying your opinions, then decide on one which you all agree is the greatest.

VOCABULARY: *way*

1 What do you understand by the highlighted expression with *way* in paragraph 7 of the text?

2 Complete the sentences with the adjectives in the box.

> bad   big   long   roundabout   wrong

1   He was holding the camera **the _____ way round** and he took a photo of himself!
2   Sally and I **go back a _____ way** – we were in the same class at primary school.
3   He was rushed to hospital – the doctors say he's **in a _____ way**.
4   I wish he was more direct – he always says things **in such a _____ way**.
5   The mini skirt caught on **in a _____ way** in the sixties – everyone was wearing one.

3 Complete the sentences with the correct form of the verbs in the box.

> change   get   give   go   know   work

1   She would kick, scream and cry to **_____ her own way** as a child, and she usually succeeded.
2   She went through a lazy period at school, but then **_____ her ways** and did well in her exams.
3   She's been working in the company for over a year now, so she **_____ her way around**.
4   She's still in a junior position but she hopes to **_____ her way up** to a management post.
5   She's very friendly: whenever someone new joins the firm, she **_____ out of her way to** make them feel welcome.
6   She holds fast to her beliefs, and will never **_____ way on** anything in an argument.

4 Which, if any, of the sentences in exercise 3 describe you, either now or in the past?

5 Work in pairs, A and B. You and your partner must try to decide what topics you are each speaking about.

A: Turn to page 147.   B: Turn to page 154.

The Rise of the Bicycle

Recently, listeners to BBC Radio 4 voted the bicycle the greatest technological innovation since 1800.

1 _____

It is the most revolutionary form of transport ever invented. When it went into mass production in the 1890s, it changed everything, from the way we dress to the course of human evolution. According to geneticist Steve Jones, the bicycle expanded the human gene pool as never before. People no longer had to marry the girl or boy next door: they could hop on their bike and pedal off to find a mate miles away.

2 _____

Throughout the 17th and 18th centuries, inventors had tried to build a human-powered vehicle as a cheap alternative to the horse. One early attempt was the Velocimano – a tricycle resembling a sea monster which moved forward when the driver flapped its wings. In 1818 the German baron Karl von Drais invented what became known as the 'hobbyhorse'. Shaped like a bicycle, it had wooden wheels but no pedals, so that the rider had to push it along with his feet. For a while, the hobbyhorse was the height of fashion among rich young dandies, until the London College of Surgeons warned that it could cause 'ruptures'.

3 _____

Many brilliant minds struggled to improve upon Van Drais' design, but it wasn't until 1861 that a Parisian blacksmith named Pierre Michaux fixed a set of pedals to the front wheel, and the bicycle (or 'pedal velocipede', as he advertised it) was finally born. It was as heavy as a modern fridge, but easy and fun to ride. To drum up interest in his new machine, Michaux organized a women's bicycle race. A racecourse in Bordeaux was roped off for the occasion, but when the female racers appeared in short skirts, the crowd of 3,000 burst through the barriers. Undaunted, the women sped off – a symbolic precursor of how bicycles were to liberate their sex.

4 _____

British engineers immediately set about trying to outdo Michaux. They improved his design by adding wire-spoked wheels and rubber tyres, drastically reducing the overall weight. In the absence of gears and chains, they could only increase the machine's top speed by making the front wheel bigger – which is how the rather precarious penny farthing evolved. But then, in 1885, the Rover Safety Bicycle was launched, with a low seat and chain-driven back wheel. It was safe, practical and fast – and the public loved it. Within two decades, almost every working man in Britain owned a bike.

5 _____

'Bicycling,' declared the American suffragist Susan Anthony in 1896, 'has done more to emancipate women than anything else in the world'. Previously, women had been restricted not just socially and legally, but physically, too: stuck at home in tight corsets and large, heavy skirts that made any movement difficult. The bicycle changed everything. It got them out and about (often without a chaperone to accompany them), made them strong and healthy, and prompted them to try new modes of dress.

6 _____

It caused a public scandal. One early female cyclist was pictured on the front of *The National Police Gazette*, underneath the outraged headline: 'SHE WORE TROUSERS'. Newspaper commentators thundered that these 'loose women' were pedalling along the path of destruction and doctors warned that the unusual physical exertion would cause serious harm to women.

7 _____

It revolutionized day-to-day life, especially for the middle and working classes. Instead of having to live in overcrowded, inner-city tenements, workers were suddenly able to commute in from newly-built suburbs. Cycling groups lobbied for smooth, asphalt roads to be laid down all over the country – thus literally paving the way for the bicycle's greatest competitor, the car. Indeed, the car might never have been invented if the bicycle had not got there first.

8 _____

Much of the technology involved in making bicycles was later used for making automobiles. Indeed, manufacturers such as Ford, Peugeot, Fiat and Škoda all made bicycles before they made cars. There is also, according to economists, a natural social progression from bicycles to cars. People in poor nations get on their bikes to look for work, thus invigorating the economy and making themselves rich, so that they can move on to cars. A modern example of this is China, where, increasingly, workers are exchanging their bikes for mopeds, motorbikes and cars.

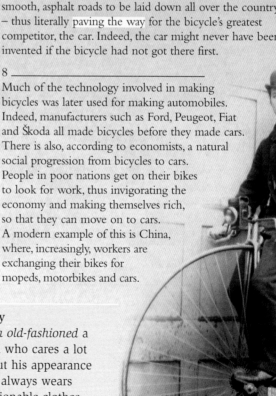

Glossary

dandy *n old-fashioned* a man who cares a lot about his appearance and always wears fashionable clothes

corset *n* a stiff piece of underwear worn by women to make their waists look thin, especially in the past

2D | A glimpse of the past

Exploratorium, San Francisco, US: a science museum with over 600 exhibits designed to let you explore, discover and play.

Jorvik, York, England: see over 800 items uncovered here, and journey through an indoor reconstruction of actual Viking-age streets.

Australian museum, Sydney, Australia: a museum of natural history and anthropology, with numerous collections covering zoology, mineralogy and paleontology.

Maison de la magie, Blois, France: dedicated to Blois-born magician Jean-Eugène Robert-Houdin (1805–1871), this museum houses a fascinating collection of magic objects and interactive exhibits.

Black Forest Open Air Museum, Gutach, Germany: a collection of farmhouses and other buildings which show how people have lived and worked in the area over the last 400 years.

LISTENING

1 Work in pairs. Answer the question.

- Which of these museums would you be most and least interested to visit?

   Compare your choices with your partner's, giving reasons for your opinions.

2 🔊 1.12 Listen to five people speaking about the museums above. Match the speakers 1–5 to the museums A–E.

3 🔊 1.12 Listen again and complete the table for the speakers 1–5.

What I liked about the museum	What I didn't like about the museum
1	
2	
3	
4	
5	

4 Work in pairs. Discuss the questions.

- Have you changed any of your views from exercise 1, after hearing speakers 1–5? Why or why not?
- Speaker 5 says: '... there's a more traditional part to it – what I understand by a "museum" – with displays of objects and things to read.' What do you understand by a 'museum'?
- What was the last museum you visited? How interactive were the displays? Did you enjoy it?

GRAMMAR: comparisons

1 There is one word missing in each sentence. Write the missing word in the correct place.

1 With his red cheeks and even redder nose he looked just a clown.
2 The older he got, less tolerant he became.
3 It's not quite such well-written book as her last, but the storyline is every bit as intriguing.
4 My new broadband connection enables me to download films much quickly than before.
5 In science this year we have to do quite lot more homework than last year.
6 With these roadworks it takes me twice long as usual to get to the office.
7 The land is farmed in very much same way as it was in the Middle Ages.
8 The beaches were nowhere near as good as last year and the hotel was far the worst we've ever stayed in.

Use *like* with nouns, pronouns or gerunds; use *as* with verb phrases.

> *You all sit in this car, a bit **like a rollercoaster car**.*
> *Getting Tom to do homework is **like getting** blood from a stone – impossible.*
> *If you work at home, **as I do/like me**, you'll know how lonely it can get.*

Use *the* + comparative, *the* + comparative when one thing is the result of another.

> ***The more** I hear the song, **the better** it sounds.*

Use *as* + adjective/adverb + *as* to show similarities and *not as/not so* to show differences. Use *not such* with nouns/noun phrases.

> *It's **not as cold as** yesterday.*
> *It's **not such a bad idea as** it sounds.*

Use these words to modify comparisons:

- before comparatives.
  a little/slightly/much/(quite) a lot/far/three times, four times etc/a great deal/even
  *I came out **a lot poorer than** when I went in.*
  *They were **far more interested** in the optical illusions.*
- before superlatives.
  by far, easily, far and away
  *It was **by far the best** day I've spent in a museum for a long time.*
- before *as* + adjective/adverb + *as*.
  not quite/(not) nearly/almost/just/half/twice, three times etc/nothing like/nowhere near/every bit
  *Some of the explanations in the dinosaur exhibition **weren't quite as clear as** they could have been.*
- before *the same (as)*.
  not quite/(not) nearly/almost/just/exactly/(very) much
  *His latest book is **much the same as** all his others.*

> ❯ SEE LANGUAGE REFERENCE PAGE 24

2 Complete the sentences with the words in the box.

> about   with   as   than   to   in

1 **There's nothing more** irritating _____ having to wait for someone who's late.
2 The food in my country is **unlike any other** _____ the world – it's fantastic.
3 **There is little to choose between** the political parties in my country. **They're all just as** bad _____ **each other**.
4 **The** worst **thing** _____ my school/work is that I have to get up so early.
5 My country's national football team **compares very favourably** _____ most others.
6 Our English teacher **bears a striking resemblance** _____ a famous TV personality.

3 Discuss each of the statements in exercise 2. Do you agree or disagree with them?

4 Use the expressions in bold in exercise 2 to write five sentences expressing your own opinions. Discuss your sentences with another student.

SPEAKING

1 Work in small groups or committees, A, B and C. You are going to prepare your proposal for a new national museum in your area.

Committee A: Turn to page 140.
Committee B: Turn to page 147.
Committee C: Turn to page 152.

2 Create new groups consisting of one member from each committee and present your proposals to each other. Then explain why your museum will be more successful than those of the other committees.

3 As a whole class, vote for one of the proposals. You may not vote for your own.

DID YOU KNOW?

1 Work in pairs. Read about Trafalgar Square statues and discuss the questions.

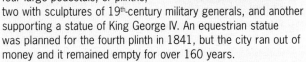

One of London's most famous statues can be found in Trafalgar Square, named in honour of Admiral Lord Nelson's naval victory over France at the Battle of Trafalgar in 1805. As well as a five-metre statue of the Admiral at the top of the imposing Nelson's Column, the square also contains four large pedestals, or plinths, two with sculptures of 19th-century military generals, and another supporting a statue of King George IV. An equestrian statue was planned for the fourth plinth in 1841, but the city ran out of money and it remained empty for over 160 years.

Then, in 2005, it was occupied by a controversial sculpture of a naked, disabled and pregnant woman. Entitled *Alison Lapper Pregnant*, it depicted a disabled artist a month before she gave birth to her son. Whilst many criticized the statue as unsuitable for such a famous public space, others welcomed it as a celebration of human diversity which challenged people's views of disability. As with its successors, the sculpture was only ever intended to occupy the plinth for a brief period, and it was replaced in 2007.

- What is your reaction to *Alison Lapper Pregnant*? Is it suitable for such a famous, historical square?
- If there were an empty plinth in a public square in your town, who or what would you like to see depicted on it? Why?

GRAMMAR
Gerunds & infinitives

The full infinitive (with *to*) is used:

- to express purpose.
  *I'm just going to the bank **to get** some money out.*
- after certain adjectives.
  eg (*I am/She was, etc*) *amazed, delighted, disappointed;*
  (*It is/was*) *easy, important, necessary*
  *We're **delighted to see** you. It's **easy to criticize** others.*
- after certain verbs.
  eg *agree, appear, arrange, attempt, demand, deserve, expect, help, hesitate, hope, learn, manage, need, offer, pretend, refuse, seem, struggle, threaten, would like, promise*
  *I've **decided to take** the exam but don't **expect to pass**.*
- after certain verbs with an object.
  eg *advise, allow, ask, enable, encourage, expect, force, help, invite, persuade, recommend, remind, teach, tell, warn*
  *The experience **taught me not to trust** anyone but myself.*
- after certain nouns.
  eg *ability, chance, decision, effort, failure, intention, opportunity, plan, power, refusal, right, tendency, way*
  *The defendant exercised his **right to remain** silent.*

The bare infinitive (without *to*) is used:

- after modal verbs.
  *You **can look** at it, but you **mustn't touch**.*
- after these verbs:
  help, had better, let, make, would rather/sooner
  *I'd **better go** – I promised to **help my dad clean** his car.*

The gerund is used:

- after prepositions.
  *She got tired **of waiting** for him and went home.*
- as the subject, object or complement of a sentence or clause.
  ***Eating** the right kind of food improves **learning**.*
- after certain verbs.
  eg *admit, adore, advise, appreciate, anticipate, avoid, consider, deny, dislike, enjoy, feel like, imagine, keep, mind, miss, prevent, recommend, resent, risk, suggest*
  *He **admitted breaking** the window, but **denied stealing** anything.*
  If the subjects of the main verb and the gerund are different, an object or possessive adjective is used.
  *I really **appreciate you/your helping** me like this.*
- after verbs which include the preposition *to*.
  eg *get round to, be/get used to, look forward to, object to.*
  *I still can't **get used to working** with a computer.*
- after these verbs and expressions:
  can't help, can't stand, have difficulty, it's/there's no use, it's (not) worth
  *It's **no use worrying** about it – it'll sort itself out.*

The gerund is used after *forget, remember, stop* and *regret* to refer to something which occurs before the act of *forgetting, remembering,* etc. The full infinitive is used for actions which occur afterwards.
*I **remember studying** this last year.*
***Remember to study** this for the exam next week.*

When followed by a gerund, *go on* means *to continue with the same activity.* With an infinitive, it means *to change to a different activity.*
*He **went on working** well after normal retirement age.*
*After outlining the problems, she **went on to offer** some solutions.*

Try + gerund means *experiment with: try* + infinitive means *attempt.*
***Try eating** it with honey – it makes it easier to digest.*
*I **tried to arrange** a meeting but she's always too busy.*

These verbs can be followed by the gerund or the full infinitive with no change in meaning:
begin, continue, hate, intend, like, love, prefer, start
*Don't **start writing/to write** until I say so.*

Comparisons

To compare two things or people, use the comparative form of adjectives and adverbs, or *more/less* with uncountable nouns and *more/fewer* with countable nouns.
*Look **more closely** and you'll see that this coin is **older than** the other one.*
*There are **fewer** cars, which means **less** pollution.*

These words can be used to modify comparatives: (*quite*) *a bit/a little/slightly/much;* (*quite*) *a lot/far/significantly/ considerably/three times, etc/a great deal/miles/even*
*Nadal is **considerably** better than his opponent.*

The + comparative, *the* + comparative shows that one thing is the result of another.
***The more often** you practise, **the easier** it becomes.*
***The more** I think about it, **the less** I like the idea.*

To compare more than two things or people, use the superlative form of adjectives and adverbs, or *the most/the least* with uncountable nouns and *the most/the fewest* with countable nouns. Modifying words: *by far, easily, far and away.*
*She's **the youngest** student in the class – and **by far the most intelligent**.*
*The winner is the person with **the fewest** points.*

as + adjective/adverb + *as*
Modifying words: *not quite/(not) nearly/almost/just/half/ twice, three times, etc/nothing like/nowhere near/every bit/so* can replace the first *as* in negative sentences.
*I'm **every bit as good as** him.*
*He's **not quite so tall as** me.*

the same as and _the same_ + noun + _as_
Modifying words: _not quite/(not) nearly/almost/just/exactly/(very) much_

> They look **almost the same as** each other.
> We think in **much the same way**.

Use _not such_ before adjective + uncountable and plural countable nouns; use _not such a_ before adjective + singular countable nouns.

> This is**n't such a good hotel** as last year. But then, last year we did**n't** have **such good weather**.

Like is used with nouns, pronouns or gerunds to make comparisons; _as_ is used with verb phrases.

> He's arrogant, just **like his father**.
> He worked down the mine, just **as his father had done**.

There are a number of common expressions which can be used to make comparisons:

> There is nothing worse/better/more annoying, etc than …
> The worst/best/hardest, etc thing about … is …
> There is little to choose between … and …
> … bears a striking/a close/a slight/no resemblance to …
> … is unlike …
> … compares (un)favourably with …

WORD LIST

Memory

bring back memories of (sth)
/ˌbrɪŋ bæk ˈmem(ə)riːz əv/

have a good/poor memory for
/ˌhæv ə ˈɡʊd, ˈpɔː(r), ˈpʊə(r) ˌmem(ə)ri fə/

have bittersweet/fond/painful/vague/ vivid memories of (sth)
/hæv ˌbɪtəˈswiːt, ˈfɒnd, ˈpeɪnf(ə)l, ˈveɪɡ, ˈvɪvɪd ˌmem(ə)riːz əv/

know (sth) by heart
/ˌnəʊ baɪ ˈhɑː(r)t/

names and faces n pl
/ˌneɪmz ən(d) ˈfeɪsɪz/

Playing cards

ace n C	/eɪs/
bet v **	/bet/
blackjack n U	/ˈblækˌdʒæk/
card counting n U	/ˈkɑː(r)d kaʊntɪŋ/
clubs n pl ***	/klʌbz/
deal v ***	/diːl/
deck n C **	/dek/
diamonds n pl **	/ˈdaɪəməndz/
draw v ***	/drɔː/
face up/down	/ˌfeɪs ˈʌp, ˈdaʊn/
face value n C	/ˌfeɪs ˈvæljuː/
hand n C ***	/hænd/
jack n C *	/dʒæk/
joker n C	/ˈdʒəʊkə(r)/
keep track of (sth)	/ˌkiːp ˈtræk əv/
odds n pl **	/ɒdz/
pack n C **	/pæk/
shuffle v *	/ˈʃʌf(ə)l/
spades n pl	/speɪdz/
suit n C ***	/suːt/

Way

change one's ways	/ˌtʃeɪndʒ wʌnz ˈweɪz/
get one's own way	/ˌget wʌnz ˈəʊn weɪ/
give way on (sth)	/ˌgɪv ˈweɪ ɒn/
go back a long way	/ˌgəʊ ˌbæk ə ˈlɒŋ weɪ/
go out of one's way to do (sth)	/ˌgəʊ ˌaʊt əv wʌnz ˈweɪ tə duː/
in a bad way	/ˌɪn ə ˈbæd ˌweɪ/
in a big way	/ˌɪn ə ˈbɪg ˌweɪ/
in a roundabout way	/ˌɪn ə ˈraʊndəˌbaʊt ˌweɪ/
know one's way around	/ˌnəʊ wʌnz ˈweɪ əˈraʊnd/
pave the way for (sth)	/ˌpeɪv ðə ˈweɪ fɔː(r)/
the wrong way round	/ðə ˌrɒŋ weɪ ˌraʊnd/
work one's way up	/ˌwɜː(r)k wʌnz ˈweɪ ˈʌp/

Other words & phrases

A-grade student n C	/ˈeɪˌɡreɪd ˈstjuːd(ə)nt/
automaton n C	/ɔːˈtɒmətən/
bar v ***	/bɑː(r)/
blacksmith n C	/ˈblækˌsmɪθ/
blanket ban n C	/ˈblæŋkɪt ˌbæn/
boost v **	/buːst/
chaperone n C	/ˈʃæpərəʊn/
cognition enhancer n C	/kɒɡˈnɪʃ(ə)n ɪnˌhɑːnsə/
come up with v	/ˌkʌm ˈʌp wɪð/
commit (sth) to memory	/kəˈmɪt tə ˈmem(ə)ri/
commute v	/kəˈmjuːt/
corset n C	/ˈkɔː(r)sɪt/
dandy n C	/ˈdændi/
digit n C	/ˈdɪdʒɪt/
dispose of v	/dɪsˈpəʊz əv/
do without v	/ˌduː wɪˈðaʊt/
drum up interest in (sth)	/ˌdrʌm ʌp ˈɪntrəst ɪn/
dummy n C	/ˈdʌmi/
ease v **	/iːz/
enhancer n C	/ɪnˈhɑːnsə(r)/
enhancing adj	/ɪnˈhɑːnsɪŋ/
enlightening adj	/ɪnˈlaɪt(ə)nɪŋ/
equestrian statue n C	/ɪˈkwestriən ˌstætʃuː/
facts and figures n pl	/ˈfækts ən(d) ˌfɪɡə(r)z/
fall to bits	/ˌfɔːl tʊ ˈbɪts/
flap v	/flæp/
fringe n C *	/frɪndʒ/
gene pool n C	/ˈdʒiːn ˌpuːl/
have an edge over (sb)	/ˌhæv ən ˈedʒ əʊvə(r)/
highlight n C *	/ˈhaɪˌlaɪt/
in a row	/ˌɪn ə ˈrəʊ/
indigenous adj	/ɪnˈdɪdʒənəs/
let alone	/ˌlet əˈləʊn/
lobby for v	/ˈlɒbi ˌfɔː(r)/
memorize v *	/ˈmeməraɪz/
memory n C ***	/ˈmem(ə)ri/
moped n C	/ˈməʊped/
norm n sing **	/nɔː(r)m/
optical illusion n	/ˌɒptɪk(ə)l ɪˈluːʒ(ə)n/
outraged adj	/ˈaʊtˌreɪdʒd/
peak performance n U	/ˈpiːk pə(r)ˌfɔː(r)məns/
pedestal n C	/ˈpedɪst(ə)l/
photographic memory	/ˌfəʊtəˈɡræfɪk ˌmem(ə)ri/
plinth n C	/plɪnθ/
plot of land	/ˌplɒt əv ˈlænd/
precarious adj	/prɪˈkeəriəs/
prompt v **	/prɒmpt/
retrieve v *	/rɪˈtriːv/
roller coaster n C	/ˈrəʊlə(r) ˌkəʊstə(r)/
rope (sth) off	/ˌrəʊp ˈɒf/
rupture n C	/ˈrʌptʃə(r)/
vault n	/vɔːlt/
wear off v	/ˌweə(r) ˈɒf/
whiff n C	/wɪf/
wire-spoked adj	/ˈwaɪə(r) ˌspəʊkd/

3A | Enough is enough

VOCABULARY: (not) having enough

1 Complete the sentences with the words in the box.

> adequate   lacking   needs   plenty
> short   shortages   supply   well

1 We're _____ **off for** parks in my area.
2 This town **is sadly** _____ **in** good sports facilities.
3 In my area we often suffer from **water** _____ in summer.
4. I'd like to work or study in an English-speaking country. My level of English is **perfectly** _____ **for** either.
5 I'm a bit _____ **of** cash at the moment. I need to go to the bank.
6 Well-paid jobs are **in short** _____ in this part of the country.
7 There are a lot of things I want to do. I've got _____ **of** time before I need to think about settling down.
8 The library resources in this school are **sufficient to meet the** _____ **of** students.

2 In exercise 1, tick (✓) those sentences which describe having enough or more than enough of something. Mark with a cross (✗) those sentences which describe not having enough of something.

3 Work in pairs. Discuss the sentences in exercise 1, saying how true each one is for you or your area.

READING

1 Look at the title and cover of a book by John Naish, as well as the quotation from the first page. Work in pairs and answer the questions.

- What do you think the book will be about? What views will it express?

2 Read the extract from John Naish's book, *Enough*, ignoring the gaps. Check your ideas from exercise 1.

3 Use the context to work out the meanings of the highlighted words and expressions.

4 Read the extract again and complete the gaps 1–7 with the correct sentence beginnings a–g.

a Meanwhile, the world carries on worrying about global warming
b There's hope in the steady flow of surveys
c One of the wiser ones might wonder

d These discoveries, along with advances in evolutionary psychology, show how we have built a culture that drives us to switch on all the wrong instincts
e This isn't a question of turning the clocks back or having less
f We were built to seek comfort and food
g But this is bearing strange fruit

5 Work in pairs. Discuss the questions, giving reasons for your opinions.

- *'In the Western world we now effectively have everything we could possibly need.'* Do you feel you have enough in the following areas of your life or do you hope to have more?

> work   leisure time   money   possessions
> housing   happiness   freedom

- Do you agree with the author's assessment that *'Enoughness is a tipping point, beyond which getting more of anything makes life worse rather than better'*?
- Do you share the brand of optimism the author expresses in the final paragraph?
- Would you be interested in reading John Naish's book?

GRAMMAR: adding emphasis with auxiliary verbs

> *Do, does, did* can add emphasis in positive statements. In speech the auxiliary is stressed.
>   *And we **do** have some evolving to do.*
>
> Emphatic *do* often indicates contrast/contradiction. Words such as *but*, *however* and *although* can also be used.
>   *I'm not a great tennis fan but I **did** watch the final on Saturday.*
>   *'It doesn't work.' 'It **does** work – you have to push this button, not that one.'*
>
> Other auxiliary verbs, positive or negative, can be stressed in speech to add emphasis or show contrast/contradiction.
>   *I **am** listening. I just closed my eyes, that's all.*
>   *But he **can't** be married – he looks so young!*
>
> *Do* is also used in persuasive commands, to show politeness or express annoyance.
>   ***Do** help yourself to more meat.*
>   *Oh, **do** stop arguing, you two!*

> ❯ SEE LANGUAGE REFERENCE PAGE 34

ENOUGH

He who knows he has enough is rich.
Tao Te Ching (c. 260 BC)

If an alien spacecraft were orbiting the blackened husk of Earth in centuries' time, its pilots might be appalled to learn how the human inhabitants had produced and consumed so much of everything that they had ultimately burnt the whole planet out. 'Daft idiots,' our aliens would say, shaking their silvery heads. If those visitors also learnt how we had only got grumpier, sicker and more exhausted as our pursuit of more of everything reached its climax, they would scratch their scalps and ask: 'What were they thinking?' (1) _____, 'How on earth did they fail to evolve?'

And we do have some evolving to do. And quickly. We need to develop a sense of enough. Or, if you fancy, enoughness. Or even enoughism. We have created a culture that has one overriding message – we do not yet have all we need to be satisfied. The answer, we are told, is to have, see, be and do even more. Always more. (2) _____: levels of stress, depression and burnout are all rising fast, even though we live amid unprecedented abundance. Our planet doesn't look so happy, either.

We urgently need to stop over-stimulating the powerful ancient instincts that make us never satisfied. Instead, we must nurture our capacities to appreciate the unprecedented wonders now at our feet. In the Western world we now effectively have everything we could possibly need. There is no 'more'. We have to learn to live 'post-more'. (3) _____, it's about realizing that we've arrived. Enoughness is a path to contentment. It's about personal ecology, about each of us finding our own sustainable balance as individuals. Enoughness is a tipping point, beyond which getting more of anything makes life worse rather than better.

We have at least now spotted the basic problem. In my research for this book, I've found that you can't enter a meeting of psychologists, economists or politicos without someone warning that half of us wealthy westerners are certifiably miserable, and that getting rich no longer makes us any happier. These pundits also complain that we're suffocating on our own exhaust pipes. But then they blame the economy. Or the Government. Or 'society'. Or they even say it's a sickness. (4) _____, grumbling about overwork and complaining of not being happy – while still chasing, making and consuming evermore, in the hope that it will cheer everyone up.

So long as it's someone else's problem, the cycle will continue until the planet is fit only for cockroaches. It's time to ditch our ancient habits. We rely on instincts that give old answers to new challenges – in particular the challenge of living amid abundance when our minds are still programmed to fear scarcity and to consume everything that we can. (5) _____, but not designed to find them all the time. We are lumbered with 'wanting' brains. Now, thanks to breakthroughs in neuroscience and medical technology, we can glimpse these ancient responses as they fire up in our heads.

(6) _____ – ones that respond to excess by seeking even more, that react to convenience by encouraging us to work harder, that make us hurry more when our leisure time increases, and that even make us eat more whenever we hurry. All of this creates a feedback loop where our needless desires drive our culture's economy more, and our culture's economy in turn drives our needless desires more. As Robert Trivers, an evolutionary biologist at Rutgers University, says, 'We've evolved to be maximizing machines. There isn't necessarily a stop mechanism in us that says, "Relax, you've got enough".'

Am I downhearted? No. (7) _____ – reporting how modern life increasingly leaves us miserable, tetchy, fearful and mad. Amid the global warming, we are seeing more personal warming – more stress and depression, more melting of our circuits. That's dismal for individuals. But, hey, it's our one hopeful sign of potential cultural shift. It may push growing numbers of us to embrace enoughism, to balance our personal ecologies in the pursuit of contentment, sanity and sustainability. As individuals, we can try to find balance by seeking only the things that we truly desire, rather than chasing manufactured rainbows. The knock-ons for our planet would grow if we could shift focus from ever-more to enoughness.

---

1 Use *do, does* or *did* to add emphasis to the verbs in bold. Make any other necessary changes.

*It **makes** me angry.*
It does make me angry.

1 I **think** he's right on this occasion.
2 She **told** me but I can't remember.
3 If anything **goes** wrong, phone me.
4 I **like** your hat.
5 I **did** my homework last night.
6 **Stop** worrying!

2 Include each of the sentences you wrote for exercise 1 in a short dialogue.

A: *Don't listen to him – I'm sure you're all right. You know he always talks nonsense.*
B: *Yes, I know. But I do think he's right on this occasion – I'm going to phone the doctor.*

Practise reading your dialogues with your partner. Make sure you stress the auxiliary verb.

3 Work in pairs, A and B. You are going to practise adding emphasis.

A: Turn to page 138.   B: Turn to page 146.

3B Rubbish!

SPEAKING & VOCABULARY: rubbish

1 Work in pairs and describe each pair of photos. Discuss the similarities and differences and say what you think might be happening in each.

2 Which of the photos has the greatest effect on you? Why?

3 Choose the correct words to complete the texts.

A Plastics go in one bag and we put food (1) *scraps / ends / rests* in another – they're for the garden. We take glass to the bottle (2) *account / bank / deposit* and if we want to throw away something big and bulky we take it in the car to the civic amenity site (more commonly known as the (3) *tap / tip / top*), where they have about a dozen enormous metal (4) *skips / junks / bowls* for all the different types of household refuse.

B We (5) *give away / put out / set off* our rubbish last thing at night, and the dustmen usually come about five in the morning to take it away. The noise of their (6) *rubbish dump / waste basket / dustcart* often wakes me up. There is no (7) *collection / compilation / gathering* on Sundays, so by Monday there are always huge (8) *lots / piles / masses* of rubbish in our street.

C Our local parks are full of (9) *matter / waste / litter*. People can't be bothered to put it in a bin so they just (10) *let fall / drop / dispose* it anywhere. I pick up any paper or cans I see and take them home.

4 Work in pairs. To what extent do the texts A–C in exercise 3 apply to you or your area?

LISTENING

1 Work in pairs. Discuss the questions.

- What recycling facilities are there in your area?
- To what extent does the public use them?

2 💿 **1.13** You are going to hear part of a radio programme investigating a recycling initiative in the English county of Dorset. Listen and answer the questions.

1 What does the initiative consist of?
2 What is its principal objective?
3 What is said about the following?
a) organic matter   b) a fishing boat   c) flashy jewellery

3 💿 **1.13** Listen again and decide whether these statements are true (T) or false (F). Correct the false statements.

1 The local council runs the recycling centres.
2 Dorset recycles about a third of domestic rubbish.
3 The recycling centres produce compost on site.
4 Rubbish from small businesses is not accepted at the centres.
5 Employees at the centres do not have to pay for items they take home.
6 There are no restrictions on what they sell to the public.
7 Some of the jewellery Gerry takes home is quite valuable.
8 The two students have come to look for some chairs.

4 Work in pairs. Discuss the questions.

- Would you buy rubbish from the centre? Why or why not?
- How much e-waste have you generated in recent years? How did you dispose of it?

SPEECH FEATURE: fronting

Who or what do the words in bold refer to in these sentences from the listening?

*Huge **it** was.*

*£150 **he** paid for **it**, and very happy **he** was too!*

*Really comfortable **they** are.*

The above sentences contain examples of 'fronting': the complement or object is placed before the subject and verb to give it emphasis.

It was huge. ➔ ***Huge** it was.*

He paid £150. ➔ ***£150** he paid.*

How is used with adjectives; *what* with nouns.

***How lucky** you are!*   ***What an idiot** I am!*

Whole clauses can be fronted, particularly those beginning with a question word.

Why anyone would want to bring a fishing boat to a place like this, *I have no idea.*

Clauses are often fronted before expressions such as *I'm not sure, I don't know, I couldn't tell you.*

> ❯ SEE LANGUAGE REFERENCE PAGE 34

1 Rewrite the sentences using fronting to create emphasis. Begin with the words in italics.

1   It was really expensive. *Really*
2   It cost me six hundred euros. *Six*
3   It's lovely to see you again. *How*
4   He's an awful man. *What*
5   I just don't know how she puts up with him. *How*
6   I couldn't tell you why they decided to buy me a walking stick. *Why*

2 🔊 **1.14–1.15** Listen to these two people. What objects are they describing?

3   Look at audioscripts 1.14–1.15 on page 156 and underline the examples of fronting.

4   Write your own description of something you bought or were given without mentioning the name of the object. Include some fronting.

5   Read your description to other students. Can they guess what you are describing?

DID YOU KNOW?

1   Work in pairs. Read about the PlasTax and discuss the questions.

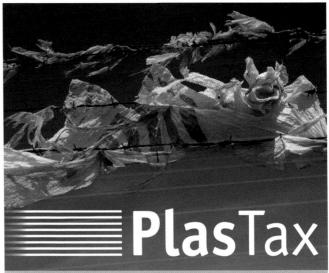

In 2002, the Republic of Ireland became the first country to charge a tax on disposable plastic shopping bags. The Plastic Bag Environmental Levy, or 'PlasTax', was introduced to change consumer behaviour and reduce the number of bags littering the Irish streets and countryside. The fifteen-cent tax on each bag was hailed as a success, with consumption falling by more than 90 per cent in the first year, from 1.2 billion to just under 90 million. In addition, over ten million euros was raised from the tax and paid into a new Environmental Fund to support waste management and other environmental initiatives.

Critics of the tax claim that plastic bags represent a relatively small percentage of total litter and a more comprehensive approach is needed to tackle the problem. They also complain that many shops have switched to using paper bags, which are more bulky than plastic bags and therefore more expensive to store and transport. The environmental group, *Friends of the Earth*, called for the tax to be doubled after the initial effect had worn off. They pointed out that rather than avoiding the tax by taking reusable bags when they went shopping, consumers were gradually becoming used to paying the fifteen cents.

- Would you be for or against such a tax in your country? Why?
- What other solutions to the problem of litter are there?

3c | Competitive eating

SPEAKING

1 Read the following information.

> The photo on page 31 shows Korean-born American Sonya Thomas, who takes part in competitive eating contests. These involve consuming large quantities of food, such as hot dogs or apple pie, in a short period of time, usually twelve minutes or less. Sonya holds over 20 eating records and earns as much as $60,000 a year.

2 Work in pairs, Pairs A and Pairs B. You are going to prepare for an interview with Sonya Thomas.
Pairs A: Turn to page 141 and prepare your questions.
Pairs B: Turn to page 152 and prepare your answers.

3 Change pairs, so that a student from a Pair A and a student from a Pair B work together. Roleplay the interview.

READING

1 Read the article. Which of the questions asked in your roleplay in Speaking exercise 3 is/are answered in the article?

2 Read the article again and decide whether the sentences are true (T) or false (F). Explain with reference to the text why the false sentences are incorrect.

1 The writer suggests that Sonya's achievements are surprising.
2 In Baltimore she is attempting to regain a record she recently lost.
3 Early success encouraged her to participate in more eating contests.
4 The writer says that the thinner a person is, the better they will be at competitive eating.
5 The first eating contest was held some six years ago.
6 In Baltimore, contestants are not allowed to drink during the contest.
7 Doctors are always present at competitive eating contests.
8 Sonya is unhappy with her performance in Baltimore.

3 Match the highlighted verbs in the article to the definitions 1–8.

1 tell someone a secret
2 pick something up suddenly and roughly
3 eat very quickly
4 chew
5 put food into liquid before eating it
6 make something wet with one's tongue
7 think about something carefully
8 be unable to breathe because your airway is blocked

4 Work in pairs. Discuss the questions.

• What type of criticism do you think competitive eating comes in for? What is your own reaction to such contests?
• Do you consider competitive eating to be a sport? Why or why not?

VOCABULARY: excess

1 Work in pairs and discuss the questions. Use a dictionary if necessary.

1 How often do you do the following?
 • **overeat**
 • **oversleep**
 • **go overdrawn**
2 Which of these adjectives apply to you?
 • **overworked**
 • **overtired**
 • **oversensitive**
3 Give examples of the following:
 • a film which is **overrated**
 • a profession which is **overpaid**
 • a person who is **overexposed** on television
 • something you bought which was **overpriced**

2 Complete the sentences with the prepositions in the box.

> in   in   of   over   to   to   with

1 There are no easy solutions to the growing problem of **binge-drinking**, the practice among young people of **drinking** _____ **excess**.
2 People who drive at **speeds** _____ **excess** _____ 120kph should lose their licence for six months.
3 Sexual equality is all very well but some people **take it** _____ **extremes**.
4 Junk mail is not effective: **bombarding** people _____ information, advice and offers leads to **overkill** and people stop reading it.
5 It's alright for films to have some violence, but some really do **go** _____ **the top**.
6 'Moderation _____ **all things**': that's the best way to live life.

3 Work in pairs. Discuss the statements in exercise 2.

Me and my BIG MOUTH

When you first see Sonya Thomas you wonder whether she might be blown away by the breeze that is bouncing off Baltimore's inner harbour this bright and sunny morning. She is a very
5 **slim woman indeed, just seven stones zero by her own reckoning, and around 5ft 5in*. Yet as unlikely as it seems, Sonya, or 'The Black Widow' as she calls herself, is America's number one eater.**

10 What is even more remarkable is that Sonya is the overall eating champion – not just in the skinny women category. She routinely destroys men more than twice her size, wolfing down her food as they stand nauseated and unable to push any more into their mouths. To give some
15 idea of this woman's ability, consider just some of the records she currently holds: 552 oysters in ten minutes, 5.95lbs of meatballs in twelve minutes, 162 chicken wings in twelve minutes, and 52 hard-boiled eggs in five minutes. Last August in Harrington, Delaware, Sonya ate
20 an astonishing 40 crabcakes in twelve minutes. It is that record she is here this morning to defend, or rather, to break. She has a plan to make it happen. 'It's actually easier if you can dunk them in water,' she confides.

Her first try at competitive eating came in 2003 during a
25 qualifier for the World Cup of competitive eating – the 4 July hot dog challenge at Coney Island. In that qualifier Sonya managed eighteen dogs, giving her a slot in the final where she ate 25, which was a new record for women eaters. 'I didn't know I was good at this,' she
30 says. 'The first time I did it, it was just for fun. It just came out good so I thought, "OK, let's do it".'

Many have pondered Sonya's talent. One idea is the 'band of fat theory', which suggests larger eaters struggle to expand their stomachs because they are constrained
35 by the fat. They point out that the world champion eater, the near-legendary Takeru Kobayashi of Japan, is also as skinny as Sonya. Dedication is also a factor. Sonya regularly practises for contests.

The so-called sport of eating contests – while dating
40 back decades to events held at county fairs around the country – has only really had a national profile for the last half-dozen years since being sponsored by the International Federation of Competitive Eating, a New York marketing company which 'governs' 100 or so
45 events and annually pays out $250,000 in prize money.

On a stage alongside the harbour, the lightly-grilled crabcakes, made from blue crab meat and a number of other ingredients, are set on metal trays and placed on tables. Each crabcake has 160 calories. The judge

50 – 'Hungry' Charles Hardy, a former competitive eater himself – has some disturbing news for Sonya. There will be no dunking of the crabcakes in water, he declares. 'It's too hard to measure.'

Hardy reveals that, as at every eating contest, there are
55 medics on hand. While there are no studies showing actual proven dangers, doctors have warned of the potential risks of speed eating and in Japan – another stronghold of competitive eating – several people choked to death during contests in the 1990s.

60 It's time to get started. As the biggest name at the contest, Sonya comes on last and stands centre-stage. She licks her fingers. The countdown begins. They're off. Sonya grabs a handful of crabcake and pushes it into her mouth. It is gone in an instant and she pushes
65 in more, masticating like a machine. She eats with one hand, using the other to take sips from a bottle. After one minute it is announced she has eaten eight.

All around her are scenes of farce and horror. Food and water and a combination of the two drip down faces as
70 the contestants seek to push in more. Nine minutes in and Sonya has eaten 43 crabcakes. The last seconds are excruciating and messy as the competitors try to force in a few last mouthfuls. It looks terribly painful. Then, at last, it is over.

75 There is a pause as the judges add up the numbers. And then it is announced that Sonya has eaten 46 crabcakes. It is a new record. She is thrilled. 'I went very fast at the start. Then after about five or six minutes, I slowed down,' she says. 'I feel OK – I could eat more.'

80 She stands for photographs, a huge smile across her face and her skinny arms holding the oversized prize-winner's cheque above her head.

*7 stones = 44 kilograms;
5ft 5in = 1m 65cm

Glossary
nauseated *adj* made to feel sick
excruciating *adj* very
    unpleasant to experience

3D | A cautionary tale

SPEAKING

1 Work in small groups. Imagine that you all live on the beautiful but remote tropical island of Nauru, where the discovery of mineral resources has brought great wealth to the population. Everyone has benefited financially and nothing is lacking.

Discuss how you would each spend your time and money on the island. What would be the positive and negative aspects of such a life?

LISTENING

1 🎧 **1.16** Listen to the radio programme about Nauru. Put the following in the order they are mentioned. The recording is divided into six different parts. Write numbers 1–6 in the boxes below.

- ☐ Nauru's mineral wealth
- ☐ Present-day life on the island
- ☐ An island of superlatives
- ☐ The President's hopes for the future
- ☐ A life of leisure
- ☐ The road to ruin

2 🎧 **1.16** Listen again and answer the following questions, making brief notes. There is one question for each part.

1 Which 'world-beating statistics' does Rob Crossan mention in relation to Nauru?
2 How was the rock on Nauru formed and why was it so important to Australia?
3 How were profits distributed to Nauruans and what did they spend them on?
4 What 'ill-advised rescue schemes' were implemented to save the island?
5 How do many Nauruans spend their mornings now?
6 What does the President of Nauru think will attract tourists to the island?

3 🎧 **1.16** Listen and check. Work in pairs. Discuss the questions.

- Would you be interested in visiting Nauru? Why or why not?
- Do you know any other 'riches to rags' stories? What happened and why?

GRAMMAR: cleft sentences

Cleft sentences add emphasis to a noun, a person, a time, a phrase or a clause using the structures *It is/was … that/who …* or *What … is/was …* In the following examples, the underlined part of the sentence is being emphasized.

> **It was** <u>an Australian, Albert Ellis,</u> **who** *made the discovery from which Nauru is still reeling.*
> **It was** <u>only in 1968</u> **that** *the Nauruans could begin to benefit from their riches.*
> **What** *strikes one first about the island* **is** <u>its size</u>.
> **What** *they did* **was** *(to)* <u>ship the phosphate to Australia.</u>

A number of other words can be used instead of *what*, eg *the thing (that), something (that), the person/people (who/that), someone (that)*.

> **The people** *who extracted the phosphate* **were** <u>Chinese labourers</u>.

All can be used instead of *what* to mean 'the only thing that'.

> **All** *the islanders did in the way of exercise* **was** <u>walk to the government offices once a week.</u>

> ❯ SEE LANGUAGE REFERENCE PAGE 34

1 Rewrite the sentences, emphasizing the underlined part.

1 I began to make changes in my life <u>after I read John Naish's book *Enough*</u>.
It _____.

2 I just <u>looked at the cover</u> and I knew the book would interest me.
All _____.

3 I'm curious to know <u>what kind of people come to the recycling centre to buy things</u>.
One thing _____.

4 I mostly look out for <u>flashy jewellery</u>.
What _____.

5 We've only got <u>a wooden crate</u>.
All _____.

6 <u>Sonya is the overall eating champion</u> – that's remarkable.
What _____.

7 Sonya ate 40 crabcakes in 12 minutes. She is here this morning to defend <u>that record</u>.
Sonya ate 40 crabcakes in 12 minutes.
It _____.

8 <u>British sailor John Fearn</u> was the first outsider who laid eyes on Nauru.
The first _____.

🌐 1.17 Listen and check.

2 Complete the sentences using your own ideas.

1 What I like most about _____ is
_____.

2 It was when I was _____ that
_____.

3 Something I've always wanted to do is
_____.

4 The person I most admire is/was
_____.

5 All _____ ever talk(s) about is
_____.

6 What the government ought to do is
_____.

3 Read out your sentences from exercise 2 to your partner, giving more details for each one.

VOCABULARY: adjective affixes

1 Use the correct adjective form of the words in capitals to complete these extracts from the recording. One of the adjectives requires a negative prefix.

… the rising tides caused by _global_ warming.	GLOBE
1 Rob Crossan tells a _____ tale.	CAUTION
2 Phosphate (is) a must for _____ agriculture.	SUCCESS
3 These included the purchase of _____ properties abroad.	NUMBER
4 The President (has) the _____ task of recovering the mined-out ruin of Nauru.	ENVY
5 He tells me his _____ plans to bring tourists to Nauru.	IMAGINE

2 Use the same suffixes as in exercise 1 to form adjectives from the following words. Use the same suffix for all three nouns in each group.

origin	person	environment
original	*personal*	*environmental*
1 represent	inform	compare
2 advise	forget	apply
3 literature	volunteer	imagine
4 advantage	courtesy	humour
5 harm	power	faith

3 Complete the text with the correct form of the words in brackets. Use the suffixes in the box. You may also need to use a negative prefix.

-ive   -~~ful~~   -ial (x2)   -able (x2)   -ible (x2)   -y   -ed   -less

It must be rather _stressful_ (*stress*) to win or come into a (1) _____ (*substance*) amount of money and suddenly become rich. There'd be all those unwanted begging letters and (2) _____ (*expect*) visits from long-forgotten friends – lots of would-be (3) _____ (*finance*) 'experts' telling you what to do with it all. Some people can be very (4) _____ (*persuade*) in these matters and sound extremely (5) _____ (*knowledge*) despite having absolutely no idea – you'd have to be very careful. If it happened to me, I'd be very (6) _____ (*sense*) as to how I spent it. I think it's (7) _____ (*response*) to go out and blow it all on a huge house or a luxury yacht, but I'd probably buy a new car. I'd also give some to a deserving cause, like a charity for (8) _____ (*home*) people, and then save the rest for a (9) _____ (*rain*) day. Life is so (10) _____ (*predict*), so it's best to be prepared.

Work in pairs. Discuss the question.

• What would you do with the money if you suddenly became rich?

GRAMMAR
Adding emphasis

A number of techniques can be used to add emphasis in spoken and written English. For information on inversion, see page 94.

Auxiliary verbs

In spoken English, auxiliary verbs can be stressed to give more emphasis to a sentence, and to express, for example, surprise, enthusiasm, criticism or certainty.

> I **must** remember to post that letter.
> Goodness me, you **have** lost weight!

If there is no auxiliary verb, *do, does* and *did* can be used in affirmative sentences. This use is found in both spoken and written English, though it is more common in conversation.

> I **do** like your new dress!
> He **does** worry a lot, doesn't he?
> I **did** enjoy the party last night.

Further emphasis can be added by using adverbs such as *really, certainly* or *definitely* before a stressed auxiliary verb.

> I **really do** think you should phone her.
> She **certainly is** looking better, isn't she?

Auxiliary verbs, both positive and negative, can be used to show contrast/contradiction, often with the addition of *but, however* or *although*.

> 'Why did you hit him?' 'I **didn't** hit him!'
> I'm not very sporty but I **do** like playing tennis.

Do is also used in persuasive commands, to show politeness or express annoyance.

> **Do** come in! **Do** be careful! **Do** hurry up!

Fronting

Fronting involves moving information to the front of a sentence, often to give it emphasis.

- Some features are more typical of informal spoken English.
  > **Really good** it was – the best film I've seen all year.
  > **Ten quid** it cost me – daylight robbery!

  How can be used before adjectives and *what* before nouns:
  > **How clever** you are! **What a great party** it was!

- Some types of fronting involve inversion of the subject and verb and occur more frequently in written English.
  > **Far more important** is an applicant's experience.
  > **Enclosed** is a cheque for £125.
  > **Waiting at the station** was his Aunt Clarissa.

- Also more common in written English is the following structure:
  > **Tired as/though she was**, she kept on walking.
  > (= Although she was tired, she kept on walking.)

- Whole clauses can be fronted without subject-verb inversion in both spoken and written English.
  > **What he does for a living** I couldn't tell you.
  > **Whether he loved her or not** she did not know.

Clefting

The structures *It is/was ... that ...* and *What ... is/was ...* together with variations of these, can be used in the following ways:

1 *It is/was ... that ...* can be used in both spoken and written English:

- to emphasize a thing or a person; *who* can be used in place of *that* when referring to people.
  > **It was** his age **that** prevented him getting the job.
  > **It's** her husband **who** does all the cooking.

- with *because* to emphasize reasons.
  > **It was because** he refused to give up drinking **that** she left him.

- with *(only) when, while, not until* + verb clause to emphasize a time.
  > **It was only when/It wasn't until** I got home **that** I realized I didn't have my keys with me.
  > **It was while** I was in hospital **that** he proposed to me.

- to emphasize prepositional phrases.
  > **It was after dinner that** he phoned, not before.

2 *What ... is/was ...* is more frequent in conversation and can be used to emphasize:

- nouns and noun phrases, including gerunds.
  > **What** irritates me most about her **is** her laugh/the way she laughs.
  > **What** I most enjoyed about the holiday **was** not having to set the alarm clock.

- an action or series of actions.
  > **What** you do **is** (to) fold the two end pieces like this.
  > **What** happened **was** (that) I overslept and missed my plane.

- embedded questions.
  > **What** I've never understood **is** why he resigned.
  > **What** I'd like to know **is** when you're leaving.

Alternatives to the word *What* in the structure above are *The thing, One thing* and *Something. All* can also be used, meaning 'the only thing that'.

> **One thing** I won't tolerate **is** rudeness.
> What a boring job – **all** I did **was** count cars all day.

The person, One person and *Someone* can be used to emphasize a person.

> **One person** I'd like to meet **is** Johnny Depp.

The order of clauses can be, and often is, reversed.

> Rudeness **is one thing** I won't tolerate.
> Her laugh **is what** irritates me most.

WORD LIST

(not) having enough

(perfectly) adequate for *adj*	/ˈpɜː(r)fɪk(t)li ˈædɪkwət fɔː(r), fə(r)/
(sadly) lacking in *adj*	/ˈsædli ˈlækɪŋ ɪn/
have plenty of	/hæv ˈplenti əv, ɒv/
in short supply	/ɪn ʃɔː(r)t səˈplaɪ/
short of *adj*	/ʃɔː(r)t əv, ɒv/
sufficient to meet the needs of	/səˈfɪʃ(ə)nt tə miːt ðə niːdz əv, ɒv/
water shortage *n C*	/ˈwɔːtə(r) ˈʃɔː(r)tɪdʒ/
well off for *adj*	/wel ɒf fɔː(r), fə(r)/

Rubbish

bottle bank *n C*	/ˈbɒt(ə)l ˌbæŋk/
bulky *adj*	/ˈbʌlki/
civic amenity site *n C*	/ˌsɪvɪk əˈmiːnəti saɪt/
drop litter	/ˌdrɒp ˈlɪtə(r)/
dustcart *n C*	/ˈdʌs(t)ˌkɑː(r)t/
dustman *n C*	/ˈdʌs(t)mən/
food scraps *n pl*	/ˈfuːd ˌskræps/
piles of rubbish	/ˌpaɪlz əv ˈrʌbɪʃ/
put the rubbish out	/ˌpʊt ðə ˈrʌbɪʃ aʊt/
refuse *n U*	/ˈrefjuːs/
rubbish collection *n C*	/ˈrʌbɪʃ kəˌlekʃ(ə)n/
skip *n C*	/skɪp/
throw (sth) away *v*	/ˌθrəʊ əˈweɪ/
tip *n C* **	/tɪp/

Excess

binge drinking *n U*	/ˈbɪndʒ ˌdrɪŋkɪŋ/
bombard (sb) with	/ˌbɒmˈbɑː(r)d wɪθ/
do (sth) to excess	/ˌduː tʊ ɪkˈses/
go over the top	/ˌgəʊ ˈəʊvə(r) ðə ˌtɒp/
go overdrawn	/ˌgəʊ əʊvə(r)ˈdrɔːn/
in excess of	/ˌɪn ɪkˈses əv, ɒv/
overeat *v*	/ˌəʊvərˈiːt/
overexposed *adj*	/ˌəʊvərɪkˈspəʊzd/
overkill *n U*	/ˈəʊvə(r)ˌkɪl/
overpaid *adj*	/ˌəʊvə(r)ˈpeɪd/
overpriced *adj*	/ˌəʊvə(r)ˈpraɪst/
overrated *adj*	/ˌəʊvəˈreɪtɪd/
oversensitive *adj*	/ˌəʊvə(r)ˈsensətɪv/
oversleep *v*	/ˌəʊvə(r)ˈsliːp/
overtired *adj*	/ˌəʊvə(r)ˈtaɪə(r)d/
overworked *adj*	/ˌəʊvə(r)ˈwɜː(r)kt/
take (sth) to extremes	/ˌteɪk tʊ ɪkˈstriːmz/

Adjective affixes

caution *n U* **	/ˈkɔːʃ(ə)n/
cautionary *adj*	/ˈkɔːʃ(ə)nəri/
envy *n U*	/ˈenvi/
(un)enviable *adj*	/(ʌn)ˈenviəb(ə)l/
expect *v* ***	/ɪkˈspekt/
(un)expected *adj* **	/(ʌn)ɪkˈspektɪd/
faith *n U* ***	/feɪθ/
faithful *adj* *	/ˈfeɪθf(ə)l/
globe *n C*	/gləʊb/
global *adj* ***	/ˈgləʊb(ə)l/
home *n C* ***	/həʊm/
homeless *adj* *	/ˈhəʊmləs/
imagine *v* ***	/ɪˈmædʒɪn/
imaginative *adj* *	/ɪˈmædʒɪnətɪv/
number *n C* ***	/ˈnʌmbə(r)/
numerous *adj* **	/ˈnjuːmərəs/
persuade *v* ***	/pə(r)ˈsweɪd/
persuasive *adj* *	/pə(r)ˈsweɪsɪv/
rain *n C* ***	/reɪn/
rainy *adj*	/ˈreɪni/
response *n C* ***	/rɪˈspɒns/
(ir)responsible *adj* ***	/(ˌɪ)rɪˈspɒnsəb(ə)l/
substance *n U* ***	/ˈsʌbstəns/
substantial *adj* ***	/səbˈstænʃ(ə)l/

Other words & phrases

amiable *adj*	/ˈeɪmiəb(ə)l/
appalled *adj*	/əˈpɔːld/
at a premium	/ət ə ˈpriːmiəm/
blacklist *v*	/ˈblækˌlɪst/
book price *n C*	/ˈbʊk ˌpraɪs/
bottom line *n sing*	/ˌbɒt(ə)m ˈlaɪn/
breakthrough *n C* *	/ˈbreɪkθruː/
buck *n C*	/bʌk/
bulging *adj*	/ˈbʌldʒɪŋ/
burnout *n U*	/ˈbɜː(r)naʊt/
cash handout *n C*	/ˌkæʃ ˈhændaʊt/
cheapskate *n C*	/ˈtʃiːpˌskeɪt/
choke *v* *	/tʃəʊk/
chuck (sth) out *v*	/ˌtʃʌk ˈaʊt/
come in for criticism	/ˌkʌm ɪn fə ˈkrɪtɪˌsɪz(ə)m/
compost *n U*	/ˈkɒmpɒst/
confide *v* *	/kənˈfaɪd/
conman *n C*	/ˈkɒnmæn/
countless *adj* *	/ˈkaʊntləs/
crate *n C*	/kreɪt/
criticism	/ˈkrɪtɪˌsɪz(ə)m/
crockery *n U*	/ˈkrɒkəri/
decay *v* *	/dɪˈkeɪ/
decompose *v*	/ˌdiːkəmˈpəʊz/
dismal *adj*	/ˈdɪzm(ə)l/
disposable *adj* *	/dɪˈspəʊzəb(ə)l/
ditch *v*	/dɪtʃ/

downhearted *adj*	/ˌdaʊnˈhɑː(r)tɪd/
dunk *v*	/dʌŋk/
e-waste *n U*	/ˈiːˌweɪst/
excruciating *adj*	/ɪkˈskruːʃiˌeɪtɪŋ/
fake *adj*	/feɪk/
fire up *v*	/ˌfaɪə(r) ˈʌp/
flashy *adj*	/ˈflæʃi/
glimpse *v*	/glɪmps/
grab *v* **	/græb/
grumpy *adj*	/ˈgrʌmpi/
hail (sth) as a success	/ˈheɪl əz ə səkˌses/
have (*distance*) on the clock	/ˌhæv ɒn ðə ˈklɒk/
husk *n C*	/hʌsk/
junk shop *n C*	/ˈdʒʌŋk ˌʃɒp/
knock-on *n C*	/ˈnɒk ˌɒn/
landfill site *n C*	/ˈlæn(d)fɪl ˌsaɪt/
lick *v* *	/lɪk/
life expectancy *n U*	/ˌlaɪf ɪkˈspektənsi/
lumbered with *adj*	/ˈlʌmbə(r)d ˌwɪð/
masticate *v*	/ˈmæstɪkeɪt/
money- laundering *n U*	/ˈmʌni ˌlɔːnd(ə)rɪŋ/
nauseated *adj*	/ˈnɔːziˌeɪtɪd/
needless *adj*	/ˈniːdləs/
nurture *v*	/ˈnɜː(r)tʃə(r)/
overriding *adj*	/ˌəʊvəˈraɪdɪŋ/
oversized *adj*	/ˌəʊvə(r)ˌsaɪzd/
pallet *n C*	/ˈpælət/
scratch one's scalp	/ˌskrætʃ wʌnz ˈskælp/
perk *n C*	/pɜː(r)k/
pick up a bargain	/ˌpɪk ˌʌp ə ˈbɑː(r)gɪn/
ponder *v*	/ˈpɒndə(r)/
quarry *n C*	/ˈkwɒri/
reel *v*	/riːl/
rust *v*	/rʌst/
shed *n C* **	/ʃed/
sip *n C*	/sɪp/
slot *n C* *	/slɒt/
snap (sth) up *v*	/ˌsnæp ˈʌp/
stronghold *n C*	/ˈstrɒŋˌhəʊld/
stuffing *n U*	/ˈstʌfɪŋ/
suffocate *v*	/ˈsʌfəkeɪt/
sustainable *adj*	/səˈsteɪnəb(ə)l/
tackle a problem	/ˌtæk(ə)l ə ˈprɒbləm/
tax haven *n C*	/ˈtæks ˌheɪv(ə)n/
tetchy *adj*	/ˈtetʃi/
thrilled *adj*	/θrɪld/
tipping point *n C*	/ˈtɪpɪŋ ˌpɔɪnt/
unprecedented *adj* *	/ʌnˈpresɪˌdentɪd/
wear off *v*	/ˌweə(r) ˈɒf/
wolf (sth) down	/ˌwʊlf ˈdaʊn/

4A | Voicing complaints

SPEAKING

1 Work in groups of three. Take turns to describe the photos. Talk about why the people might be complaining, the way in which they are complaining and how they might be feeling.

2 Tell each other about a time when you made a complaint. Say **why** you complained, **how** you complained and what the **outcome** was.

READING

1 Read the blogs A–C and answer these questions.

- What is each blogger complaining about?
- Do you sympathize with their views? Why or why not?

2 Read the blogs again and decide which blogger ...

1 almost suffered a serious misfortune.
2 complains that an existing problem is being made worse.
3 says their reaction towards certain people has changed.
4 feels the name of a certain organization is inappropriate.
5 wonders if their view is widely shared.
6 points out the benefits of complaining on their blog.
7 complains about a lack of originality.
8 says that the same problem occurs with great frequency.
9 talks about the aggressive attitude of some people.
10 urges readers to take action.

3 Underline those words and expressions which the bloggers use to express irritation.

drive me to distraction

4 Work in small groups. You are going to 'have a good old moan', like the bloggers. Tell each other about something which irritates you using some of the words and expressions you found in exercise 3.

VOCABULARY: ways of speaking

1 Match the definitions a and b to the verbs in bold in sentences 1 and 2 from blog B.

1 *... you can hear them ... **muttering** under their breath about you as you walk away.*
2 *I'm **moaning** about nothing again, aren't I?*
a speaking in a quiet voice when you are annoyed about something
b complaining in an annoying way, usually about something unimportant (informal)

2 Complete each sentence beginning 1–8 with the appropriate ending a–h.

1 'Please keep your voice down!' the librarian
2 The news came as a shock. 'D-d-dead?' he
3 'He gave me his autograph!' the young girl
4 'Get to your classroom this instant!'
5 'Oh! Why can't I have some sweets?' he
6 'How did the date go?' I asked. 'Alright,' he
7 'Good morning!' 'What's good about it?' she
8 'Oh, no, not another delay,' she

a **shrieked**, excitedly.
b **bellowed** the headmaster loudly.
c **whispered,** fiercely.
d **snapped** back angrily, throwing her bag down.
e **stuttered**, hardly daring to believe it.
f **sighed**, wondering if it would ever take off.
g **grunted**, and disappeared to his bedroom.
h **whined** tearfully to his mother. 'It's not fair!'

3 🔊 1.18 Listen to check your answers, then practise saying the utterances in 1–8 in exercise 2 as you heard them on the recording.

4 Work in pairs, A and B. You will practise different ways of speaking.

A: Turn to page 141.   B: Turn to page 150.

5 Complete the sentences with the words in the box.

teeth   lips   voice   tongue   mouth   word

1 **The question on everyone's** _____ **at the moment is** 'Who will be the next president?'
2 I find it hard to **get my** _____ **round** Welsh place names – there are too many consonants.
3 The main opposition party was first to _____ **criticism of** the proposed reforms.
4 **You can't believe a** _____ **of what** Laura **says** – she **lies through** her _____.
5 I've learnt to **keep my** _____ **shut** when my dad starts talking politics – it's safer that way.

6 Use the words in bold in exercise 5 to write your own true sentences. Discuss your sentences with your partner.

A Our buses drive me to distraction

I've had it up to here with buses! To be more precise, I am sick to death of the service offered by the shambolic outfit that masquerades as our local bus company and which dares to call itself Reliabus – a misnomer if ever there was one, since
5 its exhaust-fume-coughing, atmosphere-choking buses are anything but reliable. Nine times out of ten they arrive late, and when they do eventually turn up, there's no guarantee you'll get on. I've lost count of the times I have watched as a full-to-bursting number 26 – which I try to catch home from
10 college – sails past the bus stop (another misnomer), leaving weary travellers like myself to wait for at least another 20 minutes until the next one comes along. Unless of course that's full as well, in which case we have to wait even longer. It's so infuriating! Why don't they lay on more buses?

15 It annoys me to think that our public transport service is in the hands of these incompetents. They are turning people away from travelling by public transport, encouraging them to use their cars and causing traffic chaos in our already heavily-congested town centre. I wrote them an email and
20 gave them a piece of my mind. If you're as fed up as I am, why not do the same? If enough of us kick up a fuss, they might just sit up and take notice.

B Leave me alone!

Friday 12th May

If there's one thing that gets on my nerves, it's people who keep trying to sell me things I don't want. It drives me mad when I'm in the middle of my dinner or watching a film and some
5 smooth-talking idiot phones up and asks me if I'm interested in new kitchen units, a subscription to a book club or a superfast internet connection. No, I'm not, thank you very much, and if I was, I'd get in touch with you! I very nearly burnt the
10 house down the other day answering one of their ridiculous calls. I forgot I'd left a couple of fillets frying in the kitchen – just got back to the blackened remains in time.

It's even worse outside of the home – sometimes
15 you can't move for people handing out fliers in the street, advertising computer classes or urging you to buy this, that or the other. They push one into your face, and if you don't take it, they give you a nasty look and you can hear them
20 swearing and muttering under their breath about you as you walk away. Not nice at all.

I know, I know, I'm moaning about nothing again, aren't I? But I don't see anything wrong in having a good old moan every now and then to get
25 things off your chest – and what better place to do it than here? You can release all your tensions, vent your anger and frustrations and you don't upset anyone – well, not knowingly, anyway!

C I HATE clowns

READ MORE

Don't you just hate circuses? It amazes me that they still exist, quite frankly. Don't get me wrong, I have no problem with performing animals. I'm not one of these animal rights defenders.
5 In fact, I think the lions and tigers have a good time running round, jumping through hoops and things. No, what I object to are the human performers: trapeze artists in silly clothes swinging upside down in the air, and fire-eaters,
10 acrobats and jugglers all showing off, doing things everyone's seen millions of times before.

And then there are the clowns. When I was a little kid the clowns used to really freak me out and give me nightmares. Now I just find them
15 unfunny and irritating – they really get up my nose. Who wants to see a load of grown men falling over and throwing things at each other? Pathetic. Maybe it's just me, I don't know. Am I alone in this or is this a commonly held opinion?

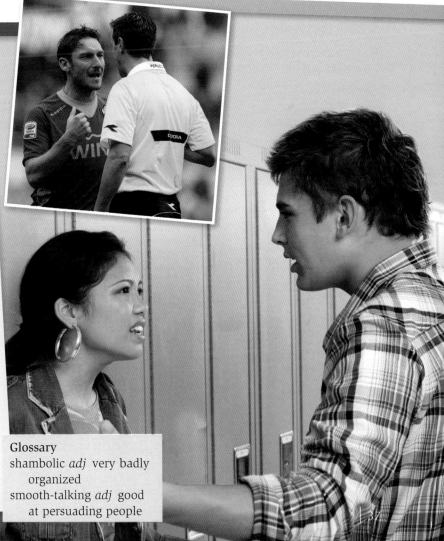

Glossary
shambolic *adj* very badly organized
smooth-talking *adj* good at persuading people

4B | Voice complaints

VOCABULARY: voice

1 Work in pairs. Give examples of situations when you might *lower*, *raise*, *strain* or *disguise* your voice.

2 The adjectives in the box can all be used to describe types of voice. Arrange them into pairs of words with similar meanings.

shaky & trembling

~~shaky~~	deep	soft
flat	hoarse	~~trembling~~
gentle	squeaky	croaky
expressionless	high-pitched	
booming		

3 For each pair of adjectives in exercise 2 think of someone, famous or otherwise, that they describe. Compare your ideas with your partner.

4 How would you describe your own voice? In what circumstances, if any, does it change?

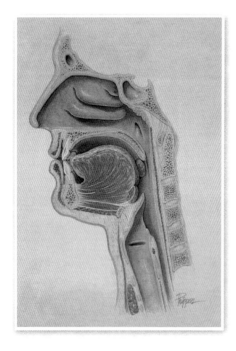

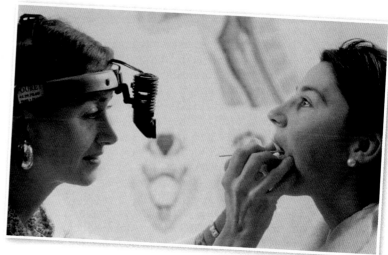

LISTENING

1 Work in pairs. Discuss the question.

* If you lost your voice for a prolonged period, how would it affect your daily life?

2 🔘 1.19 Listen to this radio interview about voice complaints and medical problems with the voice. Put the following in the order in which they are discussed.

☐ Examples of voice complaints   ☐ Threats to the voice at work
☐ Taking care of our own voice   ☐ Exercising the voice
☑ Numbers of people affected   ☐ Types of people affected
☐ Possible treatment   ☐ Surgery for cosmetic purposes

3 🔘 1.19 Listen to the interview again and complete the sentences with one word.

1 One in _____ workers in modern economies suffers regular voice problems.
2 The two professions which suffer most are _____ and call centre workers.
3 Odynophonia is soreness in the throat and makes _____ painful.
4 The new term used to describe a number of voice problems is 'repetitive voice _____'.
5 A good _____ therapist can help people recover their voice.
6 Vocal cord surgery for cosmetic purposes is called a 'voice _____'.
7 Throat infections can be caused by offices with central heating and low _____.
8 Teachers can suffer voice strain in classrooms with poor _____.
9 Drinks which contain caffeine should be avoided as they _____ out the vocal cords.
10 During vocal warm-ups, correct breathing and a good _____ are important.

Check your answers in audioscript 1.19 on page 156.

4 Work in pairs. Discuss the questions.

* How voice-friendly are the conditions where you work or study? How could they be improved?
* How well do you look after your voice? Which of Ellen's recommendations would you follow?
* Would you ever consider changing your voice with cosmetic surgery? Why or why not?

GRAMMAR: reported speech

1 A large number of reporting verbs are followed by a *that* clause: *claim, estimate, predict, remark, say, stress, tell.*
  The presenter **remarked (that) his voice had been hoarse** more than once recently.

  Tense changes in the *that* clause need not be made if the statement is still relevant:
  Ellen stressed **(that) prevention is/was better than cure.**

2 Use normal word order without *do, does, did* in reported questions.
  The presenter **asked why so many people experienced** problems with their voice.

3 Use an object + infinitive after these verbs: *advise, ask, encourage, invite, persuade, recommend, remind, tell, warn.*
  He **invited Ellen to demonstrate** some vocal warm-ups.

4 Use an infinitive without an object after these verbs: *agree, ask, claim, offer, promise, refuse.*
  She **agreed to do** some vocal exercises.

5 Use a gerund after these verbs: *admit, advise, deny, recommend, regret, suggest.*
  She **suggested asking** questions to give the voice a rest.

6 Use these verbs with *should* + bare infinitive: *advise, agree, demand, insist, recommend, suggest.*
  She **recommended that we should drink** lots of water.

7 Many verbs can be followed by a preposition: *accuse of, admit to, advise against, apologize for.*
  She advised against drinking coffee or tea.

➤ SEE LANGUAGE REFERENCE PAGE 44

1 Report the direct speech using the verb at the end of each line.

'You really should apply for the job,' he told me.　ENCOURAGE
He encouraged me to apply for the job.

1 '**I really wish I hadn't** left the cake next to the radiator,' he said.　REGRET
2 '**It's not a good idea** to wear a pink shirt with your green trousers,' she told me.　ADVISE
3 '**I think there's a good chance** it'll rain tomorrow,' she said.　PREDICT
4 '**There's no way I'm going to** sing karaoke with you,' he said to his mother.　REFUSE
5 '**The authorities ought to** provide more litter bins in our parks,' he said.　SUGGEST
6 '**Why do some people** have to get so angry when they drive?' she asked.　WONDER
7 '**Believe it or not, I** can name the capital city of every country in the world,' he said.　CLAIM
8 '**Don't forget to** hand in your essay next Friday,' she told me.　REMIND
9 '**The government has failed** to keep its promise to reduce inflation,' she said.　ACCUSE
10 '**I think there are about 700** students in the school,' he said.　ESTIMATE

2 Write three of your own sentences using the phrases in bold in exercise 1. The sentences must be true and/or reflect your opinions.

3 Compare and discuss your sentences with another student, making brief notes about what your partner says.

4 Work with a different student and report your dialogues in exercise 3.

PRONUNCIATION: voiced & unvoiced sounds

1 Voiced sounds are produced by moving your vocal cords, eg /z/ in *was* and /b/ in *job*.

  Unvoiced sounds are produced without moving your vocal cords, eg /s/ in *bus* and /p/ in *top*.

  For each of the following pairs of sounds, decide which is voiced and which is unvoiced.

1 /f/ in *life*　　/v/ in *live*
2 /d/ in *seed*　/t/ in *seat*
3 /k/ in *back*　/g/ in *bag*
4 /ð/ in *mother*　/θ/ in *mouth*
5 /ʃ/ in *sugar*　/ʒ/ in *usual*

2 In each group of words, one of the underlined sounds is pronounced differently. Circle the different one. Is it voiced or unvoiced?

rise　　*lose*　　(case)　　*unvoiced*

1 thank　third　those
2 bathe　smooth　health
3 wife　of　roof
4 choose　loose　goose
5 picked　loved　robbed
6 chaos　antique　league
7 possess　missing　scissors
8 Stephen　photo　graph
9 collision　occasion　tension
10 insure　measure　pressure

3 Try saying the following tongue twister quickly three times in succession.

Silly Susan says Sarah sells sausages.

4 Write your own tongue twister using one of the pairs of sounds in exercise 1. Invite other students to say it.

4c | A speech problem

Speaking

1 Imagine you had to do one of the following activities. Rank them from the one which you would be most willing to do (1) to the one which you would least like to have to do (6).

☐ sing a few songs in a crowded karaoke bar
☐ give a ten-minute presentation in English to the rest of the class
☐ appear on a reality television show of your choice
☐ play a lead role in an amateur stage play
☐ give an interview about a recent achievement for the front page of your local newspaper
☐ give a guided tour of your school to the mayor in the presence of television cameras

2 Compare your list with your partner, giving reasons for your choices. Do you enjoy being the focus of attention? Why or why not?

Reading

1 Work in pairs. Tell each other what you know about the film *The King's Speech*. If you have seen it, did you enjoy it? Why or why not?

2 Read the article and answer these questions:

1 Does Nicholas Mosley have good or bad memories of Lionel Logue?
2 Did Mosley's stammer prove to be an obstacle to his army career?

3 Read the article again and choose the correct words to complete the sentences.

1 Before watching *The King's Speech*, Mosley *had been told what to expect / was apprehensive about seeing the film / almost had an accident.*
2 In the second paragraph, we are told that Mosley *was upset by one aspect of the film / was not only assessing Firth's portrayal of a stammerer / recognized the actor playing Logue.*
3 According to Mosley, the real Lionel Logue was *calmer / less independent / more manipulative* than his on-screen version.
4 Logue asked Mosley to *read with more emotion / speak before an audience / memorize a speech.*
5 Mosley felt that talking as if he were singing *made him stammer more / made him sound like an animal / was no better than stammering.*
6 Mosley was *embarrassed / surprised / unconvinced* by Colin Firth's portrayal of a stammerer.
7 At prep school, Mosley *realized the true extent of his stammer / began to stammer more / stammered only in certain situations.*
8 When Mosley applied to become an officer, *his voice appeared strange / he was desperate for power / he was not confident of success.*

4 Work in pairs. Discuss the questions.

- If you could interview Nicholas Mosley, what questions would you ask him?
- Which people involved in public life in your country are known as much for the way they speak as for what they say? How are they treated by the media?

Vocabulary: emotional reactions

1 Which emotions do these two sentences from the article describe?

1 It then became a real sorrow.
2 I was so cheered up by that.

2 Choose the correct alternatives to complete the sentences.

1 I was **close** *of / to / on* **tears** but I didn't actually cry.
2 It was so sad – I **cried my eyes** *out / in / from.*
3 It was so funny – I **roared** *for / with / by* **laughter**.
4 It's such a funny book – it had me **laughing** *up / out / off* **loud**.
5 I **got** very **worked** *out / on / up* and I was **trembling** *with / to / over* **anger**.
6 The news **took me completely** *from / in / by* **surprise**. I just **couldn't get** *up / over / above* **it**.
7 It **frightened the life** *out of / up to / down from* me.
8 I'd never do that. Just the thought of it **scares** me *with / to / by* **death**.
9 It always cheers me up and **puts** me *through / to / in* **a good mood**, no matter how fed up I've been feeling.
10 It's so depressing – it really **gets** me *along / down / off.*

3 Work in small groups. Choose five of the sentences in exercise 2 and for each one think of an example which is true for you. Describe your examples to your group, who must guess which sentences you are illustrating.

Treated by the King's Speech therapist

Author Nicholas Mosley's stammer was treated by Lionel Logue, speech therapist to King George VI.

A tall, stooping man, walking stiffly with two sticks, folded himself into a front row seat at the cinema and prepared to see
5 his life's affliction exposed, examined and perhaps for the first time, properly understood. It was a precarious moment.

Like other stammerers, the author Nicholas Mosley had a nervous interest in *The King's Speech*, the film that so brilliantly charts George VI's painful efforts to overcome his
10 speech impediment. But in his case, there was more to it than measuring Colin Firth's award-winning performance as George VI by his own experience: Mosley had been a patient of the King's specialist, Lionel Logue, too. On screen, he not only saw another man suffer as he had; he watched his own therapist
15 trying to cure him.

Mosley was sent by his aunts to the unorthodox Australian speech therapist who was known to have helped the King. 'I was due to go into the army and my aunts thought my terrible stammer would be an enormous obstacle to getting
20 on,' he said. 'He was more straightforward, more controlled, than Geoffrey Rush plays him, and very charming to me as a 17-year-old. He was very still and very authoritative. He encouraged me to talk like someone singing, because he said stammerers don't stammer when they sing or act. He got me
25 reading by heart a famous speech by William Pitt the Younger* which I still remember. It included the phrase: "I am accused of the atrocious crime of being a young man." He told me to speak it as though I were addressing Parliament.

'I could talk all right in sing-song mode when I was with him
30 but when I went out to get a taxi I sounded completely half-witted. I thought: Oh hell, what's the difference between
35 feeling like an

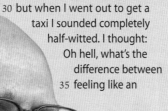

absolute ass and stammering. I couldn't go home and talk like this to my family. Logue didn't really help me, and he never
40 became a friend and mentor as he was to the King, but he gave me confidence. He gave me hope.'

The King's Speech gripped him.
45 He never believed an actor could capture a stammerer's complex verbal and facial contortions with such accuracy, or convey the intensity of shame and frustration. He watched Firth's strangled performance in amazement. 'People think stammering is about repeating the
50 first letter of a word. But it's either not making any noise at all or making strange sucking noises: you breathe in instead of breathing out and get stuck with your lips. I had been told as a child to talk more slowly and carefully but that makes it worse. You become self-conscious and choke it back.

55 'There is a wonderful scene early in the film where Bertie (Logue insisted on calling the King by his first name) has headphones on, and Logue makes him read Hamlet's soliloquy with music roaring. That struck a chord so much that I think Logue must have tried the technique with me.' Mosley's
60 impediment began, as did the King's, when he was a young boy. 'I wasn't aware how bad it was till I went to prep school when I was nine. It was hell when one had to stand up in class and spout. I became extremely self-conscious. It then became a real sorrow.'

65 After Nicholas's mother died, his aunt Irene took the boy under her wing. Determined he shouldn't be disqualified from the army because of his stammer, she paid for him to visit Lionel Logue. Mosley was mysteriously fluent when giving orders on the parade ground, but at other times his stammer was as bad
70 as ever and he expected to be refused a commission. 'In a very minor way, I was being put in the position of Bertie. Being an officer was like being a very minor king.'

The young major interviewing him sounded sombre: 'Well, Nicholas, you must realize we would never recommend a
75 commission to a chap with a stammer as bad as yours.' Pause. 'But with you we are going to make an exception.' 'I thought for a moment and ventured: "Why?" He said: "I don't know." Such a lovely answer. I was so cheered up by that. He felt that ultimately if I made a good officer, the stammer wasn't the most
80 important thing. Eventually, it stopped making a difference.'

*William Pitt the Younger: British Prime Minister 1783–1801 and 1804–1806

4D | Speech!

LISTENING

1 Work in small groups. Discuss the questions.

- On what occasions do people give speeches in your country?
- Have you ever given a speech? If so, how did you feel? If not, how do you think you would feel?

2 You are going to hear a man talking about how to write speeches.

What advice do you think he might give?

3 🌐 1.20 Listen to the recording and complete the Speech Writing Tips.

4 What advice do you think he will give regarding delivering the speech?

5 🌐 1.21–1.25 Listen to the extracts from five different speeches. For each extract answer the following questions:

- What is the occasion and who is speaking?
- Which of the techniques in the Speech Writing Tips are used?

6 Work in pairs. Choose one of the situations on page 140 and write a brief speech. Include at least one of the techniques mentioned in the Speech Writing Tips.

7 Listen to each other's speeches and for each one answer the questions in exercise 5 above.

SPEECH WRITING TIPS

(1) _____: the most important part of speech writing.

Three factors to consider:

* (2) _____: Not always appropriate to include (3) _____.
* audience: If familiar with the audience, use (4) _____.
             This brings you closer and improves your (5) _____.
* purpose: Have clear goals. Remember social conventions.

BEGINNING
The first (6) _____ are the most important.
Get the audience interested – use a statement, question, comparison, (7) _____ or joke.

MIDDLE
Don't include (8) _____.

END
Finish on a positive note – make a thought-provoking comment.

NB Good idea to (9) _____ the speech as you write it.

GRAMMAR: modal verbs 1

must, might, may, could

1 When making deductions, use *must* if you have reason to think something is true, and *couldn't/can't* if you think it is untrue.
*I **must** have done something right for so many of you to want to be here with me on my final day.*
*She **couldn't** be at work – her car's still here.*

2 Use *might (not)*, *may (not)*, *could* to express possibility and to speculate.
*Too many points **might** confuse your audience.*
*He **may** have left the country – we can't say for sure.*

3 Use *might have/could have* to talk about a past possibility which did not happen.
*It **could have** been worse. I **might have** become a poet.*

4 Use *might/could* (but not *may*) to express annoyance.
*You **might** at least offer to pay for the damage.*
*She **could** have told me she was vegetarian – I'd cooked a lovely chicken dish.*

5 Use *might/may* to express concession or contrast.
*He **may** be a good leader, **but** his speeches are boring.*
*You **might** like her, **but** I don't.*

6 Use *might as well/may as well* to suggest the best course of action, without having much enthusiasm for it.
*The next bus doesn't come for another hour, so we **might as well** walk.*

> SEE LANGUAGE REFERENCE PAGE 44

1 Match the sentences 1–8 to the replies a–h.

1f You look a real mess! You could have put on some clean trousers.

1 You look a real mess!
2 My phone didn't ring once all day.
3 She was crying her eyes out.
4 You really should drive more carefully.
5 How can you say it was a good party?
6 I'm not sure what to do tonight.
7 I can't find that book you lent me anywhere.
8 It's pouring with rain so we can't go out.

a You must have really upset her.
b You may have enjoyed it but I certainly didn't.
c I might just have a meal out on my own.
d You couldn't have called me; you're lying.
e We might as well have a game of cards instead.
f You could have put on some clean trousers.
g I think I may have left it on the train.
h You could have had a serious accident.

2 Match the grammar points 1–6 in the grammar box to some of the replies a–h in exercise 1.

a1 must *for making deductions*

3 Choose four of the replies from exercise 1 and have four separate dialogues, using a different reply to start each dialogue.

1 **A:** *You look a real mess. You could have put on some clean trousers.*
B: *What do you mean?! They **are** clean – I washed them yesterday.*
A: *You couldn't have washed them very well. Look at those stains …*

DID YOU KNOW?

1 Work in pairs. Read about the Queen's Speech and the State of the Union Address and discuss the questions.

One of the high points in the British parliamentary calendar is the annual Queen's Speech, which contains an outline of the government's policies and legislative agenda for the coming year. It is written by the government and delivered by the Queen as part of an annual ceremony known as the State Opening of Parliament. There is a great deal of formality and tradition surrounding the event, which takes place in the House of Lords, usually in November.

In the United States of America, the President reports on the condition of the country and sets out the government's legislative programme in the State of the Union Address. Tens of millions of people watch the speech live on television and the internet when it is delivered in January or February each year to Congress, which consists of members of the House of Representatives and the Senate.

- Is there a similar ceremony in your country? If so, how does it compare to those described above?
- How interested are people of your age in politics? How typical are you of your generation in this respect?
- Which politicians in your country do you consider to be the most …
  a) charismatic? b) boring? c) intelligent?

GRAMMAR
Reported speech

1   verb + *that* clause

add, admit, announce, assure, claim, complain, confirm, estimate, explain, mention, point out, predict, remark, remind, repeat, reply, say, stress, tell, warn

When reporting direct speech, tense changes may occur in the *that* clause: present tenses change to past; present perfect and past tenses change to past perfect. Pronouns and words referring to time and place may also change, depending on when the person reporting the statement/ question is speaking and where he or she is at the time of speaking.
'She doesn't live here any more,' he said.
He told me (that) she **didn't live there** *any more.*

'I didn't leave the house yesterday,' she claimed.
She claimed (that) **she hadn't left** *the house* **the previous day.**

Modal verbs *can, will, may, shall* change to *could, would, might, should. Must* can remain unchanged or we can use *had to* instead when expressing obligation. Other modals do not change.
*'You **cannot** wear jeans and you **must** wear a tie.'*
*He said he **couldn't** wear jeans and he **must/had to** wear a tie.*

There is often no tense change if a present tense of the reporting verb is used and/or if the statement being reported is still true.
He told/tells me he's thinking of buying a new car.

In reported questions, *do, does, did* only appear in negative questions and the subject comes before the verb. *Yes/No* questions are reported with *if* or *whether* and question marks are not used.
'Why don't you want to go?' he asked.
He asked her why she didn't want to go.

'Do you work for Mr Beasley?' she asked.
She asked him if he worked for Mr Beasley.

2   verb + infinitive with *to*

agree, ask, claim, demand, offer, promise, refuse, threaten
*I **offered to help** her and **refused to accept** payment.*

3   verb + object + infinitive with *to*

advise, ask, beg, convince, encourage, instruct, invite, order, persuade, recommend, remind, tell, urge, warn
*She **told him to leave** and **warned him not to tell** anyone.*

4   verb + gerund

admit, advise, deny, recommend, regret, suggest
*He **admitted breaking** the window but **denied stealing** anything.*

5   verb + preposition

*argue, protest, advise, warn **against**, apologize, blame, forgive, tell off, thank **for**, speak, accuse **of**, insist, congratulate **on**, admit, confess, object **to***
*She **thanked** me **for** helping her and **insisted on** paying me.*

6   verb + *that* clause (+ *should*)

advise, agree, ask, demand, insist, propose, recommend, request, suggest, urge
*I **suggested (that) he (should)** report it to the police.*

Modal verbs: *must, might, may, could*

1   Use *may (not), might (not)* and *could*:
*   to talk about the possibility of something happening in the future.
    *I **might** apply for that job – I **may not** get it but it's worth a try.*
*   to speculate about the present or the past.
    *She's not answering the phone – she **could** be in bed or she **might** have gone out.*

    The addition of *well* after these modal verbs expresses more probability.
    *She **could well** win an award. You **may well** be right.*

2   For deductions about the present or past, use:
*   *must* if you have good reason to believe something is true.
    *Why haven't you got a coat on? You **must** be freezing!*
*   *couldn't/can't* if you think it is untrue.
    *He **couldn't** have taken the car – the keys are still here.*

For information on obligation and prohibition see Unit 10 on page 104.

3   Use *could/couldn't* to talk about:
*   general ability or inability in the past.
    *He **could** play a number of instruments but he **couldn't** read music.*

    For specific ability on one occasion in the past, use *was/ were able to, managed to* or *succeeded in.*
    *I **managed to** shut the suitcase, but then I **couldn't** get it open again.*

    Use *could have* to talk about something we were able to do, but didn't.
    *Why didn't you ask me? I **could have** helped you.*

4   Use *might* and *could* to express:
*   annoyance.
    *I do think he **might** have phoned to apologize.*
    *You **could** at least make your bed in the morning.*
*   a past possibility which did not happen.
    *Without that map we **might** have got lost.*

5 Use **may/might as well** to suggest what could be done even though you may not really want to do it.
*I can't get back to sleep so I **might as well** get up.*
*She knows we're lying so we **may as well** tell her the truth.*

6 Use **may/might … but** to express:

- concession.
  *You **might** be tired, **but** you've got work to do.*

- contrast.
  *She **may** have found him funny, **but** I thought he was rude.*

WORD LIST

Ways of speaking

be on everyone's lips	/biː ɒn ˈevriwʌnz ˌlɪps/
bellow *v*	/ˈbeləʊ/
get one's tongue round (sth)	/get wʌnz ˈtʌŋ ˌraʊnd/
grunt *v*	/grʌnt/
keep one's mouth shut	/kiːp wʌnz ˌmaʊθ ˈʃʌt/
lie through one's teeth	/ˈlaɪ θruː wʌnz ˌtiːθ/
moan *v* *	/məʊn/
mutter *v* **	/ˈmʌtə(r)/
shriek *v*	/ʃriːk/
sigh *v* **	/saɪ/
snap *v* **	/snæp/
stutter *v*	/ˈstʌtə(r)/
voice criticism of (sth)	/ˌvɔɪs ˈkrɪtɪsɪz(ə)m əv/
whine *v*	/waɪn/
whisper *v* **	/ˈwɪspə(r)/

Voice

booming *adj*	/ˈbuːmɪŋ/
croaky *adj*	/ˈkrəʊki/
disguise one's voice	/dɪsˈɡaɪz wʌnz ˌvɔɪs/
expressionless *adj*	/ɪkˈspreʃ(ə)nləs/
high-pitched *adj*	/ˌhaɪˈpɪtʃt/
hoarse *adj*	/hɔː(r)s/
lower one's voice	/ˌləʊə(r) wʌnz ˈvɔɪs/
raise one's voice	/ˌreɪz wʌnz ˈvɔɪs/
shaky *adj*	/ˈʃeɪki/
squeaky *adj*	/ˈskwiːki/
strain one's voice	/ˌstreɪn wʌnz ˈvɔɪs/
trembling *adj* **	/ˈtremblɪŋ/

Emotional reactions

cheer (sb) up	/ˌtʃɪə(r) ˈʌp/
close to tears	/ˌkləʊs tə ˈtɪə(r)z/
come over all tearful	/kʌm ˌəʊvə(r) ɔːl ˈtɪə(r)f(ə)l/
cry one's eyes out	/ˌkraɪ wʌnz ˈaɪz aʊt/
frighten the (sb) life out of	/ˈfraɪt(ə)n ðə ˈlaɪf aʊt əv/
get (sb) down	/ˌget ˈdaʊn/
get over *v*	/ˌget ˈəʊvə(r)/
get worked up	/ˌget ˈwɜː(r)kt ʌp/
lachrymose *adj*	/ˈlækrɪməʊs/
laugh out loud	/ˌlɑːf aʊt ˈlaʊd/
put (sb) in a good mood	/ˌpʊt ɪn ə ˈgʊd muːd/
roar with laughter	/rɔː(r) wɪθ ˈlɑːftə(r)/
scare (sb) to death	/ˌskeə(r) tə ˈdeθ/
sorrow *n U*	/ˈsɒrəʊ/
the sniffles *n pl*	/ðə ˈsnɪf(ə)lz/
take (sb) by surprise	/ˌteɪk baɪ sə(r)ˈpraɪz/
tremble with anger	/ˌtremb(ə)l wɪð ˈæŋgə(r)/

Other words & phrases

affliction *n C*	/əˈflɪkʃ(ə)n/
all manner of ills	/ˌɔːl mænə(r) əv ˈɪlz/
apprehensive *adj*	/ˌæprɪˈhensɪv/
atrocious *adj*	/əˈtrəʊʃəs/
award-winning *adj*	/əˈwɔː(r)d ˌwɪnɪŋ/
be sick to death of (sth)	/ˌbiː ˌsɪk tə ˈdeθ əv/
catchy *adj*	/ˈkætʃi/
chart *v* *	/tʃɑː(r)t/
choke (sth) back *v*	/ˌtʃəʊk ˈbæk/
collagen *n U*	/ˈkɒlədʒ(ə)n/
commission *n C* ***	/kəˈmɪʃ(ə)n/
contortion *n C*	/kənˈtɔː(r)ʃ(ə)n/
drive (sb) mad/ to distraction	/draɪv ˈmæd, tə dɪˈstrækʃ(ə)n/
flier *n C*	/ˈflaɪə(r)/
freak (sb) out *v*	/ˌfriːk ˈaʊt/
full-to-bursting *adj*	/ˌfʊl tə ˈbɜː(r)stɪŋ/
get on one's nerves	/ˌget ɒn wʌnz ˈnɜː(r)vz/
get things off one's chest	/ˌget θɪŋz ɒf wʌnz ˈtʃest/
get up one's nose	/ˌget ʌp wʌnz ˈnəʊz/
give (sb) a piece of one's mind	/ˌgɪv ə ˈpiːs əv wʌnz ˌmaɪnd/
give (sth) one's best shot	/ˌgɪv wʌnz ˈbest ʃɒt/

half-witted *adj*	/ˌhɑːf ˈwɪtɪd/
have a good old moan	/hæv ə ˈgʊd əʊld ˌməʊn/
have had it up to here with (sth)	/həv hæd ɪt ʌp tə ˈhɪə(r) wɪð/
hoop *n C*	/huːp/
human resources *n pl*	/ˌhjuːmən rɪˈzɔː(r)sɪz/
hunched *adj*	/hʌntʃt/
inaugurate *v*	/ɪˈnɔːgjʊreɪt/
infuriating *adj*	/ɪnˈfjʊərieɪtɪŋ/
juggler *n C*	/ˈdʒʌglə(r)/
kick up a fuss	/ˌkɪk ʌp ə ˈfʌs/
larynx *n C*	/ˈlærɪŋks/
lay (sth) on	/ˌleɪ ˈɒn/
make a difference	/ˌmeɪk ə ˈdɪfrəns/
masquerade as *v*	/ˌmæskəˈreɪd/
mentor *n C*	/ˈmentɔː(r)/
misnomer *n C*	/mɪsˈnəʊmə(r)/
navel *n C*	/ˈneɪv(ə)l/
opt *v* **	/ɒpt/
outfit *n C* *	/ˈaʊtfɪt/
outline *n C* **	/ˈaʊtlaɪn/
portrayal *n C*	/pɔː(r)ˈtreɪəl/
precarious *adj*	/prɪˈkeəriəs/
sail past *v*	/ˌseɪl ˈpɑːst/
set (sth) out *v*	/ˌset ˈaʊt/
shambolic *adj*	/ʃæmˈbɒlɪk/
show off *v*	/ˌʃəʊ ˈɒf/
sloping *adj*	/ˈsləʊpɪŋ/
smooth-talking *adj*	/ˌsmuːð ˈtɔːkɪŋ/
soliloquy *n C*	/səˈlɪləkwi/
sombre *adj*	/ˈsɒmbə(r)/
speech impediment *n C*	/ˈspiːtʃ ɪmˌpedɪmənt/
speech therapist *n C*	/ˌspiːtʃ ˈθerəpɪst/
spout *v*	/spaʊt/
stammer *v*	/ˈstæmə(r)/
stammerer *n C*	/ˈstæmərə(r)/
stooping *adj*	/ˈstuːpɪŋ/
swanky *adj*	/ˈswæŋki/
take a beating	/ˌteɪk ə ˈbiːtɪŋ/
toast *n C* *	/təʊst/
toast *v*	/təʊst/
trapeze artist *n C*	/trəˈpiːz ˌɑː(r)tɪst/
tummy button *n C*	/ˈtʌmi ˌbʌt(ə)n/
turn out en masse	/ˌtɜː(r)n ˌaʊt ɒn ˈmæs/
unorthodox *adj*	/ʌnˈɔː(r)θədɒks/
vocal cords *n pl*	/ˈvəʊk(ə)l ˌkɔː(r)dz/
voice lift *n C*	/ˈvɔɪs ˌlɪft/
weary *adj*	/ˈwɪəri/

5A Entrepreneurs

SPEAKING & LISTENING

1 Work in pairs. Match the famous people 1–4 to the area of business a–d which made them successful.

1	Oprah Winfrey	a	oil
2	Richard Branson	b	entertainment
3	Roman Abramovich	c	computers
4	Michael Dell	d	music and air travel

What else do you know about each one?
Share your ideas in groups.

2 🔵 **2.1–2.4** Listen and check your ideas. Make notes on their achievements.

3 Who are the leading entrepreneurs in your country? How did they become successful?

READING

1 The following words and phrases all occur in the article. Discuss their possible relevance to the Swedish furniture company Ikea and its founder, Ingvar Kamprad.

> 18.5 billion   vineyard   frugality   cigarette lighters
> revolution   300 million   cult

2 Read the article, ignoring the gaps, and check your ideas in exercise 1.

3 Complete the gaps 1–7 in the article with the sentences a–g.

a Even senior executives travel around Europe on budget airlines and always stay, they insist, in cut-price hotels.

b But instead of a chauffeur-driven limo, he drives a 10-year-old Volvo and whenever he flies, even long haul, it's in economy.

c It also offloaded on to customers an expensive part of selling furniture – actually putting the stuff together.

d Kamprad's idea of a break is fishing or rowing in his native Sweden.

e In his teens, he discovered an aptitude for business and began importing and selling anything he thought he could make a profit on.

f Kamprad long gave up the day-to-day running of Ikea and lives with his second wife in Switzerland, apparently for tax purposes.

g Having a company enabled Kamprad to bid for a contract to supply pencils and he was soon sending goods out with the daily milk round.

4 Use context to work out the approximate meanings of the highlighted phrasal verbs in the article.

5 Work in pairs. Discuss the questions.

- Which multinationals like Ikea have branches or own companies in your country?
- What contribution, positive and/or negative, do multinationals make to a country?

GRAMMAR: relative clauses

> Read the sentences 1–4 from the article and answer the questions a–e.
>
> 1 Kamprad set up his company, Ikea, which took its name from his initials …
> 2 He opened a showroom to reassure people who felt his prices were simply too good to be true.
> 3 His big breakthrough came in 1955 with the birth of a product which would become a market leader.
> 4 He began importing and selling anything he thought he could make a profit on.
>
> a Why is a comma used before the relative pronoun in 1, but not in 2 or 3?
> b Which of the relative pronouns in sentences 1–4 could be replaced by the pronoun *that*?
> c Which relative pronoun has been omitted from 4? Why is this possible?
> d Rewrite sentence 4 in the following way:
> He began importing and selling anything on …
> e Complete the sentences with a relative pronoun.
> a) Kamprad, _____ fortune is estimated at $18.5bn, is one of the world's wealthiest people.
> b) He sometimes travels by bus and subway, _____ enables him to benefit from his pensioner's discount.

> ❯ SEE LANGUAGE REFERENCE PAGE 54

1 In each sentence there is one word missing. Write the missing word in the correct place.

1 The managing director, worked his way up through the company from the factory floor, now earns over £1 million a year.

2 He was banned from driving for two years, meant he lost his job as a sales representative.

3 I don't think I know anyone attitude to work is quite so positive as his.

4 It is very difficult to determine the extent to charity concerts help resolve the problem of poverty in developing countries.

5 I can't remember when exactly my fascination for astronomy began – I think it's something I've always been interested in.

INGVAR KAMPRAD:
leader of the flatpack

The Swedish furniture company Ikea has made its founder, Ingvar Kamprad, one of the world's wealthiest people, with a fortune estimated at $18.5bn.

5 (1) _____ Rather than travelling by taxi, he's even been known to use Stockholm's subway and public buses to take advantage of his pensioner's discount.

And forget holidays in St Tropez. (2) _____ He once said that his idea of luxury is buying the occasional nice shirt.

10 Kamprad's sole extravagance is having a small vineyard in Provence, which he describes, with characteristic dourness, as a 'very expensive hobby'.

His frugality is not born of a desire simply to build up his billions, but also to offer a guiding example to Ikea's 76,000 15 staff. His penny-pinching permeates Ikea. (3) _____ He reasons that if Ikea is to provide customers with low prices, its brutal control of costs has to extend to every level in the company.

Born in southern Sweden, Kamprad grew up on a village 20 farm. (4) _____ He traded in cigarette lighters, Christmas cards and pens, and at the age of seventeen, Kamprad set up his company, Ikea, which took its name from his initials and the first letters of his family farm Elmtaryd and nearby village Agunnaryd.

25 (5) _____ He discovered that by buying goods in bulk he could sell them to his customers at low prices and still make a profit. Kamprad then acquired a disused factory and began turning out furniture. His low prices undercut Swedish cartels and in 1952 he opened a showroom 30 in the town of Almhult to reassure people who felt his prices were simply too good to be true. Kamprad tinkered with furniture designs to keep costs low, but his big breakthrough came in 1955 with the birth of a product which would become a market leader.

35 While trying to pack and ship a bulky table, Gillis Lundgren, an early employee and later the chief designer, hit upon the idea of taking the legs off and mailing them packed flat under the tabletop. Enter the flatpack. The secret of Ikea's products is functionality. The flatpack 40 eliminated the cost of shipping vast quantities of air whenever a product was sent from factory to shopfloor. (6) _____ Flatpacks allowed furniture to be made so cheaply that, instead of accumulating emotional weight as it was passed down the generations, it would come to 45 seem transient and disposable. This started a revolution in interior furnishing and now more than 300 million people worldwide frequent Ikea each year, even though it has only about 200 branches.

Employees have described Ikea as a 'cult'. The company 50 structure is less hierarchical than similar businesses – titles and privileges are taboo – and every year Kamprad personally hands out Christmas presents to each of Ikea's 2,500 staff members at its Almhult headquarters.

The company never releases profit figures but sources 55 suggest they are massive – around 18 per cent – while rival firms operate on single-figure margins. (7) _____ He has also sheltered his company from Sweden's taxes and death duties by creating trusts and holding companies, ensuring that Ikea will continue after he is gone. Flatpacks 60 are here to stay.

---

2 Work in pairs. Complete the sentences in an appropriate way. Then compare your sentences with your partner's.

1 The situation at work was becoming intolerable; **it got to the point where** ... .
2 There is a strong possibility that I'll lose my job, **in which case** ... .
3 Many of those attending the demonstration criticized **the way in which** ... .
4 The activities of the paparazzi can cause friction. Indeed, there have been **a number of cases where** ... .
5 I'll never forget **the day when** ... .

5B | A new business

VOCABULARY: setting up in business

1 Complete the text with the words in the boxes. Do not change the words.

Nouns:	**Verbs:**
design identity plan return share target	build pitch secure ~~set up~~ source strike

If you have a new invention or an innovative idea and you want to (1) _set up_ **in business** to market it, here are some basic steps you'll need to follow.

First of all, you need to **put together a** comprehensive **business** (2) _____, in which you **set out** your **goals** and provide information on your (3) _____ **market** (the potential customers), short-term **sales forecasts**, profitability, marketing strategies and so on.

Then, in order to (4) _____ **financial backing** for your business, you will probably need to (5) _____ your **idea** to investors, with the aim of convincing them there is a market for it, and that they will **obtain a good** (6) _____ **on their investment**. Before you (7) _____ a **deal**, you will need to decide how much **percentage equity** you are prepared to give away, that is, the (8) _____ **in the business** that investors will receive in return for their money.

If necessary, this **investment capital** can be used to (9) _____ a **prototype**, the first example of your product from which all others will be developed. To do so, of course, you'll need first to (10) _____ **suppliers**; find companies who can provide you with the right materials to manufacture your product.

Finally, you should give thought to developing the **brand** (11) _____, the name and visual appearance of the product by which consumers will recognize it and differentiate it from competitors. Clearly, the (12) _____ of your **logo** is very important in this respect.

LISTENING

1 The photo shows a recent invention called the Snowbone. Work in pairs and discuss the questions.

- How would you describe the Snowbone?
- Who do you think it would appeal to?

Part 1

2 🔵 **2.5** You are going to hear an interview with Paddy Radcliffe, the managing director of the company which developed the Snowbone. Listen to Part 1 of the interview and decide whether the sentences are true (T) or false (F). Say why the false sentences are incorrect.

1 The Snowbone is produced using old bicycle parts.
2 It was not designed by Paddy.
3 It is primarily targeted at people in their mid- to late-twenties.
4 Paddy says he aims to produce one and a half million Snowbones.
5 Paddy and Nick were both business students.
6 After the business course, Paddy devoted all his energies to the Snowbone.

Part 2

Paddy and Nick appeared as contestants on the BBC television series *Dragons' Den*. This is a reality programme where people pitch their ideas to a panel of elite business entrepreneurs known as "dragons" in the hope of securing investment capital.

3 🔘 **2.6** Listen to Part 2 and underline the correct alternative to complete the sentences.

1 Paddy and Nick *did not prepare for / were fully familiar with / underwent selection for* the TV programme.
2 Their pitch took place *before / while / after* they had lunch.
3 On view next to each dragon was *a cheque book / an amount of money / a gold credit card*.
4 Paddy says the pitch *went reasonably well / was constantly interrupted / was partly improvised*.
5 The dragons *were quick / needed time / failed to* understand the nature and potential of the Snowbone.
6 Rachel Elnaugh *took to / had heard of / was amused by* Paddy and Nick.
7 Rachel's investment would buy her a *quarter / third / half* share in the business.

Part 3

4 🔘 **2.7** Listen to Part 3 and answer these questions.

1 What were the immediate benefits of Rachel's offer of investment?
2 What setback did Paddy and Nick suffer?
3 What is the significance of London and Taiwan?
4 How does Paddy feel about the future?
5 What advice does he give to other would-be entrepreneurs?

5 Work in pairs. Discuss the questions.

• Would you enjoy the entrepreneurial lifestyle? Why or why not?

Speech feature: question tags

1 🔘 **2.8** Listen again to these sentences from the interview and mark the intonation pattern on the underlined question tags. Write either ⤴ or ⤵. Then answer the questions below.

BMX, that's a kind of bike, <u>isn't it</u>?
But she did eventually invest her money, <u>didn't she</u>?

• How are question tags formed?
• What do the different intonation patterns indicate?

Check your ideas in sections A and B of the Language reference section on pages 54–55.

2 Complete the sentences with an appropriate question tag.

1 I'm older than you, _____?
2 Nobody in this class has been to Australia, _____?
3 Remind me what happens with imperatives, _____?
4 There are several possible question tags, _____?
5 You hardly ever wear jeans, _____?
6 We'd better hurry up and finish this exercise, _____?
7 Let's have a little rest now, _____?

3 Work in pairs. Take turns to read out the questions in exercise 2. Respond to your partner's questions in an appropriate way.

4 Read the information in the box on same-way question tags and follow the instructions.

> A positive question tag can also be added to a positive statement. The speaker repeats, rephrases or interprets what he/she has just heard and uses the tag with rising intonation to express interest, surprise, anger or concern.
>
> *'Peter gave me a lift.' 'So Peter can drive, can he?'*
> *'Don't be stupid.' 'Oh, so I'm stupid now, am I?'*

Write four positive statements, either true or invented, which will either interest, surprise, anger or cause concern for your partner.

5 Read out your sentences to your partner, who will respond using a same-way question tag. Keep each dialogue going as long as possible.

Speaking

1 Work in four groups, A–D. You are going to make a pitch for an idea or product.

Group A: Turn to page 142.
Group B: Turn to page 146.
Group C: Turn to page 151.
Group D: Turn to page 153.

2 Form new groups, each consisting of one student from each of the four original groups.

Make your pitch to the other students in your group, who take on the role of potential investors. At the end of your pitch, the 'investors' may ask you questions about your idea or product.

3 When all students have made their pitch, you should each say which idea you will invest in and why. You must choose one and you may not invest in your own idea.

5c | Women's work?

SPEAKING

1 Work in groups of three, A–C. You have just moved into rented accommodation together and are discussing the housework rota for the next three months. You are keen to ensure an equal distribution of labour.

Student A: Turn to page 141.
Student B: Turn to page 147.
Student C: Turn to page 153.

2 Was it easy to come to a decision as a group? Would/Do you find it easy or difficult to share a house or flat? Why?

READING

1 Look at the photos and read the title and first paragraph of the article.

What do you think the article will say about:

1 men, women and housework?
2 women and marriage?

2 Read the article and check your predictions in exercise 1.

3 Read the article again and decide whether the following are stated (✓) or not stated (✗).

1 Susan's behaviour after her honeymoon was atypical of her.
2 She would not allow her husband to do any of the housework.
3 She thinks there are more disadvantages than advantages to getting married.
4 Women are reluctant to admit they do more housework than their husbands.
5 Susan considered her fiancé's attitude towards her smoking to be unreasonable.
6 She was amused by his initial attempts at washing his own clothes.
7 Men are more keen to get married after a divorce than women.
8 Marriage is gradually going out of fashion.

4 Work in pairs. Discuss the questions.

• Compare the situation described in the article to that in your country.
• Describe the 'division of labour' in your household now and/or when you were growing up.
• Is the institution of marriage 'worth saving'? Why or why not?

VOCABULARY: intensifying adverbs

A number of adverbs collocate with certain adjectives, often to intensify or emphasize them as in these examples from the article.

*perfectly **normal** behaviour*
*highly **revealing** nuggets of information*

1 Underline one adverb in each group which is very different in meaning or intensity to the other three.

1 I can clearly remember a time when I felt *acutely / mildly / deeply / highly* **embarrassed**.
2 The sports facilities where I live are *pitifully / hopelessly / woefully / rather* **inadequate**.
3 I failed an exam once – I was *sorely / slightly / bitterly / deeply* **disappointed**.
4 I am *particularly / strongly / vehemently / fiercely* **opposed** to smacking children.
5 The atmosphere where I work/study is *highly / fiercely / fairly / intensely* **competitive**.
6 If I was alone in a foreign city, I'd be *perfectly / quite / fully / reasonably* **capable** of looking after myself.
7 It's *practically / virtually / completely / almost* **impossible** to escape the noise of cars in my region.
8 People in my country are *fully / vaguely / well / only too* **aware** of the need to protect the environment.

2 Work in pairs. Discuss the sentences in exercise 1. How true is each one, assuming one of the three similar adverbs is used?

A woman's work is never done

When the 27-year-old Susan Maushart arrived at her marital home with her new husband after their honeymoon, she found herself suddenly acting very strangely. She proceeded directly to the bathroom
5 **and started cleaning and didn't stop until it had been scrubbed and polished from top to bottom.**

When that was done, she moved to the kitchen, pulled out a recipe book and started work on a casserole. Perfectly normal behaviour for some blushing brides
10 maybe, but for Maushart, an ardent feminist and hardened New Yorker who'd previously existed on fast food, this was decidedly out of character. 'It was like some weird way of marking out female territory,' she says. 'Scrubbing the bathroom felt good. Wifely, even.'

15 What Maushart had unwittingly found herself doing was participating in what she now terms 'wifework' – that is the extra, unpaid labour that a woman takes on when she ties the knot. 'I thought I was the last person it would happen to,' she says. 'But when I got married a
20 metamorphosis happened to me, it was bizarre.'

In her book, entitled *Wifework*, Maushart sets out to explain why an intelligent PhD student like herself should suddenly regress into archetypal Fifties housewife mode. And by contemplating marriage in terms of a
25 simple calculation – a balance sheet, if you like, of the cost of getting hitched weighed up against the benefits – Maushart draws some disturbing conclusions.

'The moment a man gets married,' Maushart says, 'his domestic workload almost disappears. He immediately
30 gets about 70 per cent less cleaning, 50 per cent less cooking and 90 per cent less laundry. There are nowhere near these benefits for a woman when she gets married. And these days you're at pains to deny that you're doing it, because apart from being exhausted by it, you're
35 ashamed of yourself.'

Maushart's motivation comes from her own marital experiences. Perhaps the alarm bells should have started ringing prior to tying the knot on her own happy day. 'I remember being surprised when he requested,
40 rather firmly, that I refrain from smoking during our outdoor wedding reception,' she writes of her husband-to-be in the book. 'But why now?' I wanted to know. 'My cigarettes have never bothered you before. And everybody else will be smoking.' 'I'd just prefer that
45 you didn't,' he replied evenly.

Things quickly went from bad to worse. 'The first day he grumbled about the lack of clean jocks in his underwear drawer, I honestly thought it was a joke,' she says. 'The day I started lying to him about line-drying his shirts,
50 I knew it had gotten way beyond one.' Within three years, the marriage had broken down and they went their separate ways.

Drawing together research from the UK, America and Australia, *Wifework* is littered with some highly revealing
55 nuggets of information. That two-thirds to three-quarters of divorces are initiated by women, that ex-wives are much slower to re-marry than husbands, and that wives reported levels of depression two or three times higher than unmarried women.

60 One woman in the book, an ex-wife, summed it up neatly. 'It just got too tiresome. I woke up one day and decided I'd rather keep my money for myself. I had a good job, I was the one who really raised the kids, I did all the housework. I even mowed the lawns. And I just decided
65 that the husband had to go. There was no advantage in keeping him.'

Instead of the seven-year itch, Maushart points out how the four-year mark is actually far more common these days. Along with that, we're now starting to see the rise
70 of the 'mini-marriage' – the one that doesn't even last a year. This may make for depressing reading, but Maushart says it's not. She believes marriage is an institution that is simply in a state of flux. Our attitudes towards it may have changed enormously compared to those of our mothers
75 and grandmothers, but the reality of it, or the division of labour within it, hasn't caught up.

As a result, there is a mismatch, and it is this that Maushart believes is causing our spiralling divorce rate. 'We are so much out of tune with our changing
80 environment, what else can we expect?' Ultimately, however, if the institution of marriage is worth saving, and for the sake of children Maushart thinks it is, then wifework simply has to go.

Glossary
tie the knot *v informal* get married
seven-year itch *n informal* a married person's
    feeling of being bored with their partner after
    seven years

5D | Sexual discrimination

VOCABULARY: gender

1 Work in pairs. When hearing the words in the box, do you immediately think of a man, woman or both? Explain your reactions to your partner.

> nurse   farmer   au pair   detective
> butcher   secretary   surgeon   babysitter

2 To specify the gender of the workers in exercise 1, you can use the words *male* or *female*, eg *male nurse*, *female detective*. Gender can be specified in other ways. Complete the table with the words in the box.

> man   woman   person   master   fighter
> officer   teacher   mistress   attendant

male	female	neutral
police ＿＿	police ＿＿	police ＿＿
sales ＿＿	sales ＿＿	sales ＿＿
fire ＿＿		fire ＿＿
air steward	air stewardess	flight ＿＿
head ＿＿	head ＿＿	head ＿＿

3 Some people consider the underlined words below offensive to women. Suggest a neutral alternative for each.

1 The company will not meet its targets unless there is a substantial increase in <u>manpower</u>.
2 The huge blaze at the petrol depot left the fire station seriously <u>undermanned</u>.
3 After the accident it took just 100 <u>man-hours</u> to get the plane back in the air.
4 We use both natural and <u>man-made</u> fabrics in the manufacture of our carpets.
5 The neolithic revolution is one of the most important events in the history of <u>mankind</u>.

4 Work in pairs, A and B. Turn to page 148 and read the instructions for your role.

When you have finished, change roles.

LISTENING

1 Read the following information and answer the question.

What legislation, if any, exists in your country to prevent sexual discrimination at work?

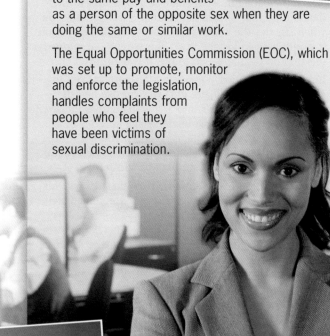

The Sex Discrimination Act came into force in Britain in 1975 and makes it unlawful for an employer to discriminate on grounds of sex in matters of recruitment, treatment at work and dismissal.

The Equal Pay Act, which also became effective in 1975, gives an individual the right to the same pay and benefits as a person of the opposite sex when they are doing the same or similar work.

The Equal Opportunities Commission (EOC), which was set up to promote, monitor and enforce the legislation, handles complaints from people who feel they have been victims of sexual discrimination.

2 🔘 **2.9–2.13** Listen to the speakers 1–5 talking about their experiences with the Sex Discrimination Act and answer this question about each one:

Does the speaker have a positive (*P*) or negative (*N*) attitude towards the current legislation?

3 🔘 **2.9–2.13** Listen again and match one of the statements a–h to the speakers 1–5. Three of the statements are not required.

a Someone hid an important fact from me.
b I missed an opportunity to defend my rights.
c I wasn't attractive enough for the job.
d I have some regrets about taking legal action.
e I was being paid less for doing more than others.
f I came under pressure to leave my job.
g Women generally work harder than men.
h Typical male behaviour can be a key factor for success.

4 How much sympathy, if any, do you have for the employer in the following situations mentioned by the speakers? Give reasons.

1 He wouldn't give me time off work for antenatal appointments.
2 He said it was better for the company's image to have women on the front desk.
3 There was a woman here who told me the day after I gave her the job that she was three months pregnant.

GRAMMAR: hypothetical past situations

Conditional sentences and *wish* can be used to hypothesize about the past.
In the following sentences from the recording decide if **I'd** stands for *I would* or *I had*, then answer the questions.
a) If **I'd** known (she was three months pregnant) at the interview, **I'd** never have taken her on.
Did the speaker know she was pregnant?
Did he take her on?

b) I just wish **I'd** realized (the SDA applies to men as well as women) at the time.
Did he realize the SDA also applied to men?

Note the following more formal alternative to the *if* clause when talking about hypothetical past situations.
Had I made *the connection, I would have taken them to an employment tribunal.* (= If I had made)

❯ SEE LANGUAGE REFERENCE PAGE 54

1 The following sentences from the recording all describe hypothetical past situations. Write the correct form of the verbs in brackets.

1 If it _____ (*not/be*) for the Sex Discrimination Act, my fight _____ (*not/be*) possible.
2 Part of me wishes I _____ (*not/take*) my case to the Employment Tribunal.
3 If I _____ (*not/inherit*) some money, I might never _____ (*be*) able to take my claim to the Employment Tribunal.
4 If the SDA _____ (*not/bring*) in, we almost certainly _____ (*not/have*) so many women in full-time employment now.

Check your answers in audioscripts 2.9–2.13 on page 157.

2 Complete the sentences in two different ways.

1 I wish I'd made more of an effort to _____ when I was younger.
2 If I'd been born twenty years earlier, _____.
3 If the mobile phone hadn't been invented, _____.
4 Had I known five years ago what I know now, _____.
5 If it hadn't been for _____, I wouldn't _____ now.

3 Work in pairs. Discuss your sentences.

DID YOU KNOW?

1 Work in pairs. Read about the Anglican Communion and discuss the questions.

In June 1990 Penny Jamieson was made Bishop of Dunedin in New Zealand, and so became the first woman bishop in the Anglican Communion to be given her own diocese, or area, to control. The Anglican Communion is an association of churches around the world which share the same beliefs as the Church of England. The acceptance of women into the Communion varies from country to country: whilst the first women priests were ordained in the Episcopal Church in the US in 1974 and in the Church of New Zealand in 1977, the Church of England did not authorize their ordination until 1992.

• Which are the most male-dominated professions in your country?
• Which jobs, if any, do you feel women do better than men, and vice versa? Why?
• Have there been any 'firsts' for women in your country recently?

GRAMMAR
Relative clauses

1   **Defining relative clauses** identify who or what we are talking about and are an essential part of the meaning of a sentence. No commas are required at the beginning or end of the relative clause. The relative pronouns *who* and *which* can both be replaced by *that*.
    *He looks just like that man **who/that** advertises flatpack furniture on the telly.*
    *And this is the actual pen **which/that** was used to sign the historic agreement.*
    *I've got a friend **whose** surname is Christopher.*

    The relative pronoun can be omitted if it refers to the object of the verb in the relative clause.
    *The oak tree **(which/that)** we planted ten years ago is as tall as the shed now.*

    Prepositions can be placed at the end of the relative clause. In more formal English they often appear before the relative pronoun. Compare:
    *It's something **(which/that)** he's very concerned **about**.*
    *It is an issue **about which** he expressed concern.*

    Whom is usually used in place of *who* after prepositions.
    *The 'payee' is the person **to whom** the cheque is made out.*

2   **Non-defining relative clauses** add extra information which is not essential to our understanding of who or what is being spoken about. *That* cannot be used and the relative pronoun cannot be omitted. Commas are used before and, where relevant, after non-defining clauses.
    *My father, **who** died last year, outlived my mother by sixteen years.*
    *The venue, **which** has yet to be decided, will probably be somewhere on the south coast.*
    *Art lovers flock to Madrid, **whose** museums boast some of the finest collections in Europe.*

    Which is used in non-defining relative clauses to refer to a whole clause.
    *He had nothing to say, **which** is unusual for him.*

3   A number of nouns commonly occur with relative clauses introduced by relative adverbs *where*, *when* and *why* or as part of a prepositional phrase with *which*. *When* and *why* can be omitted in defining relative clauses.
    the way in which   the extent to which
    as a result of which   the situation/point where
    the time/day/moment/occasion when
    the reason why   by which time
    at which point in which case
    *I see no **reason (why)** I shouldn't let you do it.*
    *The neighbours were having regular parties and **it got to the point where** we had to sleep at my mother's.*
    *He got home at midnight, **by which time** I was asleep.*

Hypothetical past situations

Wish/If only + past perfect can be used to express wishes, regrets and criticisms about the past.
    *I **wish I hadn't given** me him my phone number.*
    If only you'd been wearing a seat belt.

Unreal past conditional sentences (*if* + past perfect, *would/might/could* + perfect infinitive) can be used to speculate about the past.
    *If you had told me you were having problems, I **could have helped** you.*
    (= You didn't tell me, so I couldn't help you.)
    *If it hadn't been for his bad knee, he **would have come** walking with us.*
    (= Because of his bad knee, he didn't come.)

A more formal alternative is to omit *if* and begin with *had*:
    Had she stayed longer, she would have met Brad.

Would/Might/Could + infinitive can be used to describe possible present consequences.
    If we had left earlier, we would be there by now.

Should have + past participle can be used to criticize, express regret or talk about what was supposed to happen.
    *It was chaos – I **shouldn't have invited** so many people.*
    *Hurry up! You **should have finished** that by now.*

Suppose/Supposing/Imagine can be used instead of *if*, particularly in spoken English.
    Suppose he'd invited you. Would you have gone?

Question tags
A Formation, use and intonation

In general, negative question tags appear after positive statements and positive tags appear after negative statements. We form question tags by using the same auxiliary verb which appears in the main statement, together with a subject pronoun. If the main verb in the statement is *be*, this also appears in the question tag.
    *You've seen this film before, **haven't** you?*
    *She can't swim, **can** she? He's French, **isn't** he?*

If there is no auxiliary verb or *be* in the statement, we use *do*, *does* or *did* in the question tag.
    *He likes the sound of his own voice, **doesn't** he?*

We use falling intonation on question tags when we are checking information and we expect the listener to agree.
    *It's a lovely day, **isn't** it?*

We use rising intonation to ask a real question, when we are unsure whether the statement is true or not, or when asking for information and making requests.
    *You couldn't do me a favour, **could** you?*

B Special cases

We use *will/can you?* or *would/could you?* after positive imperatives; only *will you?* is used after negative imperatives.

> *Don't be late, **will you?***

After statements containing negative words like *never, nothing* or *nobody*, as well as *hardly, barely, seldom* and *rarely* we normally use a positive tag.

> *He hardly ever phones, **does he?***

We use the pronoun *they* in question tags after statements with *nobody/no-one, somebody/someone, everybody/everyone* as the subject.

> *Everyone seemed to have a good time, **didn't they?***

Note also the following:

> *I'm right about Julie, **aren't I?***
> *Let's go for a walk, **shall we?***

C Same-way question tags

We can follow positive statements with positive question tags to express interest, surprise, anger or concern. The speaker repeats, rephrases or interprets the information he/she has just heard and uses the tag with rising intonation.

> 'He graduated last year.' 'So he went to university, *did he?*'
> 'I can't find my keys.' 'You've lost your keys now, *have you? It'll be your head next.*'

WORD LIST

Setting up in business

brand identity *n C*	/ˌbrænd aɪˈdentɪti/
build a prototype	/ˌbɪld ə ˈprəʊtətaɪp/
investment capital	/ɪnˈves(t)mənt ˌkæpɪt(ə)l/
logo *n C* *	/ˈləʊgəʊ/
obtain a return on an investment	/əbˌteɪn ə rɪˌtɜː(r)n ɒn ən ɪnˈves(t)mənt/
percentage equity	/pə(r)ˈsentɪdʒ ˌekwəti/
pitch an idea	/ˌpɪtʃ ən aɪˈdɪə/
put together a business plan	/pʊt təˌgeðə(r) ə ˈbɪznəs ˌplæn/
sales forecast *n C*	/ˈseɪlz ˌfɔː(r)kɑːst/
secure financial backing	/sɪˌkjʊə(r) faɪˈnænʃ(ə)l ˌbækɪŋ/
set out one's goals	/set ˌaʊt wʌnz ˈgəʊlz/

set up in business	/set ˌʌp ɪn ˈbɪznəs/
share in the business	/ˌʃeə(r) ɪn ðə ˈbɪznəs/
source suppliers	/ˌsɔː(r)s səˈplaɪə(r)z/
strike a deal	/ˌstraɪk ə ˈdɪːl/

Intensifying adverbs

perfectly normal
highly revealing
acutely/deeply/highly embarrassed
hopelessly/pitifully/woefully inadequate
bitterly/deeply/sorely disappointed
fiercely/strongly/vehemently opposed
fiercely/highly/intensely competitive
fully/perfectly/quite capable
practically/virtually impossible
fully/only too/vaguely/well aware

Gender

man-hours *n pl*	/ˈmænˌaʊə(r)z/
mankind *n U* *	/mænˈkaɪnd/
man-made *adj*	/ˌmænˈmeɪd/
manpower *n C*	/ˈmænˌpaʊə(r)/
undermanned *adj*	/ˌʌndə(r)ˈmænd/

Other words & phrases

antenatal *adj*	/ˌæntiˈneɪt(ə)l/
ardent *adj*	/ˈɑː(r)d(ə)nt/
at pains to do (sth)	/ət ˈpeɪnz tə ˌduː/
avid *adj*	/ˈævɪd/
back to square one	/bæk tə ˌskweə(r) ˈwʌn/
be green	/ˌbiː ˈgriːn/
bid for *v*	/ˈbɪd ˌfɔː(r)/
bindings *n pl*	/ˈbaɪndɪŋz/
blatantly *adj*	/ˈbleɪt(ə)ntli/
breakthrough *n C* *	/ˈbreɪkθruː/
budget airline *n C*	/ˈbʌdʒɪt eə(r)laɪn/
build (sth) up *v*	/ˌbɪld ˈʌp/
buy (sth) in bulk	/ˌbaɪ ɪn ˈbʌlk/
cartel *n C*	/kɑː(r)ˈt(ə)l/
catch up *v*	/ˌkætʃ ˈʌp/
coastguard *n C*	/ˈkəʊstˌgɑː(r)d/
come into force	/ˌkʌm ɪntʊ ˈfɔː(r)s/
come up with *v*	/ˌkʌm ˈʌp wɪð/
death duties *n pl*	/ˈdeθ ˌdjuːtiːz/
demote *v*	/diːˈməʊt/
diocese *n C*	/ˈdaɪəsɪs/
dourness *n U*	/ˈdʊə(r)nəs, ˈdaʊə(r)nəs/
draining *adj*	/ˈdreɪnɪŋ/
employment tribunal *n C*	/ɪmˌplɔɪmənt traɪˈbjuːn(ə)l/
entrepreneur *n C*	/ˌɒntrəprəˈnɜː(r)/
flux *n U*	/flʌks/
fly long haul	/flaɪ ˈlɒŋ ˌhɔːl/

frequent *v*	/frɪˈkwent/
from top to bottom	/frəm ˈtɒp tə ˌbɒtəm/
frugality *n U*	/fruːˈgæləti/
get (sth) off the ground	/get ˈɒf ðə ˌgraʊnd/
get (sth) underway	/get ˌʌndə(r)ˈweɪ/
get hitched *v*	/ˌget ˈhɪtʃt/
give (sth) a go	/ˈgɪv ə ˌgəʊ/
grumble *v*	/ˈgrʌmb(ə)l/
hand (sth) out *v*	/ˌhænd ˈaʊt/
handlebars *n plural*	/ˈhænd(ə)lˌbɑː(r)z/
hang around *v*	/ˌhæŋ əˈraʊnd/
heavy hitter *n C*	/ˌhevi ˈhɪtə(r)/
hit upon *v*	/ˈhɪt əˌpɒn/
hold (sb) back	/ˌhəʊld ˈbæk/
husband-to-be *n C*	/ˈhʌzbənd tə ˌbiː/
impoverished *adj*	/ɪmˈpɒvərɪʃt/
jocks *n pl*	/dʒɒks/
knockback *n C*	/ˈnɒkˌbæk/
laundry *n U* *	/ˈlɔːndri/
limo *n C*	/ˈlɪməʊ/
littered with *v*	/ˈlɪtə(r)d ˌwɪð/
market leader *n C*	/ˌmɑː(r)kɪt ˈliːdə(r)/
maternity leave *n U*	/məˈtɜː(r)nəti ˌliːv/
mismatch *n C*	/ˈmɪsˌmætʃ/
nerve-racking *adj*	/ˈnɜː(r)v ˌrækɪŋ/
not be one for doing (sth)	/ˌnɒt bi wʌn fə ˈduːɪŋ/
offload (sth) on to (sb)	/ˌɒfˈləʊd ɒn tə/
on cloud nine	/ɒn ˌklaʊd ˈnaɪn/
ordain *v*	/ɔː(r)ˈdeɪn/
ordination *n U*	/ˌɔː(r)dɪˈneɪʃ(ə)n/
out of tune with (sth)	/aʊt əv ˈtʃuːn wɪð/
outlet *n C* **	/ˈaʊtˌlet/
pass (sth) down *v*	/ˌpɑːs ˈdaʊn/
pay dividends	/ˌpeɪ ˈdɪvɪdendz/
penny-pinching *n U*	/ˈpeni ˌpɪntʃɪŋ/
permeate *v*	/ˈpɜː(r)mieɪt/
prompt *v* **	/prɒmpt/
reap *v*	/riːp/
scrub *v*	/skrʌb/
self-made *adj*	/ˌself ˈmeɪd/
seven-year itch *n*	/ˌsev(ə)n jɪə(r) ˈɪtʃ/
sizeable *adj*	/ˈsaɪzəb(ə)l/
sole *adj* **	/səʊl/
stunt *n C*	/stʌnt/
team up with *v*	/ˌtiːm ˈʌp wɪð/
tie the knot	/ˌtaɪ ðə ˈnɒt/
toing and froing *n U*	/ˌtuːɪŋ ən ˈfrəʊɪŋ/
trade in (sth) *v*	/ˌtreɪd ˈɪn/
transient *adj*	/ˈtrænziənt/
turn (sth) out *v*	/ˌtɜː(r)n ˈaʊt/
undercut *v*	/ˌʌndə(r)ˈkʌt/
unscrupulous *adj*	/ʌnˈskruːpjʊləs/
unwittingly *adv*	/ʌnˈwɪtɪŋli/
ups and downs *n pl*	/ˌʌps ən(d) ˈdaʊnz/
weigh (sth) up against	/weɪ ˈʌp əˌgenst/
workload *n C* *	/ˈwɜː(r)kˌləʊd/

6A | Body care

Speaking

1 Rank the following activities from the one which would give you most pleasure if you could do it tomorrow (1) to the one which you would least like to do (8).

- ☐ a day in a health spa
- ☐ a few hours in a gym
- ☐ a long walk in the countryside
- ☐ a lazy day at home
- ☐ a clothes-shopping expedition
- ☐ a day on a hot, sunny beach
- ☐ a competitive sporting activity
- ☐ a meal in a posh restaurant

2 Compare your list with your partner, giving reasons for your choices. Is there any other activity you would add to the list?

Reading

1 Work in pairs. Read the texts A–C and discuss the questions.

- Have you ever done any of the activities described?
- Which, if any, of them would you enjoy doing? Why?

2 Read the texts again and match the sentences 1–9 to the texts A–C.

1 You should not take what you read too seriously.
2 It can achieve two things at once.
3 You can wear what you like.
4 You can pass on your own ideas to others.
5 The nature of the location helps prevent potential embarrassment.
6 It is ideal for people who are pressed for time.
7 You will probably hurt yourself doing it.
8 It can be tailored to individual needs.
9 Low-cost alternatives can be used in place of more expensive equipment.

3 Work in groups. Discuss the questions.

- What forms of exercise do you do?
- Do you agree that we have become too obsessed with fitness? Why or why not?

Vocabulary: nouns from phrasal verbs

A number of nouns are formed from phrasal verbs:
Verb: *We want people to forget they're **working out**.*
Noun: *The **workouts** are as thorough as they are light-hearted.*

1 Choose the correct word to complete the sentences. Use a dictionary to help you if necessary.

1 Supermarkets often put sweets on display at their *checkouts / payouts* – and I often buy them.
2 There was a **poor** *handout / turnout* for the last general election – less than half the electorate voted.
3 We haven't had a **heavy** *downpour / downturn* of rain here for quite a long time.
4 I had a very **strict** *uprising / upbringing* – my parents believed in firm discipline.
5 The *outlook / outset / outbreak* for the economy is **bleak**, with rising unemployment likely.
6 I quite often buy a *runaway / takeaway / getaway* but I never eat it in the street.
7 I'm generally very calm but I do have the **occasional** *outburst / outcome / outfit* **of anger.**
8 I think mapping the human genome is the most important **scientific** *breakdown / breakout / breakthrough* of recent times.

2 Work in pairs. Discuss the sentences in exercise 1, saying whether they are true or false for you or your country. Give details.

3 Write four sentences, each including one of the incorrect alternatives in exercise 2. Put gaps where the words should be:

Eighty-seven convicts escaped in a mass _____ from Beeton Prison yesterday.
Answer: *breakout*

4 Show your sentences to your partner, who will try to guess the missing words.

There's more than one way to stay in shape

You don't always have to run on a treadmill if you want to do exercise. Allan Simpson looks at three alternative ways to get fit.

A Integrative Exercise

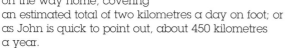

When 58-year-old accountant John Willis travels to work on the underground, he gets off two stops early and walks the
5 remaining distance at a brisk pace. Then, having arrived at his company's headquarters, he avoids the lift, taking the stairs instead to his office on
10 the 8th floor. He does the same on the way home, covering an estimated total of two kilometres a day on foot; or as John is quick to point out, about 450 kilometres a year.

15 He's doing what fitness experts have dubbed 'integrative exercise', that is, incorporating physical activity into his normal daily life. It's a kill-two-birds-with-one-stone approach and can include anything from doing squats while you load the dishwasher
20 to practising yoga in the shower, or for those with a family, lifting children up during play sessions. There's no right or wrong way of doing it – each person has to work out their own strategy, depending on the kind of life they lead.

25 So if you can't spare the time for the two-hour ordeal at the gym, this is the perfect solution, enabling you to fit regular workouts into a busy working week.

B House Gymnastics

House Gymnastics, we are told, is 'a crossbreed of yoga, break-dancing, climbing and gymnastics enacted in a domestic setting'. It's also great fun

5 and a wonderful alternative to conventional forms of exercise. The short but delightful book *House Gymnastics*, with its charming tongue-in-cheek humour shows how the home can be exploited in a variety of exciting new ways, becoming at once a playground,
10 climbing frame and meeting place for fellow gymnasts.

Simple graphics and easy-to-follow explanations talk the reader through the 25 core moves bearing names such as 'armchair handstand', 'ceiling walk' and 'X-door'. In no time at all you'll be crouching in fridges,
15 propping yourself up on furniture, wedging yourself between walls and hanging from door frames. You can also play an active part in the development of the artform by creating your own moves and submitting them to the established *House Gymnastics* website.

20 Be warned though: House Gymnastics is not for the faint-hearted. The authors, Harrison and Ford, point out that 'personal injury is a likely event' and the moves are not recommended for under-eighteens and over-84s.

C Punk Rock Aerobics

Tired of conventional gyms and the usual workout options, thirtysomething Boston punks Maura Jasper and Hilken Mancini decided to run their own aerobics classes, set to music by groups such as The Ramones,
5 Buzzcocks, Blondie and The Undertones. The emphasis is firmly on fun, but the workouts are as thorough as they are light-hearted. 'We want people to forget they're working out, even though they're working up a sweat,' says artist Jasper, now also a certified aerobics
10 instructor.

In the same way that many punk songs were written with just three chords, so too are there just three moves for each song in a typical PRA routine. These have names like Iggy's Pop (raising one knee high and
15 punching out with the opposite arm), Skank (marching in place) or Pogo (jumping up and down). If you can't afford weights, bricks can be used for strength training and a cheap piece of foam serves as a mat. Classes take place in darkly lit rock clubs and mirrors are
20 intentionally missing to prevent participants feeling intimidated or self-conscious. There is also no dress code, though you are more likely to see people working out in denim shorts and fishnet stockings than leotards and leggings. Check out the website.

6B | Medical care

SPEAKING & VOCABULARY: body collocations

1 Work in pairs. Choose the word in each group which describes a health problem when used with the noun in bold.

1 *pierced / blocked / hooked* **nose**
2 *wisdom / milk / rotten* **teeth**
3 *swollen / bare / wide* **feet**
4 *upset / full / empty* **stomach**
5 **eye** *drops / test / strain*
6 **ear** *infection / wax / plugs*

2 Work in pairs. Discuss the questions.

- What can cause each of the problems you chose in exercise 1?
- What, if anything, can be done to treat them?

3 Complete the sentences with a word from the appropriate group in exercise 1.

1 I'd hate to have a _____ **nose**: I don't want a hole there!
2 I've had two of my _____ **teeth** taken out: the other two seem OK.
3 I love walking around **in** _____ **feet** in summer.
4 I always have a big breakfast: I can't start the day **on an** _____ **stomach**.
5 I've never been for an **eye** _____: I have 20-20 vision.
6 I have to wear **ear** _____ to get to sleep: it's so noisy where I live.

4 Work in pairs. Discuss the sentences in exercise 3. How true are they for you?

LISTENING

1 Work in small groups. Try to imagine a world without the items in the box and discuss the questions.

- What consequences would this have on health?
- What alternatives could be used?

> toothbrushes   toothpaste   anaesthetics
> plaster casts   glasses   ambulances

2 🔊 2.14 Listen to the recording and decide whether the statements are true (T) or false (F). Correct the false statements.

1 The title of Lee Evans's book reflects both its style and its content.
2 Modern toothpaste first appeared in the eighteenth century.
3 Ancient Egyptians used an early form of chewing gum to clean their teeth.
4 The Chinese used horsehair to make the first toothbrushes.
5 The earliest form of toothpaste included powdered stone.
6 Modern toothpaste shares some of the same ingredients as ancient Egyptian toothpaste.
7 Before anaesthetics, alcohol was a safe alternative.
8 The anaesthetic qualities of nitrous oxide were not realized until some time after its discovery.
9 Horace Wells made his discovery after he injured his leg.
10 Wells made the first painless tooth extraction using an anaesthetic.

3 Work in pairs, A and B. You are going to tell each other about the history of glasses and ambulances.

A: Turn to page 142.   B: Turn to page 148.

WOUNDED ALLIES RELIEF COMMITTEE.

GRAMMAR: passives 1

1 Complete the passive structures with one word.

1 It was 40 years before the full potential of nitrous oxide _____ **realized** by American dentist Horace Wells.

2 All three _____ been discovered long before their properties as anaesthetics _____ **recognized**.

3 Laughing gas did eventually go on to _____ **used** as an anaesthetic.

4 William Morton _____ widely **regarded** today as the father of anaesthetics.

5 Protective gowns, masks and gloves **must** _____ **worn** when examining patients.

2 In exercise 1, the agent (the person who performs the action) is not mentioned in sentences 2–5. Match the explanations for this a–d to the passive structures 2–5 in exercise 1.

a The agent is 'people in general'.
b The agent is unknown or unimportant in this context.
c It is obvious who the agent is.
d To avoid the use of 'you' in official notices.

> • Form the passive with *be* + past participle. *The first nylon toothbrush* **was introduced** *in 1938.*
> • Use the passive to emphasize the action or the object of the action rather than the agent.
> • The choice between passive and active is often influenced by context. 'Given' or previously mentioned information usually appears towards the beginning of a sentence, and new information comes later. *Humphrey Davy found that nitrous oxide killed the pain of his inflamed gum. But the full potential of* **nitrous oxide** *(Given) was realized by an American dentist called Horace Wells (New).* **He** *(Given) was attending a demonstration (New) of the gas and …*
> • The Given/New rule conditions the use of the passive of *realize* and the active of *attend*.
>
> ❯ SEE LANGUAGE REFERENCE PAGE 64

3 Rewrite the following paragraph so that the given information in **bold** appears towards the beginning of the sentences. Make any necessary changes to verb forms and decide whether to include the agent.

> Prompt treatment of broken bones is important. Firstly, a doctor puts (1) **the bone ends** back into their correct position. After that, something has to hold (2) **the bones** together until the break heals. For many centuries they achieved (3) **this** with splints, long pieces of wood laid parallel to each other alongside the bone. The Ancient Egyptians made (4) **the first splints** from strips of tree bark which they wrapped in bandages to hold them in place. In Ancient Greece, medical practitioners used to harden (5) **the bandages** with waxes and resins. Since the mid-nineteenth century, however, hospital staff have soaked (6) **bandages** in gypsum to make plaster casts. They are gradually replacing (7) **these** now, though, with casts made of lightweight fibreglass plaster. The wearer is enabled to bathe or go swimming by (8) **fibreglass** as it is water-resistant.

PRONUNCIATION: intrusive sounds

1 Sometimes in connected speech an extra, 'intrusive' sound is added to link two vowel sounds. Look at these examples from the listening exercise, then listen and repeat.

hello‿and welcome	bamboo‿or bone	go‿on to be used
/w/	/w/	/w/

three‿anaesthetics	the‿operation	silly‿idea
/j/	/j/	/j/

for‿example	finger‿or‿a chew stick	saw‿an enormous gash
/r/	/r/ /r/	/r/

Work in pairs. Look again at the examples above from the listening exercise and discuss when /w/, /j/ or /r/ are added in connected speech.

2 Find two intrusive sounds in each of the sentences from the recording.

1 With me today is Lee Evans.
2 Spare a thought for the poor old Romans.
3 Your book contains information on other everyday aspects of healthcare.
4 I'd like to ask you about anaesthesia.
5 All three of these were already known to science.
6 Several people were invited up onto the stage to inhale some of the gas.
7 So anyway, Wells put two and two together.
8 William Morton is widely regarded today as the father of anaesthetics.

3 🔊 **2.15** Listen to the sentences in exercise 2 and practise saying them.

6c | Taken care of

SPEAKING

1 Work in small groups. Discuss the questions.

- The people in the photos have all adopted foreign children. Who are they and what do you know about the adoptions?
- Why do you think some people object to international adoptions?
- What potential problems and benefits are there for the children of famous people?

READING

1 Work in pairs. Read the blurb from the book *Natasha's Story* and discuss the question.

Michael Nicholson's nightly reports from Bosnia alerted Britain to the horrors of war in the former Yugoslavia. But when the TV war correspondent found 200 orphan children living unprotected in the outskirts of the shattered city of Sarajevo, he could no longer stand back and do nothing. Fired by anger and despair, he broke the rule of journalistic detachment and decided to smuggle a nine-year-old child back to Britain to live with his own family.

- What problems and dangers do you imagine Michael Nicholson and the girl might have faced?

2 Read the extracts and answer the questions.

1 Are any of the problems and dangers you discussed in exercise 1 mentioned?
2 How did Michael decide which child to take?

3 Read the extracts again and decide whether the sentences are true (T) or false (F). Explain with reference to the text why the false sentences are incorrect.

1 Michael had thought everything through before deciding to take a child from the orphanage.
2 Jacko did not think it was a sensible idea to return to the orphanage that evening.
3 Michael was inflexible in his decision to take Natasha.
4 Vera Zoric was reluctant to let any of the orphans out of her care.
5 According to Michael, the situation in Sarajevo was likely to get worse.
6 Michael says that some children's names were removed from the list of evacuees.
7 The children were confused about the reasons for what was happening to them.
8 It was only in the hotel that Michael began to have doubts about the wisdom of his decision.

4 Work in pairs, A and B. You are going to read what happened at the airport of departure and London Heathrow airport.

A: Turn to page 143.   B: Turn to page 149.

Summarize your extract to your partner.

5 Discuss the questions.

- Do you think Michael Nicholson's illegal action was justified? Why or why not?
- How easy or difficult might it have been for Natasha to adapt to life in England?

VOCABULARY: care

1 Choose the correct word to complete the sentences.

1 I **take good care** *about / of / for* my teeth.
2 Most people in my country **couldn't care less** *in / to / about* the environment.
3 Hospital patients are very **well cared** *about / of / for* in my country.
4 I've been learning English for **longer than I care** *I / to / can* remember.
5 I've been told to **take greater care** *by / on / with* my written English.
6 I can honestly say that at the moment I don't **have a care** *in / of / over* **the world**.

2 Match the meanings in the box to the expressions in **bold** in the sentences 1–6 in exercise 1.

be more careful   look after well
not be worried about anything
a very long time   look after well
not be at all interested in

3 Work in pairs. How true are the sentences in exercise 1 for you?

NATASHA'S STORY

EXTRACT 1
Thursday, 16 July 1992

I had scribbled in my diary as if to make it irrevocable: 'I shall take a child out of Sarajevo when I leave. Check orphanage
5 about little girl Natasha!' A decision had been made and that was that! But I had overlooked a rather crucial point; would the orphanage allow Natasha to leave and did she want to go with a complete stranger?

That evening I persuaded our interpreter, Jacko, against his
10 better judgement, to take me back up to the Ljubica Ivezic orphanage, a dangerous journey at dusk through the hills, when the gunners began to adjust their sights on the city in readiness for their night's deadly employment. The streets were empty, the city's people already back in their attics or their
15 cellars to hide the night away in darkness and much fear.

'Why Natasha?' Vera Zoric, the director, was not as surprised as I had expected. I explained there were other children in her care I could choose if she thought Natasha was not the right choice or if she felt another boy or girl had a greater
20 priority. I would leave it to her to decide, assuming I had her agreement and support.

'But why Natasha?' she asked again. I shrugged. Why do you select one among so many? Why is one face remembered above the rest? 'She shines,' I said.
25 Mrs Zoric did not understand but Jacko explained and she laughed.

I went on: 'She doesn't seem to belong here.'

'None of them belong here.'

'She seems different to me.'
30 She came to me and held my hand in both of hers. 'You want to take this child out of Bosnia and in normal times you could not. But these are not normal times. My children are in danger and every day I am working to find a way to get them out … anywhere, to anyone who will look after them. I do
35 not care where they go as long as they are safe, where there are no shells and no bombing, away from Sarajevo.'

EXTRACT 2
Saturday, 18 July 1992

**(Nicholson secures a place for Natasha on a coach
40 evacuating children from Sarajevo. He is able to travel with them covering the story for television.)**

The incessant shelling, the remorseless sniper fire and the prospect of a winter under siege, made the city despair; each day bleaker than the day before, with the prospect of
45 tomorrow bleaker still. Getting the children out to safety had become everybody's imperative, even if it meant handing them to strangers who would take them to who knew where, for who knew how long. Sarajevo might be destroyed but a generation must be saved to rebuild it.
50 The coaches arrived at the stadium at first light and families immediately surrounded them, little groups huddled together, some fathers but mostly only mothers, fussing about their children, tying a belt tighter, pulling a sock higher, tidying a headscarf, rechecking the contents of little rucksacks and
55 carrier bags … leaving their goodbyes until the very last moment. And all the time looking to the mountains, to the gunners who were certainly watching them.

Soon it was time to go, time to hug and kiss and join the queue. Names were ticked off the list and a dozen helping
60 hands guided children to their seats, tearful children taken from tearful mothers who kissed the window that separated them, mothers who perhaps only then understood what it was they were doing, suddenly uncertain and afraid they would never see their child again. But they knew that to love
65 their children was to save them and to save them was to lose them.

How the children of Sarajevo cried as we pulled out of the stadium, dazed by the abruptness of it all, wondering why, having survived so much for so long, they had been
70 abandoned by the only people who had loved and protected them. At the back of the coach, in seat number 28, a little girl sat watching. She had seen the others kiss and cry their last goodbyes but she had no one to kiss and no reason to cry. Natasha was leaving Sarajevo and its war, and that morning
75 she was happy.

EXTRACT 3

(Nicholson and Natasha reach the safety of a neighbouring country and spend the night in a hotel.)

Soon it would be Tuesday, 21 July, and at eleven o'clock that
80 morning, flight 490 would take off for London. I intended both of us to be on it. It was our last, most difficult and perhaps insurmountable obstacle. But if we failed, what then? I would be arrested of course. Trying to smuggle a child out of any country, whatever the circumstances, was a criminal
85 offence. Arrest meant jail for as long as it took the British Ambassador to arrange my release, assuming such was the Foreign Office's pleasure. Arrest would mean the authorities taking charge of Natasha, and she would be treated like any other illegal immigrant and sent to a transit hostel until
90 somebody decided what to do with her. Not for the first time that past week, the night panicked me, as if only after dark were my foolish schemes exposed and all the reasons for not pursuing them explained.

On the writing table was my passport, number B 466188. I
95 opened it and carefully wrote under my name in the columns provided: 'Accompanied by one child, Natasha. Daughter. Born 7.10.82.'

Glossary
sniper *n* someone who shoots at people from a hidden place
under siege *phrase* surrounded and prevented from receiving supplies

6D | Childcare

VOCABULARY & SPEAKING: babies & babysitting

1 Label the items in the picture with the words in the box.

> nappy dummy feeding bottle
> rattle cot high chair bib
> teddy bear pushchair pram

2 Work in small groups. You are going to discuss some situations you might encounter as a babysitter.

Turn to page 145.

3 Discuss the questions in your groups.

- What qualities do you think are required to be a good babysitter?
- Are you/Would you be a good babysitter? Why or why not?

LISTENING

1 🔘 **2.16** Listen to the recording about a babysitting agency and complete the sentences with one or two words.

1 The agency has been operating for nearly _____.
2 John and Barbara have always aimed to offer clients a _____.
3 Nearly a third of the agency's sitters have worked in the _____.
4 John helps Barbara do some of the _____.
5 John ensures that sitters do not have a _____.
6 Each class on the babysitting course lasts _____.
7 Participants practise nappy changing skills on a _____.
8 When learning how to deal with older children, participants do a lot of _____.
9 On weekdays the hourly rate for a sitter is _____.
10 On each visit sitters take a _____ which they leave with the children.

2 Complete the sentences from the recording with the nouns in the box.

> occasion references ice hand
> care books touch thought doubt

1 **Help is at** _____.
2 We have**n't** really **given it much** _____.
3 **No** _____ we'll be opening a bottle of champagne to **mark the** _____.
4 We **take great** _____ **to** ensure we have the right type of people working for us.
5 We even have a paediatric nurse **on the** _____.
6 I **take up the** _____ and I always do that by phone.
7 John **gets in** _____ **with** the CRB.
8 It helps to **break the** _____.

🔘 **2.17** Listen and check.

3 Explain the meanings of the expressions in bold in exercise 2 in your own words.

GRAMMAR: passives 2

- Use the gerund or passive infinitive after *need* when the meaning is passive.
  *... teaching students what to do if a nappy **needs changing** or a baby **needs to be fed**.*

- Use *have* + object + past participle:
  to show that the subject arranges for something to be done by someone else.
  *We **have all our applicants checked out** by the CRB.*
  to talk about events beyond the subject's control.
  *He **had his wallet stolen** on holiday.*
  Get is an informal alternative to *have*.
  *We managed to **get the car fixed**.*

- Use the infinitive or perfect infinitive after the passive of *believe, discover, expect, find, know, report, say, think, understand* and *be rumoured* to give generalized facts or opinions.
  *If they **are found to have** one, we may not employ them.*
  *She **is thought to have left** the country.*

> SEE LANGUAGE REFERENCE PAGE 64

1 Rewrite the sentences using an infinitive after a passive construction. Begin with the underlined words.

1 They say that <u>Michael Jackson</u> had a fascination for Peter Pan.
2 We understand that <u>Justin Bieber</u> enjoys playing tricks on other people.
3 Many believe that <u>Judy Garland's $500-a-week salary</u> was lower than that of the other *Wizard of Oz* stars.
4 It is known that <u>Scarlett Johansson</u> auditioned for the film *Jumanji* at the age of ten.
5 There were rumours that <u>Haley Joel Osment</u> had been picked by Spielberg to play Harry Potter.
6 It was once reported that <u>Miley Cyrus</u> was worth over $100 million.

2 Write three more sentences using the passive structure about these child stars and/or others from your country.

Read them to your partner who will try to guess who you have written about.

3 There are two mistakes in each sentence. Find and correct the mistakes.

1 I ought to test my eyes at the optician's – I think my lenses need be changed.
2 I used to get my shirts ironing by my mum, but she said I needed learning to do it myself.
3 Our roof needs being fixed – we had several tiles blew off in the storm last week.
4 The car needed service so I took it to the garage this morning to have got it done.
5 I had stolen my keys yesterday so now all the locks need of changing.

4 Work in pairs. Tell your partner about four things of yours that need doing. Say which you will do yourself and which you will have done by someone else.

DID YOU KNOW?

1 Work in pairs. Read about attitudes to children in the UK and discuss the questions.

Britons are often considered to have an intolerant attitude towards children. Fortunately, things have come a long way since Victorian times, when the cruel treatment of children was commonplace, if one is to believe the novels of Charles Dickens. But the proverb 'Children should be seen and not heard' is still sometimes used to illustrate the current situation, and many British parents have been known to complain that they feel uncomfortable when they go out as a family. Indeed, there are still pubs which are more welcoming to dogs than they are to children.

However, attitudes are thought to be changing and many pubs, restaurants and other public places now cater specifically for families. In 2003 the National Family and Parenting Institute launched a ten-year Family Friendly Campaign, aiming to 'promote a culture of acceptance, tolerance and support for parents, children and young people'. As part of this it campaigned to make local neighbourhoods more child-friendly, with speed restrictions for traffic and more play areas and youth facilities. It also supported the right of parents to have greater flexibility at work in order to enable them to balance their working lives with the task of bringing up children.

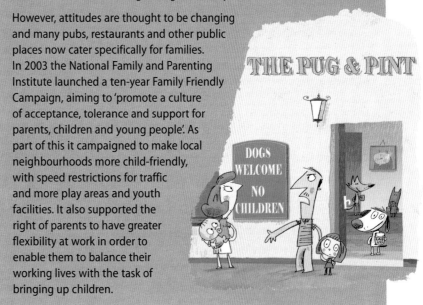

- How would you describe current attitudes towards children in your country?
- How child-friendly is your local area?
- How easy or difficult is it in your country for working parents to spend time with their children?

GRAMMAR
Passives

Form

The passive is formed with the appropriate tense or form of the verb *to be* and the past participle of the main verb:

> *Over 50,000 workers* **have been made** *redundant.*
> *A man* **is being questioned** *in connection with the theft.*

Make is followed by *to* when used in the passive.

> *We always* **make** *our guests* **feel** *very welcome.*
> *Our guests are always* **made to feel** *very welcome.*

Get is often used in informal English instead of *be*.

> *He* **got stopped** *by the police for drink driving.*

It can be used to avoid the awkward present perfect continuous passive.

> *He's* **been getting told off** *a lot recently.* (Instead of *He's been being told off.*)

Use

The passive can be used:

* to create a more impersonal, objective style. It is characteristic of more formal English.
* to focus attention on the action or the object of the action, rather than on the agent, the person or thing that performs the action.

The use of either the active or passive is often determined by context. 'Given' or previously mentioned information generally comes towards the beginning of a clause or sentence and new information towards the end.

In the second sentence of the following example, the given information is *This magnificent work of art*: it is mentioned in the first sentence (*a lifesize portrait*). As it is not the agent of the verb, the passive form, *was painted*, is required.

> *In the next room one can observe a lifesize portrait of the writer as a young man. This magnificent work of art* **was painted** *by an unknown Flemish artist around 1650.*

The agent

If we want to mention the agent, the doer of the action, the preposition *by* is used:

> *First prize was won* **by** *Mr G Hunt of Worthing.*

The agent is not normally included in passive sentences:

* if it is obvious who the agent is.
  He **was sentenced** *to life imprisonment.*
* if the agent is unknown or unimportant.
  The drink **is sold** *in over 50 countries.*
* if the agent is 'people in general'.
  Nitrous oxide **is** *also* **known** *as 'laughing gas'.*
* in official notices, where the agent is the reader of the notice (ie 'you').
  The completed form **should be** *returned by March 5th.*

Further structures

Causative *have*

We can use *have* + object + past participle to say that we arrange for something to be done by other people.

> *She* **had her portrait painted** *by a professional artist.*
> *I'm seriously thinking of* **having my nose pierced**.

The same structure can be used to talk about unpleasant events which are outside of the subject's control.

> *We* **had our flat broken into** *at the weekend.*

Get can be used as an informal alternative to *have*. It is the preferred choice in imperatives.

> *I* **got my photos done** *at the shop on the corner.*
> **Get your hair cut**!

In some cases, *get* conveys the idea that some degree of difficulty is involved.

> *It was several years before he managed to* **get his first novel published**.

need + gerund

Both the gerund and the passive infinitive can be used after *need* to indicate that something should be done.

> *The flat* **needs painting/to be painted** *again.*

Passive constructions with the infinitive

Verbs such as *allege, believe, claim, consider, discover, estimate, expect, find, know, report, be rumoured, say, think* and *understand* are often used in the passive and followed by the present infinitive (*to do, to be doing, to be done*) or the perfect infinitive (*to have done, to have been doing, to have been done*). This structure is common in journalism, when reporters may wish to distance themselves from the facts or opinions expressed.

> *She* **is believed to be suffering** *from heart disease.*
> *He* **is reported to have spoken** *to the actress shortly before her death.*
> *They* **were said to be** *'delighted' at the news of their daughter's engagement.*
> *He* **was** *widely* **rumoured to have earned** *his millions through dishonest means.*

WORD LIST

Nouns from phrasal verbs

breakdown n C **	/'breɪkˌdaʊn/
breakout n C	/'breɪkaʊt/
breakthrough n C *	/'breɪkθruː/
checkout n C	/'tʃekaʊt/
downpour n C	/'daʊnˌpɔː(r)/
downturn n C	/'daʊnˌtɜː(r)n/
getaway n C	/'getəˌweɪ/
handout n C	/'hændaʊt/
outbreak n C *	/'aʊtˌbreɪk/
outburst n C	/'aʊtˌbɜː(r)st/
outcome n C ***	/'aʊtˌkʌm/
outfit n C *	/'aʊtfɪt/
outlook n sing *	/'aʊtˌlʊk/
outset n sing *	/'aʊtˌset/
payout n C	/'peɪaʊt/
runaway n C	/'rʌnəˌweɪ/
takeaway n C	/'teɪkəˌweɪ/
turnout n sing	/'tɜː(r)naʊt/
upbringing n sing *	/'ʌpˌbrɪŋɪŋ/
uprising n C	/'ʌpˌraɪzɪŋ/
workout n C	/'wɜː(r)kaʊt/
work out v	/ˌwɜː(r)k 'aʊt/

Body collocations

blocked nose	/ˌblɒkt 'nəʊz/
ear infection n C	/'ɪə(r) ɪnˌfekʃ(ə)n/
ear wax n U	/'ɪə(r) ˌwæks/
earplug n C	/'ɪə(r)ˌplʌg/
eye drops n pl	/'aɪ ˌdrɒps/
eye strain n U	/'aɪ ˌstreɪn/
eye test n C	/'aɪ ˌtest/
hooked nose	/'hʊkt ˌnəʊz/
in bare feet	/ɪn ˌbeə(r) 'fiːt/
milk tooth n C	/'mɪlk ˌtuːθ/
on a full stomach	/ɒn ə ˌfʊl 'stʌmək/
on an empty stomach	/ɒn ən 'empti ˌstʌmək/
rotten adj *	/'rɒt(ə)n/
swollen adj *	/'swəʊlən/
upset stomach	/ˌʌpset 'stʌmək/
wisdom tooth n C	/'wɪzd(ə)m ˌtuːθ/

Care

take good care of (sb/sth)	/teɪk ˌgʊd 'keə(r) əv/
couldn't care less	/kʊd(ə)nt ˌkeə(r) 'les/
be well cared for	/bi ˌwel 'keə(r)d fɔː(r)/
longer than (sb) cares to remember	/lɒŋgə(r) ðæn ˌkeə(r)z tə rɪ'membə(r)/
take great care with (sth)	/teɪk ˌgreɪt 'keə(r) wɪð/
not have a care in the world	/nɒt hæv ə 'keə(r) ɪn ðə ˌwɜː(r)ld/

Babies & babysitting

bib n C	/bɪb/
bully v *	/'bʊli/
burp v	/bɜː(r)p/
burst into tears	/ˌbɜː(r)st ɪntʊ 'tɪə(r)z/
cot n C	/kɒt/
crybaby n C	/'kraɪˌbeɪbi/
cuddle v	/'kʌd(ə)l/
dummy n C	/'dʌmi/
feeding bottle n C	/'fiːdɪŋ ˌbɒt(ə)l/
high chair n C	/'haɪ tʃeə(r)/
nappy n C	/'næpi/
nosebleed n C	/'nəʊzˌbliːd/
nostril n C	/'nɒstrəl/
pick one's nose	/ˌpɪk wʌnz 'nəʊz/
pram n C	/præm/
pushchair n C	/'pʊʃˌtʃeə(r)/
rattle n C	/'ræt(ə)l/
smack v *	/smæk/
squabble v	/'skwɒb(ə)l/
stay up v	/ˌsteɪ 'ʌp/
teddy bear n C	/'tedi ˌbeə(r)/
throw a temper tantrum	/θrəʊ ə 'tempə(r) ˌtæntrəm/

Other words & phrases

ammonia n U	/ə'məʊniə/
anaesthesia n U	/ˌænəs'θiːziə/
anaesthetic n C/adj	/ˌænəs'θetɪk/
bash v	/bæʃ/
bewildered adj	/bɪ'wɪldə(r)d/
bifocal adj	/baɪ'fəʊk(ə)l/
break the ice	/ˌbreɪk ði 'aɪs/
brisk adj	/brɪsk/
canvas n U *	/'kænvəs/
childminder n C	/'tʃaɪldˌmaɪndə(r)/
chloroform n U	/'klɒrəˌfɔː(r)m/
commonplace adj	/'kɒmənˌpleɪs/
concave adj	/'kɒnkeɪv, kɒn'keɪv/
convex adj	/'kɒnveks, ˌkɒn'veks/
crossbreed n C	/'krɒsˌbriːd/
cussed adj	/'kʌsɪd/
dazed adj	/deɪzd/
deaden v	/'ded(ə)n/
déjà vu n U	/ˌdeɪʒɑː 'vuː/
dress code n C	/'dres ˌkəʊd/
dusk n U	/dʌsk/
emerald n C	/'em(ə)rəld/
ether n U	/'iːθə(r)/
evacuee n C	/ɪ'vækjuːiː/
faint-hearted adj	/ˌfeɪnt 'hɑː(r)tɪd/
fiasco n C	/fi'æskəʊ/
fibreglass n U	/'faɪbə(r)ˌglɑːs/
first aid n U	/ˌfɜː(r)st 'eɪd/
flick v *	/flɪk/
foam n U	/fəʊm/
frayed adj	/freɪd/
gash n C	/gæʃ/
grubby adj	/'grʌbi/

gypsum n U	/'dʒɪps(ə)m/
help is at hand	/'help ɪz ət ˌhænd/
huddle together v	/'hʌd(ə)l təˌgeðə(r)/
inhale v	/ɪn'heɪl/
irrevocable adj	/ɪ'revəkəb(ə)l/
kill two birds with one stone	/kɪl 'tuː bɜː(r)dz wɪð wʌn ˌstəʊn/
leggings n pl	/'legɪŋz/
leotard n C	/'liːəˌtɑː(r)d/
lifelike adj	/'laɪfˌlaɪk/
light-hearted adj	/ˌlaɪt 'hɑː(r)tɪd/
mark an occasion	/ˌmɑː(r)k ən ə'keɪʒ(ə)n/
nauseous adj	/'nɔːziəs, 'nɔːsiəs/
nitrous oxide n U	/ˌnaɪtrəs 'ɒksaɪd/
on the books	/ˌɒn ðə 'bʊks/
ordeal	/ɔː(r)'diːl/
paediatric nurse n C	/ˌpiːdi'ætrɪk nɜː(r)s/
plaster cast n C	/'plɑːstə(r) ˌkɑːst/
pluck up courage	/ˌplʌk ʌp 'kʌrɪdʒ/
posh adj	/pɒʃ/
pressed for time adj	/ˌprest fə 'taɪm/
prop oneself up on (sth)	/ˌprɒp wʌnself 'ʌp ɒn/
pull out v	/ˌpʊl 'aʊt/
pumice stone n C	/'pʌmɪs ˌstəʊn/
put two and two together	/pʊt ˌtuː ən(d) tuː tə'geðə(r)/
recruitment n U *	/rɪ'kruːtmənt/
remorseless adj	/rɪ'mɔː(r)sləs/
resin n C/U	/'rezɪn/
scribble v	/'skrɪb(ə)l/
shattered adj	/'ʃætə(r)d/
shelling n U	/'ʃelɪŋ/
short-sightedness n U	/ˌʃɔː(r)t 'saɪtɪdnəs/
smuggle v	/'smʌg(ə)l/
sniper n C	/'snaɪpə(r)/
splint n C	/'splɪnt/
squat n C	/skwɒt/
stamp v **	/stæmp/
stay in shape	/ˌsteɪ ɪn 'ʃeɪp/
stretcher n C	/'stretʃə(r)/
strip n C **	/strɪp/
take (sth) for granted	/ˌteɪk fə 'grɑːntɪd/
take up a reference	/teɪk ˌʌp ə 'ref(ə)rəns/
think (sth) through	/ˌθɪŋk 'θruː/
tongue-in-cheek adj	/ˌtʌŋ ɪn 'tʃiːk/
treadmill n C	/'tredˌmɪl/
twig n C	/twɪg/
under siege	/ˌʌndə(r) 'siːdʒ/
urine n U	/'jʊərɪn/
usher v	/'ʌʃə(r)/
wax n C/U	/wæks/
wedge oneself between (sth)	/ˌwedʒ wʌnself bɪ'twiːn/
weighty adj	/'weɪti/
wild boar n C	/ˌwaɪld 'bɔː(r)/
work up a sweat	/ˌwɜː(r)k ˌʌp ə 'swet/
writhe around v	/ˌraɪð ə'raʊnd/

7A | Behaving badly

SPEAKING & LISTENING

1 When talking about your secondary school, how would you describe each of the nouns in bold? Circle one or more adjectives for each noun as appropriate.

School
single-sex   mixed   private   state
Teachers
easy-going   unapproachable   strict   lenient
Pupils
well-behaved   disruptive   keen   unenthusiastic
Discipline
rigid   relaxed   poor   non-existent
Punishments
severe   light   effective   unfair
Teaching Methods
progressive   traditional   effective   ineffective

2 Work in pairs. Explain your choices in exercise 1, giving examples.

3 🔘 **2.18–2.22** You will hear five people speaking about different acts of misbehaviour at school. For the speakers 1–5 answer these questions:

1 What act(s) of misbehaviour do they describe?
2 What was the punishment?

4 🔘 **2.18–2.22** Listen again. What is each speaker's attitude to the punishment handed out?

5 Work in pairs. What are your own views on the punishments in the recording?

READING

1 Ignoring the gaps, read the extract from a book by Marie Stubbs, who writes of her experience as headmistress at an inner-city comprehensive school. Discuss the question in pairs.

• What measures does she take to improve discipline and motivation at the school?

2 Complete the gaps 1–6 in the extract with the sections a–f.

a They're a wonderful looking bunch of children, a rich mixture of races and physical types, some watching me with interest, others making it clear they have better things to do.

b Order and discipline are said to have broken down, with physical attacks on teachers and ferocious fights between pupils. The school is now on 'Special Measures', which means it's on the brink of permanent shutdown.

c I put my head round the door one lunchtime to be met by total hush, as everybody silently eats their chips with their eyes glued to *Lord of the Flies*. Lots of clubs have sprung up, and the whole building seems to have come alive during the lunch hours.

d They separate easily – the shock of being physically restrained by a 60-year-old grandmother is enough. But the incident reminds me how little there is for the children to do in the playground.

e To help me in my seemingly impossible task, I've brought with me two of the best teachers from my last job: Sean Devlin and Tracey O'Leary. Both are brilliant at dealing with troublesome, overwrought teenagers.

f I can see from the faces of the staff that some of them think I'm mad. They can't believe that these 'kids' will ever behave well enough to attend a social event in a formal setting.

3 Work in pairs. Discuss the meaning of the highlighted words and expressions in the extract.

4 Work in pairs. Discuss the questions.

• How big a problem is indiscipline in schools in your country?
• Who or what do you think is to blame?

GRAMMAR: ellipsis

Ellipsis involves omitting words to avoid unnecessary repetition. Which words have been omitted in these sentences?

1 I look out of the window and (_____) see a crowd of children.
2 Some pupils keep the books but they're not supposed to (_____).
3 I'm confident they will behave well, but many of the staff aren't (_____).
4 'We should inform his mother and (_____) father.' 'I already have (_____).'
5 'Are you going to the May Ball?' 'I'd like to (_____) but I can't (_____).'
6 'Is the cafeteria open yet?' 'It should be (_____).'

Look at sentences 1–6 again and decide which one of the following statements is incorrect.

• Words are often omitted after *and* or *but*.
• *To* can be used on its own instead of a full infinitive clause.
• The main verb can be omitted after an auxiliary verb.
• Adverbs (eg *probably, already*) can be placed before the auxiliary verb which remains.
• *Be* can be omitted after a modal verb.

▶ SEE LANGUAGE REFERENCE PAGE 74

A NEW BROOM

I have just come out of retirement. At the age of 60, when I should be putting my feet up, I have been asked to take the helm at St George's Roman Catholic Secondary School in Maida Vale. St George's has descended into chaos.
5 (1) _____ I have just four terms to turn it round.

I arrive at St George's a day before the pupils return to school. The playground is a bleak, empty place, a large expanse of tarmac pitted with chewing gum. Inside, the school is painted a uniform, washed-out magnolia, and there
10 are very few posters or noticeboards. An air of exhaustion and despair hangs over the school.

(2) _____ The three of us decide to put up posters at strategic points along the corridors: Welcome Back, Respect Each Other, Walk Don't Run, Talk Don't Shout, Get to Lessons
15 on Time, Put Rubbish in the Bin. At Tracey's suggestion we've had the posters printed with Arabic, Spanish, Portuguese, Farsi and Yoruba translations underneath. More than half the children at St George's speak English only as a second language. Some are refugees who have arrived in Britain
20 unaccompanied, knowing nobody.

We've decided to stagger the children's return, and today we have only the Year 11s in, aged fifteen and sixteen. Their response to us is crucial, because it will provide a template for the rest of the school. We walk purposefully into the
25 school hall for our first assembly. (3) _____ I tell them that the past is over, and that from now on we will all pull together. 'And for Year 11 only,' I say, 'there will be a special event: a May Ball at a top London hotel.' There is a gasp, and a ripple of excited chatter. (4) _____

30 One lunchtime in our second week I hear ragged shouts which unify into a chant: 'Fight! Fight!' I look out of the window and see a crowd of children swarming towards one corner of the playground. Two big fifteen-year-olds are embroiled in a vicious fight: kicking, swearing, thumping, grabbing one
35 another's hair. I rush out and grab one of the youths by the arm. Sean gets a grip on the other one. (5) _____ I ask one of the school technicians: 'If I give you £200 from the Governor's Fund, would you go over to B&Q and spend it on the playground?' Soon we have a playground full of benches
40 and tables. The tarmac is painted with zigzag shapes and lines for basketball and football.

We redecorate inside the school next. A different colour for each floor – a sunshine yellow, a brilliant red, and a very bright blue. I buy some electronic signs, which are updated
45 hourly with birthday greetings and other announcements. We start playing music on the Tannoy™ system. There's nothing like a bit of Bob Marley to lift the spirits. If I feel the school is getting too lively I put on a CD by Enya. It's what I call 'beauty shop music': it has a useful soothing effect.

50 We spend a fortune restocking books for every classroom. The pupils are allowed to take books home, and if the odd one disappears because a child can't bear to give it back, that's all right with me. One of the English teachers sets up a screen in the cafeteria. Every day she projects on to it the
55 text of a selected book, slowly scrolling it down to give the children a taste. (6) _____ I love to walk around it, hearing the sounds of dance music drifting out of the gym and catching glimpses of groups absorbed in other activities. I'm always keen to know what the children themselves
60 want, and I put suggestion boxes around the school asking for their ideas. Some of the suggestions are just flippant – 'Burn the place down', 'More sex education' – but there are heartfelt messages too: 'Get more black teachers', 'I'd like bigger dinners', 'Can we have football teams?'
65 Touchingly, some are thank-you messages. 'I don't have any suggestions, but if I did I know you would listen,' one child wrote.

1 Cross out those words which could be omitted. In item 5 you will need to change the order of some of the remaining words.

1 I can't play a musical instrument but I really wish I could play a musical instrument.
2 **A:** Do you watch a lot of television?
  B: I don't watch a lot of television now but I used to watch a lot of television before.
3 I often spend the evening at home on weekdays but I never spend the evening at home on Saturday.
4 **A:** Will you still be in bed at 10 on Sunday morning?
  B: I may well still be in bed at 10 on Sunday morning. I don't get up till late.
5 I don't smoke. I've never smoked and I'll probably never smoke.

2 Work in pairs. How true for you are the statements or answers in exercise 1? Tell your partner.

7B Rudeness

VOCABULARY & SPEAKING: good & bad behaviour

1 Complete the questions with the nouns in the box.

> manners   queues   language   offence
> trouble   parties   behaviour   hooligans

1   Do people in your country generally **form orderly** _____?
2   How would you and your family define **good table** _____?
3   When might a child be told to be **on his or her best** _____?
4   Do your neighbours ever keep you awake with **rowdy** _____?
5   What is the cause of the **loutish behaviour of football** _____?
6   Was there a time at school when you **got into serious** _____?
7   Can you name a public figure whose remarks often **cause** _____?
8   Do you take offence when other people **use foul** _____?

2 Work in small groups. Discuss the questions in exercise 1.

LISTENING

1 You are going to hear three friends, Jenny, Lucy and Simon, talking about rudeness. They will discuss some of the following topics:

* Careless drivers _____
* Bad manners in the office _____
* Rudeness to certain types of employee _____
* The effects of city life _____
* Saying 'please' and 'thank you' _____
* The right and wrong way to greet people _____
* Mobile phone abuse _____
* Kissing and cuddling in public _____
* Traditional etiquette _____
* Rudeness leading to fights _____
* The essence of good manners _____
* Negative influences _____

Work in pairs. Predict the kinds of things they might say in relation to each one.

They might say how careless driving causes other motorists to become angry and abusive. This may take the form of bad language or even violence.

2 🔘 **2.23** Listen to the dialogue and tick (✓) the topics in exercise 1 which they discuss.

3 🔘 **2.23** Listen again and make notes on what they say about each of the topics you have ticked.

4 Work in pairs. Discuss the questions.

* Which of their opinions expressed in the recording do you share?
* Which do you disagree with? Why?
* What forms of rude behaviour annoy you?

SPEECH FEATURE: ellipsis in conversation

In spoken English, unstressed words are often left out at the beginning of sentences if the meaning remains clear. Words omitted can be:

* subject pronouns.
  (*We*) *Might see some better behaviour at football matches.*
  (*It*) *Keeps me amused.* (*It*) *Doesn't take much, does it?*
* auxiliary verbs or *be* in questions.
  (*Does*) *Anybody want another piece of cake?*
  (*Are*) *Your parents back from their holiday yet?*
* subject pronouns and auxiliary verbs (or *be*).
  (*I was*) *Just trying to offer an explanation.*
  (*Do you*) *Do that kind of thing very often on the train?*
  (*There's*) *No eye contact, of course.*

In some cases other words may be omitted.
  (*Would you like some*) *More coffee?*
  (*Do you have*) *Any idea what happened?*

> **SEE LANGUAGE REFERENCE PAGE 74**

1 Match the questions 1–8 to the replies a–h, then cross out any words which can be omitted.

1 Is there anything else you need for the journey?
2 Did you have any luck with the tickets?
3 Are you sure you're all right?
4 Would you like a cup of tea?
5 Is your mum any better?
6 Are you coming out tonight?
7 Did you enjoy your holiday?
8 Have you got any aspirins?

a No, thanks. I never touch the stuff. It makes me feel sick.
b Yes, it was fantastic! We've just got back, actually.
c Yes, thanks. She should be home next week.
d No, they were sold out, unfortunately. It's a pity, really.
e I'm sorry. I'm afraid I can't help you.
f I don't think so. Are you coming to the airport to see me off?
g I can't, I'm afraid. I've got to work.
h I'm absolutely positive. I've never felt better.

🔊 **2.24** Listen and check your answers to exercise 1.

2 Work in pairs. Practise reading the exchanges in exercise 1.

3 With your partner, write an eight-line dialogue which begins or ends with one of the exchanges in exercise 1. Include some further examples of ellipsis.

4 Read out your dialogue to the class, but without the exchange from exercise 1. The other students must guess which exchange you chose.

SPEAKING

1 You are going to discuss something in groups, A and B.

The national tourist board is concerned that the bad manners and behaviour of its citizens, both at home and abroad, is putting foreign tourists off visiting the country. It has decided to launch a campaign in an attempt to encourage better behaviour and improve the country's image.

Group A: Turn to page 143.
Group B: Turn to page 149.

2 Work with a student from the other group. Explain your choices to each other.

3 With your partner decide on **two** posters, one from each group of three, which will be used in a press release to launch the campaign.

Explain your choices to the rest of the class.

Useful language

Discussing relative importance
This is *a/an fairly/relatively/particularly/equally* important area.
This issue is *quite a lot/a great deal/far/even more* important than that one.
It is *vital/essential/more important* that we try to encourage/discourage this behaviour.

Discussing effectiveness
This poster would have a *limited/positive/significant* effect on people's behaviour.
This one would be *only moderately/reasonably/highly* effective in changing attitudes.

Describing the posters
It is *colourful/eye-catching/visually (un)attractive/ (un)imaginative/dull.*
It *makes a good point/gets the point across well/doesn't grab my attention.*

7c | Whodunnit?

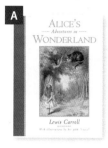

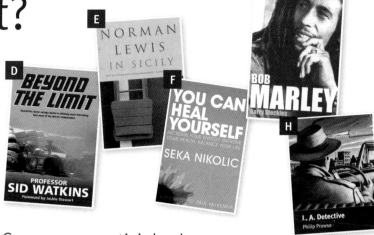

SPEAKING

1 Match the types of book 1–8 to the book covers A–H.

- ☐ 1 self-help
- ☐ 2 poetry
- ☐ 3 literary classic
- ☐ 4 crime novel
- ☐ 5 romance
- ☐ 6 travel story
- ☐ 7 sports
- ☐ 8 biography

2 Rank the books in exercise 1 according to how pleased you would be to receive them on your birthday (1 is 'extremely pleased' and 8 is 'not pleased at all').

Compare your list with your partner's, giving reasons for your choices.

3 Work in pairs and talk about your reading habits. What types of books do you enjoy reading, when do you read them and where?

READING

1 Read the extract from the crime novel *A Dark Devotion* and answer the questions.

1 What are the names of the two characters who speak in the extract?

2 What do you think their relationship is with a) each other? b) Grace?

2 Read the blurb on page 154 to check your ideas.

3 Work in groups of three, A, B and C. You will each read a further extract from *A Dark Devotion*.

A: Turn to page 144.   C: Turn to page 154.
B: Turn to page 150.

4 Summarize your extract to the others in your group, then discuss together what might have happened to Grace.

GRAMMAR: participle clauses

Participle clauses can be used instead of relative clauses. Present participles replace verbs in the active; past participles replace verbs in the passive.
> Will, **listening** hard, slowed down and I almost bumped into him. (= who was listening)
> Above the fireplace was a carriage clock, **given** to him on his retirement. (= which had been given)

Participle clauses can also be used:
- in place of conjunctions such as *after, as, if, once, when, while.*
  > **Reaching** the path, Will paused. (= when he reached)
  > **Walking** on, we fell into step. (= as we walked on)
- after some conjunctions.
  > **When asked** who he had met, he refused to comment.
- to describe the cause or result of something.
  > **Having lost** his wallet, he had to walk home.
  > He fell off a ladder, **breaking** his leg in three places.

> ❯ SEE LANGUAGE REFERENCE PAGE 74

1 Rewrite the underlined sections in the sentences using the words in the box.

if	after	while	who	which
because		with the result that		

Anyone earning less than £20,000 will remain unaffected by the changes in tax rates.
Anyone who earns less than £20,000

1 A pencil portrait of the musician, <u>drawn on an envelope</u>, has been sold for £300,000.

2 <u>Not wanting to appear rude</u>, we accepted their invitation to see their wedding video.

3 <u>Stored in an airtight container</u>, the cakes will remain fresh for up to two weeks.

4 High winds brought down power lines, <u>leaving 30,000 residents without electricity</u>.

5 <u>Walking by the river yesterday</u>, I heard the unmistakeable call of a cuckoo.

6 <u>Having discussed it further with his wife</u>, he decided not to accept the job.

2 Combine the following pairs of sentences using participle clauses.

Torrential rain continued to fall yesterday. It caused extensive flooding in many areas.
Torrential rain continued to fall yesterday, causing extensive flooding in many areas.

1 She tripped and fell. She cut her knee quite badly and sprained her ankle.
2 He had worked at the factory for over 40 years. He was devastated at the news of its impending closure.
3 This book is a first edition. It was signed by the author.
4 He was told he had won the award. He broke down in tears. (Begin *When* …)
5 She spoke to journalists after the trial. She said that justice had been done.

3 Complete each sentence in a suitable way.

1 Having lived in Spain for fifteen years,
_____.

2 Driving through the city centre last night,
_____.

3 When asked why he had stolen the traffic sign,
_____.

4 _____,
causing serious delays for travellers.

5 Not wanting to appear greedy,
_____.

4 Work in pairs. Take turns to read out the clauses you have written for sentences 1–5 above in random order. For each clause your partner will try to identify which sentence in sentences 1–5 you have completed.

A **MISSING** person

'So who was the last person to see Grace before she disappeared?'

'We don't know.' His voice rose again in agitation. 'Well, the police aren't sure, which amounts to the same thing.
5 After Charlie got back from school Grace took him over to Mum's …'

'She drove?'

'Yes. She stayed for a while, then drove back home.'

'At what time?'

10 'About four, I think.'

'So after Maggie, no one else seems to have seen her?'

'Well, no one so far. But someone might well have seen her driving back or parking the car or going into the house. Or …'

15 I thought he was being rather optimistic. Marsh House stood alone at the end of the quay some distance from the nearest house. It was perfectly possible that she had returned home – or travelled elsewhere – unseen.

We reached the edge of the meadows and the promise of
20 drier ground.

'Well, it seems to me that there are at least three areas worth looking into,' I announced, following close behind Will as he advanced up the slope in long strides. 'The first is to check out the London end, which I'll arrange. The second
25 is to make sure that no local information has been missed – make sure the police have made sufficient house-to-house enquiries, asked the neighbours if they saw anything odd, that sort of thing. Sometimes neighbours don't realize the value of what they've seen, don't think of telling anyone
30 about it until they're actually asked. The third …' Will, listening hard, slowed down and I almost bumped into him. '… is to decide if the police search was adequate, to make sure they haven't missed any obvious places that Grace might have gone to or' – it had to be said – 'been taken to.

35 I would add a fourth area – forensic testing, fingerprints and so on – but if it wasn't done almost immediately …'

'It wasn't,' he reported darkly.

'And you didn't notice anything when you got back that morning – or since? Tyre marks, smears of dirt, footprints,
40 things like that?'

'No!'

The agitation had come back into his face and I added hastily, 'It was only a thought. It's very rare to find anything like that.'

45 Reaching the path, Will paused. 'Look … perhaps it might be best if you did go and talk to the police,' he said awkwardly. 'You know which questions to ask.'

I said, in a rush, 'Of course.'

'I always get so angry when I see them! I feel they're being
50 so bloody useless! And the way they look at me, Alex! I know what they're thinking – they make it so bloody obvious!' He gave a short bitter laugh before shooting me a quick glance to see if I could guess what was coming. 'They think I'm responsible! They think I must have done away with her.'

55 'They're bound to think that.'

He wasn't quite sure how to take this remark.

'The great majority of disappearances are linked to family situations,' I explained. 'To stress or money worries. Or violence within the family. It's a statistic that gets drummed
60 into the police, I'm afraid. They're apt to get tunnel vision.'

He gave a long ragged sigh which was almost a laugh. 'So I shouldn't take it personally?'

'Absolutely not.'

'You're sure about that?'

65 But he wasn't really expecting an answer and, walking on, we fell into step. Aware of his eyes on me, I looked across at him. He said, in a rough voice, 'Glad you're here, Alex.'

'Me too.' And I reached for his hand and squeezed it.

Glossary

quay *n* a hard surface next to an ocean or river, where boats can stop
meadow *n* a field where grass and wild flowers grow

71

7D | Crime reports

LISTENING

1 Work in pairs. Look at the web page and discuss the possible stories behind the different news headlines.

2 🔘 **2.25–2.27** You are going to hear radio news reports on three of the headlines on the web page. As you listen, match the reports 1–3 to the correct headline A–F and write down who each of the following people are:

Report 1	Report 2	Report 3
Peter Simpson	Sheila Danbury	Sally Blofeld
James Boyle	Paula Banes	Jerry Wexford
David Westwood	Ian Stride	Daniel Roberts
Anna Coleby		

3 🔘 **2.25–2.27** Listen again and make notes on what is said by and/or about each of the people in exercise 2.

4 Work in small groups. Discuss the following statements. Give reasons for your opinions.

- Householders should have the right to use any force they consider necessary to defend themselves and their homes.
- Parents should be punished if their children play truant or commit other offences.
- Courts should hand out prison sentences to officials of companies which commit environmental crimes.

VOCABULARY: legal matters

1 Complete the sentences with the prepositions in the box. You will need to use two of the prepositions more than once.

> against   for   of   on   to   with

1 A pensioner who stabbed a would-be burglar … has been **cleared** _____ assault.
2 Peter Simpson had been **charged** _____ the offence following a failed burglary at his home.
3 Boyle … **pleaded guilty** _____ six counts of burglary.
4 Sheila Danbury was **sentenced** _____ 60 days' imprisonment _____ failing to ensure that her eldest daughter attended school regularly.
5 Ms Danbury's lawyer said his client would be **appealing** _____ the sentence.
6 Fines **imposed** _____ companies **convicted** _____ polluting the environment are insufficient.
7 Jerry Wexford called for tougher penalties for organizations **found guilty** _____ causing pollution.
8 A spokesman … **accused** the environmentalists _____ exaggerating the extent of the problem.

Check your answers in audioscripts 2.25–2.27 on pages 157–158.

RADIO Ambria

NEWS   SPORT   WEATHER   TRAVEL NEWS   FEATURES   PICTURES

LATEST NEWS

WEATHER
3 Day Forecast
Friday   Saturday   Sunday

E Unpaid traffic fines abroad 'will not go unpunished'

C Pensioner used 'reasonable force' to defend himself

A Mayor arrested in housing corruption scandal

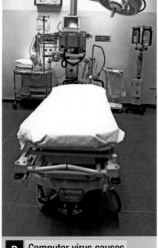

B Computer virus causes hospital treatment delays

D 'Polluters must pay more,' say environmentalists

F Mother jailed for teenage daughter's truancy

2 Complete the sentences with the appropriate noun form of the verb in capital letters. You may need to write a plural form.

1 A leading politician is to **go on** _____ for fraud next week.   TRY
2 They **denied** all _____ of money laundering.   ACCUSE
3 Police have **made** a number of _____ in connection with the bombing.   ARREST
4 She is being **held** by police **on** _____ of arson.   SUSPECT
5 Smith **entered a** _____ of 'not guilty' **to** tax evasion.   PLEAD
6 He **had** several **previous** _____ **for** traffic offences.   CONVICT
7 Police have **dropped** all _____ of bribery and corruption **against** him.   CHARGE
8 The jury **returned a** guilty **verdict** and he was **given** three **life** _____ for the murders. SENTENCE

3 Work in pairs. Describe two recent high-profile court cases in your country using some of the verbs and nouns in exercises 1 and 2.

SPEAKING

1 Work in small groups. Look at the situations 1–5 and discuss the questions.

- How much sympathy do you have for the people involved?
- How should the law deal with them?

1 An elderly lady is having trouble making ends meet. She goes to her local supermarket and puts a tin of meat into her bag. A security guard notices this and intercepts her as she attempts to leave without paying.

2 A car travelling at 165kph is stopped by police on its way to the airport. The speed limit is 120kph. The driver explains that he and his family will miss their flight and a three-week holiday in Thailand if they do not check in within half an hour.

3 A number of undergraduates throw a party to celebrate the end of their final exams. As a result of complaints from neighbours, the police call at 12.30am to break it up. A week later they have a bigger party to celebrate their results.

4 A young man refuses to do military service on ideological grounds. The alternative is eighteen months' community service; he again refuses.

5 After a hazardous sea crossing, a small boat full of men, women and children lands on foreign shores. The occupants hope to find work there, but none of them has either a work permit or a passport.

DID YOU KNOW?

1 Work in pairs. Read about the Canadian Mounties and discuss the questions.

THE ROYAL CANADIAN MOUNTED POLICE is one of Canada's best-known symbols internationally. The image of the police officer, or 'Mountie', riding a horse in his scarlet tunic and wide-brimmed Stetson hat has been glamorized by Hollywood and used to promote Canada abroad for over a century.

Created in 1873, when it was known as the North West Mounted Police, its original function was to bring law, order and Canadian authority to the Northwest Territories, wipe out the illegal whisky trade and improve relations with First Nations, the Canadian term for indigenous people.

Nowadays, the RCMP is responsible for an unusually wide range of duties across the whole country. It enforces federal laws, but also provides policing services under contract to Canada's three territories, eight of its provinces, more than 200 municipalities and over 150 aboriginal communities.

The Mounties' distinctive uniform, known as the Red Serge, is now only worn on special occasions, and has been replaced by more conventional attire for day-to-day police work. Similarly, recruits are no longer taught to ride and care for horses when they join the force, and the car has become their favoured mode of transport.

- How is the police force organized in your country?
- What do you know about its history?
- What reputation does it have both at home and abroad? Why?

GRAMMAR
Participle clauses

Clauses which begin with a participle are known as participle clauses; they are more common in written than in spoken English. Generally speaking, present participles replace verbs in the active and past participles replace verbs in the passive.

1 Participle clauses can be used:

- in place of relative clauses.
  *Residents most seriously **affected** by the flooding will receive compensation.* (= **who were ... affected**)
  *The royal newly-weds were cheered by thousands of people **lining** the route.* (= **who lined/were lining**)

- to show that one action occurred immediately after another.
  ***Closing** the door quietly behind her, she tiptoed up the stairs to bed.* (= **after she closed**)
  A perfect infinitive stresses that the first action has finished before the second begins:
  ***Having read** the letter, he tore it up and put it in the bin.*

- to show that one action occurred at the same time as another.
  *We sat there for ages **waiting** to be served.*

- to describe the cause of something.
  ***Not knowing** her postal address, he sent her an email instead.* (= **because he didn't know**)
  ***Having had** a particularly stressful day at work, she was in no mood for screaming children.*

- to describe the result of something.
  *The building collapsed, **sending** up a cloud of dust.*

- in place of *if* in conditional sentences.
  ***Left** on his own in the kitchen, my husband wouldn't know where to begin.* (= **if he were left**)

- after the object of verbs of perception such as *see, hear, watch, notice, feel.*
  *She felt something **crawling** up her back.*

- after conjunctions such as *after, if, once, when, while.*
  *He was attacked **while walking** his dog.*
  ***Once installed**, the device is simple to use.*
  ***If passed**, the law will come into immediate effect.*

2 The subject of a participle clause is usually the same as the subject of the main clause.
  ***Coming** from London, **she** knows all about city life.*

  However, participle clauses can have their own subject.
  ***His car being** at the garage for its annual service, **he** caught the bus to work.*

  With is sometimes used to introduce a different subject.
  ***With fierce northerly winds slowing** their progress, **they** decided to set up camp for the night.*

Ellipsis

When they are obvious from context, words can be 'ellipted' (= omitted) to avoid repetition.

1 Words are often omitted after *and* and *but*.
  He's made friends with some of the older boys and (***the older***) *girls in the school.*

2 The main verb (and its object) can be omitted after an auxiliary verb.
  *I've seen the film but Mike **hasn't** (**seen the film**).*
  *She wanted to come with us but she **couldn't**.*

  Be or *been* cannot be omitted after a modal verb.
  *'Is it time for dinner?' 'It **must be** – I'm starving.'*
  *'Was Paul there?' 'He **might have been**.'*

  Adverbs can be placed before an auxiliary verb if the main verb has been omitted.
  *I'll **almost certainly** go and Tom **probably will** too.*

  When there is no auxiliary verb, *do, does* or *did* are added to avoid repeating the main verb.
  *I enjoyed the film and I think Peter **did**, too.*

(See Substitution on page 10 of Unit 1.)

3 *To* can be used instead of a full infinitive clause.
  *She told him the truth – she didn't **want to** but felt she **had to**.*

Ellipsis in conversation

Words can also be omitted from the beginning of sentences, provided of course that the meaning of the sentence is clear from the context. This is a feature of spoken English.

Subject pronouns can be omitted before both ordinary and auxiliary verbs.
  ***Said** he wasn't coming.* (= **he** *said*)
  ***Might** change her mind.* (= **she** *might*)

Auxiliary verbs or the verb *be* can be omitted in questions, except before *I* or *it*.
  She get back home OK? (= Did she get back home OK?)
  Anybody else coming? (= Is anybody else coming?)
  You serious about that? (= Are you serious about that?)

But no omission is possible in this sentence:
  ***Am I** imagining things or **is it** really snowing?*

If it is clear who or what the subject is, then both auxiliary verb (or *be*) and pronoun can be omitted.
  Been fishing lately? (= Have you been fishing lately?)
  Catch anything? (= Did you catch anything?)
  Happy, darling? (= Are you happy, darling?)

Be, keep, take and *get* can sometimes be omitted from imperatives.
  (Be) careful! (Take your) elbows off the table, please.
  (Keep your) hands off my things! (Get) off the chair!

In some situations more words can be left out.
  (Do you have) any comments?
  (Would you like it) with or without sugar?

WORD LIST

Good & bad behaviour

be on one's best behaviour	/biː ɒn wʌnz ˈbest bɪˌheɪvjə(r)/
cause offence	/ˌkɔːz əˈfens/
form orderly queues	/fɔː(r)m ˌɔː(r)də(r)li ˈkjuːz/
foul adj *	/faʊl/
get into serious trouble	/get ɪntu ˌsɪəriəs ˈtrʌb(ə)l/
loutish adj	/ˈlaʊtɪʃ/
rowdy adj	/ˈraʊdi/
table manners n pl	/ˈteɪb(ə)l ˌmænə(r)z/

Legal matters

accuse (sb) of v	/əˈkjuːz ɒv/
appeal against v	/əˌpiːl əˈgenst/
arson n U	/ˈɑː(r)s(ə)n/
bribery n U *	/ˈbraɪb(ə)ri/
charge (sb) with v	/ˈtʃɑː(r)dʒ wɪð/
clear (sb) of v	/ˈklɪə(r) ɒv/
convict (sb) of v	/kənˈvɪkt ɒv/
count n C **	/kaʊnt/
deny accusations of	/dɪˌnaɪ ækjuˈzeɪʃ(ə)nz ɒv/
drop charges of (sth) against (sb)	/drɒp ˈtʃɑː(r)dʒɪz ɒv əˌgenst/
enter a plea of	/ˌentə(r) ə ˈpliː ɒv/
find (sb) guilty of v	/ˌfaɪnd ˈgɪlti əv/
fraud n U **	/frɔːd/
give (sb) a life sentence for	/gɪv ə ˈlaɪf ˌsentəns fɔː(r)/
go on trial for	/ˌgəʊ ɒn ˈtraɪəl fɔː(r)/
hold (sb) on suspicion of	/ˌhəʊld ɒn səˈspɪʃ(ə)n ɒv/
impose fines on	/ɪmˈpəʊz ˌfaɪnz ɒn/
make an arrest	/ˌmeɪk ən əˈrest/
money laundering n U	/ˈmʌni ˌlɔːnd(ə)rɪŋ/
plead guilty to	/ˌpliːd ˈgɪlti tu/
previous convictions	/ˈpriːviəs kənˌvɪkʃ(ə)nz/
return a verdict	/rɪˌtɜː(r)n ə ˈvɜː(r)dɪkt/
sentence (sb) to	/ˈsentəns ˌtuː/
tax evasion n U	/ˈtæks ɪˌveɪʒ(ə)n/

Other words & phrases

acquittal n C	/əˈkwɪt(ə)l/
allegation n C **	/ˌæləˈgeɪʃ(ə)n/
animosity n U	/ˌænɪˈmɒsəti/
apt adj *	/æpt/
attire n U	/əˈtaɪə(r)/
avidly adv	/ˈævɪdli/
be glued to	/ˌbiː ˈgluːd tu/
betray v **	/bɪˈtreɪ/
bitter adj **	/ˈbɪtə(r)/
bleak adj *	/bliːk/

catch a glimpse of	/ˌkætʃ ə ˈglɪmps əv/
catty adj	/ˈkæti/
chatter n U	/ˈtʃætə(r)/
chivalry n U	/ˈʃɪvəlri/
contagious adj	/kənˈteɪdʒəs/
contempt n U *	/kənˈtempt/
courtesy n U *	/ˈkɜː(r)təsi/
crack down on v	/ˌkræk ˈdaʊn ɒn/
dead adj ***	/ded/
deceit n U	/dɪˈsiːt/
detention n C *	/dɪˈtenʃ(ə)n/
disarmingly adv	/dɪsˈɑː(r)mɪŋli/
disruptive adj	/dɪsˈrʌptɪv/
drag v **	/dræg/
dread v	/dred/
drum (sth) into	/ˌdrʌm ˈɪntuː/
embroiled adj	/ɪmˈbrɔɪld/
empathy n U	/ˈempəθi/
enforce v **	/ɪnˈfɔː(r)s/
etiquette n U	/ˈetɪket/
expel v	/ɪkˈspel/
fall into step	/ˌfɔːl ɪntu ˈstep/
fingerprint n C	/ˈfɪŋgə(r)ˌprɪnt/
flippant adj	/ˈflɪpənt/
forensic adj	/fəˈrensɪk/
fry-up n C	/ˈfraɪ ˌʌp/
gasp n C	/gɑːsp/
get a grip on	/ˌget ə ˈgrɪp ɒn/
grossly adv	/ˈgrəʊsli/
grumpy adj	/ˈgrʌmpi/
guidelines n pl **	/ˈgaɪdˌlaɪnz/
hastily adv	/ˈheɪstəli/
have a go at	/ˌhæv ə ˈgəʊ æt, ət/
have the good grace to	/ˌhæv ðə ˌgʊd ˈgreɪs tʊ, tə/
hazardous adj *	/ˈhæzə(r)dəs/
heartfelt adj	/ˈhɑː(r)tˌfelt/
householder n C	/ˈhaʊsˌhəʊldə(r)/
house-to-house enquiries	/ˌhaʊs tə ˈhaʊs ɪnˌkwaɪriːz/
hush n U	/hʌʃ/
impending adj	/ɪmˈpendɪŋ/
indigenous adj	/ɪnˈdɪdʒənəs/
intercept v	/ˌɪntə(r)ˈsept/
intruder n C *	/ɪnˈtruːdə(r)/
jail term n C	/ˈdʒeɪl ˌtɜː(r)m/
lead (sb) on v	/ˌliːd ˈɒn/
leak v *	/liːk/
lenient adj	/ˈliːniənt/
leopard n C	/ˈlepə(r)d/
let (sb) off v	/ˌlet ˈɒf/
magistrate n C *	/ˈmædʒɪˌstreɪt/
make ends meet	/ˌmeɪk ˈendz miːt/
malevolence n U	/məˈlevələns/
marsh n C *	/mɑː(r)ʃ/
mess around v	/ˌmes əˈraʊnd/
mimic v	/ˈmɪmɪk/
negligent adj	/ˈneglɪdʒ(ə)nt/
on the brink of	/ˌɒn ðə ˈbrɪŋk əv/
overpowering adj	/ˌəʊvə(r)ˈpaʊərɪŋ/
overwrought adj	/ˌəʊvə(r)ˈrɔːt/
pitted adj	/ˈpɪtɪd/

play truant	/ˌpleɪ ˈtruːənt/
premises n pl **	/ˈpremɪsɪz/
press release n C	/ˈpres rɪˌliːs/
pull together v	/ˌpʊl təˈgeðə(r)/
put (sb) off v	/ˌpʊt ˈɒf/
put one's feet up	/ˌpʊt wʌnz ˈfiːt ʌp/
put up with v	/ˌpʊt ˈʌp wɪð/
quay n C	/kiː/
ragged adj	/ˈrægɪd/
recruit n C *	/rɪˈkruːt/
relish n U	/ˈrelɪʃ/
remorse n U	/rɪˈmɔː(r)s/
restock v	/ˌriːˈstɒk/
restrain v *	/rɪˈstreɪn/
retort v	/rɪˈtɔː(r)t/
revive v **	/rɪˈvaɪv/
righteousness n U	/ˈraɪtʃəsn(ə)s/
rigid adj **	/ˈrɪdʒɪd/
ripple n C	/ˈrɪp(ə)l/
sceptical adj *	/ˈskeptɪk(ə)l/
scroll (sth) down v	/ˌskrəʊl ˈdaʊn/
see (sb) off v	/ˌsiː ˈɒf/
self-help book n C	/ˌself ˈhelp bʊk/
self-restraint n U	/ˌself rɪˈstreɪnt/
set (sth) off v	/ˌset ˈɒf/
sewage n U	/ˈsuːɪdʒ/
sewer n C	/ˈsuːə(r)/
shoot (sb) a glance	/ˌʃuːt ə ˈglɑːns/
single-sex adj	/ˌsɪŋg(ə)l ˈseks/
slam v **	/slæm/
slob n C	/slɒb/
slope n C **	/sləʊp/
smear n C	/smɪə(r)/
softly-softly adj	/ˌsɒftli ˈsɒftli/
soothing adj	/ˈsuːðɪŋ/
sprain v	/spreɪn/
spring up v	/ˌsprɪŋ ˈʌp/
squeeze v **	/skwiːz/
stagger v *	/ˈstægə(r)/
stall v *	/stɔːl/
stand out v	/ˌstænd ˈaʊt/
stick (sth) out v	/ˌstɪk ˈaʊt/
stride n C *	/straɪd/
swarm v	/swɔː(r)m/
take the helm	/ˌteɪk ðə ˈhelm/
tart (sth) up v	/ˌtɑː(r)t ˈʌp/
template n C	/ˈtemˌpleɪt, ˈtemplət/
throw a party	/ˌθrəʊ ə ˈpɑː(r)ti/
thump v *	/θʌmp/
trespass v	/ˈtrespəs/
troublesome adj	/ˈtrʌb(ə)ls(ə)m/
truancy n U	/ˈtruːənsi/
tunic n C	/ˈtjuːnɪk/
tunnel vision n U	/ˌtʌn(ə)l ˈvɪʒ(ə)n/
turn (sth) round	/ˌtɜː(r)n ˈraʊnd/
vicious circle	/ˌvɪʃəs ˈsɜː(r)k(ə)l/
washed-out adj	/ˌwɒʃt ˈaʊt/
wide-brimmed adj	/ˌwaɪd ˈbrɪmd/
wipe (sth) out v	/ˌwaɪp ˈaʊt/
zigzag adj	/ˈzɪgzæg/

8A | It takes all sorts

READING

Mr Hilditch

Robert and Lizzie

1 Work in pairs and do the following.

- Describe the people in the pictures.
- Say which of the pictures A–H you would associate with Mr Hilditch and which with Robert and/or Lizzie.

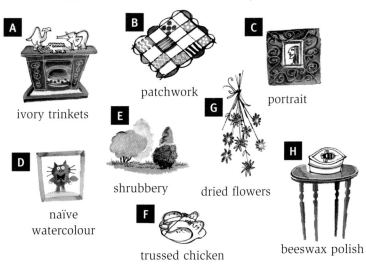

A

ivory trinkets

B

patchwork

C

portrait

D

naïve watercolour

E

shrubbery

F

trussed chicken

G

dried flowers

H

beeswax polish

2 Read the two extracts from different novels and compare your ideas in exercise 1. In what ways do the literary descriptions differ from your own more informal descriptions?

3 Use context to match the highlighted words in the extracts to the definitions a–h.

a able to move quickly and skilfully
b not solid
c not covering much of the body
d a long time ago
e very different and not well-suited to each other
f very full
g spreading in different directions
h unable to see very clearly

4 Read the extracts again. In pairs, discuss what, if anything, is said about each of the following categories, both for Mr Hilditch and for Robert and Lizzie.

> age   physical appearance   clothes   family
> work   house   furniture and decoration   habits

Mr Hilditch is 54, but we don't know how old Robert and Lizzie are. The college photo was taken 'in those far-off days' so they must be …

Using the information given, discuss in pairs what type of personality you imagine the characters to have. The following adjectives might help you.

> ambitious   easygoing   introverted   sociable
> meticulous   (dis)organized   outgoing

5 Work in pairs, A and B, and turn to page 155. You are each going to describe someone.

GRAMMAR: noun phrases

noun + noun is used:
- in commonly-accepted compound nouns. (1)
  picture frames   salesrooms
- to talk about what things are made of. (2)
  ivory trinkets   velvet cap
- for things that occur or appear regularly. (3)
  the Tuesday market   a night shift
- for containers, but not their contents. (4)
  a beer bottle   a matchbox

noun *of* noun is used:
- for containers and their contents. (4)
  a bottle of beer   a box of matches
- where no compound noun exists. (5)
  the roof of the house   the sound of the rain
- to describe the characteristics of people or things. (6)
  a woman of great intelligence
  a house of average size   a look of surprise

noun + *'s/s'* + noun is used to talk about:
- possession by or part of a particular person. (7)
  my parents' car   Elisa's toys
- things intended for people in general.
  a children's playground   men's shoes
- things occurring at a specific time.
  last Tuesday's meeting   next month's election
- the duration of something.
  three weeks' work   a day's holiday

> ● SEE LANGUAGE REFERENCE PAGE 84

Mr Hilditch

Although he does not know it, Mr Hilditch weighs nineteen and a half stone, a total that has been steady for more than a dozen years, rarely increasing or decreasing by as much as a pound. Christened Joseph Ambrose fifty-four years ago, Mr Hilditch wears spectacles
5 that have a pebbly look, keeps his pigeon-coloured hair short, dresses always in a suit with a waistcoat, ties his striped tie into a tight little knot, polishes his shoes twice a day, and is given to smiling pleasantly. Regularly, the fat that bulges about his features is rolled back and well-kept teeth appear, while a twinkle livens the blurred
10 pupils behind his spectacles. His voice is faintly high-pitched.

Mr Hilditch's hands are small, seeming not to belong to the rest of him: deft, delicate fingers that can insert a battery into a watch or tidily truss a chicken, this latter a useful accomplishment, for of all things in the world Mr Hilditch enjoys eating. Often considering that
15 he has not consumed sufficient during the course of a meal, he treats himself to a Bounty® bar or a Mars® or a packet of biscuits. The appreciation of food, he calls it privately.

Once an invoice clerk, Mr Hilditch is now, suitably, a catering manager. Fifteen years ago, he was summoned by the factory
20 management and the notion of a change of occupation was put to him. He was aware that computers were increasingly taking their toll on office staff and when the offer was made he knew better than to hesitate: as a reward for long and satisfactory service, redundancy was being forestalled.

25 Mr Hilditch occupies on his own, a detached house standing in shrubberies that run all around it, Number 3 Duke of Wellington Road. In 1979 his mother died in this house; he never knew his father. Left on his own at the time of the death, he committed to auction the furniture that had accumulated in his mother's lifetime
30 and from then on made Number 3 solely his. Visiting salesrooms at weekends, he filled it with articles, large and small, all of them to his personal taste: huge mahogany cupboards and chests, ivory trinkets for his mantelpieces, second-hand Indian carpets and elaborately framed portraits of strangers.

Robert and Lizzie

Robert and Lizzie had started the Middleton Gallery in a tiny shop in one of Langworth's rambling side streets. They had met at art college – Lizzie a sculptor, Robert a graphic
5 designer – and become inseparable. There was a photograph of them in those far-off days pinned up in the Gallery office, Robert wearing a frown of seriousness and bell-bottomed trousers and Lizzie – an
10 extraordinary, almost skinny, Lizzie – in a skimpy jersey and platform-soled shoes, her hair pushed up into a huge, floppy-peaked velvet cap. They weren't much older than that when they opened the Gallery, renting
15 the shop and the damp, rickety flat above it, furnished with ill-assorted items their parents had given them.

Robert went to evening classes in Bath, and learned to make picture frames. Lizzie
20 reluctantly abandoned her clay for patchwork making, flower drying and the patient beeswaxing of indifferent but fashionable pieces of pine furniture. They both discovered that they had a commercial eye.
25 By the time that Harriet was born, in 1978, the original shop, which by now resembled the perfect seventies' fantasy of an Anglo-Saxon rural idyll, all naïve watercolours, spongeware mugs and wooden spoons, was both highly
30 successful and bursting at the seams. With a loan from Lizzie's father, William, and another from the bank, the Middleton Gallery moved into a former florist's shop, in Langworth High Street.

1 Match the noun phrases a–i from the extracts to the appropriate categories 1–7 in the grammar box. One category is used more than once.

a a packet of biscuits
b art college
c evening classes
d Mr Hilditch's hands
e pine furniture
f watercolours
g at the time of the death
h lifetime
i a frown of seriousness

2 Correct the two mistakes in the use of noun phrases in each description.

1 a children television's programme I used to enjoy
2 the last time I drank a wine glass with my meal of evening
3 the best Sunday's new's paper in my country
4 an advice piece for cars' owners in my area
5 the tomorrow forecast of weather
6 an exceptional talent sports' man or woman in my country
7 a great natural beauty area within an hour drive of here
8 a rather ridiculous clothing's item which was once the fashion height

3 Work in pairs. Think of someone or something answering each description in exercise 2 and tell your partner.

8B | Birth order

SPEAKING

1 Work in small groups. Read the quotations about sisters and discuss these questions about each one:

- What point is it making?
- Could it apply equally well to brothers? Why or why not?
- To what extent do you agree with the sentiments expressed?

> 1 *A sister is a little bit of childhood that can never be lost.*
> Marion C. Garretty

> 2 *A sister is both your mirror and your opposite.*
> Elizabeth Fishel

> 3 *You can kid the world. But not your sister.*
> Charlotte Gray

> 4 *If you don't understand how a woman could both love her sister dearly and want to wring her neck at the same time, then you were probably an only child.*
> Linda Sunshine

> 5 *Having a sister is like having a best friend you can't get rid of. You know whatever you do, they'll still be there.*
> Amy Li

2 How would you complete the sentences? Compare your thoughts with the rest of the group.

1 Having a brother or sister means

_____

2 Being an only child means

_____

LISTENING

1 🔘 **2.28** You are going to hear a dialogue between three friends. They are talking about brothers and sisters, and how the order in which they are born, their 'birth order', helps to determine their personality. Listen to the dialogue and choose the correct words to complete each sentence.

1 Rob read that many first-born children *are more intelligent than their siblings / copy their parents' behaviour / spend too much time with their parents.*
2 In her late teens Christina was unhappy about *her parents' high expectations / her relationship with her brother / her choice of subject at university.*
3 Ann is not entirely convinced that *she is a very good artist / the article is based on fact / she fits the description in the article.*
4 Christina's brother developed *a career as an actor / accounting skills / strategies to attract attention.*
5 Ann says that her sister *is often ill / worries unnecessarily / is a light sleeper.*
6 Rob says he enjoys *receiving attention / helping to solve problems / having arguments.*
7 Birth order is thought to influence *people's chances of becoming famous / banking procedures / consumers' buying habits.*

2 Work in small groups. Discuss the questions.

- To what extent do you feel that birth order, or being an only child or a twin, has affected your personality?
- How important do you think the words and phrases in the box are in determining personality?

> gender   genetics   sibling relationships   astrology
> the attitude and behaviour of parents   life events

VOCABULARY: character traits

1 Complete the sentences from the recording with the nouns in the box.

> nature   lack   types   sense   tendency   attitude   streak

1 First-borns are more likely to be **hard-working, conscientious** _____.
2 Their younger brothers and sisters have a more **rebellious** _____.
3 That accounts for that **very bubbly, outgoing** _____ of his.
4 Younger children have a more **relaxed** _____ **to life**.
5 She has **a real** _____ **to fuss**.
6 She suffers from **a** _____ **of confidence**.
7 Some first-borns develop **a** _____ **of anxiety** when a brother or sister is born.

🔘 **2.29** Listen and check.

2 Work in pairs. Look at the character traits in exercise 1 and discuss the extent to which you feel each one is positive (*P*) or negative (*N*).

3 Choose the words which do **not** describe an aspect of a person's character when used with the words in bold.

1 **a sense of** *fun / responsibility / superiority / adventure / touch*

2 **a tendency to** *put on weight / act hastily / worry / lose one's temper / be negative*

3 **a/an** *competitive / independent / white / ruthless / vicious* **streak**

4 **a/an** *gentle / obsessive / temporary / easygoing / generous* **nature**

5 **a** *positive / happy-go-lucky / down-to-earth / government / single-minded* **attitude**

4 Tell your partner about three different people, each of whom possesses one or more of the character traits in exercise 3.

PRONUNCIATION: changing word stress

1 Some two-syllable verbs and nouns with the same spelling have a different pronunciation. Read these sentences from the recording. How is **rebel** pronounced in each case?

1 I've always seen you as a bit of a rebel.
2 My brother didn't exactly rebel.

🔊 **2.30** Listen and check.

What determines which stress pattern to use?

2 Mark the stress on the words in bold.

1 The chief **suspect** arrived at court under police **escort**, **protesting** her innocence.
2 I took the **present** back to the shop but they **refused** to give me a **refund** without a receipt.
3 The **produce** is **transported** across the **desert** in enormous refrigerated lorries.
4 The huge **increase** in personal debt was **recorded** in a recent **survey conducted** by the Institute of Finance.
5 The Republican caused a major **upset** by defeating Burns, but the Democrats **contested** the result and demanded a **recount**.

🔊 **2.31** Listen to the recording to check your answers, then read out the sentences.

3 Write five sentences, each including at least one of the words in bold from exercise 2, but with a different pronunciation.

His comments about her clothes up<u>set</u> her.

4 Read out your sentences to another student.

DID YOU KNOW?

1 Work in pairs. Read about famous American siblings and discuss the questions.

A number of famous Americans seem to confirm the view that the first-born in a family achieves the most success in life. Forty-third US President George W Bush, for example, is the eldest of five surviving siblings. His predecessor, Bill Clinton, has a younger half-brother, Roger, who spent time in jail in the 1980s. And 39th President Jimmy Carter's younger brother, Billy, is perhaps best remembered for drinking beer and endorsing the failed brand 'Billy Beer'. Many American astronauts are also first-borns, including the first man on the Moon, Neil Armstrong, whose younger brother and sister led far more 'down-to-earth' lives.

However, there are many other famous American siblings who have achieved success in more or less equal degree. These include tennis stars, Venus and Serena Williams, actors, Shirley MacLaine and Warren Beatty and singers, the Jonas brothers.

- What other famous siblings, either from your own country or elsewhere, do you know? What have they each achieved?
- Why do you think fame often runs in families?

8c | A close bond

VOCABULARY & SPEAKING: relationships

1 Choose the correct word to complete the sentences.

1 Your *immediate / near* **family** consists of your parents, brothers and sisters; other family members make up your *extensive / extended* **family**. How important is each to you?

2 In each of these pairs, what could the first people do in order to help **build a good** *report / rapport* **with** the second?

- teachers with pupils
- bosses with employees
- doctors with patients
- shopkeepers with customers

3 Are you **on friendly** *terms / words* with all your neighbours?

4 Have you read about any *stormy / thundery* **relationships** or **marriage** *breakouts / breakups* in the gossip columns recently?

5 Do the police in your area do much to **foster close** *joints / links* with the local community?

6 Which country or countries has your own traditionally had **close** *strings / ties* with? Are there any with which it has no **diplomatic** *relations / relationships*?

2 Work in pairs. Discuss each of the questions in exercise 1.

READING

1 Work in pairs. Tell each other about one or more friends you once had but who you are no longer in touch with. Why did the friendship(s) end?

2 Read the article on page 81 and answer the questions.

1 Who ended the friendship and why?
2 What is the current situation?

3 Read the article again and decide whether the statements are true (T) or false (F). Explain with reference to the text why the false statements are incorrect.

1 Nothing had happened to suggest the writer's friendship with Tula might end.
2 They became friends after almost a decade working together for the same company.
3 The writer comforted Tula at a difficult moment in her life.
4 The writer admits to breaking contact with people she once knew.
5 Figures show an increasing dependence on family relationships.
6 Mark Vernon thinks we expect too much from friendship.
7 He says that modern communication methods have ensured the survival of many friendships.
8 Vernon's experiences as a bachelor confirm certain commonly-held beliefs about friendship.

4 Work in pairs. Discuss the questions.

- For each of Aristotle's three categories of friendship talk about one friend you have. How solid do you think these friendships are?
- To what extent do you share the views expressed by Mark Vernon?

GRAMMAR: attitude adverbials

A number of adverbs and adverbial phrases can be used to express the writer or speaker's attitude to what follows in a sentence.

> But **surely** close friends are not consumer goods to be discarded or replaced at the first hint of trouble?
> **Worse still**, he says, friendships are becoming harder to maintain.

Most can also be placed within the clause or at the end of it.

> She was **understandably** upset.
> I can't swim, **unfortunately**.

Some adverbs can be used before *enough*.

> **Funnily enough**, I didn't recognize him at first.

Some can be rephrased using *to-* clauses.

> **Amazingly/To my amazement**, I passed.

> SEE LANGUAGE REFERENCE PAGE 84

1 Complete the sentences in a suitable way.

1 Ten vehicles were involved in a multiple collision on the M1 motorway today. **Miraculously**, …

2 My son stayed up to watch the World Cup Final last night. **Not surprisingly**, …

3 Just before the start of her university course, Adele was offered a major role in a new TV series. She **very wisely** …

4 The conversation turned to the subject of housework. **Predictably enough**, …

5 We chose Australia for our holiday last year. **Much to our disappointment**, …

2 Compare your sentences with those of another student. How similar are they?

END OF A FRIENDSHIP

For the first time in my life I have been dumped by a friend. I should have seen it coming: the phone calls not returned, the excuses about 'not feeling very sociable right now', the emails that languished unreplied in the
5 ether. Yet the letter suggesting that the time had come for us to move on still came as a shock.

It didn't seem to fit in with our modern ideal of friendship. As growing numbers of us live alone, friends are becoming more important. They are our families of choice,
10 we're told, taking on the roles of parent, spouse, sibling – and best friend.

Tula and I had been firm friends for nearly ten years. We met at a singing workshop and took to each other immediately. She was warm and vivacious, and we shared
15 an enthusiasm for grappling with life's conundrums over glasses of wine or long walks in the country. She helped me to move house and, when her long-term partner walked out, I put the kettle on and supplied tissues.

But life changed for both of us: I got married and she
20 responded to her newly single status by developing a fresh set of social networks. Then she took a long holiday, reviewed her life and decided what to keep and what to throw out. In her letter she described our friendship as a 'borderline' case and suggested it might be time we 'let
25 each other go'.

I'm all for letting go of bad habits and boxes of old school exercise books. I've even deleted the names of acquaintances not seen from one year to the next from my address book. But surely close friends are not
30 consumer goods to be discarded or replaced at the first hint of trouble? We are encouraged to believe that friends will be around for ever. 'You've got a friend,' sang Carole King and 'I'll be there for you' promised the theme tune of *Friends*. Such sentiments have sunk deep into the
35 collective unconsciousness, or into mine, at least.

Certainly, the statistics indicate that we need friends more than ever. Government figures predict that the proportion of married men and women aged from 45 to 54 will fall by a quarter in the next two decades. The last census shows
40 that already a third of all households contain one solitary person. A recent British survey found that two-thirds of 18–35-year-olds in Britain turn to friends before family for help and advice. Yes, the argument goes, in a fast-moving, ever-changing world, friendship is our rock, the
45 one thing we can truly rely on.

But in his book, *The Philosophy of Friendship*, Mark Vernon suggests otherwise. He cautions that we place unrealistic burdens on friendship, that it's
50 unreasonable to expect friends to fulfil family members' roles. 'Aristotle identified three categories of friendship,' he says.

'There are "utility friendships", where people are useful to each other, such as boss and employee; "friendships of
55 pleasure", when you enjoy doing something together such as playing football; and "friendships of excellence", when you love the person for who they are. The first two types depend on the activity. When that stops, often, so does the friendship.'

60 Worse still, he says, friendships are becoming harder to maintain. 'There are lots of perils in the way we live today. It's harder to put time and effort into knowing someone. Mobiles, email and so on, all these are secondary ways of communicating. There's not the depth.'

65 Vernon's experience of being a long-term single prompted him to write his book. 'The friendships I enjoyed when single only went so far,' he says. 'The limits were most obvious when compared to the relationships I witnessed between lovers or within families. When a lover calls they
70 automatically get first priority and family commitments are, well, family commitments.' His experience seemed very different from the way friendship was portrayed at a cultural level 'where it is frequently heralded as the defining relationship of our age'.

75 So, what did I do with Tula's letter? I re-read it umpteen times, agonized over where I'd gone wrong. And then I wrote back. 'Yes, you're right,' I wrote, 'things have changed. But aren't we good enough friends to hang in there?' Since then we have exchanged a couple of emails.
80 A walk has been suggested. It would be easy not to make the effort and let this friendship go but, as Louisa May Alcott, author of *Little Women*, said: '"Stay" is a charming word in a friend's vocabulary.' I think she's right.

> **Glossary**
> kettle *n* a container that is used for boiling water
> herald *v* praise something in a public way

8D | Singles

SPEAKING

1 Work in groups, A and B. You are going to talk about four people.

Group A: Turn to page 144.
Group B: Turn to page 150.

2 Work with a student from the other group. Tell your partner what you imagine your four people are like.

3 Discuss which, if any, of the people might be suitable as flatmates or housemates sharing accommodation for at least six months. Give reasons for your opinions.

LISTENING

1 You read in the article on page 81 that in Britain 'a third of all households contain one solitary person'. What different reasons are there for people being single?

2 2.32–2.37 Work in pairs. Listen to the speakers 1–6 and answer this question for each of them.

Is the speaker happy (*H*) or not happy (*N*) about not having a partner?

3 2.32–2.37 Listen again and match the statements a–i to the speakers 1–6 in exercise 2. Three of the statements are not required.

a I've changed my way of thinking.
b Running my own business takes up all my time.
c I object to people feeling sorry for me.
d I recognize my own failings.
e My parents show little sympathy towards me.
f I remain optimistic that my situation will change.
g My current situation is unlikely to change soon, unfortunately.
h I can't stop thinking about my ex-partner.
i I am able to spend more time with my friends.

4 Work in small groups. Discuss the following statements from the recording.

- Living with your parents does have its advantages.
- There's a lot to be said for being single.
- As a rule, women are much better able to cope on their own than men.
- They're bone idle, most men, aren't they?

GRAMMAR: discourse markers

1 Discourse markers are words and expressions which help to structure continuous discourse and guide the reader or listener through it.

Look at audioscripts 2.32–2.37 on pages 158–159. Match the highlighted discourse markers from speakers 1–3 to the explanations a–i.

a Adding extra information: *In fact*
b Making a general statement: _____
c Explaining what you have said: _____
d Correcting what someone has said: _____
e Returning to the original subject: _____
f Showing you do not intend to offend: _____
g Introducing information which should be obvious to the listener: _____
h Enumerating a series of points: _____ & _____
i Contrasting with previous ideas: _____ & _____

2 Explain the use of the highlighted discourse markers from speakers 4–6.

3 Complete the texts with the discourse markers in the boxes. More than one answer may be possible.

> after all   to be honest   admittedly
> anyway   for one thing

(1) '*Admittedly*, there are certain disadvantages to working alone at home. (2) _____, there isn't the human contact you get if you work for a company. (3) _____, though, that doesn't bother me too much, as I get to see much more of my wife and children – (4) _____, they're the people that really matter, aren't they? And (5) _____, in my last job, there was always lots of backbiting and other unpleasantness, so I'm happy to be out of all that.'

| at least | of course | generally | all the same | I mean |

(6) '_____ speaking, it's much better to go on holiday alone than with a group of friends. (7) _____, that's what I think, anyway. (8) _____, for example, if you're with other people, there are always disputes and arguments about what to do and where to go next, and that doesn't happen if you're on your own. (9) _____, if it's just you, there will be times when you get lonely and you don't know what to do with yourself. But (10) _____, I still think the advantages outweigh the disadvantages.'

| actually | ultimately | in fact | mind you | anyway |

'… home alone because my husband went away on a golfing holiday with his friends, lucky thing. (11) _____, though, he deserved it – he's been working really hard lately and he needed a break. (12) _____, as I was saying, I had the house to myself for the whole week. And I thought I was going to enjoy being on my own all that time, but I (13) _____ got quite bored. (14) _____, after a couple of days I invited a friend to stay to keep me company. The whole thing made me realize that (15) _____, I'm a social animal and I'm just not very good at being alone.'

4 Work in pairs. Talk about how happy you would be on your own in the three situations in exercise 3.

Discourse markers perform a number of functions including:

- enumerating a series of points.
  for one thing, for another thing, plus, as well as that
- making a general statement.
  as a rule, on balance, generally speaking, ultimately
- inviting and/or indicating honesty.
  let's be honest, to be (perfectly) honest, admittedly
- showing contrast.
  still, all the same, even so, mind you
- clarifying and explaining.
  *I mean, to put it another way, **after all***
- limiting, modifying or correcting.
  *at least, **anyway**, actually, **in (actual) fact***

After all is used to give a reason to explain what you have just said.
Anyway is also used to return to the original subject or to support a previous statement.
In (actual) fact is also used to add extra details.

❯ SEE LANGUAGE REFERENCE PAGE 84

VOCABULARY: adverbs with two forms

1 Some adverbs have two forms, as in these two sentences from speaker 4 in the listening.

One of the things I miss <u>most</u> is the regular conversation.
My boss keeps sending me away on business – Eastern Europe <u>mostly</u>.

Which of the underlined words in the examples above:

1 means *mainly* or *most often*?
2 is the superlative of *much*?

2 Choose the correct word to complete the sentences.

1 a) I find it hard to study: I'm very *easy / easily* **distracted**.
  b) I'm stressed out: I need to **take things** *easy / easily*.
2 a) I feel *wide / widely* **awake** at the moment.
  b) I've **travelled** *wide / widely* in my own country.
3 a) I tend to **travel** *light / lightly* – just a small bag.
  b) I tend to **sleep** *light / lightly* – I wake up at the slightest sound.
4 a) Apparently, I **snore** *loud / loudly*.
  b) I rarely **laugh out** *loud / loudly* in the cinema.
5 a) I rarely **arrive** *late / lately* for anything.
  b) I haven't been to the theatre *late / lately*.
6 a) I'm going on holiday *short / shortly*.
  b) I once had to **cut** *short / shortly* my holiday due to illness.
7 a) I **aim** *high / highly* in most things I do.
  b) I'm a *high / highly* **motivated** English student.
8 a) I've eaten *hard / hardly* **anything** today.
  b) I'm **trying** *hard / hardly* to lose weight.

3 Work in pairs and discuss the question. How true are the sentences in exercise 2 for you?

Grammar

Noun phrases

1 **noun** + **noun** is used in a large number of commonly-accepted compound nouns to describe a single idea. Some compound nouns are usually written as one word, some as two. They may even be hyphenated.
bookshop car keys shell-fish (or shellfish)

Where no compound noun exists **noun** + **preposition** + **noun** is often used.
a film about racism my chances of success

2 Use **noun** *of* **noun** to describe the characteristics of people or things: use **noun** + **noun** to talk about what something is made of.
a man of average height a decision of great importance
a metal bridge a brick wall a stone bench

Use **noun** *of* **noun** with *top, bottom, back, front, beginning, middle, end* for parts of things.
the top of the page the front of the class the end of May

3 Use **noun** + **'s/s'** + **noun** to talk about:
- possession by a particular person or animal.
Tom's socks the students' books the dog's lead
- part of a particular person or animal.
Sarah's finger the children's hair the cat's ears
- things intended for people in general.
women's clothes children's books

4 **Note the following:**

Use **noun** + **noun** for:
- things occurring or appearing regularly, but noun + **'s/s'** + noun if they occur at a specific time.
a Saturday job (= a job you do every Saturday)
last Saturday's match (refers to one match)
- for duration use noun + **'s/s'** + noun or singular hyphenated noun + noun.
three days' journey or a three-day journey
an hour's flight or a one-hour flight

Use **noun** + **noun** for containers, and **noun** *of* **noun** to refer to the contents of things.
a wine bottle (= a bottle used for putting wine in)
a bottle of wine (refers to the quantity of wine)

Use **noun** + **noun** for products from dead animals, but **noun** + **'s/s'** + **noun** for products from living ones.
chicken soup sheepskin fox fur
a chicken's egg sheep's wool cow's milk

Attitude adverbials

1 A number of adverbs can be used to express the attitude of the writer or speaker. They include: *amazingly, astonishingly, certainly, clearly, disappointingly, foolishly, (un)fortunately, ironically, miraculously, naturally, regrettably, remarkably, surely, (not) surprisingly, understandably, undoubtedly, wisely, (even) worse*

They often appear at the beginning of a clause, but they may also appear at the end.
***Regrettably**, we have had to postpone the concert.*
*He felt nervous before the exam, **naturally**.*

They can also be placed before the main verb, after the verb *be* and before adjectives.
*I **foolishly** threw away all my notes.*
*She kept **remarkably** calm. He is **undoubtedly** very clever.*

2 *Surely* and *certainly* have different uses.

Surely can be used to express surprise and to show that you find something difficult to believe. The sentence often appears as a question.
***Surely** there's something we can do to help him?*
(= I can't believe there's nothing we can do.)
***Surely** they're not going to build yet another airport?*
(= It's difficult to believe they intend to.)

Certainly can be used to emphasize and confirm what has been said.
*He seems destined for a career in science. **Certainly**, his exam marks in physics and chemistry were way above those of the rest of the class.*

3 Some attitude adverbs can be used before *enough*. These include: *amazingly, curiously, funnily, interestingly, ironically, oddly, predictably, strangely, understandably.*
***Oddly enough**, I don't feel sad about what happened.*

4 *To*-clauses with nouns can be used in place of some attitude adverbs. Nouns used in this way include: *amazement, disappointment, disgust, regret, surprise.*
*They rejected my application, **much to my disappointment**.*

Discourse markers

In addition to attitude adverbials, there are a number of other discourse markers which help to structure extended pieces of spoken and written English. They often prepare the reader or listener for the type of information which follows. They may also indicate the connection between what is about to be said and what was said before.

In particular, discourse markers can be used to:
- enumerate a series of points.
to start with, for one/another thing, moreover, on top of that, besides, anyway, in addition.

To start with gives the first and most important reason:
*Well, **to start with**, it won't fit into the bedroom.*

Besides and *anyway* introduce an extra, often stronger, reason to support your argument.
*I don't think the job would suit me. And **besides/anyway**, it's too late to apply now.*

- make a general statement.
as a rule, on balance, generally speaking, all in all, by and large, on the whole, ultimately

Ultimately shows that what you are saying is the most important point.

Ultimately, *it's taxpayers' money, so we're the ones who should enjoy the benefits.*

- invite and/or indicate honesty.
let's be honest, let's face it, quite honestly/frankly, in all honesty, to be (perfectly) honest/frank, admittedly

*I had the radio on, but **to be honest**, I wasn't listening.*

- introduce an idea which contrasts with a previous one.
still, all/just the same, even so, mind you, however, nevertheless

Mind you makes the previous statement less strong.

*I feel sorry for her. **Mind you**, it was partly her fault.*

- clarify and explain.
I mean, to put it another way, that's to say, after all

After all is used to give a reason to explain what you have just said.

*Don't eat too much. **After all**, you are on a diet.*

- limit, modify or correct.
at least, anyway, actually, in (actual) fact

*I'd never go there. **At least** not on my own, **anyway**.*

*Most people think he's Spanish, but **actually** he's Swedish.*

In (actual) fact is also used to add extra details.

*I loved that film. **In fact**, I went to see it four times.*

- change the subject (back).
By the way and *incidentally* introduce a new subject.

By the way, *did I tell you what happened to Joe?*

Anyway indicates a return to the original subject.

Anyway, *as I was saying, Joe got caught speeding.*

Word list

Character traits

bubbly nature	/ˌbʌbli ˈneɪtʃə(r)/
conscientious type	/ˌkɒnʃiˈenʃəs ˈtaɪp/
down-to-earth *adj*	/ˌdaʊn tə ˈɜː(r)θ/
happy-go-lucky *adj*	/ˌhæpi gəʊ ˈlʌki/
lack of confidence	/ˌlæk əv ˈkɒnfɪd(ə)ns/
rebellious *adj*	/rɪˈbeljəs/
relaxed attitude to life	/rɪˈlækst ˌætɪˌtjuːd tə laɪf/
ruthless *adj*	/ˈruːθləs/
sense of superiority	/sens əv suˌpɪəriˈɒrəti/
single-minded *adj*	/ˌsɪŋg(ə)l ˈmaɪndɪd/
tendency to act hastily	/ˌtendənsi tʊ ækt ˈheɪstəli/
winning streak *n C*	/ˌwɪnɪŋ ˈstriːk/

Relationships

build a good rapport with (sb)	/ˌbɪld ə gʊd ræˈpɔː(r) wɪð/
close ties	/ˌkləʊs ˈtaɪz/
diplomatic relations	/ˌdɪpləˈmætɪk rɪˈleɪʃ(ə)ns/
extended family	/ɪkˌstendɪd ˈfæm(ə)li/
foster close links with (sb)	/ˌfɒstə(r) ˌkləʊs ˈlɪŋks wɪð/
immediate family	/ɪˌmiːdiət ˈfæm(ə)li/
marriage breakup *n C*	/ˌmærɪdʒ ˈbreɪkʌp/
on friendly terms	/ɒn ˈfren(d)li ˌtɜː(r)mz/
stormy relationship	/ˌstɔː(r)mi rɪˈleɪʃ(ə)nʃɪp/

Adverbs with two forms

aim high	/ˌeɪm ˈhaɪ/
cut (sth) short	/ˌkʌt ˈʃɔː(r)t/
easily distracted	/ˌiːzɪli dɪsˈtræktɪd/
highly motivated	/ˌhaɪli ˈməʊtɪveɪtɪd/
laugh out loud	/ˌlɑːf aʊt ˈlaʊd/
shortly *adv ****	/ˈʃɔː(r)tli/
sleep lightly	/ˌsliːp ˈlaɪtli/
snore loudly	/ˌsnɔː(r) ˈlaʊdli/
take things easy	/ˌteɪk θɪŋz ˈiːzi/
travel light	/ˌtræv(ə)l ˈlaɪt/
travel widely	/ˌtræv(ə)l ˈwaɪdli/
wide awake	/ˌwaɪd əˈweɪk/

Other words & phrases

a handful *n sing*	/ə ˈhæn(d)fʊl/
be given to	/ˌbiː ˈgɪv(ə)n tʊ/
blurred *adj **	/blɜː(r)d/
bone idle *adj*	/ˌbəʊn ˈaɪd(ə)l/
bulge *v*	/bʌldʒ/
bursting at the seams	/ˌbɜː(r)stɪŋ ət ðə ˈsiːmz/
by the same token	/baɪ ðə ˌseɪm ˈtəʊkən/
census *n C **	/ˈsensəs/
chest *n C ****	/tʃest/
chum *n C*	/tʃʌm/
clay *n U ***	/kleɪ/
clown around *v*	/ˌklaʊn əˈraʊnd/
deft *adj*	/deft/
discard *v*	/dɪsˈkɑː(r)d/
dump *v ***	/dʌmp/
elusive *adj*	/ɪˈluːsɪv/
far-off *adj*	/ˌfɑː(r) ˈɒf/
firstborn *n C*	/ˈfɜː(r)stˌbɔː(r)n/
forestall *v*	/fɔː(r)ˈstɔːl/
frown *n C **	/fraʊn/
fuss over *v*	/ˌfʌs ˈəʊvə(r)/
good riddance	/ˌgʊd ˈrɪd(ə)ns/
goody-two-shoes *n pl*	/ˌgʊdi ˈtuː ˌʃuːz/
grapple *v*	/ˈgræp(ə)l/
herald *v*	/ˈherəld/
hint *n sing ***	/hɪnt/
ill-assorted *adj*	/ˌɪl əˈsɔː(r)tɪd/
ivory *n U ***	/ˈaɪvəri/
kettle *n C **	/ˈket(ə)l/
kid *v*	/kɪd/
laid-back *adj*	/ˌleɪd ˈbæk/
languish *v*	/ˈlæŋgwɪʃ/
liven *v*	/ˈlaɪv(ə)n/
mahogany *n U*	/məˈhɒgəni/
mantelpiece *n C*	/ˈmænt(ə)lˌpiːs/
mimic *v*	/ˈmɪmɪk/
on the shelf	/ˌɒn ðə ˈʃelf/
patch things up	/ˌpætʃ θɪŋz ˈʌp/
patchwork *n U*	/ˈpætʃˌwɜː(r)k/
pebbly *adj*	/ˈpeb(ə)li/
peril *n C*	/ˈperəl/
personality clash *n C*	/ˌpɜː(r)səˈnæləti ˈklæʃ/
pop in *v*	/ˌpɒp ˈɪn/
rambling *adj*	/ˈræmblɪŋ/
rickety *adj*	/ˈrɪkəti/
rock the boat	/ˌrɒk ðə ˈbəʊt/
sibling *n C **	/ˈsɪblɪŋ/
skimpy *adj*	/ˈskɪmpi/
sky-high *adj*	/ˌskaɪ ˈhaɪ/
spongeware *n U*	/ˈspʌndʒˌweə(r)/
steady *adj ***	/ˈstedi/
stroppy *adj*	/ˈstrɒpi/
suffocating *adj*	/ˈsʌfəˌkeɪtɪŋ/
take its toll on	/ˌteɪk ɪts ˈtəʊl ɒn/
tied down *adj*	/ˌtaɪd ˈdaʊn/
tissue *n C ***	/ˈtɪʃuː, ˈtɪsjuː/
trinket *n C*	/ˈtrɪŋkɪt/
turn to *v*	/ˈtɜː(r)n ˌtʊ/
twinkle *n C*	/ˈtwɪŋk(ə)l/
umpteen *adj*	/ˌʌmpˈtiːn/
vivacious *adj*	/vɪˈveɪʃəs/
velvet *n U*	/ˈvelvɪt/
wear off *v*	/ˌweə(r) ˈɒf/
whitewater rafting *n U*	/ˌwaɪtwɔːtə(r) ˈrɑːftɪŋ/
wring (sb's) neck	/ˌrɪŋ ˈnek/

9A | A place called home

READING

1 Work in groups. Discuss the question.

- What images come to mind when you think of Paris?

2 Look at the photo, read the introductory sentence to the article and discuss the questions in your groups.

1 Why do you think Le Corbusier's plan is described as 'drastic'?
2 Why might such a plan have been considered necessary?

3 Read the article and compare your ideas in exercise 1.

4 Read the article again and choose the correct words to complete the sentences.

1 The writer says that Chez Antoine was *very near the National Library / owned by his hotel / being restored.*
2 He did not feel *lonely / safe / happy* in Paris.
3 At the beginning of the twentieth-century Paris was *one of the poorest European cities / extremely overcrowded / a mainly industrial city.*
4 Le Corbusier was concerned about *the negative consequences of his proposed changes / political situation in France / living conditions in cities.*
5 He believed his plans would help stop *further migration to the city / the uncontrolled development of the city / unfair property speculation.*
6 Le Corbusier felt that cars *should be banned / drove too fast / should not be hindered by pedestrians.*

5 Work in pairs. Discuss the meaning of the highlighted words and expressions in the article.

6 Discuss the questions.

- What are the potential problems of Le Corbusier's vision of a modern city centre?
- How attractive and convenient for residents are the buildings and streets in your capital city or the town in which you live? What changes, small or drastic, would you make?

SPEAKING

1 Work in small groups. You are going to submit a plan for a new town. Turn to page 139.

2 One member from your group should present your plan to the rest of the class, explaining the various decisions you have made.

3 Vote for one of the plans. You may not vote for your own.

GRAMMAR: modal verbs 2

> *will, would, shall*
>
> Use *will* and *would* for habitual behaviour, annoying behaviour, willingness, refusal and requests.
> > I **would** often sit in a café adjacent to my hotel.
> > He **will** wear that ridiculous hat when we go out.
> > She**'ll** help you but I certainly **won't**.
> > **Would** you turn that music down a little, please?
>
> Use *will* for predictions, intentions and present assumptions.
> > No pedestrian **will** ever meet an automobile, ever!
> > We**'ll** leave at about 6.00.
> > You've had a hard day – I imagine you**'ll** be tired now.
>
> Use *would* to express the future from a past perspective and imaginary situations.
> > People **would** have footpaths all to themselves.
> > I **wouldn't** care if I never saw him again.
>
> Use *shall* for arrangements, suggestions and offers.
> > Where **shall** we meet? **Shall** we go? **Shall** I help?

> ❯ SEE LANGUAGE REFERENCE PAGE 94

1 Complete the sentence beginnings 1–8 with the appropriate endings a–h.

1 He**'ll** often spend two or three hours there,
2 She **won't** see you without an appointment,
3 They **will** keep moving things around –
4 **Shall** we meet in the reception area? I**'ll**
5 It **would** be closed down just two years later
6 **Would** you kindly stop fidgeting? You're
7 Ten past three? He**'ll** have left there by now,
8 I **wouldn't** be surprised if they closed a branch or two:

a the frozen foods are next to the wines now.
b unless he's been given a detention, of course.
c just have a quick shower after my class.
d reading the newspapers or surfing the net.
e and most of the exhibits sold off at auction.
f unless it's an emergency, of course.
g a lot of people do their transactions via the internet now.
h ruining my enjoyment of the play.

2 The sentences in exercise 1 either make reference to or are said in a particular place. Identify the places.

3 What is the function of each of the modal verbs in bold in sentences 1–8 in exercise 1? Use the terms in the grammar box on this page.

1 habitual behaviour

4 Work in pairs, A and B. You are going to practise using *will*, *would* or *shall*.

A: Turn to page 154. B: Turn to page 142.

THE CITY OF
Tomorrow

Alain de Botton describes how in 1925 French architect Le Corbusier proposed a drastic plan to rebuild the historic centre of Paris.

5 I once spent a summer in a small hotel in the second arrondissement of Paris, a stone's throw away from the chilly seriousness of the old National Library, where I repaired every morning in a vain attempt to research a book I hoped to write. It was a lively part of town, and I would often sit in a café adjacent to my hotel named, as if out of a tourist guide,
10 Chez Antoine.

Everyone, it seemed, dropped by Chez Antoine at some point in the day. Elegant women would have coffee and a cigarette at the counter in the morning. Policemen lunched there, students whiled away the afternoons on the covered terrace,
15 and by evening there'd be scholars, politicians, divorcees and tourists, flirting, arguing, having dinner, smoking and playing pinball. As a result, although I was alone in Paris, and went for days hardly speaking to anyone, I felt none of the alienation with which I was familiar in other cities. That
20 summer I imagined no greater happiness than to be able to live in Paris for ever, pursuing a routine of going to the library, ambling the streets and watching the world from a corner table at Chez Antoine.

I was therefore surprised to find out, some years later, that
25 the very area in which I had stayed had fallen within a zone which one of the most intelligent and influential architects of the twentieth century had wanted systematically to dynamite and replace with a great park punctuated at intervals with eighteen 60-storey cruciform towers stretching up to the
30 lower slopes of Montmartre.

Le Corbusier had drawn up his Parisian scheme at a moment of unequalled urban crisis. Across the developing world, cities were exploding in size. In 1800 the French capital was home to 647,000 people. By 1910 three million were squeezed within
35 its inadequate confines. In apartment buildings, several families typically shared a single room. In 1900, in the poorer districts of Paris, one toilet generally served 70 residents. A cold-water tap was a luxury. Factories and workshops were sited in the middle of residential areas, emitting smoke and deadly effluents.
40 Children played in courtyards covered with raw sewage. Cholera and tuberculosis were a constant threat. Streets were choked by traffic day and night. There was not much that was picturesque about the early twentieth-century city.

45 Le Corbusier was horrified by such conditions. 'All cities have fallen into a state of anarchy,' he remarked. 'The world is sick.' Given the scale of the crisis, drastic measures were in order, and the architect was in no mood to feel sentimental about their side effects. 'The existing centres must come down,' he said. 'To save itself every great city must rebuild
50 its centre.' In order to alleviate overcrowding, the ancient low-rise buildings would have to be replaced by a new kind of structure only recently made possible by advances in reinforced concrete technology: the skyscraper. '2,700 people will use one front door,' marvelled Le Corbusier.

55 By building upwards, two problems would be resolved at a stroke: overcrowding and urban sprawl. With room enough for everyone in towers, there would be no need to spread outwards and devour the countryside in the process. There would be ample green space as well, as up to 50 per cent of
60 urban land would be devoted to parks. The new city would itself be a vast park, with large towers dotted among the trees. On the roofs of the apartment blocks, there would be games of tennis, and sunbathing on the shores of artificial beaches.

Simultaneously, Le Corbusier planned to abolish the city
65 street. He resented the fact that the legitimate demands of both cars and people were constantly and needlessly compromised, and he therefore recommended that the two be separated. In the new city, people would have footpaths all to themselves, winding through woods and forests (no
70 pedestrian will ever meet an automobile, ever!), while cars would enjoy massive and dedicated motorways, with smooth, curving interchanges, thus guaranteeing that no driver would ever have to slow down for the sake of a pedestrian.

The division of cars and people was but one element
75 in Le Corbusier's plan for a reorganization of life in the new city. All functions would now be untangled. There would no longer be factories, for example,
80 in the middle of residential areas. The new city would be an arena of green space, clean air, ample accommodation
85 and flowers.

9B | Squatters

VOCABULARY & SPEAKING: describing homes

1 Work in pairs. Discuss which type of home you would prefer in each of the pairs. Money is no object.

- A detached house in the country or a large town-centre flat.
- A caravan by the sea or a log cabin in the mountains.
- A brand new flat overlooking a motorway or a 60-year-old flat in need of renovation and overlooking a park.
- A house with no running water or one with neither gas nor electricity.

2 Choose the correct words to complete the sentences. Use a dictionary if necessary.

1 This *newly-* / *freshly-***built** house is *comfortably* / *conveniently* **located** near the town centre.
2 The building is **in poor** *condition* / *state* and **in urgent need of** *repair* / *reform*.
3 It's a lovely old *straw* / *thatched* **cottage**, full of *antique* / *elderly* **furniture**.
4 The **house** is very *broken-down* / *run-down* and the **garden** completely *grown-up* / *overgrown*.
5 It's a **warm** and *cosy* / *draughty* little flat, and very *tastily* / *tastefully* **decorated**.
6 This nineteenth-century *period* / *history* **house** would suit the *FAQ* / *DIY* **enthusiast**.
7 The family of six live **in** *cramped* / *close* **conditions** in a *brightly lit* / *gloomy* one-bedroomed flat with no electricity.
8 It's *weakly* / *poorly* **furnished** – the **chairs** are *rickety* / *sickly* and likely to collapse and the **carpets** are *threadbare* / *trodden*.

3 Work in pairs. Answer the questions.

- Which of the sentences in exercise 2 give a positive (*P*) and which a negative (*N*) description?
- How would you describe your own home?

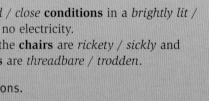

4 You are going to do a roleplay in pairs, A and B.

Student A
You saw an advertisement for the house below and have come to view it. Express your doubts to the owner.

Student B
You are the owner of the house below and are showing it to a prospective buyer. Respond to his/her doubts, highlighting its positive aspects.

5 Change roles and do the roleplay on page 155.

LISTENING

1 Work in pairs. Read the dictionary definition of *squatter* and discuss the questions.

squatter /ˈskwɒtə(r)/ *noun*
someone who lives in a place without permission and without paying the owner

- What type of people do you think squat and why?
- How do you think you might react if squatters came to live near you?

2 💿 **3.1** Listen to a radio programme about squatting and answer these questions.

1 What does Annie's job entail?
2 Is she sympathetic towards squatters?
3 How did Gerry get into his current squat?
4 How does he feel about squatting?

3 💿 **3.1** Listen again and complete the sentences with no more than three words.

1 There are nearly _____ squatters in the UK.
2 Annie points to a nationwide shortage of _____ as one reason for squatting.
3 She says there are _____ a million empty homes in Britain.
4 There is an increasing number of foreign squatters from _____ countries.
5 The presenter says that squatting is not a _____ in the UK.
6 The SRA advises squatters to display a copy of the document known as _____.
7 Gerry is squatting in a _____ house.
8 Before moving in, Gerry and his friends looked in the _____ every day.
9 He hopes to get a _____ soon.
10 _____ suppliers in particular often refuse to connect houses with squatters in.

💿 **3.2** Listen and check.

4 Complete the sentences from the recording with the prepositions in the box.

> in   out   out   through   on   up   up   down

1 … run-down houses and flats that **bring** _____ **property values** in the local area.
2 … the SRA, the group that **carried** _____ **the study**.
3 There are over 100,000 families **queuing** _____ **for** this type of housing.
4 … young people who cannot afford to **get** _____ **the property ladder**.
5 It's a document **spelling** _____ what your rights are.
6 They have to **go** _____ **the courts**.
7 … little by little you **get settled** _____.
8 We **do their houses** _____ for them.

Check your answers in audioscript 3.1 on pages 159–160.

5 Work in pairs. Discuss the questions.

- How do you think you would cope if you had to squat?
- How important is it in your country for people to buy their own house or flat rather than rent? Is it easy to get on the property ladder?

DID YOU KNOW?

1 Work in small groups. Read about listed buildings in the UK and discuss the questions.

Buildings in the UK which are considered to be of special architectural or historical interest are placed on an official list in order to protect them by law. The owner of a listed building cannot make any alterations to it without first receiving permission or 'listed building consent' from the local planning authority.

Buildings are graded to show their relative significance. In England and Wales there are currently three grades, I, II* and II, with Grade I buildings being the most important. Buckingham Palace is an example of a Grade I listed building.

There are approximately half a million listed buildings in England. They are mainly old buildings, although there are also a few examples of modern architecture, such as the BT Tower in London, as well as bridges, sculptures, signposts, lampposts, bandstands, seaside piers and telephone boxes.

- What system exists in your country for protecting buildings of architectural and/or historical interest?
- Which buildings or other structures would you include on such a list? Why?

9c | A place in the sun

SPEAKING

1 During a Caribbean cruise you have one full day on the small island of Tobago. Look at the list of activities on page 152 and choose **four** which interest you.

2 Work in pairs. Explain your choices to each other and agree on **three** that you will do together.

3 Explain your choices to another pair of students and agree on **two** that you will all do together.

Compare your choices with the rest of the class.

READING

1 Work in pairs. Discuss the questions.

- The article speaks of two Caribbean hotels which take 'environmentally friendly measures'. What might these measures consist of?
- It also advises tourists to 'help support the local economy'. How might they do this?

2 Read the article and compare your ideas in exercise 1.

3 Match the phrases 1–9 to the sections A–C of the article in which they are mentioned.

1 trying to pay less for something
2 attracting celebrities
3 avoiding other holidaymakers
4 an appeal for parents to educate their children
5 the benefits of restricting size (two sections)
6 giving away unwanted cups and plates
7 a prohibition
8 clearing up rubbish
9 a carefully thought-out restoration

4 Work in pairs. Discuss the questions.

- In what ways did your last holiday benefit and/or harm the environment and the local culture?
- These items are all used at the Blue Haven Hotel. How widespread is their use in your country?
  - solar heating
  - biodegradable detergents
  - energy-saving light bulbs
  - organically-grown produce

GRAMMAR: inversion

*Not only **will you get** under the skin of the island, but you can also ensure your money goes …*

Inversion of the subject and auxiliary verb is required when certain adverbials are placed at the beginning of a sentence for emphasis.
*Never before **had he seen** anything so beautiful.*
*Only now **are the effects** becoming apparent.*
*On no account **must exhibits be touched.***

Do, does or did is inserted where an auxiliary verb (or the verb *to be*) is not present.
*Rarely **do you find** a coin of this age in such good condition.*
*Not until/Only when she got home **did she realize** what had happened.*

 **SEE LANGUAGE REFERENCE PAGE 94**

1 Rewrite the following sentences beginning with the words in brackets.

1 There isn't a city anywhere in the world with as many beautiful monuments as Rome. (*Nowhere*)
1 Nowhere in the world is there a city with as many beautiful monuments as Rome.

2 You very rarely come across anyone nowadays who hasn't been abroad. (*Very rarely*)
3 You can only really learn a language by living in a country where it is spoken. (*Only by*)
4 Tourists should not be allowed to visit the Antarctic under any circumstances. (*Under no circumstances*)
5 You won't truly know what good food is until you've tried French cuisine. (*Not until*)
6 I hated visiting monuments as a child and I couldn't stand going into museums. (*Not only*)
7 I've only recently started going on holiday without my parents. (*Only recently*)
8 I'll never go back to that place I went to last year on holiday! (*Never again*)

2 Work in pairs. Discuss the sentences in exercise 1. How true are they for you?

3 Imagine you have just spent a disappointing fortnight in a Caribbean ecotourism hotel. Write five sentences complaining about different aspects of your stay. Begin each sentence with one of the following:

At no time, Not once, Only when, Not until, Hardly, No sooner, Not only, Nowhere, Never again

Compare your sentences with your partner's.

A happy marriage

The pressure created by hordes of holidaymakers and their increasing demands is leaving a depressing litany of damage on the Caribbean. Two-thirds of the beaches are eroded, wildlife is being displaced by huge hotel
5 complexes, water sports cause coastal, coral-reef and marine pollution, while more and more wetlands are being destroyed to develop golf courses. Fortunately, though, the area is beginning to enjoy the effects of ecotourism.

Section A

10 Take Tobago's Blue Haven Hotel, an antidote to so many of the fenced-off and homogenized resorts in the region. It is renowned for several things: incredible food, a spectacular setting and, above all, its commitment to the happy marriage of ecology and tourism.

15 It wasn't always so. Once the favourite haunt of film stars such as Rita Hayworth and Robert Mitchum, the hotel lay abandoned for more than 25 years. Planning a complete renovation, its new owners were committed to both preserving the original architecture and installing modern
20 environmentally-friendly measures.

The result is stunning thirties colonial chic underpinned by a nature-conscious strategy. The hotel uses solar heating, biodegradable detergents, energy-saving light bulbs, rainwater irrigation, plus
25 local, organically-grown produce and toiletries. It has also banned polluting motor water sports. Only local staff are employed there, and the scale of the hotel is kept small enough to safeguard the highest quality service and lowest impact tourism.

Section B

30 Glitter Bay in Barbados is equally grand, with impeccably-furnished rooms, a crisply-uniformed staff and immaculate lawns. Children are welcome, with club activities scheduled throughout the day and a pool of nannies on tap. On a recent family visit, my son helped
35 monitor turtle nest-sites and went on a scavenger hunt for throwaway plastics that threaten the marine life. Meanwhile, Glitter Bay's dedicated Green Team got to grips with waste management, donating used hotel crockery to local hospitals, composting garden waste and recycling bed covers into pillow
40 shams. The aim is to saturate Caribbean holiday spots with a renewed beauty that's more than skin deep. The challenge is to match tour companies that deliver on their promises with family holidaymakers that care enough to make a difference.

'It would be fabulous if all families could instill in their
45 kids the idea that when we're on holiday we are all guests in somebody else's home,' says Tricia Barnett, of the campaigning organization Tourism Concern. 'While it is your holiday for just two weeks, it is someone else's home for a lifetime.'

Section C

50 When booking your island holiday, consider scaling back on accommodation. Few visitors to the Caribbean realize that staying in huge, all-inclusive hotel complexes or using luxury cruise liners provides almost no benefit to the island people. Many less scrupulous hotel chains use disproportionate
55 amounts of valuable local resources (water, for example), while cruise ships create pollution and erosion which affect the livelihood of local fishermen. By staying in smaller, locally-run hotels you can minimize your family's impact on both the environment and the culture.

60 Once you arrive, help support the local economy by buying produce that has been made or grown nearby. And be sure to pay a fair price for the goods or services you buy. Haggling for the lowest possible price might save you pennies, but deprive the vendor of a day's salary. Use public transport, hire
65 a bike, visit local restaurants and carnivals, find out where the locals go, and get off the well-trodden tourist route. That way, not only will you get under the skin of the island, but you can also ensure your money goes into the pockets of those who need
70 it most.

Glossary
litany *n* a long list of things
underpin *v* be an important,
basic part of something

9D | Experimental travel

'Sick of sightseeing? Tired of tour guides? Then why not try experimental tourism, a novel approach to travel that starts with a quirky concept and can lead anywhere from Bora Bora to a bus stop.'

1 The travel options 1–5 all appear in *The Lonely Planet Guide to Experimental Travel*. Match the travel options 1–5 to the descriptions a–e.

☐ 1 Alternating Travel ☐ 4 Slight-hitch Travel
☐ 2 Chance Travel ☐ 5 Ero Tourism
☐ 3 Blind Man's Bluff Travel

a Arrange to take a holiday with your loved one. Travel there separately by different means and don't arrange a meeting time or place. Then look for each other.

b Leave your home or hotel on foot. Take the first road on the right, then the next on the left, then the next on the right, and so on.

c Look up the name of your home town in the index of a world atlas. Throw a pair of dice, then count that number of lines down from the name of your town. The line that your finger lands on is your destination.

d Write the name of a faraway destination on a large piece of card. Stand at the side of your nearest motorway (or similar) with your backpack, stick your thumb out and wait.

e Spend 24 hours blindfolded in a new location with a friend to guide you.

2 Rank the travel options from the book in exercise 1 from the one which you would find most interesting (1) to the one which least appeals to you (5).

3 Work in pairs. Compare your list with your partner's and give reasons for your choices.

LISTENING

1 🔘 **3.3–3.6** Listen to four extracts from a dialogue between friends who recently tried out some of the ideas in *The Lonely Planet Guide to Experimental Travel*. For each extract 1–4 answer the questions.

- Which of the travel options 1–5 from Speaking exercise 1 is being described?
- Did the speaker(s) enjoy the experience?

2 🔘 **3.3–3.6** Listen to the extracts again and decide whether these statements are true (T) or false (F). Say why the false statements are incorrect.

Sally
1 Sally already knew the city of York very well.
2 She had problems when trying to drink.
3 She was able to touch some of the museum exhibits.

Dave
4 Dave had done something similar to this before.
5 He was almost involved in a serious accident.
6 He stayed in a hotel in Munich.

Helen
7 Helen hadn't expected to enjoy the experience so much.
8 She particularly liked the element of uncertainty.
9 The living conditions in some areas made her feel depressed.

Emma and Steve
10 Emma started looking for Steve in some of the bars.
11 They both went to the same places.
12 They didn't see each other in Madrid.

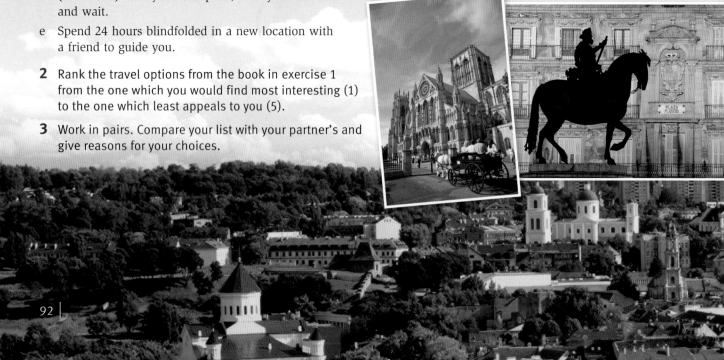

SPEECH FEATURE: vague language

> A number of expressions are used in conversation to show vagueness or a lack of precision. Here are some examples from the listening.
> I **sort of** became aware of every sound.
> I could smell every coffee or sandwich **or whatever**.
> There was loads of greenery, you know, trees and grass **and stuff like that**.

1 Complete the vague expressions from the first extract of the recording with the words in the box.

> anything   everything   something
> thing   kind   all   so   like

1 I think wearing it really did _____ of sharpen my other senses.
2 We did all the sights **and** _____ – the cathedral, the city walls, the historic buildings **and** _____ **on.**
3 What about things like eating and washing **and** _____ **that?**
4 Did you _____ go into any museums **or** _____?
5 Paul took me into an exhibition by some local sculptor – Anna Kirby, **or** _____, I think her name was.
6 It was all modern stuff, from local stone – lots of curves and holes **and that sort of** _____.

2 Check your answers in audioscript 3.3 on page 160. Underline further examples of vague language in extracts 2 and 3 in audioscripts 3.4 and 3.5.

3 Work in small groups. Imagine you have each just returned from the experimental travel experience you ranked number 1 in Speaking exercise 2. Tell each other about your experience using some of the expressions in exercise 2.

VOCABULARY: adjectives formed with particles

> A number of adjectives are formed using particles such as *in, out, on, off, up, down, over, under, away.* These may be written with or without a hyphen or as one word. The following examples are all from the recording:
> *head-on collision   run-down estates   built-up area*
> *worn out   fed up   cheesed off   faraway place*
> *oncoming lorry   overnight train*

1 Complete the questions with the adjectives in the box.

> sit-down   outdoor   uphill   off-the-peg
> out-of-the-way   online   comfortably off
> up-to-date   outspoken   indoor   out-of-town

1 Is learning English an _____ **struggle** for you or a relatively easy task?
2 Do you prefer _____ **superstores** or town centre shops?
3 Would you rather have a holiday in an _____ **place** or a crowded resort?
4 Do you do more _____ or _____ **activities** in your free time?
5 Are you more a supporter or an _____ **critic** of your government?
6 For weddings and other celebrations do you prefer a _____ **meal** or a finger-food buffet?
7 Are you more likely to buy an _____ **suit** or a made-to-measure one?
8 Which do you do more – use _____ **banking** services or visit your local branch?
9 Do you **keep** _____ **with** the latest celebrity gossip or does it bore you?
10 Are you hard up or _____ at the moment?

2 Work in pairs. For each question in exercise 1, underline the alternative which you think your partner is most likely to choose in answer to the question.

3 Check and discuss your ideas for exercise 2 with your partner. How accurate were they?

GRAMMAR
Modal verbs: *will, would, shall*

1 Use *will* and *would*:

- to talk about present and past habits.
  *I'**ll** often have just a biscuit for breakfast.*
  *She **would** always cook fish on Fridays.*

- to talk about typical annoying behaviour. In speech the modal verb is stressed.
  *She **will** keep sniffing all the time.*
  *He **would** be late, wouldn't he? He always does this.*

- to make requests.
  ***Will/Would** you make me a cup of tea, please?*

- to express willingness to do something.
  *If you'**ll** put the dishes away, I'**ll** do the ironing.*
  *If you'**ll/would** take a seat, I'**ll** tell her you're here.*

- to express refusal to do something in the present and the past.
  *He **won't** do anything I ask him to.*
  *She just **wouldn't** listen to me.*

2 Use *will* to express:

- predictions.
  *I think she'**ll** pass – she's been studying very hard.*
  *There's every/a good/a fair/a slight/little/no chance (that) they'**ll** lose tomorrow.*

- intentions.
  *I'**ll** give him a ring later.*

- assumptions about the present.
  *They **won't** have got there yet – they'**ll** still be on the motorway somewhere.*

- future facts.
  *It's Sam's birthday tomorrow – he'**ll** be eighteen.*

See also Futures Unit 10.

3 Use *would*:

- to express future from a past perspective.
  *As a child he dreamed he **would** one day be famous.*

- to talk about imaginary situations.
  *You'**d** look smarter in a suit.*

- to give advice.
  *I **wouldn't** eat it if I were you – it's very bitter.*
  *I'**d** put a coat on – it's quite chilly outside.*

4 Use *shall* to make:

- offers.
  ***Shall** I pick you up from the station?*

- suggestions.
  ***Shall** we try that new Indian restaurant tonight?*

- requests for instructions and advice.
  *Here you are. Where **shall** I put it?*
  *I'm so nervous – what **shall** I say to her?*

- arrangements.
  *What time **shall** we meet?*

Inversion

The position of the subject and auxiliary verb is inverted (= reversed) when certain negative or restrictive adverbials are placed at the beginning of a sentence for emphasis.

> *She would never feel able to trust him again.*
> ***Never again would she feel** able to trust him.*

If neither an auxiliary verb nor the verb *to be* is present, *do, does* or *did* is inserted.

> *He realized only then the full extent of the damage.*
> ***Only then did he realize** the full extent of the damage.*

Inversion occurs mainly, though not exclusively, in written English or more formal speech. It is used:

- after certain phrases with *not*.
  ***Not since** their wedding **had he told** Diana he loved her.*
  ***Not only did she have** to pay a fine, but she also lost her driving licence.*

Also: *not until, not once, not for one minute*

- after certain phrases with *only*.
  ***Only occasionally do they fail** to agree.*
  ***Only when** we know she is safe **will we agree** to pay the ransom.*

Also: *only now, only then, only recently, only later, only very rarely, only by -ing, only in the last few days*

- after certain phrases with *no*.
  ***At no time did we consider** giving up.*

Also: *nowhere (else), under no circumstances, on no account, (in) no way*

- after the frequency adverbs *rarely, seldom, hardly ever, never (before/again)*.
  ***Rarely have I seen** such a talented young musician.*
  ***Hardly ever do we have** time for a cooked lunch.*

- with *hardly ... when ...* and *no sooner ... than ...*
  ***Hardly had he started** in the job **when** he fell ill.*
  ***No sooner had she unpacked** her bags **than** the phone rang.*

WORD LIST

Vague language

and all that
and everything
and so on
and stuff like that
and that sort of thing
I mean
kind of
like
or anything
or something
or whatever
sort of
you know

Describing homes

antique *adj* *	/æn'tiːk/
conveniently located	/kən,viːniəntli ləʊ'keɪtɪd/
cosy *adj* *	/'kəʊzi/
DIY enthusiast *n C*	/,diː aɪ 'waɪ ɪn'θjuːziæst/
draughty *adj*	/'drɑːfti/
gloomy *adj* *	/'gluːmi/
in cramped conditions	/ɪn 'kræmpt kən,dɪʃ(ə)nz/
in poor condition	/ɪn 'pɔː(r), 'pʊə(r) kən,dɪʃ(ə)n/
in urgent need of repair	/ɪn 'ɜː(r)dʒ(ə)nt niːd əv rɪ,peə(r)/
log cabin *n C*	/,lɒg 'kæbɪn/
mobile home *n C*	/,məʊbaɪl 'həʊm/
newly built	/,njuːli 'bɪlt/
overgrown *adj*	/,əʊvə(r)'grəʊn/
period *adj*	/'pɪəriəd/
poorly furnished	/,pɔː(r)li, pʊə(r)li 'fɜː(r)nɪʃt/
rickety *adj*	/'rɪkəti/
run-down *adj*	/,rʌn 'daʊn/
running water *n U*	/,rʌnɪŋ 'wɔːtə(r)/
tastefully decorated	/,teɪstfəli 'dekəreɪtɪd/
thatched *adj*	/'θætʃt/
threadbare *adj*	/'θred,beə(r)/

Adjectives formed with particles

built-up *adj*	/'bɪlt ,ʌp/
cheesed off *adj*	/,tʃiːzd 'ɒf/
comfortably off *adj*	/,kʌmftəbli 'ɒf/
faraway *adj*	/,fɑːrə'weɪ/
hard up *adj*	/,hɑː(r)d 'ʌp/
head-on *adj*	/'hed ,ɒn/
indoor *adj* *	/'ɪndɔː(r)/
made-to-measure	/,meɪd tə 'meʒə(r)/
off-the-peg *adj*	/,ɒf ðə 'peg/
oncoming *adj*	/'ɒn,kʌmɪŋ/
online *adj* **	/'ɒnlaɪn/
outdoor *adj* *	/,aʊt'dɔː(r)/
out-of-the-way *adj*	/,aʊt əv ðə 'weɪ/
out-of-town *adj*	/,aʊt əv 'taʊn/
outspoken *adj* *	/,aʊt'spəʊkən/
overnight *adj* *	/,əʊvə(r)'naɪt/
sit-down meal	/,sɪt daʊn 'miːl/
uphill struggle	/,ʌphɪl 'strʌg(ə)l/
up-to-date *adj* *	/,ʌp tə 'deɪt/
worn out *adj*	/,wɔː(r)n 'aʊt/

Other words & phrases

adjacent to	/ə'dʒeɪs(ə)nt tuː/
alienation *n U*	/,eɪliə'neɪʃ(ə)n/
alleviate *v*	/ə'liːvieɪt/
amble *v*	/'æmb(ə)l/
ample *adj* *	/'æmp(ə)l/
at a stroke	/,æt ə 'strəʊk/
bandstand *n C*	/'bæn(d),stænd/
biodegradable *adj*	/,baɪəʊdɪ'greɪdəb(ə)l/
blindfolded *adj*	/'blaɪn(d),fəʊldɪd/
boast *v* *	/bəʊst/
branch *n* ***	/brɑːntʃ/
breathtaking *adj* *	/'breθ,teɪkɪŋ/
bring (sth) down *v*	/,brɪŋ 'daʊn/
carry (sth) out *v*	/,kæri 'aʊt/
choked *adj*	/tʃəʊkt/
coat of paint *n C*	/,kəʊt əv 'peɪnt/
confines *n pl*	/'kɒnfaɪnz/
coral reef *n C*	/,kɒrəl 'riːf/
crisply uniformed	/,krɪspli 'juːnɪfɔː(r)md/
cruciform *adj*	/'kruːsɪ,fɔː(r)m/
crumbling *adj*	/'krʌmblɪŋ/
dead end *adj*	/,ded 'end/
devour *v*	/dɪ'vaʊə(r)/
do (sth) up *v*	/,duː 'ʌp/
dotted *adj*	/'dɒtɪd/
draw (sth) up *v*	/,drɔː 'ʌp/
drop by *v*	/,drɒp 'baɪ/
dynamite *v*	/'daɪnəmaɪt/
effluent *n C*	/'efluənt/
enlightening *adj*	/ɪn'laɪt(ə)nɪŋ/
evict *v*	/ɪ'vɪkt/
fenced off *adj*	/,fenst 'ɒf/
fidget *v*	/'fɪdʒɪt/
flirt *v*	/flɜː(r)t/
for the sake of	/,fɔː(r) ðə 'seɪk ɒv/
get settled in	/,get 'set(ə)ld 'ɪn/
get to grips with	/,get tʊ 'grɪps wɪð/
go through the courts	/,gəʊ ,θruː ðə 'kɔː(r)ts/
greenery *n U*	/'griːnəri/

haggle *v*	/'hæg(ə)l/
hairy *adj* *	/'heəri/
hands-on *adj*	/,hændz 'ɒn/
hassle *n C* *	/'hæs(ə)l/
haunt *n C*	/hɔːnt/
hinder *v*	/'hɪndə(r)/
horde *n C*	/hɔː(r)d/
house-hunting *n U*	/'haʊs ,hʌntɪŋ/
immaculate *adj*	/ɪ'mækjʊlət/
impeccably *adv*	/ɪm'pekəbli/
instill *v*	/ɪn'stɪl/
interchange *n C*	/'ɪntə(r),tʃeɪndʒ/
layabout *n C*	/'leɪə,baʊt/
listed building	/,lɪstɪd 'bɪldɪŋ/
litany *n C*	/'lɪtəni/
lousy *adj*	/'laʊzi/
low-rise *adj*	/,ləʊ 'raɪz/
lush *adj* *	/lʌʃ/
marshland *n U*	/'mɑː(r)ʃ,lænd/
needlessly *adv*	/'niːdləsli/
on tap	/,ɒn 'tæp/
pier *n C* *	/pɪə(r)/
pillow sham *n C*	/'pɪləʊ 'ʃæm/
pinball *n U*	/'pɪn,bɔːl/
property ladder *n*	/'prɒpə(r)ti ,lædə(r)/
queue up for *v*	/,kjuː 'ʌp fɔː(r)/
refuse point blank	/rɪ,fjuːz pɔɪnt 'blæŋk/
renowned for *adj*	/rɪ'naʊnd ,fɔː(r)/
rookie *n C*	/'rʊki/
rowdy *adj*	/'raʊdi/
safeguard *v*	/'seɪf,gɑː(r)d/
scattered *adj* *	/'skætə(r)d/
scavenger hunt *n C*	/'skævɪndʒə(r) ,hʌnt/
scrape *n C*	/skreɪp/
sewage *n U*	/'suːɪdʒ/
snorkelling *n U*	/'snɔː(r)k(ə)lɪŋ/
spell (sth) out	/,spel 'aʊt/
sprawl *n U*	/sprɔːl/
squat *v* *	/skwɒt/
squatter *n*	/'skwɒtə(r)/
squeeze *v* **	/skwiːz/
steelpan band *n C*	/,stiːlpæn 'bænd/
stunning *adj* *	/'stʌnɪŋ/
tactile *adj*	/'tæktaɪl/
take in the sights	/,teɪk ɪn ðə 'saɪts/
tiered *adj*	/tɪə(r)d/
turtle *n C*	/'tɜː(r)t(ə)l/
underpin *v*	/,ʌndə(r)'pɪn/
untangle *v*	/ʌn'tæŋg(ə)l/
well-trodden *adj*	/,wel 'trɒd(ə)n/
wetlands *n pl*	/'wetlændz/
while (sth) away *v*	/,waɪl ə'weɪ/
wind *v*	/waɪnd/

10A | Achieving the impossible

In 1970, the Japanese alpinist Yuichiro Miura skied 2,000 metres down Mount Everest in two minutes and 20 seconds.

In 1974, Frenchman Philippe Petit walked on a tightrope between the Twin Towers of the World Trade Centre in New York.

In 2009, British yachtswoman Dee Caffari became the first woman to sail solo, non-stop both ways around the world.

In 2011, Canadian Jean Beliveau completed his round-the-world walk, having covered 75,000 kilometres across 64 countries in eleven years.

SPEAKING

1 Look at the photos and read about the four achievements.

2 Work in pairs. Discuss the questions.

- What difficulties and dangers might each of these four adventurers have faced?
- What type of personality would you need to have in order to take on these kinds of challenges?
- What other feats of this kind do you know of?

READING

1 Work in pairs. Read the article about Philippe Petit and answer the question.

- What impression do you gain of Petit's personality?

2 Read the article again and choose the correct words to complete the sentences.

1 Petit's World Trade Centre walk led to *a number of traffic accidents / worldwide exposure for the Twin Towers / the publication of a novel.*
2 In paragraph 2 we learn that James Marsh *approached Petit several times about making a film / was the subject of a criminal investigation / was the first director Petit agreed to work with.*
3 Petit left the dentist's *before receiving treatment / feeling worse / with a pile of magazines.*
4 James Marsh wanted his film to *arouse strong feelings in Petit / be a detailed account of Petit's walk / mirror the pace at which Petit lives his life.*

5 Marsh's film *is interspersed with lighthearted episodes / paints a negative picture of Petit / condemns New York customs officials.*
6 The writer criticizes Petit for his *lack of organization / treatment of colleagues / frivolous attitude during preparations for the walk.*
7 Petit was angry with Blondeau for *repeatedly delaying the walk / disappearing at a crucial moment / informing the police.*
8 When the police arrived at the Twin Towers, they *took action which endangered Petit's life / were initially ignored by Petit / were amused by Petit's performance.*

3 Work in pairs. Tell each other about an important objective you would like to achieve at some time in your life. For what reasons, if any, is it not possible to achieve your objective now?

VOCABULARY: success

1 Complete the sentences with the correct form of the verbs in the box.

| achieve | stand | do | pay |
| turn | go | further | give |

1 Something you did which _____ **badly** at first but _____ **out well in the end**.
2 A time when all your **hard work** _____ **off** and you _____ **your aim**.
3 Something you did which _____ you an **enormous sense of achievement**.
4 A time when you _____ **very well** in your exams.
5 An ambition you _____ **a reasonable chance of** fulfilling in the future.
6 Something you could do to _____ **your career**.

The poet in the sky

One morning in August 1974, thousands of employees hurrying to work in Manhattan's business district stopped in their tracks to watch something unforgettable high above them in the sky, at the twin peaks of the World Trade Centre. Cars were
5 abandoned in the middle of streets as their drivers stopped to get a better view and the skyscrapers' security went into red alert. This particular event, though, was benign – 'a gift', the novelist Paul Auster called it, 'of astonishing, indelible beauty to New York'. By tightrope-walking across the space between the
10 Twin Towers, Frenchman Philippe Petit brought the landmark's existence to a global audience.

In the subsequent decades the self-titled 'Poet in the sky' received dozens of offers to turn his existential tour de force into a film, but accepted only when the director James Marsh,
15 a veteran of the BBC, suggested a collaboration. *Man on Wire*, named after the police report that followed this 'artistic crime of the century', as Petit proudly called it, is an extraordinary, gripping account, more thriller than documentary, that won two Sundance Film Festival awards in 2008. 'The idea,' Marsh
20 says, 'was to put on a good show like Philippe did. His is the oldest story there is: the hero on a journey to achieve a seemingly impossible objective.'

The idea for the walk was born in a dentist's waiting-room when Petit saw an illustration of a planned building whose twin towers would
25 'tickle the clouds'. With a pencil the eighteen-year-old instinctively traced a line between its rooftops, then ripped out the page, disguising the noise with a sneeze, and walked out, his tooth aching, to file the clipping in a red box marked 'projects'. The dream turned to obsession. 'I will become the emperor of the American sky,' he told
30 anyone who would listen.

There were of course disagreements over *Man on Wire*. 'When we first started working together,' Marsh says, 'Philippe sent me this beautifully hand-written manifesto that said, "At some point you will take over and I will hate you for it." He is obsessed with details and was shocked
35 at how much I left out, but it was important for the film to gallop the way he does. If Philippe objects to something, he does it passionately, relentlessly. We're like fire and ice. He's French, I'm British. Ultimately, he did recognize me as the filmmaker, and let go of the film.'

At every turn there is frustration, irritation, fuming and sulking, but
40 these explosions are counterbalanced with frequent moments of humour. On his trip to New York, he is stopped by customs. What are all these ropes for? 'I'm a tightrope walker,' Petit says. 'I've come to walk between the towers of the World Trade Centre.' Laughing, the official waves him through.

45 Petit is hopelessly chaotic in laying the groundwork, and the ensuing comedy of errors, clashing personalities and cultures, and miraculous luck is mainly held in check by Petit's long-standing assistant, Blondeau, who insists on meticulous planning in order to save the coup and his friend's life. The walk is postponed eleven times. Sadly,
50 Blondeau blows it at the last minute, photographing Petit's first steps on the wire, but running off when the police show up, and thereby failing to capture the unrepeatable event on film. 'I wanted to kill him!' Petit says, and Blondeau's tears to camera so many years later are poignant. Now, Petit loves 'the idea that something marvellous – like a
55 glass of fabulous port – is ephemeral'.

The walk was euphoric for Petit. Over the course of eight crossings he knelt in traditional salute, displayed his 'torero's walk' and his 'promenader's walk' and lay down and 'dialogued with a hovering seagull' while 100,000 people clamoured below. Petit gave himself
60 up to the waiting police, who were threatening to loosen the rope. Sgt Charles Daniels reported his own experience thus: 'Upon seeing us he started to smile and laugh and he started going into a dancing routine on the high wire … And when he got to the building we asked him to get off … but instead he turned around and ran back out into
65 the middle … He was bouncing up and down. His feet were actually leaving the wire … Everybody was spellbound'.

Immediately following the coup, Petit was handcuffed and led away to cheers from labourers. 'Why did you do it?', journalists asked him. 'When I see three oranges, I juggle,' he said. 'When I see two towers, I walk.'

---

2 Complete the sentences with the nouns in the box.

life	charts	region	future	flier	success

1 An up-and-coming recording artist or sports personality who **has a bright** ____ ahead.
2 A film or music album which was **an overnight** ____.
3 A song which is currently **riding high in the** ____ in your country.
4 Someone in your family who is an academic **high-**____.
5 The kind of thing parents do to ensure their children **get on in** ____.
6 **A thriving** ____, company or industry in your country.

3 Work in pairs. Think of examples for six of the descriptions in exercises 1 and 2 and tell your partner about them.

> **Glossary**
> tour de force *n* something that impresses people because it is successful and done very skilfully
> ephemeral *adj* lasting for only a short time
> coup *n* achievement

10B | What is success?

LISTENING

1 Work in small groups. Discuss how you would answer these two questions.

- What do you understand by 'success'?
- What is the best way to achieve it?

2 🔊 **3.7–3.12** Listen to six people talking about success and match the pictures A–F to the speakers 1–6.

3 🔊 **3.7–3.12** Listen again and complete the table for speakers 1–6.

What is success?	How do you achieve it?
1	
2	
3	
4	
5	
6	

4 In your groups, discuss each of the views expressed in the listening, saying how much you agree or disagree with them.

GRAMMAR: futures

1 Look at audioscripts 3.7–3.12 on pages 161–162. Explain the choice of the highlighted verb tenses, all of which refer to the future.

I'll be 83 next month.
Will here is used to talk about future facts.

2 Read the grammar box and do exercise 3.

- *be* + adjective + *of* + noun/gerund
  eg *confident, doubtful, hopeful, (un)sure*
  *They're **confident of winning** the next election.*
- *be* + adjective + full infinitive
  eg *bound, certain, due, (un)likely, sure*
  *He **is due to appear** in court next Friday.*
- *be (just) about to* + infinitive, *be on the point of* + gerund to talk about the immediate future
  *The film's **about to start** – hurry up.*
- *be* + full infinitive in formal English to talk about scheduled events
  *The funeral **is to take place** on Monday.*
- modal verbs eg *may/might/could* (*well*), *should*
  *I **should** be there at six, but Sue **may well** be delayed.*
- verb + gerund eg *anticipate, consider, think of*
  *We don't **anticipate leaving** until tomorrow.*
- verb + full infinitive eg *aim, expect, hope, plan*
  *We **aim to get** the job finished by the end of the week.*
- verb + *will* + infinitive eg *believe, expect, hope* (*hope* can also be used with a present tense)
  *I **hope they (will) remember** to lock the door.*

▶ SEE LANGUAGE REFERENCE PAGE 104

3 Choose the correct words to complete the sentences.

1 I'm *thinking / hoping / wishing* to buy <u>a new car</u> in the not too distant future.
2 We *should / likely / expect* see <u>a decrease in petrol prices</u> by the end of the month.
3 <u>DVDs are</u> *confident / definite / bound* to become obsolete before the decade is out.
4 <u>United</u> stand a good *chance / intention / occasion* of winning the league this season.
5 I really *expect / hope / want* that <u>it rains</u> in the next few days.
6 <u>My sister</u> is *just / on the point / about* to <u>have a baby</u>.
7 I may *like / well / consider* <u>get married</u> at some time in the future.
8 <u>She's</u> *hopeful / doubtless / lucky* of success in <u>her forthcoming exams</u>.
9 The <u>next European election</u> *expects / is / due* to be held in three months' time.
10 If I don't <u>study</u>, I'm *probably / likely / certainly* to <u>forget this grammar</u> within a week.

4 Choose five of the sentences in exercise 3 and write new ones by changing the underlined sections. Your new sentences should be either true or express your opinion. You may also change the time expressions at the end of the sentences.

5 Work in pairs. Compare and discuss your sentences from exercise 4.

PRONUNCIATION: contrastive stress

1 Stress can be used to indicate contrast or to correct previous information. Read out the following sentence.

*Success is not about accumulating **wealth**, it's about achieving **happiness**.*

🔘 **3.13** Listen and check.

2 Underline the words with contrastive stress in these sentences from the recording.

1 He seems sure I won't be able to do it, but I know I will.
2 It's not so much what you achieve as how you achieve it that counts.
3 When, or rather, if I get to old age …
4 He wrote several books, but he wasn't suggesting that everyone has to do that.
5 It's not the winning, it's the taking part that's important.
6 That's fair enough, particularly if, like me, you're an amateur, rather than a professional.

3 🔘 **3.14** Listen to the sentences to check your answers, then practise reading them aloud.

4 Work in pairs. Tell your partner six things about him or her which you know or believe to be untrue. Your partner will correct you using contrastive stress.

A: You're twenty-two years old.
B: No, I'm twenty-<u>five</u>.

VOCABULARY: three-part phrasal verbs

1 Work in pairs. Discuss the meaning of the three-part phrasal verbs in these sentences from the recording.

*I **put** my success **down to** self-discipline and perseverance.*
*I've just **signed up for** a computer course.*
*We all **come up against** problems – we just have to **face up to** them.*

2 Complete the sentences with the correct form of the verbs in the box.

crack	come	get	go	look	make	put

1 The money associated with fame and success more than _____ **up for** the constant intrusions of the media that celebrities have to _____ **up with**.
2 It is incomprehensible that youngsters should _____ **up to** sportsmen and women as role models – they are not worthy of such respect.
3 There isn't one successful, well-known person who doesn't _____ **in for** some kind of criticism from the media.
4 People who _____ **in for** TV competitions like *Big Brother* clearly have personality problems.
5 In my country, celebrities often _____ **away with** crimes for which normal people are imprisoned.
6 The authorities in my country are really _____ **down on** drug taking in professional sport.

3 Match the meanings a–g to the phrasal verbs in the sentences 1–6 in exercise 2.

a receive
b tolerate
c take part in
d deal more strictly with
e respect and admire
f compensate for
g not be punished for

4 Work in pairs. Discuss the statements and opinions in exercise 2. Give examples to support your views.

10c | Going wrong?

SPEAKING

1 Work in small groups. Discuss what you would do in the following situations and why.

1 While you are cooking chips in a deep-fat fryer, the phone rings in the lounge and you go to answer the call. When you return to the kitchen, you find the chip pan is on fire.

2 You are driving on a dual carriageway when your accelerator jams. Your car reaches speeds of 180 kilometres per hour.

3 The leader of your country is visiting your workplace with a television camera crew and has just walked into your department. Your colleague says he/she reminds him of a frog and you break into an uncontrollable fit of giggles. The leader approaches your desk.

4 You are hillwalking alone in a remote part of Scotland. It is early evening and you are still three hours from the nearest village when fog descends. You have no navigation aids or mobile phone.

2 Tell each other about a time when something went wrong for you.

READING

1 Read the text about the cloud formation in the photo on page 101.

How common is it to see Cumulonimbus clouds in your area?

The clouds are our fluffy friends – except, perhaps, for one: the cumulonimbus. When it comes to extreme and destructive weather, you can be sure that a cumulonimbus will be in the thick of the action. With torrential downpours, hail, storms, snowstorms, lightning, gales, tornados and hurricanes the enormous thundercloud can lead to untold loss of life and damage to property. When it is mature, this cloud can be considerably taller than Mount Everest.

Pilots do all they can to avoid flying too close to these storm clouds. If they can't pass around one, and their plane is capable of flying at high altitudes, they will generally climb over the top.

And that is exactly what Lieutenant-Colonel William Rankin, a pilot in the US Air Force, was attempting to do in the summer of 1959 when his jet fighter's engine seized completely and he had to eject.

2 You are going to read about what happened to Lieutenant Colonel Rankin. Work in groups of three, A, B and C.

A: Read Part 1 on page 101.
B: Read Part 2 on page 138.
C: Read Part 3 on page 155.

3 Your teacher will give you ten definitions. Match your definitions to the highlighted words in your part of the text.

4 Read your part of the story again, then take turns to summarize your part to the others in the group. Give the main points but include two factual errors. You might, for example, change a figure or other detail, include an event which did not take place or misquote William Rankin.

5 Read the other two parts of the story and find the errors.

6 Do you know any other stories of people who survived an extreme situation? Tell the others in your group.

VOCABULARY: weather

1 Work in pairs. The following words and phrases appear in the text. When was the last time you experienced these weather conditions? Which of them do you like or dislike most? Why?

hailstones   claps of thunder   a bolt of lightning
snowstorms   torrential downpours

2 Complete each gap with a word from the box which can be used in combination with all three words or phrases in the group.

ice   rain   snow   sun   thunder   wind

1	_____ drift	fall	flake
2	_____ light	shine	beam
3	_____ cloud	storm	bolt
4	_____ fall	water	drop
5	patch of	sheet of	layer of _____
6	gust of	blast of	breath of _____

3 Which of the words in the box in exercise 2 do you associate with the following?

flash flood   severe frost   howling gale
sweltering heatwave   fierce blizzard

4 Write five sentences, each with one of the words or phrases from exercises 1–3. Leave a gap where the word or phrase should be.

5 Give your sentences to another student to complete.

Part 1

Rankin was on a 70-minute routine navigational flight from the South Weymouth Naval Air Station in Massachusetts to his squadron's headquarters in Beaufort, North Carolina. Before take-off, he'd had a word with the meteorologist at the air base, who'd told him to expect isolated thunderstorms en route. The thunderclouds could be expected to reach altitudes of 30,000 to 40,000 feet*. He knew his jet could reach 50,000 feet comfortably and so he was confident of being able to fly over any storms without difficulty.

Four minutes into the flight, as he was approaching Norfolk, Virginia, Rankin spotted the distinctive shape of a Cumulonimbus ahead. A storm was raging in the town below and the cloud rose in an enormous tower of puffy convection mounds, mushrooming out into a broad, wispy canopy at its top. The summit was at around 45,000 feet – somewhat higher than he'd been led to expect by the official back at South Weymouth – so the pilot began a climb to 48,000 feet to be sure of clearing it.

Rankin was directly over the top, at an altitude of 47,000 feet and a speed of mach 0.82, when he heard a loud bump and rumble from the engine behind him. He watched in disbelief as the rpm indicator on his dashboard spiralled to zero in a matter of seconds and the bright red 'FIRE' light began flashing urgently.

Sudden and unexplained engine seizure like this is a one-in-a-million kind of emergency and Rankin knew that he would have to act fast. Without power, the jet's controls became ineffective and he instinctively reached for the lever that deployed the auxiliary power package to restore emergency electricity. As he pulled the lever, however, he was horrified to feel it come away in his hands. He was wearing just a lightweight summer flying suit. It was unheard-of to eject at this altitude at the best of times. To do so without a pressure suit would surely be suicide.

'The temperature outside was close to –50°C,' Rankin later recounted. 'Perhaps I would survive frostbite without permanent injury, but what about "explosive" decompression at almost ten miles up? And what about that thunderstorm directly below me? If it could be hazardous for an aeroplane in flight, what would it do to a mere human?'

There was little time to ponder the dangers. In a matter of seconds, Rankin realized he had no option but to reach behind his head and yank with all his might on the ejection seat handles. He exploded out of the cockpit and began his descent towards the clouds below.

*10,000 feet = 3,048 metres

DID YOU KNOW?

1 Work in pairs. Read about tornados and discuss the questions.

Tornados, or 'twisters' as they are also called, are huge columns of air rotating violently between cumulonimbus clouds and the surface of the Earth. An average of over 800 twisters are reported in the United States every year and most of these are to be found in spring and early summer in the Great Plains of the central states. This flat area, which extends into the Prairies of Canada, is commonly known as Tornado Alley.

Storm chasers are people who drive hundreds, sometimes thousands of miles to witness these twisters. Some are journalists or research scientists, but most are amateurs who do it for the thrill of the chase, and the prospect of photographing this most beautiful of severe weather phenomena. Many chasers are also trained storm spotters, who report their observations to the NWS, the National Weather Service. The almost 300,000 volunteers in the SKYWARN® programme provide information which enables the NWS to save lives by issuing more up-to-date and accurate warnings for tornados, severe thunderstorms and flash floods.

- If you were invited on a storm-chasing trip, would you accept? Why or why not?
- What are the most severe weather phenomena in your country? Are sufficient and accurate warnings given by the weather authorities?
- What is your favourite type of weather? Why?

10D | A stabbing incident

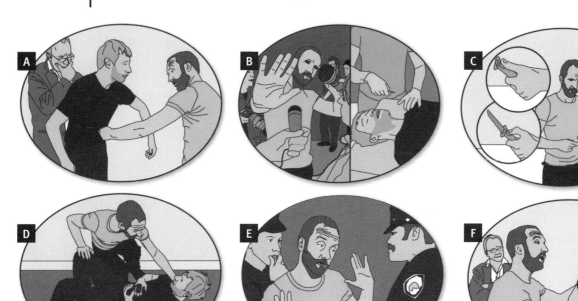

LISTENING & SPEAKING

1 Work in pairs. The pictures tell a story but they are in the wrong order. Discuss the possible order with your partner and tell the story.

2 Look at the final picture for the story on page 152. Does this affect your version of events?

3 🔘 3.15 Listen to the recording and put the pictures in the correct order. How accurate were your ideas in exercises 1 and 2?

4 🔘 3.15 Listen again and choose the correct words to complete the sentences.

1 At the time, David found the incident in *La Bohème amusing / frightening / annoying*.
2 In Milwaukee, he initially objected to the fact that the knife *was too sharp / seemed so authentic / weighed so much*.
3 It became clear to David that something was wrong when he saw *the director's face / Kimm change colour / the amount of blood*.
4 The police thought that David had *murdered Kimm / committed adultery / stabbed his wife*.
5 David says that the stabbing incident proved beneficial to *his family / the opera's success / his own career*.
6 In the first performance, *there was almost a repetition of / David was still affected by / the audience demanded an explanation for* the stabbing incident.

5 Complete the sentences from the recording with the correct form of either *take* or *turn*.

1 Things didn't _____ **out** quite **as planned**.
2 _____ my Covent Garden debut in 1976.
3 I saw Kimm's face _____ **white**.
4 The police _____ **it seriously**.
5 Farce was _____ **into** nightmare.
6 Reporters _____ **up** at our house.
7 He _____ **it all in the best of spirits**.
8 I _____ **lessons** on a special way of tucking the knife up my sleeve.

6 Work in pairs. Discuss the meaning of the expressions in bold with *turn* and *take* in exercise 5.

7 With your partner, retell David's story, using the pictures to help you.

GRAMMAR: modal verbs 3

must, need, should

must
- Use *must have* + past participle for deductions about the past.
  *He **must have** felt terrible about stabbing Kimm.*
- Use *had to* instead of *must* for past obligation.
  *He **had to** go with the police into another room.*
- Use *couldn't* or *wasn't/weren't allowed to* instead of *mustn't* for past prohibition.
  *He **wasn't allowed to** speak to anyone.*

Must and *mustn't* can remain unchanged after past reporting verbs.
*I hadn't felt any resistance when I stabbed Kimm, so I **thought** everything **must** be OK.*
*They **told** me I **mustn't** speak with my mouth full.*

need
- Use *didn't need to* + infinitive for actions that were not necessary: context makes it clear whether they were performed or not.
- Use *needn't have* + past participle for actions that were performed but were not necessary.
  *Fortunately, I **didn't need to** work on Saturday – I finished it all on Friday.*
  *I **needn't have** cooked so much – only five people came.*

should
- Use *should/shouldn't have* + past participle to criticize past actions (or omissions) or express regret.
  *You **should have** given me a toy knife.*
  *I **shouldn't have** let myself be persuaded.*

> SEE LANGUAGE REFERENCE PAGE 104

1 Complete the sentences with the phrases in the box. You need to use one of the phrases twice.

> must have   should have   shouldn't have
> needn't have   didn't need   mustn't
> wasn't allowed   had to

I *wasn't allowed* to go **there** – they wouldn't let me. At least, not until I was eighteen.

1 I told her she _____ ever put **it** on top of the heater to dry, otherwise it might catch fire.
2 I _____ let my little brother ride **it** as well – in fact, I shared nearly all my toys with him.
3 **They** used to think I _____ eyes in the back of my head – I knew what they were up to even when I was facing the board.
4 I _____ left **it** on the bus. Oh well – I'll just have to get wet.

5 You threw **it** away?! You _____ done that – we won't be able to get a refund now.
6 You _____ come earlier – **it**'s nearly all gone now.
7 I _____ to take **one** – I'd read on the website that bedding would be provided.
8 I'm glad we had **it** with us but to be honest, we _____ taken it – everyone spoke English.

2 Work in pairs, A and B. Discuss the possible context for each sentence in exercise 1. What might the word in bold refer to?

The word 'there' might refer to a nightclub or somewhere similar. The speaker is probably talking about a prohibition imposed by his or her parents.

3 Work in pairs, A and B. You are going to roleplay different situations. Turn to page 141.

VOCABULARY: not turning out well

1 Complete the sentences with the correct form of the verbs in the box.

> make   fall   go   come   work

1 All her **hard work and effort** _____ **to nothing** – the book was never published.
2 Our holiday **plans have** _____ **through** – we can't get a cheap enough flight.
3 Last year's champions **didn't** even _____ **it to** the quarter finals this year.
4 It was a beautiful wedding – shame **the marriage didn't** _____ **out**.
5 Business was bad and the firm _____ **bankrupt**.

2 Complete the sentences with the nouns in the box.

> mess   grief   good   cause   flop

1 I watered the plants every day but it **didn't do any** _____ – they all died.
2 The film was **a box-office** _____, and even less successful on DVD.
3 I **made a real** _____ **of** my driving test – almost had an accident.
4 My son is **a lost** _____ – I just accept that I'll never get him interested in reading.
5 The negotiations **came to** _____ after the unions insisted on higher overtime rates.

3 Write five sentences about situations you have experienced, witnessed or read about using the expressions in bold from exercises 1 and 2.

4 Work in pairs. Compare and discuss your sentences.

GRAMMAR
Futures

When referring to the future, we use:

- present simple for timetabled or scheduled events and after time conjunctions such as *if, when, before, after*.

- present continuous for arrangements.

- *going to* + infinitive for intentions, plans and predictions.

- *will* + infinitive for spontaneous decisions, future facts and to make predictions.

- future perfect to talk about actions which will be completed by a certain time in the future.

- future continuous to talk about actions which will be in progress at a certain time in the future. Also, to talk about actions that will happen because they are regular or decided:

  I'll be seeing Jane tomorrow – I'll ask her then.

  and to ask about someone's plans politely:

  Will you be coming *to the party on Saturday?*

Verbs of thinking such as *believe, doubt, expect, hope, think, wonder* can be followed by *will* when referring to the future. A present tense can also be used after *hope*.

  'I hope she **won't/doesn't** *get angry with me.'*

Modal verbs express degrees of certainty about the future.

  Tomorrow **should** *be sunny in the north.* (probability)
  It **might** *rain in the south* (possibility) *and there* **may well** *be thunderstorms on the coast.* (probability)

A full infinitive can be used after a number of verbs to refer to a future event: *aim, arrange, expect, hope, intend, plan.*

  I've **arranged to meet** *him tomorrow morning.*

Gerunds are used after certain other verbs in the same way: eg *anticipate, consider, fancy, feel like, think of.*

  Do you **fancy coming out** *with us later?*

The following adjectives can be used to refer to the future:

- *Be + bound/certain/sure +* full infinitive expresses certainty.

  She's **bound to win** *– she's a much better player.*

- *Be + (un)likely +* full infinitive expresses probability.

  It's **unlikely to rain** *but take a coat just in case.*

- *Be + due +* full infinitive is used for scheduled events.

  We're **due to arrive** *on Friday around midday.*

In formal English, *be +* full infinitive is also possible.

  The Minister **is (due) to make** *a statement later today.*

A number of adjectives can be used with *of +* noun or gerund with future reference: *assured, (un)certain, confident, doubtful, fearful, hopeful, (un)sure.*

  He has a degree but he can't **be certain of finding** *work.*

Be (just) about to + infinitive and *be on the point of +* gerund can be used to talk about the immediate future.

  We **are on the point of acquiring** *new premises.*
  We're **just about to sign** *the contract.*

MODAL VERBS: *must, need, should*

must

Present & Future

We use *must* to express obligation or strong advice. The authority comes from the speaker. We can also use *have to*, particularly when the authority comes from someone other than the speaker.

  You **must** *do exactly as I say.*
  You really **must** *get yourself a computer.*
  I **have to** *be home by 10 – my dad said.*

We also use *must* for deductions: see Unit 4 page 43.

We use *must not/mustn't* to express prohibition.

  Residents **must not** *use the shower after 10pm.*

Past

There is no past form of *must* to express past obligation, so we use *had to* instead; *must have +* past participle is used to make deductions about past situations and events.

  'I didn't see the match – I **had to** *go to a meeting.'*
  'You **must have** *been fed up about that.'*

There is no past form of *mustn't* to express past prohibition, so we use *couldn't* or *wasn't/weren't allowed to* instead.

  We **couldn't** *use the shower after 10pm.*

In reported speech *mustn't* for prohibition can remain unchanged or we can use *couldn't* or *wasn't/weren't allowed to*.

  He said we **mustn't/couldn't** *use the shower after 10pm.*

Must can remain unchanged in reported speech. *Had to* can be used when reporting obligations.

  I told her she **must** *be crazy and she* **must/had to** *abandon the whole silly idea immediately.*

need

Present & Future

Need as a modal verb (ie + infinitive without *to*) normally only occurs in negative sentences; *need to/have to* is much more common for expressing necessity.

  I **need to** *eat something.* (not: *I* **need** *eat*)
  Do you **need to** *go to the toilet?* (not: **Need** *you go?*)

Usually there is no difference in meaning between *needn't* and *don't need/have to*: both forms indicate a lack of obligation or necessity.

  You **needn't do/don't need to do** *it if you don't want to.*

Past

We use *needn't have* + past participle to express an action that was completed but that was not necessary.

> *I was a bit nervous before the party, but I needn't have worried – everything went very well.*

We use *didn't need to* + infinitive to express an action that was not necessary. The context usually makes it clear whether the action was performed or not.

> *They said we **didn't need to** take a torch, so I didn't.*

should

Present & Future

We use *should(n't)* to give advice, to say what we think is right or wrong, and to talk about probability. We use *ought (not) to* to express the same ideas.

> *You **should/ought to** see the doctor about that cough.*
> *Children of that age **shouldn't** be left on their own.*
> *They're both strong teams, so it **should** be a good game.*

Past

We use *should(n't) have* + past participle to criticize past actions and express regrets about the past. The use of *ought to* is much less common, particularly in the negative.

> *You **shouldn't have** said that – it's not very nice.*
> *He's so lazy – I **should** never **have** employed him.*

We use the same structure to talk about events which you expect to have happened already and those which were supposed to happen but did not.

> *Her plane **should have** landed by now – I'll phone her.*
> *Her plane **should have** taken off at ten o'clock, but it was delayed.*

WORD LIST

Success

achieve an aim	/əˌtʃiːv ən ˈeɪm/
bright future	/ˌbraɪt ˈfjuːtʃə(r)/
do well	/ˌduː ˈwel/
further one's career	/ˌfɜː(r)ðə(r) wʌnz kəˈrɪə(r)/
get on in life	/ˌget ˈɒn ɪn ˌlaɪf/
give (sb) a sense of achievement	/gɪv ə ˌsens əv əˈtʃiːvmənt/
go badly	/ˌgəʊ ˈbædli/
high-flier *n C*	/ˌhaɪ ˈflaɪə(r)/
overnight success	/ˌəʊvə(r)naɪt səkˈses/
pay off *v*	/ˌpeɪ ˈɒf/
ride high in the charts	/raɪd ˈhaɪ ɪn ðə ˌtʃɑː(r)ts/
stand a chance of	/ˌstænd ə ˈtʃɑːns ɒv/
thriving *adj*	/ˈθraɪvɪŋ/
turn out *v*	/ˌtɜː(r)n ˈaʊt/

Three-part phrasal verbs

come in for *v*	/ˌkʌm ˈɪn fɔː(r)/
come up against *v*	/kʌm ˌʌp əˈgenst/
crack down on *v*	/ˌkræk ˈdaʊn ɒn/
face up to *v*	/ˌfeɪs ˈʌp tʊ/
get away with *v*	/ˌget əˈweɪ wɪð/
go in for *v*	/ˌgəʊ ˈɪn fɔː(r)/
look up to *v*	/ˌlʊk ˈʌp tʊ/
make up for *v*	/ˌmeɪk ˈʌp fɔː(r)/
put (sth) down to *v*	/ˌpʊt ˈdaʊn tʊ/
put up with *v*	/ˌpʊt ˈʌp wɪð/
sign up for *v*	/ˌsaɪn ˈʌp fɔː(r)/

Weather

blast of wind *n C*	/ˌblɑːst əv ˈwɪnd/
bolt of lightning *n C*	/ˌbəʊlt əv ˈlaɪt(ə)nɪŋ/
breath of wind *n C*	/ˌbreθ əv ˈwɪnd/
clap of thunder *n C*	/ˌklæp əv ˈθʌndə(r)/
gust of wind *n C*	/ˌgʌst əv ˈwɪnd/
layer of ice *n C*	/ˌleɪə(r) ɒv ˈaɪs/
patch of ice *n C*	/ˌpætʃ ɒv ˈaɪs/
sheet of ice *n C*	/ˌʃiːt ɒv ˈaɪs/
fierce blizzard *n C*	/ˌfɪə(r)s ˈblɪzə(r)d/
flash flood *n C*	/ˌflæʃ ˈflʌd/
howling gale *n C*	/ˌhaʊlɪŋ ˈgeɪl/
severe frost *n C*	/sɪˌvɪə(r) ˈfrɒst/
sweltering heatwave *n C*	/ˌswelt(ə)rɪŋ ˈhiːtˌweɪv/
torrential downpour *n C*	/təˌrenʃ(ə)l ˈdaʊnˌpɔː(r)/
hailstone *n C*	/ˈheɪlˌstəʊn/
raindrop *n C*	/ˈreɪnˌdrɒp/
rainfall *n U*	/ˈreɪnˌfɔːl/
rainwater *n U*	/ˈreɪnˌwɔːtə(r)/
snowdrift *n C*	/ˈsnəʊˌdrɪft/
snowfall *n C*	/ˈsnəʊˌfɔːl/
snowflake *n C*	/ˈsnəʊˌfleɪk/
snowstorm *n C*	/ˈsnəʊˌstɔː(r)m/
sunbeam *n C*	/ˈsʌnˌbiːm/
sunlight *n C* **	/ˈsʌnˌlaɪt/
sunshine *n C* **	/ˈsʌnˌʃaɪn/
thunderbolt *n C*	/ˈθʌndə(r)ˌbəʊlt/
thundercloud *n C*	/ˈθʌndə(r)ˌklaʊd/
thunderstorm *n C*	/ˈθʌndə(r)ˌstɔː(r)m/

Not turning out well

a lost cause	/ə ˌlɒst ˈkɔːz/
box-office flop *n C*	/ˌbɒks ɒfɪs ˈflɒp/
come to grief	/ˌkʌm tʊ ˈgriːf/
come to nothing	/ˌkʌm tʊ ˈnʌθɪŋ/
fall through *v*	/ˌfɔːl ˈθruː/
go bankrupt	/ˌgəʊ ˈbæŋkrʌpt/
make a mess of (sth)	/ˌmeɪk ə ˈmes əv/
make it to	/ˈmeɪk ɪt ˌtʊ/
not do any good	/nɒt duː ˌeni ˈgʊd/
work out *v*	/ˌwɜː(r)k ˈaʊt/

Other words & phrases

arch *v*	/ɑː(r)tʃ/
billow *v*	/ˈbɪləʊ/
boom *v*	/buːm/
brandish *v*	/ˈbrændɪʃ/
break into a fit of giggles	/ˌbreɪk ˈɪntʊ ə ˌfit ɒv ˈgɪg(ə)lz/
buffet *v*	/ˈbʊfeɪ/
chunk *n C*	/tʃʌŋk/
cockpit *n C*	/ˈkɒkˌpɪt/
dashboard *n C*	/ˈdæʃˌbɔː(r)d/
debut *n C* *	/ˈdeɪbjuː/
deploy *v* *	/dɪˈplɔɪ/
drag *v* **	/dræg/
dual carriageway	/ˌdjuːəl ˈkærɪdʒweɪ/
flail *v*	/fleɪl/
give (sb) the shivers	/ˌgɪv ðə ˈʃɪvə(r)z/
glimpse *n C* *	/glɪmps/
gloom *n U* *	/gluːm/
hassle *v*	/ˈhæs(ə)l/
hazardous *adj* *	/ˈhæzə(r)dəs/
holster *n C*	/ˈhəʊlstə(r)/
hound *v*	/haʊnd/
hurl *v*	/hɜː(r)l/
hurtle *v*	/ˈhɜː(r)t(ə)l/
jam *v* *	/dʒæm/
jolt *n*	/dʒəʊlt/
leak out *v*	/ˌliːk ˈaʊt/
legacy *n C* **	/ˈlegəsi/
let one's hair down	/ˌlet wʌnz ˈheə(r) ˌdaʊn/
lever *n C*	/ˈliːvə(r)/
mere *adj* **	/mɪə(r)/
numb *v*	/nʌm/
ooze *v*	/uːz/
ordeal *n C* *	/ɔː(r)ˈdiːl/
plead with *v*	/ˈpliːd ˌwɪð/
pose a challenge	/ˌpəʊz ə ˈtʃælɪndʒ/
prop *n C*	/prɒp/
puffy *adj*	/ˈpʌfi/
pull off a deal	/ˌpʊl ˌɒf ə ˈdiːl/
pull out of *v*	/ˌpʊl ˈaʊt ɒv/
retract *v*	/rɪˈtrækt/
rumble *n C*	/ˈrʌmb(ə)l/
soar *v* *	/sɔː(r)/
spark *n U*	/spɑː(r)k/
surge *v*	/sɜː(r)dʒ/
toss *v* **	/tɒs/
trail *v* **	/treɪl/
trapdoor *n C*	/ˈtræpˌdɔː(r)/
tuck *v* **	/tʌk/
unfold *v*	/ʌnˈfəʊld/
win (sb) over *v*	/ˌwɪn ˈəʊvə(r)/
wispy *adj*	/ˈwɪspi/

READING & PRONUNCIATION: stress patterns & rhyming schemes

1 Work in pairs. Discuss the questions.

- How do you think you might feel if you were greeted with the sight of a field full of daffodils?
- What metaphors could be used to describe the sight and movement of a large number of flowers?

2 Read the poem by the English Romantic poet William Wordsworth (1770–1850) and choose the best word to complete the lines.

Note that the **rhyme scheme** for the poem is **ababcc**. This means that the last words of the first and third lines rhyme with each other, as do those of the second and fourth lines and the fifth and sixth lines.

3 🔘 **3.16** Listen and compare your answers with the actual poem.

4 The stressed syllables in the first seven lines of the poem are marked in bold. Underline the stressed syllables in the remainder of the poem.

Note that the stress pattern for the poem is iambic tetrameter. An iamb consists of one weak beat (unstressed syllable) followed by one strong beat (stressed syllable). In iambic tetrameter there are four iambs in each line.

5 🔘 **3.16** Listen again to the poem to check your answers. Then practise reading it aloud to each other.

---

a   I **wa**ndered **lon**ely **as** a **cloud**
b   That **floats** on **high** o'er **vales** and **hills**,
a   When **all** at **once** I **saw** a (1) _____,   *load / flood / row / crowd*
b   A **host**, of **gold**en **daf**fo**dils**:
c   Be**side** the **lake**, be**neath** the **trees**,
c   **Flut**tering and **danc**ing in the (2) _____.   *peace / skies / breeze / mist*

Continuous as the stars that shine
And (3) _____ on the Milky Way,   *twinkle / sprinkle / jingle / mingle*
They stretched in never-ending line
Along the margin of a (4) _____: *spray / quay / bay / hay*
Ten thousand saw I at a glance,
(5) _____ their heads in sprightly dance.   *bowing / tossing / losing / shaking*

The waves beside them danced; but they
Out-did the sparkling waves in glee:
A poet could not but be (6) _____,   *grey / gloomy / gay / cheery*
In such a jocund company:
I gazed – and gazed – but little thought
What wealth the show to me had (7) _____: *brought / sought / caught / fought*

For oft, when on my (8) _____ I lie   *self / time / way / couch*
In vacant or in pensive mood,
They (9) _____ upon that inward eye   *flash / smash / squash / brush*
Which is the bliss of solitude;
And then my heart with (10) _____ fills,   *measure / leisure / pleasure / treasure*
And dances with the daffodils.

Glossary
o'er *prep* over
a host *n* a large number
sprightly *adj* lively
glee *n* delight
jocund *adj* cheerful
oft *adv* often
bliss *n* extreme happiness

VOCABULARY: descriptive verbs

1 What different ways of seeing do the underlined words from the poem describe?

Ten thousand saw I at a <u>glance</u> …
I <u>gazed</u> and gazed …

These and several other words of seeing can be used either as verbs or as nouns.

2 Complete the sentences with the words in the box. Use the same word for both sentences, a and b. You may need to change the form of the word.

gaze	glance	browse	view	stare

1 a) I **had a quick** _____ **at the newspaper** this morning.
   b) She kept _____ **surreptitiously at her watch**, desperate for the meeting to end.
2 a) We don't have an encyclopaedia at home – we just _____ **the Web**.
   b) No visit to the museum would be complete without a _____ **in the bookshop**.
3 a) I can't see much from my house – there's another building **blocking the** _____.
   b) When house-hunting, you should _____ as many **properties** as possible.
4 a) My parents always told me that it's rude to _____.
   b) She met his friendly greeting with a **blank** _____ – she clearly didn't recognize him.
5 a) I'd hate to be a celebrity, always **in the public** _____.
   b) He _____ **lovingly** at her photograph and sighed.

3 Work in pairs. How true are the *a* sentences in exercise 2 for you?

4 Put the verbs in the box from the poem into the appropriate column below.

~~wander~~	~~shine~~	flutter	float
twinkle	toss	sparkle	flash

Light	**Movement**
shine	*wander*

5 Complete the gaps with the verbs in exercise 4. The verb must collocate with all four nouns.

Nouns as subjects

1 eyelids   heart   hands   flags   _____
2 eyes   sea   jewellery   glass   _____
3 eyes   thoughts   attention   mind   _____
4 eyes   lightning   neon signs   warning lights   _____

Nouns as objects

5 _____   a coin   one's hair   a ball   a salad
6 _____   a light   a torch   shoes   silver

6 Choose five of the noun/verb collocations in exercise 5 and write a sentence for each. Leave gaps where the verbs should be and ask your partner to complete them.

DID YOU KNOW?

1 Work in pairs. Read about Romanticism and discuss the questions.

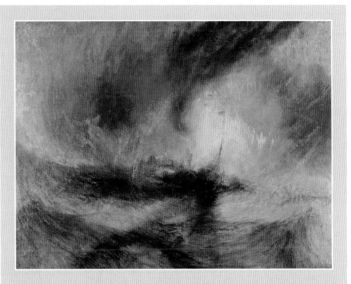

Romanticism was a literary and artistic movement originating in Europe in the late 18ᵗʰ and 19ᵗʰ century. It emphasized the importance of the emotions and imagination over reason and intellect, and was characterized by love of nature, individualism and sentimentality.

In **literature**, Wordsworth and Coleridge were among the first Romantic poets in Britain, followed by Shelley, Keats and Lord Byron. Sir Walter Scott, author of historical novels such as *Ivanhoe* and *Rob Roy*, and Mary Shelley, who wrote *Frankenstein*, were both prominent figures of British Romanticism. In the United States, well-known writers of the period include James Fennimore Cooper (*The Last of the Mohicans*), Herman Melville (*Moby Dick*) and Washington Irving (*Sleepy Hollow*).

In **art**, John Constable's quiet English landscapes contrasted with JMW Turner's dramatic seascapes, such as *Snow Storm – Steamboat off a Harbour's Mouth* (above), for which Turner claimed he had been tied to the mast of the steamboat in order to observe the storm.

Washington Allston introduced Romanticism to the United States with his poetic landscapes.

- Who are your favourite writers, artists and composers? Why do you like them?
- Which contemporary authors, artists and musicians do you think will continue to be popular in the next century? Why?

11B | Affordable art

LISTENING

1 You are going to hear an interview with Will Ramsay, owner of Will's Art Warehouse, a London art gallery.

🔘 **3.17** Listen to Part 1 of the interview and complete the sentences with one or two words.

1 Will's aim is to make art more _____ to the general public.
2 He wanted to remove the _____ from buying art.
3 He says his staff are _____.
4 Artworks at this gallery cost between _____ and three thousand pounds.
5 Will says an art gallery should be like a _____ in terms of the variety it offers.
6 He says that art helps to improve the _____ in an organization.
7 Art Warehouse gift vouchers for employees can have the _____ printed on them.

2 🔘 **3.18** In Part 2 Will talks about his Affordable Art Fairs. Listen and decide whether the statements are true (T) or false (F). Say why the false statements are incorrect.

1 The London Affordable Art Fair is restricted to UK art galleries.
2 The Fair includes an exhibition of work by recent art school entrants.
3 Children can create their own works of art at the fairs.
4 Most buyers at the fairs look upon art primarily as an investment.
5 One quarter of all visitors to the art fairs buys something.
6 Will says his previous career gave him some useful experience.

3 🔘 **3.19** Listen to Part 3, in which Will offers tips to first-time buyers of art. Make notes on what he says about each of the items in the box.

> guaranteed investment   artists' CVs
> art fairs   auctions   prints

4 Work in pairs. Discuss the questions.

• What work do you think is involved in organizing an art fair such as Will Ramsay's?
• Would you be interested in buying original works of contemporary art for your own home? Why or why not?

SPEAKING

1 Work in pairs. You work for an art gallery which has been asked to provide works of art to decorate the reception areas of the buildings in the box.

> a large hospital   a sports centre
> a modern five-star hotel in a capital city
> the offices of an established law firm

Discuss the suitability of the works above for each building. Which, if any, would you select and why?

If you have not chosen a work of art for a particular building, what type of work would you commission?

2 Compare your ideas with the rest of the class.

3 Work in groups. Discuss the questions.

• What pictures do you have in your school or workplace? How much do you like them?
• If you were to buy or commission a painting, photograph, print or sculpture for your school or workplace, what would it be like?

GRAMMAR: determiners, pronouns & quantifiers

1 Complete the sentences from the recording with the words in the box.

all	most	no	any
a little	little	another	these

1 Can you tell us _____ about the gallery?
2 They might be asked something which gives away the fact that they know very _____.
3 _____ important point is that we also enable buyers to choose works from a variety of artists.
4 You can search through _____ the work we have in stock on our website.
5 _____ of them want to offer incentives and bonuses to attract and retain key talent.
6 We will produce vouchers of _____ amount.
7 _____ now all take place on a regular basis in a number of cities all over the world …
8 Reproductions are worthless, they have _____ value at all.

🔊 **3.20** Listen and check.

2 Read the information in the grammar box and decide whether the words you wrote in exercise 1 are being used as a determiner (*D*), pronoun (*P*) or quantifier (*Q*).

Determiners come before nouns and indicate which people or things you are referring to, as well as quantities and amounts.
> *I wanted to take **this** fear factor out of buying art.*
> *You can often pick up **some** good bargains there.*

Most determiners can also be used as **pronouns**, that is, instead of a noun. *Every*, *no* and *other* cannot be used as pronouns: *each*, *none* and *others* are used instead.
> ***All** are run by experienced professionals.*
> *There are eight rooms with 20 paintings in **each**.*

The pronouns can also be used as **quantifiers**, before *of* + pronoun, or *of* + *the, this, that, these, those, my, your,* etc + noun. The word *of* is optional with *all* and *both* before a noun.
> ***Many** of them feel embarrassed about their lack of knowledge.*

❯ SEE LANGUAGE REFERENCE PAGE 114

3 Choose the correct words to complete the sentences.

1 **I've been** painting **for quite** *some / a lot / much* **time now** – over ten years, I think.
2 **In** *other / another / more* three **months I'll have** finished this commission.
3 **I try to** go to an art museum **once every** *few / each / other* week – so that's twice a month.
4 **There's** *all / many / every* **chance I'll** study art at university.
5 **Few, if** *any / some / none*, **of my** friends could name more than about six artists.
6 **I have** *neither / no / enough* **time for** art critics – they talk utter nonsense.
7 **For** *all / most / many* his **faults, I think** Picasso was a great painter.
8 **I think** Madrid is **second to** *none / no / any* **for** art – you can't beat it.

4 Work in pairs. Use five of the words and expressions in bold (including the words you selected) in exercise 3 to tell your partner things which are true for you. Give details.

VOCABULARY: prepositional phrases

1 In the recording Will used these prepositional phrases.

*put work **on display*** *work we have **in stock*** *buy **at leisure***

Complete the phrases with a preposition from the box which can be used before all five nouns in each group.

at	in	on	off	by	out of	in	on

1 _____ danger practice retrospect custody person
2 _____ risk ease stake fault gunpoint
3 _____ fire offer loan leave tiptoe
4 _____ flames tears ruins arrears droves
5 _____ date sight breath character work
6 _____ duty balance course limits work
7 _____ paper strike trial bail hold
8 _____ chance mistake nature force law

2 Complete the sentences with an appropriate noun from exercise 1.

1 The idea looks good **on** _____, but will it work in _____?
2 She's a very calm person **by** _____: that angry outburst was completely **out of** _____.
3 Jane's been **off** _____ for six months **on** maternity _____.
4 The goalkeeper wasn't **at** _____ for the last goal. A defender ran into him and knocked him **off** _____ – he fell over and missed the ball.
5 It was a huge turnout. People turned up **in** _____ for a chance to see their hero **in** _____: he so rarely appears in public.

3 Write five sentences, each with one of the prepositional phrases from exercise 1. Leave a gap where the noun should be, as in exercise 2.

4 Give your sentences to another student to complete.

11c | The sound of silence

SPEAKING

1 Work in groups of four students, A–D. You will each see a photo with people who are not speaking. Choose one of the people and imagine what he or she is thinking.

A: Turn to page 141.   C: Turn to page 151.
B: Turn to page 148.   D: Turn to page 146.

2 You have two minutes each to speak the thoughts of your person aloud. Do not describe your photo: imagine you are the person actually in the situation.

3 Talk about each others' photos, saying what you think each one contains. Compare your ideas by looking at the relevant pages.

READING

1 Sit in complete silence for one minute. At the end of the minute tell your partner what sounds you could hear, no matter how faint.

2 Read the article, ignoring the gaps, and answer the questions.

1 What is an anechoic chamber?
2 What is it used for?
3 How does the writer describe his experience …
   a) whilst inside the chamber?
   b) on leaving the chamber?

3 Complete the gaps 1–8 in the article with the sentences a–h.

a Anechoic chambers eliminate this problem by covering walls, ceiling and floor with wedges of fibreglass which stick out eighteen inches into the room.

b This latter device measures the opening and closing of the voice box while the subject speaks.

c And our own search for 'peace and quiet' never extends as far as wanting no noise at all.

d Once you have a silent room, you don't want to ruin it.

e As I hold my breath in order to stop this, I begin to hear a whistling noise in my ears.

f Some people, standing in an anechoic chamber, have lost their balance.

g In one of the busiest parts of campus, and next to the low hum of an electricity substation, it is hard to believe the unassuming walls can block out all sounds.

h Even the steel door is covered with a foot and a half of fibreglass.

4 Underline all instances of the noun *sound* in the article, together with any accompanying verbs, adjectives or nouns. Record each collocation in your notebook in the sentence in which it appears.

Most people cannot sleep without at least some background sound.

5 Work in pairs. Discuss the questions.

- What 'ambient sounds' might typically be heard during a performance of John Cage's *4'33"*?
- Do you agree that *our own search for 'peace and quiet' never extends as far as wanting no noise at all*?
- How important is silence to you when you are …
  - working or studying?   • reading?
  - sleeping?   • eating?

VOCABULARY: sounds

1 Complete the sentences with one word from the text.

1 The walls contain coils to cancel out the _____ of the substation.
2 I begin to hear a _____ noise in my ears.

What sounds do these words describe?

2 Choose the most appropriate words for the sentences.

1 **Bacon** *sizzled / buzzed* in the frying pan and my **stomach** *stuttered / rumbled* in anticipation.
2 When the **clock** finished *timing / chiming*, there was a sound of champagne **corks** *popping / plopping* and **glasses** *clinking / snapping*.
3 A **car horn** *bleeped / beeped* outside and she came *clattering / shattering* excitedly **down the stairs**.
4 There was a *screech / scratch* of **brakes** followed by the *croak / crack* of **gunfire**.
5 **Leaves** began to *whistle / rustle*, **windows** *rattled / muttered* and a **door** *rang / banged* shut.
6 They lay awake, relieved to hear the **door** *click / crash* quietly shut, her **keys** *hum / jingle* briefly as she returned them to her pocket and the **stairs** *creak / shriek* as she crept up to her room.

3 🔘 **3.21** Work in pairs. Listen to the sound sequences from exercise 2 and discuss what might be happening in each situation.

1 This is probably somebody preparing their breakfast.

4 Work in groups, A and B. You are going to write a short story including a number of sounds.

Group A: Turn to page 151.   Group B: Turn to page 146.

5 Work with a student from the other group and read your stories to each other.

The quietest place on Earth

Silence holds a paradoxical place in science and in human consciousness. In science, the quietest conditions that modern technology allows are invariably used to research sound. (1) ＿＿＿ Real silence is strange and disturbing, not relaxing. Most people cannot sleep without at least some background sound.

The closest humankind can get to complete silence is the inside of a heavily soundproofed anechoic chamber, a handful of which exist in universities and labs across Britain. These are used for a range of interesting research – but they also have a profound effect on the people who go into them.

My search for one leads me to University College London, whose anechoic ('without echo') room is in an anonymous, windowless building. (2) ＿＿＿ Dave Cushing, a technician in the phonetics and linguistics department, which owns the facility, shows me the stacks of equipment used in the chamber, and the extensive precautions taken to keep sound pollution inside to a minimum.

Stepping into the chamber is a strange experience, 'like being in a field in the middle of the night' according to John Fithyan who runs Southampton University's facility. The silence is profound and the room looks unusual too, with jagged sound-cancelling spikes covering the walls and ceiling that take on a menacing look in the dim light. A 70s-style padded armchair sits incongruously in this other-worldly environment. As I sit on the chair, I try to speak. My voice sounds quiet and dead, and yet I am conscious of the sound of my breathing. (3) ＿＿＿ The experience is disconcerting.

Unpleasant or not, complete silence is incredibly difficult to achieve. Insulate a room, build it within thick brick walls, and vibrations will still get in. Mount the whole thing on springs, and the vibrations will stop – but the echoes won't. (4) ＿＿＿ These absorb virtually all the sound, meaning that measurements of sound levels typically weigh in far below zero decibels, the threshold of human hearing. The Bell Labs chamber, the first ever built, featured in *The Guinness Book of Records* as the 'quietest place on Earth' after its construction in 1940.

(5) ＿＿＿ So the chamber at UCL has specially designed silent air conditioning, and the walls contain coils to cancel out the hum of the substation. The chamber is lit with light bulbs instead of noisy fluorescent tubes. And users must walk on a platform, raised above the soundproofed floor. (6) ＿＿＿

While most anechoic chambers are used for acoustic research, UCL's is used in phonetics – the scientific study of the human voice. Researchers make precise recordings of voices, using both microphones and laryngographs. (7) ＿＿＿ Linguists at UCL use the recordings to identify the root causes of speech abnormalities in children.

The silence of the anechoic room was a source of inspiration for American composer John Cage, who visited Harvard University's facility in the late 1940s. Though he was in a room with no background sound and no echo, Cage discovered that total silence is not actually possible: he claims he heard two sounds, 'one high, my nervous system in operation, one low, my blood in circulation'. After this experience, he was inspired to write his 'silent' piece, *4'33"*, in which the 'music' is made by the ambient sounds of the concert hall alone.

(8) ＿＿＿ Professor Linda Luxon, an audiologist at the Institute of Child Health, questions why this might be. 'I can't give you any rational explanation,' she says. But she does agree that people find orientation easier if they have full use of all five senses.

As I step out of the anechoic chamber and back into the control room, my sensory deprivation ends. Before going into the chamber, I had thought the control room was quiet, but I now hear the fans of the computer systems, the echoes of students chatting outside. The shock of hearing all this is as great as was the shock of hearing nothing.

Glossary

threshold *n* a limit at which an arrangement changes

sit incongruously *v* look strange or out of context

11D The sound of music

LISTENING

1 Work in pairs. Talk about how much you (would) enjoy hearing music in these situations. Give reasons for your opinions.

Recorded music:
- in a shopping mall
- in the car
- in a dentist's waiting room
- in a gym

Live music:
- in a bar
- on public transport
- in the street
- coming from a neighbour's house

2 ⊙ **3.22–3.27** Listen to dialogues 1–6, in which people talk about the music they hear in different situations. Answer this question about each one:

Does the main speaker have a positive (*P*) or negative (*N*) attitude towards the music they hear?

3 ⊙ **3.22–3.27** Listen again and choose from the statements a–i what each of the main speakers in dialogues 1–6 is expressing. Three of the statements are not required.

a   The music is affecting my ability to concentrate.
b   I like the fact that a variety of music is played.
c   I think the music should be played more quietly.
d   The quality of some of the music is unexpectedly good.
e   I produce some of my best work when music is playing.
f   The type of music should be more carefully chosen.
g   The music is played at unusual times.
h   People of any age can enjoy listening to loud music.
i   The music helps take my mind off what I am doing.

4 Which, if any, of the main speakers in dialogues 1–6 have attitudes which are similar to your own?

GRAMMAR: hypothetical present & future situations

1   Use *if/supposing/suppose/imagine* + past simple or continuous for hypothetical conditions in the present and future. Use *would/might/could* to talk or ask about possible results.
    Suppose we went *next door and said something. Do you think they* ***would*** *do anything?*
    Imagine there were *no music at all being played. It'd be a bit odd,* ***wouldn't*** *it?*

2   *Were to* + infinitive makes an event seem less probable.
    If I were to do *a survey,* ***would*** *everyone say, 'I just love the music'?*

3   Use *wish/if only* + past simple for wishes about present states.
    I ***wish I knew*** *how to play an instrument.*
    If only she wasn't/weren't *so busy all the time.*

4   Use *would* with dynamic verbs. *I wish/If only I would* is not possible: use *I wish/If only I could*.
    I just ***wish they would give*** *a little more thought to what they put on.*
    If only I could remember *her name.*

5   Use *hope* + a present or future tense if there is a real possibility that something will happen.
    I ***hope she comes*** *on Friday – she said she might.*

6   Past simple and continuous can be used after *it's time* and *would rather/sooner* to talk about what we want to happen.
    She says ***it's time*** *I grew up.*
    I'd ***rather*** *they just switched off the music.*

7   Use the infinitive with *would rather/sooner* if the subject is the same.
    I'd ***sooner*** ~~I lived~~ *live in a house than a flat.*

❯ SEE LANGUAGE REFERENCE PAGE 114

1 Correct the sentences by changing the underlined words. Write one or two words.

1 I wish I <u>wouldn't</u> have to do **that** so often.
2 If only we <u>would have</u> one of **those** at home.
3 I wish **he** <u>gets</u> in touch with me.
4 If only I <u>stopped</u> doing **that**.
5 I <u>wish</u> the weather stays fine for **it** – it'll be a shame if it rains.
6 I'd sooner <u>I walked</u> than go anywhere in a car with **him** driving.
7 **He**'d rather no one <u>to phone</u> **him** before 10am at the weekend.
8 It's time **he** <u>should buy</u> some new clothes.
9 **He** wouldn't be pleased if I <u>would</u> say **that** to **him**.
10 Imagine they stopped making **them**. What <u>did</u> we do?

2 Work in pairs. For what situations might you personally say each of the sentences in exercise 1? Who or what might the words in bold refer to? If necessary change *he/him* to *she/her*.

I might use the first sentence to talk about ironing. I have to be smart for my job, which is fine, but I wish I didn't have to iron my shirts so often.

3 Work in pairs, A and B. You are going to roleplay a situation.

Student A: Turn to page 138.
Student B: Turn to page 151.

SPEECH FEATURE: dislocation

Dislocation involves the use of both noun phrases and pronouns to clarify meaning. There are two types of dislocation: noun phrase prefaces and noun phrase tags. Speakers use **noun phrase prefaces** to announce a topic first, before going on to the main point.

> *All that music they have on at the Haywood Centre, do you think people really like **it**?*

Prefaces enable the speaker to check that the listener has recognized the topic before moving on.

> *'That music they play down at the gym.' 'Yeah?' 'It really gets you going, doesn't it?'*

Speakers use **noun phrase tags** at the end of a sentence to clarify the meaning of a preceding pronoun, particularly if it might be unclear.

> *It's depressing, **all this talk in the papers of banning live music on the underground**.*
> *Was **it** expensive, **your camera**?*

Tags may repeat a preceding noun and add information to clarify it.

> *Just about all the shops there have **music** blaring out of them – **pop music, rock music** …*

A demonstrative pronoun may be used as a tag to emphasize a feeling or opinion.

> *It's a pity, **that**. It's a good book, **this**.*

1 Complete the sentences with an appropriate word. There may be more than one possibility.

1 These ____, do you think they need **altering**? They seem a bit **long in the leg** to me.
2 I used to **know** it **by heart**, that ____. Now I can't even remember **the chorus**.
3 Those ____, they wake me up every morning. They make such a clatter with the **bins**.
4 It's so **squeaky**, his ____. He sounds just like a mouse.
5 And the ____ **facilities**, they're hopelessly inadequate. There's space for about 20 **cars**, that's all.
6 It was very **strict**, my ____. Both my **parents** were strong disciplinarians.
7 The ____, have you seen it? I only had time for **a quick glance at** the **front page** this morning.
8 I wish you'd fix it, that ____. It keeps **rattling** and it lets in a terrible **draught**.

🔘 **3.28** Listen and check your answers.

2 Work in two groups, A and B. You are going to write sentences which include dislocation.

Group A: Turn to page 140. Group B: Turn to page 153.

3 Show your sentences to someone in the other group and ask him or her to complete them.

GRAMMAR
Determiners, pronouns & quantifiers

Determiners

all, another, any, both, a couple of, each, either, enough, every, (a) few, fewer, less, a lot of, (a) little, many, more, most, much, neither, no, one, other, plenty of, several, some, this, that, these, those.

We use determiners before nouns to identify which people or things we are talking about, or to talk about quantities and amounts.

> *I'll have **some toast** with **a little jam** on it, please.*
> *Very **few records** remain of **this period**.*

We can use *quite* before *some* and *a few* to mean *a fairly large amount* or *number*.

> *We haven't seen her for **quite some time/quite a few days**.*

Each, every, neither and *either* are followed by a singular noun and a singular verb.

> ***Neither side is** prepared to give way on this issue.*

We can use *every* before nouns such as *chance, effort, intention, likelihood, reason, right, sign, success,* to emphasize what we are saying.

> *They had **every reason** to believe they would win.*

We use *for all* with a noun to mean *despite*.

> ***For all** the company's talk of equal opportunities, there are no women in management positions.*

Sometimes we can use two determiners before a noun. Note that we use *another* with *few* or numbers and a plural noun.

> *another few/five minutes   every other day   no more sweets*
> *all/both those books   many other countries   these few words*

Pronouns

We can use most of the above determiners on their own as pronouns.

> *'Do you want jam on your toast?' 'Just **a little**, please.'*

We cannot use *every* or *no* as pronouns or *other* with plural meaning: instead, we use *each, none* and *others*.

> *Don't look for problems where there are **none**.*
> *Here are just a few examples; there are **others**.*

We can use *other* as a singular pronoun after an article or determiner such as *no, any, each* or *one*.

> *Fold one arm over **the other**.   We love **each other**.*

We can use some other pronouns after determiners.

> *Try **another one**.   There's a **lot less** than before.*
> *Do you have **any others**?   Have a **few more**.*

Quantifiers

We can also use the pronouns as quantifiers:

*   before *of* + object pronoun.
    > *He ate **both of them**.   **None of us** knew the answer.*

*   before *of* + *the, this, that, these, those, my, your,* etc + noun.
    > ***Most of her friends** were there.*
    > *Do **any of these books** belong to you?*

Of is optional with *all* and *both* before a noun.

> *Where did you get **all (of) this money** from?*
> ***Both (of) my parents** are retired.*

Hypothetical present & future situations

(For past situations see page 54 in Unit 5.)

Conditional sentences

Second conditional sentences (*if* + past simple/continuous, *would/might/could* + infinitive) are used to talk and ask about imaginary, improbable or impossible situations in the present or future and their likely results.

> *How do you think he **might react if you told** him?*
> ***If it weren't for** her cats, she would be very lonely.*
> (= Thanks to her cats, she isn't lonely.)

Suppose/Supposing/Imagine are alternatives to *if*.

> ***Imagine you lost** your job. We'd have to sell the flat.*

To describe possible past consequences of a hypothetical present situation use *would/might/could* + perfect infinitive.

> ***If you weren't** so self-centred, **you might have noticed** how unhappy I was.*

Were to + *infinitive* makes the event seem more unlikely. Inversion is possible in formal contexts.

> ***If they were to win** the election, we might see some improvements in the economy.*
> ***Were he to accept** the job, he would become the youngest manager in the club's history.*

Wish/If only

Wish/If only + past simple can be used to express wishes about present states. Stative verbs such as *be, know, like* and *understand* are used.

> ***If only** Jilly **were** here – she'd know what to do.*
> *I **wish** I **didn't have to** go to work tomorrow.*

Wish/If only + *would* can be used to express what we want to happen now or in the future. Dynamic verbs (verbs describing actions) are used.

> *I **wish** you **wouldn't bite** your nails all the time.* (persistent habit)
> ***If only** he **would resign**!* (one occasion)

The past simple of dynamic verbs can also be used to express wishes about habits.

> *I **wish** she **didn't smoke** so much.*

If there is a real possibility that the action will happen, we use *hope* + a present or future tense.

> *I **hope** it doesn't rain this weekend.*

It is not possible to say '*I wish I would*'. Instead, '*I wish I could*' is used.

> *I **wish I could find** my glasses.*

Would rather/Sooner

Would rather/Sooner + past simple/ continuous can be used to express our preferences about other people's actions.

I'd rather you didn't wear that.

If the subject of *would rather/sooner* and the following verb is the same, the infinitive is used.

I'd sooner go hungry than eat that!

It's time

It's (high/about) time + past simple/ continuous can be used to talk about what we want to happen now. It implies that the action should have been done already.

It's time I was going.
It's high time you had your hair cut. *It's far too long.*

Use *it's time (for me/you, etc)* + infinitive with *to* to talk about the normal time something happens.

It's time for us to go now, but we'll be back next week for another edition of Sportsnews.

WORD LIST

Descriptive verbs

browse *v* *	/braʊz/
browse *n C*	/braʊz/
flash *v* **	/flæʃ/
float *v* **	/fləʊt/
flutter *v*	/ˈflʌtə(r)/
gaze *n C v* **	/geɪz/
glance *n C* **	/glɑːns/
glance *v* ***	/glɑːns/
shine *v* **	/ʃaɪn/
sparkle *v* *	/ˈspɑː(r)k(ə)l/
stare *n C*	/steə(r)/
stare *v* ***	/steə(r)/
toss *v* *	/tɒs/
twinkle *v*	/ˈtwɪŋk(ə)l/
view *n C v* ***	/vjuː/
wander *v* **	/ˈwɒndə(r)/

Prepositional phrases

at ease	/ˌæt, ət ˈiːz/
at fault	/ˌæt, ət ˈfɔːlt/
at gunpoint	/ˌæt, ət ˈgʌnˌpɔɪnt/
at leisure	/ˌæt, ət ˈleʒə(r)/
at stake	/ˌæt, ət ˈsteɪk/
by chance	/ˌbaɪ ˈtʃɑːns/
by mistake	/ˌbaɪ mɪˈsteɪk/
by nature	/ˌbaɪ ˈneɪtʃə(r)/
in arrears	/ˌɪn əˈrɪə(r)z/
in custody	/ˌɪn ˈkʌstədi/
in droves	/ˌɪn ˈdrəʊvz/
in person	/ˌɪn ˈpɜː(r)s(ə)n/
in retrospect	/ˌɪn ˈretrəʊˌspekt/
in stock	/ˌɪn ˈstɒk/
off balance	/ˌɒf ˈbæləns/
off course	/ˌɒf ˈkɔː(r)s/
off duty	/ˌɒf ˈdjuːti/
off limits	/ˌɒf ˈlɪmɪts/
off work	/ˌɒf ˈwɜː(r)k/
on bail	/ˌɒn ˈbeɪl/
on display	/ˌɒn dɪˈspleɪ/
on hold	/ˌɒn ˈhəʊld/
on leave	/ˌɒn ˈliːv/
on tiptoe	/ˌɒn ˈtɪptəʊ/
out of breath	/ˌaʊt əv ˈbreθ/
out of character	/ˌaʊt əv ˈkærɪktə(r)/
out of work	/ˌaʊt əv ˈwɜː(r)k/

Sounds

bang *v* *	/bæŋ/
beep *v*	/biːp/
bleep *v*	/bliːp/
buzz *v*	/bʌz/
chime *v*	/tʃaɪm/
clatter *v*	/ˈklætə(r)/
click *v* *	/klɪk/
clink *v*	/klɪŋk/
crack *n C* **	/kræk/
crash *v* **	/kræʃ/
creak *v*	/kriːk/
croak *n C*	/krəʊk/
hum *n C*	/hʌm/
jingle *v*	/ˈdʒɪŋg(ə)l/
plop *v*	/plɒp/
pop *v* **	/pɒp/
rattle *v*	/ˈræt(ə)l/
rumble *v*	/ˈrʌmb(ə)l/
rustle *v*	/ˈrʌs(ə)l/
scratch *n C* *	/skrætʃ/
screech *n C*	/skriːtʃ/
shatter *v* *	/ˈʃætə(r)/
sizzle *v*	/ˈsɪz(ə)l/
snap *v* **	/snæp/

Other words & phrases

at full blast	/ət ˌfʊl ˈblɑːst/
auction *n C* *	/ˈɔːkʃ(ə)n/
battered *adj* *	/ˈbætə(r)d/
bay *n C* **	/beɪ/
be made up of	/bi ˌmeɪd ˈʌp ɒv/
beat *n C* **	/biːt/
bid *v* **	/bɪd/
blare out *v*	/ˌbleə(r) ˈaʊt/
block (sth) out *v*	/ˌblɒk ˈaʊt/
catch (sb) out	/ˌkætʃ ˈaʊt/
cheery *adj*	/ˈtʃɪəri/
cheesy *adj*	/ˈtʃiːzi/
coil *n C* *	/kɔɪl/
daffodil *n C*	/ˈdæfədɪl/
dim *adj*	/dɪm/

disconcerting *adj*	/ˌdɪskən ˈsɜː(r)tɪŋ/
drive (sb) potty	/ˌdraɪv ˈpɒti/
emerging *adj*	/ɪˈmɜː(r)dʒɪŋ/
enhance *v* **	/ɪnˈhɑːns/
fan *n C* **	/fæn/
fluorescent *adj*	/flɔːˈres(ə)nt/
fuse *v* *	/fjuːz/
get into one's stride	/ˌget ɪntʊ wʌnz ˈstraɪd/
gift voucher *n C*	/ˈgɪft ˌvaʊtʃə(r)/
gloomy *adj* *	/ˈgluːmi/
have an eye for	/ˌhæv ən ˈaɪ fɔː(r)/
hoof *n C*	/huːf/
incongruously *adv*	/ɪnˈkɒŋgruəsli/
intimidating *adj*	/ɪnˈtɪmɪˌdeɪtɪŋ/
invariably *adv* *	/ɪnˈveəriəbli/
jagged *adj*	/ˈdʒægɪd/
let off steam	/ˌlet ɒf ˈstiːm/
margin *n C* **	/ˈmɑː(r)dʒɪn/
mast *n C*	/mɑːst/
menacing *adj*	/ˈmenəsɪŋ/
mingle *v*	/ˈmɪŋg(ə)l/
mount *v* **	/maʊnt/
odd *adj* **	/ɒd/
otherworldly *adj*	/ˌʌðə(r)ˈwɜː(r)ldli/
outdo *v*	/ˌaʊtˈduː/
padded *adj*	/ˈpædɪd/
pensive *adj*	/ˈpensɪv/
permeate *v*	/ˈpɜː(r)mieɪt/
pick up a bargain	/pɪk ˌʌp ə ˈbɑː(r)gɪn/
premises *n pl* **	/ˈpremɪsɪz/
prominent *adj* **	/ˈprɒmɪnənt/
quay *n C*	/kiː/
root canal treatment	/ˌruːt kəˌnæl ˈtriːtmənt/
set one's teeth on edge	/ˌset wʌnz ˈtiːθ ɒn ˌedʒ/
showcase *n C*	/ˈʃəʊˌkeɪs/
soundproof *v*	/ˈsaʊndˌpruːf/
spike *n C*	/spaɪk/
spring *n C* ***	/sprɪŋ/
sprinkle *v* *	/ˈsprɪŋk(ə)l/
squash *v*	/skwɒʃ/
stack *n C* *	/stæk/
stick out *v*	/ˌstɪk ˈaʊt/
take the plunge	/ˌteɪk ðə ˈplʌndʒ/
tap one's feet	/ˌtæp wʌnz ˈfiːt/
treadmill *n C*	/ˈtredˌmɪl/
turnover *n C* **	/ˈtɜː(r)nˌəʊvə(r)/
upshot *n*	/ˈʌpˌʃɒt/
upturned *adj*	/ʌpˈtɜː(r)nd/
warehouse *n C* **	/ˈweə(r)ˌhaʊs/
wedge *n C*	/wedʒ/
weigh in *v*	/ˈweɪ ˈɪn/
within the grasp of	/wɪˌðɪn ðə ˈgrɑːsp ɒv/
worthwhile *adj* **	/ˌwɜː(r)θˈwaɪl/

12A | Science fact

SPEAKING & LISTENING

1 Work in two groups, A and B.
Try to answer your group's
questions below.

Group A
1 Why is the sea salty?
2 Why does our mouth dry up
   when we are nervous?
3 Why do clothes look darker
   when they're wet?
4 What do seals drink?
5 What causes the sound
   of thunder?
6 Why are eggs egg-shaped?

Group B
1 Why is the sky blue?
2 Why don't we laugh when we
   tickle ourselves?
3 Why does a whip crack?
4 Why does a chip-pan fire explode
   if you put water on it?
5 Why do you sometimes get an
   electric shock when you touch a
   door handle?
6 Why do we close our eyes when
   we sneeze?

2 ⊙ **3.29–3.34** and ⊙ **3.35–3.40** Listen and make notes on the
answers to your questions.

3 Work with a student from the other group. Invite him/her to
answer each of your questions, then give the information which
you heard in the recording.

GRAMMAR: plurals & number

1 Underline the word in each group which is **not** a correct plural form.

fish   sheep   <u>cow</u>   deer

1 heroes   kiloes   echoes   tomatoes
2 spies   countries   monkies   berries
3 cliffs   handkerchiefs   roofs   shelfs
4 verses   horses   gooses   roses
5 sister-in-laws   down-and-outs   break-ins drive-throughs
6 analyses   theses   appendises   crises
7 nuclei   formuli   radii   cacti
8 criteria   memoranda   phenomena stimula

2 Check your ideas for exercise 1 in section A of the grammar box. Then work in pairs and justify your answers to your partner.

Some nouns require no changes or additions to form the plural. That's true of fish, sheep *and* deer, *but not* cow.

3 Choose the correct words to complete the sentences. More than one alternative may be possible.

My government <u>do</u> / <u>does</u> more to help the <u>rich</u> / riches than the <u>poor</u> / poors.

1 I remember the pyjamas I wore as a child – *it / they* had pictures of rabbits on *it / them*.
2 I received *a / some / many* good news recently – *it / they* made me feel very happy.
3 Mathematics *is / are / was / were* one of my least favourite subjects at school.
4 Our national media *is / are* generally biased in favour of the government.
5 The police in my country *is / are* very well paid.
6 My family *own / owns* a second home.
7 *This / These* school premises *is / are* very brightly decorated.
8 We get too *much / many* English *homework / homeworks* – 30 minutes *is / are* more than enough.

4 Check your ideas for exercise 3 in section B of the grammar box, then justify your answers to your partner.

5 Work in pairs. Discuss the sentences in exercise 3. Say how true each one is and give details.

A To make nouns plural:
* some require no changes or additions.
  aircraft, deer, fish, salmon, sheep, trout
* some have irregular forms.
  children, feet, geese, mice, teeth
* add *s* and/or *es* to nouns ending in *o*. Add *s* to abbreviated words.
  radios, photos, potatoes, dominoes, volcanoes/volcanos
* change *y* to *ies* except where the *y* is preceded by a vowel.
  flies, ladies, worries, days, donkeys, valleys
* change *f* or *fe* to *ves* in some cases: in others simply add *s*.
  halves, knives, loaves, shelves, chefs, safes
* add *s* to the first word of compound nouns formed with noun + preposition + noun.
  birds of prey, brothers-in-law, but *pin-ups, in-laws*
* use the original Latin or Greek form in some nouns borrowed from those languages.
  hypothesis → *hypotheses*   *fungus* → *fungi*
  curriculum → *curricula*   *automaton* → *automata*
  antenna → *antennae*   *matrix* → *matrices*

B Singular or plural?
Some nouns are always plural and take a plural verb form:
eg *pyjamas, tights, trousers, police, premises.*
  These trousers **are** too tight – I can't get **them** on.
Some nouns ending in *s* are uncountable and therefore take a singular verb form: eg *athletics, economics, mathematics, news.*
  *The athletics **is** on TV tonight – are you going to watch **it**?*
Many collective nouns can take either a singular or a plural verb form: *crew, family, government, media, press, team.*
  *The local press **has/have** been invited to the opening.*
Plural expressions of time, measurement and money are often considered as single items.
  *Three weeks **is** too long to wait.*
Some adjectives can be used as plural nouns to talk about groups of people: eg *the homeless, the blind, the deaf, the rich, the poor.*
  *The city's homeless **receive** free medical care.*

❯ SEE LANGUAGE REFERENCE PAGE 124

DID YOU KNOW?

1 Work in pairs. Read about science in UK schools and discuss the questions.

Until recently, great concern was being expressed in the UK at the lack of interest in science in schools. Despite an overall increase in A-Level entries, the number of 16–18-year-old students studying science and maths fell by as much as 35% over a fifteen-year period in the case of physics. Consequently, science graduates, teachers and research scientists have all been in shorter supply. Government initiatives and programmes such as the *Stimulating Physics Network* from the Institute of Physics have helped to reverse the trend and the uptake for science and maths at A-Level is now back on the increase.

* How popular are science and maths subjects in schools in your country?
* How interested in science are you? Why?

12B | Science fiction

SPEAKING

1 Work in pairs. Draw an object or being that you might expect to find in a science fiction novel. Do not show your picture to your partner.

2 Describe your picture in detail to your partner. He or she will draw your object or being according to your description.

3 Compare the two pictures to see how alike they are. Do you think such beings or objects actually exist?

READING

1 Read the extract from a science fiction short story and choose one word from the box to replace XXX.

> spaceship   robot   suit   alien   helmet   buggy

2 Check your answer in the extract on page 144.

3 Read the extract again and decide whether the sentences are true (T) or false (F). Explain with reference to the text why the false sentences are incorrect.

1 The narrator has just suffered an attack.
2 He rests at night because it is too dark to see.
3 The base is a thousand kilometres away.
4 The narrator says that the XXX's intelligence has its disadvantages.
5 He thinks the XXX probably saved his life.
6 The planet's surface is entirely flat.
7 He says he may have to abandon the XXX.
8 It is a source of some relief to him that the planet may be uninhabited.

4 Work in groups, A and B. With another student from your group you are going to write a short dialogue between a human being and a smart object.

Group A: Turn to page 154.
Group B: Turn to page 144.

5 Read out your dialogue to a pair of students from the other group. They should try to guess the identity of your smart object.

VOCABULARY: words with more than one meaning

1 Complete the sentences from the extracts. Use the same word for both sentences, a and b. You may need to change the form of the word.

1 a) 'How far do you think we'll _get_ today?'
   b) Whatever _got_ us must have been very small.
2 a) 'How far did we _____ yesterday?'
   b) This is what _____ of having a smart suit.
3 a) It is _____ mostly on external power.
   b) It was a close _____ thing even as it was.
4 a) Thirty-five klicks. I haven't _____ a tenth of that yet.
   b) A standard suit might have _____ almost as well.
5 a) I'll just have to keep going. I'd be _____ the suit down.
   b) There was every chance that I would never get this far, even as a cinder, _____ alone whole.
6 a) I suspect it … knows things are worse than it's _____ me.
   b) Sometimes we see a stain on a rock that might be plant life, but I can't _____.
7 a) It walked all that long _____ yesterday.
   b) I am injured, but so is the suit, which is worse in some _____.
8 a) The suit walked all of that, carrying me like a _____ weight.
   b) … mumbling about walking in a dream and being the living _____.

Check your answers in the extracts.

2 Work in pairs. For exercise 1, discuss the meaning of each word in both sentences, either on its own or together with the words in bold.

1a) *progress*; 1b) *attack*

3 Choose five words from different reading texts in Units 1–11 of this Student's Book. Write two gapped sentences for each, as in exercise 1. The first sentence should be copied from the text; the second should be your own and show a different use or meaning for the target word.

Unit 1 page 7
The Romanov Bride *is a _____ and emotional journey through one of the most turbulent times in Russian history.*
Her hands _____ the edge of the seat anxiously.
Answer: *gripping, gripped*

4 Show your sentences to your partner, who will try to complete the gaps.

I don't know what happened, which is annoying, though it wouldn't make any difference if I did know. It wouldn't have made any difference when it happened either, because there was no time for me to do anything. It was a
5 surprise: an ambush.

Whatever got us must have been very small or very far away, otherwise we wouldn't be here, still alive. If the module had taken any standard-sized warhead full on there would be only radiation and atoms left; probably
10 not an intact molecule. Even a near miss would have left nothing recognizable to the unaided human eye. Only something tiny – perhaps not a warhead at all but just something moving fast – or a more distant miss, would leave wreckage.

15 I must remember that, hold on to that. However bad I may feel, I am still alive, when there was every chance that I would never get this far, even as a cinder, let alone whole and thinking and still able to walk.

But damaged. Both of us are damaged. I am injured, but
20 so is the **XXX**, which is worse in some ways. It is running mostly on external power, soaking up the weak sunlight as best it can, but so inefficiently that it has to rest at night, when both of us have to sleep. Its communications and AG are wrecked, and the recycle and medical units are
25 badly damaged too. All that and a tiny leak we can't find. I'm frightened.

It says I have internal bruising and I shouldn't be walking, but we talked it over and agreed that our only hope is to walk, to head in roughly the right direction and hope
30 we're seen by the base we were heading for originally, in the module. The base is a thousand kilometres south of the northern ice cap. We came down north of the equator, but just how far north, we don't know. It's going to be a long walk, for both of us.

35 'How do you feel now?'

'Fine,' the **XXX** replies.'

'How far do you think we'll get today?'

'Maybe twenty kilometres.'

'That's not very much.'

40 'You're not very well. We'll do better once you heal. You were quite ill.'

Quite ill. There are still some little bits of sickness and patches of dried blood within the helmet, where I can see

them. They don't smell any more, but they don't look very
45 pleasant either. I'll try cleaning them up again tonight.

I am worried that, apart from anything else, the **XXX** isn't being completely honest with me. It says it thinks our chances are fifty-fifty, but I suspect it either doesn't have any idea at all, or knows things are worse than it's telling
50 me. This is what comes of having a smart **XXX**. But I asked for one; it was my choice, so I can't complain. Besides, I might have died if the **XXX** hadn't been as bright as it is. It got the two of us down here, out of the wrecked module and down through the thin atmosphere while I was still
55 unconscious from the explosion. A standard **XXX** might have done almost as well, but that probably wouldn't have been enough; it was a close run thing even as it was.

My legs hurt. The ground is fairly level, but occasionally I have to negotiate small ridges and areas of corrugated
60 ground. My feet are sore too, but the pain in my legs worries me more. I don't know if I'll be able to keep going all day, which is what the **XXX** expects.

'How far did we come yesterday?'

'Thirty-five kilometres.'

65 The **XXX** walked all of that, carrying me like a dead weight. It got up and walked, clasping me inside it so I wouldn't bump around, and marched off, the wispy remains of its crippled emergency photopanels dragging over the dusty ground behind it like the wings of some
70 strange, damaged insect.

Thirty-five klicks. I haven't done a tenth of that yet. I'll just have to keep going. I can't disappoint it. I'd be letting the **XXX** down. It has done so well to get us here in one piece, and it walked all that long way yesterday,
75 supporting me while I was still rolling my eyes and drooling, mumbling about walking in a dream and being the living dead … so I can't let it down. If I fail I harm us both, lessening the **XXX**'s chances of survival too.

The slope goes on. The ground is boringly uniform, always
80 the same rusty brown. It frightens me that there is so little variety, so little sign of life. Sometimes we see a stain on a rock that might be plant life, but I can't tell, and the **XXX** doesn't know, because most of its external eyes and tactiles were burned out in the fall. Maybe we are the
85 only life here, maybe there's nothing living or thinking for thousands and thousands of kilometres. The thought appals me.

Glossary
drool *v* let saliva (the liquid in your
    mouth) come out of your mouth

12c | Sport technology

LISTENING

1 Work in pairs. Discuss the different ways in which technology may influence the following sports.

> golf   athletics   cycling   swimming
> tennis   skating   football   hockey

I'm fairly sure technology has influenced the design of golf clubs and golf balls. The first clubs were wooden, but now they're made of graphite or something. And golf balls used to be made of leather, didn't they? Now, …

2 You are going to listen to a radio discussion on technology in sport.

🔘 **3.41** Listen to Part 1 of the recording and answer these questions.

1 Which of the sports in exercise 1 does the presenter mention?
2 What technological developments does he describe for each one?

3 🔘 **3.42** Listen to Part 2 and answer the question.

• What are the three main arguments put forward by each guest in support of their views?

4 🔘 **3.43** Listen to Part 3 and decide if the following statements are true (T) or false (F). Say why the false statements are incorrect.

1 Geoff thinks the use of technology for refereeing decisions adds to the excitement of sport.
2 Sally enjoys the speed at which tennis is played nowadays.
3 Geoff says that certain banned practices should be made legal.
4 He feels that there are adequate restrictions on the use of technology in sport.

5 Work in pairs. Discuss this question.

• Which of the two guests do you agree with most and why?

PRONUNCIATION: intonation (feelings)

1 Work in pairs. Read out the following exchange in the manner indicated in brackets.

Sally: *(Heavily sarcastic)* Oh right. So presumably then, doping is acceptable, as long as everyone has access to it. That's brilliant.

Geoff: *(Indignant)* I'm not suggesting that at all. That should be obvious.

🔘 **3.44** Listen to the recording, paying particular attention to the intonation of the speakers. Then read out the exchange again.

2 🔘 **3.45** Read and listen to these exchanges and match the feelings in the box to the speakers. More than one answer may be possible.

> admiration   curiosity   enthusiasm
> indifference   irritation   reassurance
> sarcasm   surprise   suspicion   worry

1 **A:** Oh, I wonder what that noise is.
  B: Oh, that always happens when you turn it on.

2 **A:** Oh, isn't he a talented cyclist?
  B: Oh, yeah. I mean, no one else could pedal like that, could they?

3 **A:** Oh, I wonder if he works with computers for a living.
  B: Oh, I don't know. Ask him if you want to.

4 **A:** Oh, are you coming with us as well?
  B: Oh, yeah, I thought I'd tag along – see what was going on.

5 **A:** Oh, yeah, John's going to be there, too.
  B: Oh, yes, I heard that, too. That's interesting.

3 Practise reading the exchanges with your partner. Use the same intonation to express the same feelings that you heard in the recording.

4 Read the exchanges again, this time expressing different feelings from the box.

SPEAKING

1 Work in two groups, A and B. You are going to discuss this statement with the other group.

There is too much technology in the home.

Group A: You agree with the statement.
Group B: You disagree with the statement.

In your group, brainstorm and note down as many different arguments as possible to support your opinion.

2 Select the three most convincing arguments from exercise 1 and choose a representative from your group. He or she has one minute to put forward these arguments to the other group.

3 All group members may now discuss the statement in exercise 1, expanding on the points your representative made. You should offer further arguments and examples, as well as counter arguments.

Useful language

Introducing arguments
Firstly … Secondly … And finally …
The main/Another argument in favour of/ against having technology in the home …
Obviously/Clearly/Naturally/Unfortunately/ Worryingly/Regrettably/Worse still …
Referring to arguments
I'd like to pick up on the point you made about …
Let's go back to what you said about …
Regarding your comment about …
You mentioned earlier …
Introducing examples
(Let's) take, for instance, the use of …
A good/perfect example of this is …
That's particularly true of …

VOCABULARY: verb affixes

1 Complete the sentences with the correct form of the word in brackets. Check your answers in audioscripts 3.42–3.43 on pages 162–163.

Technology has revolutionized (revolution) sport.

1 It _____ (able) athletes to improve their performance.
2 It helps to _____ (maximum) safety.
3 Technology _____ (sure) a greater degree of fairness.
4 Technology has come to _____ (dominant) sport.
5 We see them using technologies which _____ (danger) health.
6 The technology only serves to _____ (high) interest, to _____ (intense) the drama.
7 Tennis no longer _____ (captive) spectators like it used to.
8 There is no way we can _____ (just) the use of performance-enhancing drugs.
9 You did use the word *equipment*, perhaps we should _____ (emphasis) that.
10 Its use has to be _____ (standard) by the sporting authority.

2 Use the same affixes as those in exercise 1 to form verbs from the following groups of words. Some words require further spelling changes.

1 category	summary	stable
2 class	identity	example
3 large	courage	rage
4 assassin	difference	value
5 threat	flat	long

Verbs can also be formed using particles, as in these examples from the listening.
*The effects of technology in sport cannot be **understated**.*
*[Technology] **overshadows** human achievement.*

---

3 Choose the correct word to complete the sentences.

1 I regularly *download / downplay* music from the internet.
2 I never *overuse / overstretch* myself at school or work – I only ever do the bare minimum.
3 Our national football team is usually *outclassed / outlasted* by the opposition.
4 I never tell the shop assistant if I realize I've been *underfunded / undercharged*.
5 My great grandmother *outlived / outnumbered* my great grandfather – he passed away first.
6 I'm not the sort of person to be *overtaken / overcome* by emotion.
7 I've never had to *undercut / undergo* surgery.
8 The advantages of nuclear power *outweigh / outgrow* the disadvantages.

4 Work in pairs. Tell your partner how true the statements and opinions in exercise 3 are for you.

12D | The end?

Revision

Units 1–3

VOCABULARY

1 Complete the sentences with the correct word, A, B, C or D.

1 She found it difficult to _____ to married life.
   A vary   B transform   C alter   D adapt
2 He looks middle-aged but he's only just _____ 30.
   A turned   B gone   C taken   D had
3 I have a very _____ memory for facts and figures.
   A rich   B hard   C poor   D soft
4 The four _____ in the pack are hearts, clubs, diamonds and spades.
   A suits   B patterns   C colours   D designs
5 She went _____ her way to help me.
   A from   B out of   C around   D off
6 During the war, fresh fruit was in _____ supply.
   A lacking   B short   C failed   D unavailable
7 They live next door to the local rubbish _____.
   A scrap   B bank   C pile   D tip
8 Sure, animals have rights, but these activists take it to _____.
   A the top   B overkill   C extremes   D excess

2 Check your answers in Units 1–3.

GRAMMAR

1 Choose the correct words to complete the sentences.

1 We've *finished / been finishing* two sections of this revision page; now we *work / 're working* on the third.
2 **A:** Did she get to the station on time?
   B: I think *yes / did / so* – if *no / not / didn't* she'd have phoned by now.
3 He says he's had difficulty *finding / to find* a job, but I actually think he enjoys *being / to be* unemployed and he's given up *looking / to look*.
4 I regret *informing / to inform* you that your application has been rejected.
5 You sound just *as / like* your mother.
6 The *older / oldest* I get, the *less / least* I seem to know.
7 It wasn't until I got home *when / that* I realized what had happened.
8 All he ever does is *play / playing* computer games.

2 Check your answers on pages 9, 16 and 23.

WORD BUILDING

1 Complete the sentences with the correct form of the word in brackets.

1 I have a high level of _____ (*fluent*) and _____ (*accurate*) in both spoken and written English.
2 I have feelings of _____ (*sad*) and _____ (*disappoint*) that this course is coming to an end.
3 I am familiar with the emergency _____ (*proceed*) in this building.
4 I don't think I could write a book – I'm not creative or _____ (*imagine*) enough.
5 I'm a clean-living person with no _____ (*harm*) vices.
6 I enjoy _____ (*expect*) surprises – they add spice to life!

2 Check your answers on pages 13 and 33.

3 Work in pairs. Discuss how true the statements in exercise 1 are for you.

DID YOU KNOW?

1 How well do you remember what you learnt in the *Did you know?* sections? Answer the following.

1 Name a charity which represents the interests of elderly people in the UK.
2 Which British admiral stands at the top of a column in Trafalgar Square, London?
3 Who or what is *Alison Lapper Pregnant*?
4 Which was the first country to introduce a tax on plastic shopping bags?
5 What is the name of the tax in number 4 above?

2 Check your answers on pages 13, 23 and 29.

Units 4–12

1 Work in three groups, A, B and C. You are going to write your own revision questions. Each group will focus on the following units: Group A: Units 4–6; Group B: Units 7–9; Group C: Units 10–12. Write a total of twelve revision questions, with at least two questions for each section: *Vocabulary, Grammar, Word building* and *Did you know?*

2 Work in new groups with one student from each of Groups A, B and C. Ask your questions to each of the other two students in turn. A correct answer scores two points. If a student cannot answer, or gives an incorrect answer to a question, offer it to the other student for one point. The winner is the student with the most points after all students have asked their questions.

SPEAKING

1 Work in small groups. You are a team of photo editors who have been asked to choose photos to illustrate the final page of this Student's Book.

Discuss the suitability of each of the photos shown, then agree on two that you wish to include. At least one of the photos should be from this selection: if you cannot agree on a second, you may write a brief description outlining your requirements.

Explain your choices to the rest of the class.

2 Discuss the questions in your groups.

- What aspects of your English do you think you have developed most during this course?
- Do you intend to take further English study courses? Give reasons/details.
- What do you plan to do outside of the classroom to improve your language skills?

GRAMMAR
Plurals & number

A Plural forms

Some nouns, particularly those referring to animals or fish, have the same form for both singular and plural. They include:

Animals: *bison, deer, moose, reindeer, sheep*
Fish: *cod, (shell)fish*, mackerel, salmon, squid, trout*
Others: *aircraft, means, offspring, series, species.*
*The form *fishes* exists but is not common.

The following nouns have special plural forms:

child/children, foot/feet, goose/geese, man/men, mouse/mice, ox/oxen, tooth/teeth, woman/women.

Nouns ending in *-ch, -sh, -s* or *-z* form their plural by adding *-es*:

churches, dishes, buses, quizzes.

Nouns ending in *o* form their plural by adding *s* or *es*. Sometimes either form is used. Examples include:

Add s: *pianos, radios, solos, sopranos, studios, zoos*
Add es: *dominoes, echoes, heroes, potatoes, tomatoes, torpedoes, vetoes*
Add s or es: *ghettos/es, halos/es, mosquitos/es, tornados/es, volcanos/es.*

Plurals of abbreviated words are usually written with *s*:

autos, kilos, memos, photos, videos.

Nouns ending in *y* form their plural with *ies* except where the *y* is preceded by a vowel,

so *flies, spies, babies, berries, countries, ladies, worries*
but *boys, days, guys, donkeys, monkeys, trolleys, valleys.*

Several nouns substitute *ves* for *f* or *fe* to form their plurals:

shelf/shelves, life/lives.

Other words which behave in this way include:

calf, half, knife, leaf, loaf, scarf*, self, thief, wife, wolf.

Nouns ending in *fs* or *fes* in the plural include:

chefs, cliffs, cuffs, handkerchiefs*, hoofs*, roofs*, safes.
*The forms *scarfs, handkerchieves, hooves, rooves* are also possible.

Most compound nouns have plurals formed by adding *s* to the end of the last word:

check-ups, down-and-outs, in-laws, play-offs, pencil sharpeners.

In compound nouns formed with verb + *er* and an adverb, the first word is made plural:

hangers-on, lookers-on, passers-by, runners-up.

Compounds composed of noun + preposition + noun behave in the same way:

daughters-in-law, holes-in-one, heads of state, Members of Parliament, works of art.

Some words of Latin and Greek origin retain their original plural form. Examples include:

crisis/crises, diagnosis/diagnoses, emphasis/emphases, antenna/antennae, formula/formulae, larva/larvae, cactus/cacti, stimulus/stimuli, syllabus/syllabi, automaton/automata, criterion/criteria, phenomenon/ phenomena, erratum/errata, medium/media, stadium/stadia.

The English *s* or *es* plural is also possible in some cases, particularly in less formal or non-technical contexts:

antennas, cactuses, formulas, stadiums, syllabuses.

B Number

Some nouns which refer to single items are always plural and take a plural verb form. This applies to clothes and tools made up of two parts:

Clothes: *jeans, pants, pyjamas, shorts, tights, trousers*
Tools: *nail clippers, pliers, scissors, tweezers.*
> My trousers **have** got a hole in **them** and **they're** the only clean pair I've got.

Other nouns which are always plural include: *belongings, earnings, goods, outskirts, premises, savings* as well as *police* and *people*.
> Police **have arrested** two people who **are thought** to have taken part in the robbery.

Some words, like *news*, look plural but are actually uncountable nouns which take a singular verb form. Other examples include:

Sports: *aerobics, athletics, gymnastics*
Academic disciplines: *economics, genetics, mechanics, linguistics, mathematics, physics, politics*
Illnesses: *diabetes, measles, mumps, rabies.*

When the use of the word is different to that of the above categories, a plural verb form may be used:

Academic discipline
*Economics just **sends** me to sleep – **it's** so boring.*

Financial system
*The economics of the business **are** not easy to explain.*

Many collective nouns referring to groups can be either singular or plural. These include:

audience, band, cast, committee, crew, family, government, media, press, team (and names of teams).
> United **has/have** lost **its/their** last six games.

When referring to time, money and measurement, expressions of quantity often take a singular verb form, even if the noun is plural.

*Ten years **isn't** enough – he should have been given a life sentence.*

*Fifty pounds **was** a lot of money in those days.*

*Four miles **is** about six kilometres, isn't it?*

A limited number of adjectives can be used with the definite article to talk about groups of people. No plural s or es is added, but a plural verb form is used. They include: *the blind, the deaf, the old, the elderly, the young, the rich, the poor, the sick, the wounded, the dead, the homeless, the unemployed.*

The sick were *the first to be evacuated, followed by **the elderly** and **the very young.***

WORD LIST

Verb affixes

able *adj* ***	/'eɪb(ə)l/
enable *v* ***	/ɪn'eɪb(ə)l/
assassin *n C*	/ə'sæsɪn/
assassinate *v*	/ə'sæsɪneɪt/
class *n C* ***	/klɑːs/
classify *v* **	/'klæsɪfaɪ/
revolution *n C* ***	/ˌrevə'luːʃ(ə)n/
revolutionize *v*	/ˌrevə'luːʃəˌnaɪz/
threat *n C* ***	/θret/
threaten *v* ***	/'θret(ə)n/
download *v*	/ˌdaʊn'ləʊd/
downplay *v*	/ˌdaʊn'pleɪ/
outclass *v*	/ˌaʊt'klɑːs/
outlast *v*	/ˌaʊt'lɑːst/
outlive *v*	/ˌaʊt'lɪv/
outnumber *v*	/ˌaʊt'nʌmbə(r)/
overcome *v* **	/ˌəʊvə(r)'kʌm/
overshadow *v*	/ˌəʊvə(r)'ʃædəʊ/
overstretch *v*	/ˌəʊvə(r)'stretʃ/
overtake *v* *	/ˌəʊvə(r)'teɪk/
overuse *v*	/ˌəʊvə(r)'juːz/
undercharge *v*	/ˌʌndə(r)'tʃɑː(r)dʒ/
undercut *v*	/ˌʌndə(r)'kʌt/
underfund *v*	/ˌʌndə(r)'fʌnd/
undergo *v* **	/ˌʌndə(r)'gəʊ/
understate *v*	/ˌʌndə(r)'steɪt/

Other words & phrases

a close run thing	/ə ˌkləʊs ˌrʌn 'θɪŋ/
ambush *n C*	/'æmbʊʃ/
atom *n C* **	/'ætəm/
be down to	/ˌbiː 'daʊn tuː, tʊ/
bend the rules	/ˌbend ðə 'ruːlz/
bolt of lightning *n C*	/ˌbəʊlt əv 'laɪtnɪŋ/
buoyancy *n U*	/'bɔɪənsi/
cinder *n C*	/'sɪndə(r)/
clap of thunder *n C*	/'klæp əv ˌθʌndə(r)/
clasp *v* *	/klɑːsp/
corrugated *adj*	/'kɒrəˌgeɪtɪd/
crippled *adj*	/'krɪp(ə)ld/
cylindrical *adj*	/sɪ'lɪndrɪk(ə)l/
dead weight *n C*	/ˌded 'weɪt/
digestive system *n C*	/daɪ'dʒestɪv ˌsɪst(ə)m/
diminish *v* **	/dɪ'mɪnɪʃ/
discharge *n C* **	/'dɪstʃɑː(r)dʒ/
doorknob *n C*	/'dɔː(r)nɒb/
drool *v*	/druːl/
droplet *n C*	/'drɒplət/
dusty *adj* *	/'dʌsti/
fiery *adj*	/'faɪri/
fireball *n C*	/'faɪə(r)ˌbɔːl/
freelance *adj*	/'friːlɑːns/
grace *v*	/greɪs/
graphite *n U*	/'græfaɪt/
head for *v*	/'hed ˌfɔː(r)/
headgear *n U*	/'hedˌgɪə(r)/
heart rate *n C*	/'hɑː(r)t ˌreɪt/
ice cap *n C*	/'aɪs ˌkæp/
intake *n sing* *	/'ɪnˌteɪk/
internal bruising *n U*	/ɪnˌtɜː(r)n(ə)l 'bruːzɪŋ/
leak *n C* *	/liːk/
lessen *v*	/'les(ə)n/
let alone	/ˌlet ə'ləʊn/
let (sb) down	/ˌlet 'daʊn/
line call *n C*	/'laɪn ˌkɔːl/
loop *n C* *	/luːp/
lung *n C* **	/lʌŋ/
module *n C* ***	/'mɒdjuːl/
molecule *n C* **	/'mɒlɪˌkjuːl/
molten *adj*	/'məʊltən/
mumble *v* *	/'mʌmb(ə)l/
near miss *n C*	/ˌnɪə(r) 'mɪs/
negotiate *v*	/nɪ'gəʊʃieɪt/
octopus *n C*	/'ɒktəpəs/
ovoid *adj*	/'əʊvɔɪd/
pole vault *n sing*	/'pəʊl ˌvɔːlt/
porous *adj*	/'pɔːrəs/
radiation *n U* **	/ˌreɪdi'eɪʃ(ə)n/
rally *n C* **	/'ræli/

refract *v*	/rɪ'frækt/
replenishment *n U*	/rɪ'plenɪʃm(ə)nt/
ridge *n C* **	/rɪdʒ/
rusty *adj* *	/'rʌsti/
scalding *n U*	/'skɔːldɪŋ/
scatter *v* **	/'skætə(r)/
seal *n C* **	/siːl/
soak (sth) up *v*	/ˌsəʊk 'ʌp/
spark *n C*	/spɑː(r)k/
spherical *adj*	/'sferɪk(ə)l/
spring *n C* ***	/sprɪŋ/
squid *n C*	/skwɪd/
surpass *v*	/sə(r)'pɑːs/
tag along *v*	/ˌtæg ə'lɒŋ/
tag *v*	/tæg/
thigh *n C* **	/θaɪ/
tickle *v*	/'tɪk(ə)l/
ticklish *adj*	/'tɪk(ə)lɪʃ/
umpire *n C*	/'ʌmpaɪə(r)/
unease *n U*	/ʌn'iːz/
warhead *n C*	/'wɔː(r)ˌhed/
whip *n C* *	/wɪp/
wreck *v* *	/rek/
wreckage *n U* *	/'rekɪdʒ/
young *n pl*	/jʌŋ/

1 | Writing An autobiography

SPEAKING

1 Draw a line to represent your life, from birth to the present. Note on the line any significant events or turning points, eg

- starting school or university.
- a birth or major event.
- moving home.
- the start or end of a relationship.
- starting a new job or activity.
- a change of direction or outlook.

Continue the line into the future with plans, hopes or predictions about your life.

2 Work in pairs. Compare your lifelines and find out about some of the significant events in your partner's life.

READING

1 Read Murat's autobiography. What are the similarities and differences with your life?

2 Complete the following events in order on Murat's lifeline. Which do you think have been the happiest and unhappiest times in his life?

- working as a plumber
- did military service
- got married
- looked after by maternal grandmother
- met his wife
- set up travel agency
- moved to Scotland
- worked as a tour guide
- retrained as a plumber
- sent away to attend secondary school
- studied English at university
- won the school prize for English

I was born on March 31ˢᵗ 1985 in a small mountain village in the south-west of Turkey. I was the youngest of four siblings and part of a large extended family. My parents both worked long hours in the village store, and up to the age of five I was looked after by my
5 maternal grandmother, to whom I was very close. I went to the local primary school, and when I look back on my childhood I remember it as a happy, if largely uneventful, period.

However, all this ended abruptly when at the age of twelve I was sent away to attend secondary school in Izmir, a large coastal town, where
10 I lodged with an aunt. At first I loathed it and was terribly homesick, and used to weep bitterly every night. As time went on, however, I slowly started to make friends and even enjoy school life. It was during this period that I developed an interest in languages, and in my final year I won the school prize for English, which in retrospect
15 was probably the highlight of my school career.

After leaving school I did military service and then got a place to study English at university, financing my studies by working in a restaurant in the evenings. On graduating I worked as a tour guide, taking groups of tourists round the country's important archaeological
20 sites. While I was working on one of these trips I met Sarah, a history student from Scotland. We kept in touch afterwards, and, to cut a long story short, got married two years later and came over to Scotland to settle in Aberdeen.

Since my arrival I have retrained as a plumber and am currently
25 running my own business to support my wife and two young children. However, our long-term plan is to set up our own travel agency to take British tourists round Turkey, and I hope that in five years' time I may have achieved this ambition.

Murat's lifeline

Pre-school years	School days	After school	After university	Present	Future
1 _looked after by maternal grandmother_	2 _____ 3 _won the school prize for English_	4 _____ 5 _____	6 _____ 7 _met his wife_ 8 _____ 9 _____ 10 _____	11 _____	12 _____

3 Read the autobiography again and underline the different time expressions.

LANGUAGE FOCUS

Using time expressions

1 When describing your life you could use the following time expressions. Put them in the appropriate column for you.

at present	in six months' time	for the last five years
in those days	during my adolescence	to date
next year	currently	some day
so far	at the moment	three years later
ever since	as a child	at the age of ten

Past	Present perfect	Present	Future
I lived/I was living/I used to live	*I have met/ I have been living*	*I am living/ I like*	*I hope/plan to go, I will be living*

2 Choose an expression from each column in exercise 1 and write a true sentence about yourself.

Describing your family

3 Say whether both alternatives in italics are possible, or only one. If both are possible, explain the difference.

1 I am *an only child / a single child*.
2 There are four *members / people* in my family.
3 My *oldest / eldest* brother is doing military service.
4 My sister is three years *older / elder* than me.
5 I have three *brothers / siblings*.
6 I was *brought up / educated* by my grandmother.
7 When my father remarried, I gained two *half-sisters / step-sisters*.
8 I had a *lenient / strict* upbringing.
9 We are a *closely-linked / close-knit* family.
10 On the whole, I *spent / had* a happy childhood.

Verb-noun collocations

4 Match the verbs and nouns to make collocations.

A	B
take	school
train as	research
get	a gap year
go to	a nurse
do	a place at university
graduate from	a scholarship
leave	a solicitor
do	school
qualify as	university
apply for	a degree

5 Write four sentences about yourself using a verb-noun collocation and a suitable time expression.

WRITING

1 Choose different events or periods from your lifeline and arrange them into three or four paragraphs. Include your current situation, and future plans or hopes.

Next to each event or period, write a time expression and some more information, as in the example.

Moved to secondary school, loathed it, wept bitterly – at the age of twelve
Made friends – as time went on
Won the school prize (highlight) – in my final year

2 Work in pairs and explain the events in your plan.

3 Write your autobiography following the notes in your plan.

Useful language

In retrospect, …
Looking back, …
I remember X as …
X marked a major turning point for me …
X was the highlight of (my school days, my trip, etc) …
To cut a long story short …

REMEMBER TO …

- organize your writing into clear paragraphs.
- use time expressions to describe different periods of your life.
- give details of significant events and periods.
- use language from the units to describe family and education.
- check your writing for correct use of tenses.

2 | Writing An article

SPEAKING

1 Which of the statements best describes your attitude to sending text messages? Why?

- I couldn't manage without texting my friends.
- I like to keep in touch with people by sending text messages.
- I occasionally send texts for the sake of convenience.
- I am not sure how to use my text messaging service.
- I prefer not to send text messages.

Work in pairs. What possible problems could arise from texting too much?

2 A teenage girl got into trouble with her teacher for writing an essay in text language. Can you understand it?

> my smmr hols wr CWOT. B4,
> we used 2go2 NY 2C my bro,
> his GF &thr 3 :-@ kids FTF.
> ILNY, it's a gr8 plc

Do you know any other examples of text language?

READING

1 Read the article and match the headings 1–3 to the paragraphs A–C.

1 Suggesting strategies for change
2 Engaging the reader
3 Defining the addiction and explaining the symptoms and causes

ARE YOU A TEXTAHOLIC?

A Do you spend over an hour each day texting your friends? Do you frequently neglect work, study and leisure activities to check your phone for text messages? Are you moody and irritable if you are separated from your mobile phone? Do you hardly ever
5 use your phone to talk any more, and do your thumbs hurt from texting too much?

B If you answered 'Yes' to any of the above questions, then the chances are that you are a textaholic. A textaholic can be defined as someone who is addicted to sending and receiving text
10 messages. The main symptoms are a compulsion to text which takes precedence over everything else, and withdrawal symptoms if messages fail to come in, leading to agitation, depression and a lack of self-esteem. Other problems include insomnia, eye strain and repetitive strain injury due to constant messaging, not to
15 mention spiralling phone bills. The root of the problem, as with many addictions, is the desire to escape from emotional difficulties such as stress, anxiety and relationship problems. Experts warn that text addiction is likely to become the most common form of addiction in the future, especially among the young.

20 **C** So what can you do if you think you may be a textaholic? The key is to get your life back in balance. Make sure you resist the urge to answer every message you receive and consider leaving your mobile phone behind occasionally when you go out. Most importantly, make a point of spending quality time with friends
25 and family, and make time to re-learn the art of face-to-face conversation instead of conducting your relationships by means of text messages. Not only will you save time and money, but you may also rediscover the pleasure of true communication.

2 Decide whether these facts about textaholics are given (*G*) or not given (*NG*) in the article.

1 They prioritize sending and receiving texts over other activities.
2 They may find it difficult to sleep.
3 They lose the ability to relate to other people.
4 They may suffer from physical symptoms.
5 They tend to run up debts on their mobile phones.
6 They tend to feel miserable if they do not receive text messages.
7 Text addiction is the most prevalent form of addiction among teenagers.
8 The underlying causes of text addiction are psychological.

3 Do you agree that text addiction is a growing problem? What do you think about the advice given in paragraph C?

LANGUAGE FOCUS

Writing definitions

> A textaholic is/can be defined as …
>
> | someone | who is dependent on sending and receiving texts. |
> |---|---|
> | a person | whose compulsion to text takes precedence over face-to-face communication. |

1 Write definitions for the words and phrases 1–4, using the language in the box.

> is dependent on …
> can't live without …
> is addicted to …
> suffers from a compulsion to …
> has a craving for …
> is obsessed with …
> can't resist the urge to …
> suffers from withdrawal symptoms if …

1 a shopaholic
2 a coffee addict
3 a chocoholic
4 an email addict

Making a deduction

2 Choose one of the nouns 1–4 from exercise 1 to complete the sentences a–d. Then complete e–g with your own ideas, using one of the expressions in italics in a–d.

a Do you find yourself checking your emails at least ten times a day? *If so, then the chances are that you are …*

b Do you regularly run up debts on shopping sprees? *If the answer is yes, you could be …*

c Can you manage without a regular injection of caffeine? *If not, then you may well be …*

d Do you find it hard to resist eating a box of chocolates in one go? *If you do, then you are certainly …*

e Do you make a point of buying a lottery ticket every week? …

f Do you spend an hour every night reading your English dictionary before you go to sleep? …

g Is a burger, fries and a cola your idea of a perfect meal? …

Describing cause & effect

3 Underline the expressions used to describe cause and effect, as in the examples. Label the cause (*C*) and the effect (*E*).

Back pain (E) is often due to poor posture (C). Symptoms of stress (C) include insomnia and an inability to concentrate (E).

1 Poor education is at the root of many social problems.
2 Overwork can lead to stress.
3 Severe stress can result in high blood pressure.
4 High blood pressure is a risk factor in heart disease.
5 The underlying causes of most addictions are psychological.
6 Many emotional difficulties in adults stem from childhood insecurities.

4 Write four sentences describing either the cause or effect of each of the following.

1 air pollution   3 road rage
2 childhood obesity   4 poor posture

WRITING

1 Work in pairs. Choose one of these titles to write a website article.

- Are you an internet addict?   • Are you a workaholic?
- Are you a television addict?   • Are you an mp3 addict?

List the characteristics of the person you are writing about with addiction problems, and tips for helping them.

2 Write your article following this structure.

Paragraph 1 Ask questions to invite the reader to think about the topic.
Paragraph 2 Define the person you are describing, and describe their habits and characteristics. Describe problems that may result from the addiction.
Paragraph 3 Give tips on how to overcome the addiction.

> ### Useful language
>
> Make a point of …ing   Make time to …
> Consider …ing   Make sure you …
> Most importantly, learn how to …

REMEMBER TO …

- start each paragraph with a clear sentence to introduce the topic.
- include ideas that are lively and relevant to your readers.
- use language from the unit to write definitions, describe habits and cause and effect and give advice.
- finish the article with an engaging final sentence.

3 | Writing A work email

Speaking

1 Imagine you could go and work for a short time in an English-speaking country.

- Where would you go?
- What sort of work would you look for?
- How would you go about looking for work?
- How long would you stay?

Compare your ideas with a partner.

2 Work in pairs. Discuss the questions.

- How often do you send or receive emails in English? In what situations?
- Say whether you think these statements are true (T) or false (F).

1 Salutations (eg *Dear Anne*) and endings (eg *Best wishes*) are not always necessary.
2 Polite expressions (eg *I look forward to hearing from you*) are not used in emails.
3 Abbreviations are commonly used.
4 Emails are often no longer than one or two lines.
5 It is possible to miss out pronouns and other words at the beginnings of sentences.
6 Punctuation rules in emails are different from those in letters.
7 Spelling mistakes and typos are acceptable.
8 The register of emails (formal or informal) depends on the situation.

Reading

1 Match the emails 1–4 to their answers A–D. What happened to Halina?

1

Hi Beth

Just a quick email to say I've finally arrived in London. Can't wait to see you!!! Can you make lunch at the Tapas Bar on Weds – say 12.30ish?

Love

Halina

2

Dear Mr Rogers

I have just finished a BA in architecture at Cracow University of Technology and am now in the UK looking for work experience. I was given your name by my tutor, Mr Grzegorz Kowalski. Do you happen to have any vacancies for trainee placements at the moment? I attach my curriculum vitae for your information.

I look forward to hearing from you.

Best regards

Halina Wisniewski

3

Beth

I'm really sorry but I can't make lunch after all as I have an interview at Rogers and Eagleton. Are you free on Thurs instead?

Wish me luck!

H

4

Dear Halina

Further to our meeting on Wednesday, this is just to say that we will be able to offer you a three-month placement starting on 1st March, with terms as discussed. Could you contact me asap to let me know if this would be of interest?

All the best

Dick Rogers

A

Hi

Good news about the interview!!! Hope it goes well – I'll keep my fingers crossed for you. Thurs will be fine.

B XX

B

Dear Ms Wisniewski

Thanks for your mail. As a matter of fact we do have a vacancy for a trainee at the moment. Would you be able to drop by for lunch on Wednesday at 1.00 so that we can discuss this?

Do give my regards to Grzegorz.

Dick Rogers

C

Dear Mr Rogers

Many thanks for your email. I would be delighted to accept your offer of a placement. I look forward to hearing more details.

Best wishes

Halina

D

Sounds great. See you Weds. Looking forward to catching up!

Beth xx

2 In which of the emails (1–4) or (A–D) does the writer perform the functions 1–8?

1	make an invitation	5	accept an offer
2	accept an invitation	6	wish someone luck
3	congratulate someone	7	cancel an engagement
4	make an offer	8	make a request

Underline the expressions in the emails the writers use to perform the functions 1–8.

LANGUAGE FOCUS

Formal & informal style

1 Decide if the expressions 1–14 are a) formal, b) neutral or c) informal.

1	Hi Emma	8	(Kind) regards
2	Dear Ms Jackson	9	(Lots of) love
3	Dear Emma	10	Yours sincerely
4	Hi	11	Best (wishes)
5	Emma	12	Yours
6	Dear All	13	Yours faithfully
7	Cheers	14	All the best

Making arrangements & requests in emails

2 Choose the best alternative (formal or informal) in these extracts from email exchanges.

1 **Beth:** *Would you be able to meet for / Can you make* lunch tomorrow?
Halina: *Sounds great. / Thanks for the lunch invitation – I'd be delighted to accept.*
Beth: Re lunch, something has come up. *I'm sorry to cancel at such short notice. / Sorry about this.* Could we make it later in the week?
Halina: *How about Thursday? / Would Thursday be convenient?*
Beth: Thurs will be fine. *I look forward to seeing you. / See you then.*

2 **Mr Rogers:** *Could you send me details of / When is the* meeting?
Ms Brown: The meeting is scheduled for Friday. *Let me know if this is difficult. / Is that OK?*
Mr Rogers: *I'm afraid I'm busy. / I'm tied up on Friday. Could we make it another day? / Could we possibly reschedule this?*
Ms Brown: *Any time next week would be good. / Would next week be OK?*
Mr Rogers: *Sorry, I'm not in. / Unfortunately I'll be out of the office next week.*

3 Match the statements 1–5 to the requests a–e.

1 I need to update our personnel records.
2 Lunch will be served from 1–2 in the Barnes Hall.
3 I am attaching your revised contract.
4 I'm afraid I didn't receive your attachment.
5 I think our meeting is scheduled for the 5th.

a Could you possibly try resending it?
b Can you give me a ring to confirm?
c Please get back to me asap if there are any queries.
d Let me know if you have special dietary requirements.
e Do you think you could send me a copy of your CV?

WRITING

1 Work in pairs, A and B. Do the following:

1 Write an 'email' on a piece of paper for some of the situations below, using language studied in this unit.
2 'Send' the email to your partner.
3 'Send' a reply to the emails that you receive.

A: 1) Invite a friend to do something this week.
2) Write to a work colleague to cancel a meeting.
3) Write to a work colleague to make a request about a business arrangement.
4) Write to a friend to ask him/her to send you something.

B: 1) Write to a friend to cancel an arrangement.
2) Write to a work colleague to try to schedule a meeting.
3) Write to a friend to make a request about a party.
4) Write to a work colleague to ask him/her to resend you an attachment.

2 Work in pairs. Look again at the emails you have written. Did you follow the advice in the *Remember to …* box below?

Useful language

Here's (a copy of) …
I am sending/forwarding with this email …
Attached is/are … I attach … Please find attached …

REMEMBER TO …
- use appropriate salutations and endings.
- use language from the unit to make requests and arrangements and send attachments.
- use an appropriate style.
- use abbreviations where relevant.
- make your emails as concise as possible.
- check for spelling mistakes.

4 | Writing A narrative

Speaking

1 Work in pairs. Discuss the questions.

• Is it legal to possess a gun in your country?
• What problems does your country, or other countries you know, have with gun-related crime?

2 Do you agree or disagree with the opinions? Why or why not?

1 Guns are a deterrent. Burglars have to ask themselves when they approach a house, 'Is that family armed or not?'

2 If homeowners arm themselves, that will simply encourage potential burglars to arm themselves, too.

3 Everyone has the right to self-defence. If my granny were to be mugged, I'd rather she had the choice of pulling out her purse or her .45 Magnum.

4 Violence breeds violence. A country in which guns are legal is one which condones and encourages violence in other areas of life.

Reading

1 Read the short story about two friends from a poor housing estate in New York. What do you think is the meaning of the final sentence in the story? Choose the best meaning, 1, 2, 3 or 4.

1 I'm going to kill you.
2 Life is hopeless.
3 Violence breeds violence.
4 There is no way out from this street.

2 Read the story again. Put these events in the order in which they happened 1–10.

☐ Joey and Al gatecrashed a party.
☐ Joey pointed his gun at Brad.
☐ Joey and Al set off home.
☐ Brad attacked Al's brother.
☐ Joey and Al missed their last train home.
☐ Al handed his gun over to Joey.
☐ Joey and Al went into a café.
☐ Joey stole Brad's gun.
☐ Joey and Al arrived back at the estate.
☐ Joey and Al broke into a car.

What do you think happened next?

It was 5.00 in the morning in the backstreets of New York, and the sun was just beginning to appear over the tenement buildings. Al and Joey, two friends from a poor housing estate
5 on the outskirts of the city, were making their way home after gatecrashing a party in the city centre. Having missed their last train home, they had broken into a car parked in an alleyway, only to find, to their consternation, that neither
10 of them knew how to drive. So they had set off on foot, telling jokes and exchanging stories to keep themselves awake.

They had been walking for over an hour when they found an all-night café, so they went in and
15 ordered a coffee. Al started boasting to Joey about a fight he had had earlier that day with Brad, the leader of a rival gang on the estate. Brad had attacked Al's brother, but Al had managed to grab Brad's gun and run off. Taking
20 the gun out of his pocket, Al stroked it proudly, dreaming of revenge. 'Don't be crazy, man,' said Joey. 'Guns make you feel like a man, but violence is a dead end.'

Two hours later the two friends arrived back
25 at the estate. But no sooner had they turned into the main street than they suddenly found themselves, to their dismay, face to face with Brad, who started running towards them with his gang, revenge written all over his face. Fearing
30 for his life, Al pulled out the gun and pointed it at Brad, while the other members of Brad's gang fled. Joey gazed at the scene in horror, wondering what would happen next. It was at that moment that Al realized he would never be
35 able to pull the trigger. With eyes downcast, he handed his gun over to Joey. 'It's a dead end,' he said to Brad.

LANGUAGE FOCUS

Using narrative tenses

1 Look again at the story and find an example of the ...

1 past continuous.
2 past perfect simple.
3 past perfect continuous.
4 past simple.

2 Which tenses are used to do the following? Find examples from the story.

1 describe the main events of the story
2 set the scene of the story
3 describe events happening before the main events of the story
4 clarify that one event in the story happened before another
5 describe actions continuing up to a point in the past

Linking events

3 How are these events linked in the story?

1 They missed their last train home./They broke into a car.
2 They broke into a car./They found that neither of them knew how to drive.
3 They had been walking for over an hour./They found an all-night café.
4 Al took the gun out of his pocket./He stroked it proudly.
5 They turned into the main street./They found themselves face to face with Brad.
6 Al pointed his gun at Brad./The other gang members fled.

Look again at the story and check your answers.

4 Complete the sentence beginnings 1–5 with the endings a–e.

1 He got out his wallet
2 No sooner had he turned out the light
3 He found himself face to face with a guard dog,
4 He broke into the car
5 They had just got into their car

a while his friend kept watch for the police.
b which started growling at him.
c when a stranger started tapping on the window.
d only to discover that he had left his credit card at home.
e than there was a knock on the door.

Describing emotion

5 Choose the most appropriate words to complete the sentences.

1 When I turned on the computer, I discovered to my utter *horror / amusement* that I had lost the document I had been working on for the last three days.
2 Imagine my *relief / embarrassment* when I discovered that I had arrived at work wearing my slippers.
3 To my great *annoyance / delight*, the children started pouring cola all over my new white sofa.
4 I asked my boss for a rise and to my great *astonishment / dismay* he agreed.
5 Having arrived home, I realized to my *delight / consternation* that I had left my keys inside the house.

WRITING

1 You are going to write a story in which someone changes their bad behaviour. Work in pairs. Choose from 1 and 2 below.

1 a thief (eg a burglar, a car thief or a bank robber)
2 a person who treats his/her employees or partner badly

2 Plan the story as follows:

a Setting the scene
Where and when did the story take place?
What was happening and what was he/she doing?
What had happened before the story started?

b Telling the story
What exactly happened to make the person change his/her behaviour?
How did he/she feel? How did he/she react?

c Finishing the story
What happened at the end?

3 Write the story. Follow the advice in the *Remember to ...* box.

Useful language

Just then, ... Suddenly, ... All of a sudden, ...
It was at that moment that ...
Just as he was leaving, ... Just in the nick of time, ...

REMEMBER TO ...

* arrange your story in logical paragraphs.
* use correct verb forms/tenses to set the scene, and to describe events before and during the story.
* link events using a range of linking devices from the unit.
* introduce key events with appropriate expressions from the *Useful language box*.
* use a range of expressions to describe emotion.

5 | Writing A letter of complaint

SPEAKING

1 Imagine you have these problems with rented accommodation.

- The bathroom tap keeps dripping.
- The roof is leaking.
- The walls are paper thin.
- The hall carpet is stained and filthy.
- The toilet doesn't flush.
- The bell isn't working.
- The walls are damp.
- There are mice under the floorboards.
- The tiles in the bathroom are chipped and cracked.
- The kitchen sink is blocked.

In each case, would you ...

1 fix it yourself?
2 ask the landlord to fix it?
3 ignore it?
4 move out?

2 Work in pairs and discuss the questions.

- Have you or anyone you know had any of these problems with accommodation?
- What other problems have you had?
- How did you sort them out?

READING

1 Read the letter from a tenant to a landlord and put the paragraphs in the correct order. What helped you decide?

2 What problems does the writer mention? What were the consequences of each?

3 Give more formal equivalents for these expressions in the letter.

1 I've found some problems ...
2 It'll be obvious to you that these problems are giving me a headache ...
3 I'm writing to you to complain ...
4 ... tell me how you're going to sort out these problems ...
5 Another annoying thing is ...
6 ... as soon as you can ...
7 I want to let you know ...
8 It'd be good if you could get in touch ...
9 I'm writing about the flat ...

Dear Mr Brown

☐

The first and most serious problem is the fact that the central heating system in the flat is erratic and at times does not come on at all. I have tried adjusting the thermostat and the timer but this
5 has made no difference. A further source of irritation is that the windows in the living room do not shut properly, so that this room is extremely draughty. As a result, I have had to borrow a fan heater from a friend as a temporary measure, but even so the temperature in the flat is frequently freezing.

☐

10 As you will appreciate, these problems have been causing me a great deal of inconvenience and distress, especially in the recent spell of bad weather. I would therefore be grateful if you could contact me on the above telephone number as a matter of urgency, and let me know how you propose to resolve these problems.

☐

15 I am writing with regard to the flat in Woodstock Gardens that I am renting from you. Unfortunately, since I moved here on 1st January, I have discovered a number of problems with the accommodation. I have left several messages on your answerphone but as I have not yet received a reply, I am writing to you to express my concerns.

☐

20 I am also concerned about the fact that several of the sockets in the bedroom are loose, which constitutes a safety hazard. Finally, I would like to draw your attention to the fact that the lift in this block is frequently out of order, which is extremely annoying as the flat is on the seventh floor.

25 I look forward to hearing from you.

Yours sincerely

Alex Gibbons (Mr)

LANGUAGE FOCUS

Article use

With singular nouns, use *the*:

1 with ordinal nouns (*the first, the sixth, the tenth, the twenty-first*).
2 for something that has been mentioned before. *I have a new car. The car is red.*
3 for an attribute of something mentioned before. *The engine is very powerful.*
4 when there is normally only one in a place. *the front door, the garden*
5 when something is specified or defined. *the tree in your garden, the book I bought*
6 when something has not been mentioned but is known to the reader, eg *the war* (= *the recent war that we all know about*).

Note that the zero article is never used before a singular noun.
Not (*Flat is cold, I have problem.*)

1 Say which of the rules 1–6 in the grammar box explains the use of *the* in the extracts a–i from the letter.

a the flat in Woodstock Gardens that I am renting from you
b the first and most serious problem
c the central heating system in the flat
d the thermostat and the timer
e the windows in the living room
f the lift in this block
g the flat is on the seventh floor
h the recent spell of bad weather
i the above telephone number

Writing about results of problems

2 Match the problems 1–5 to their consequences a–e.

1 The ventilation in the bathroom is poor,
2 The washing machine has broken down,
3 The bathroom radiator is leaking,
4 The boiler is not working,
5 The wiring in the flat is faulty,

a which constitutes a fire hazard.
b so that I keep having to mop up pools of water.
c which means that the room is frequently full of condensation.
d and as a result, I have had to take my clothes to a launderette.
e which is extremely annoying as I am having to take cold showers.

3 Write consequences for these problems, using some of the expressions underlined in exercise 2.

1 The cooker is not working,

_____.

2 The carpets on the stairs are coming loose,

_____.

3 The fridge is making a very loud noise,

_____.

4 The springs on the sofa have broken,

_____.

5 The windows in the bedroom are jammed shut,

_____.

WRITING

1 Work in pairs. Imagine that you had problems with accommodation (a hotel or self-catering flat) on a recent holiday. You enjoyed the holiday but are writing to comment on problems you had with your accommodation and suggest improvements for the future.

1 Make a list of the problems you encountered and make notes on their consequences.
2 Decide what action you want taken.
3 Write a letter of complaint. Begin *I am writing to express my disappointment with aspects of my recent holiday …*

A common structure for letters of complaint is:

First paragraph
State the situation and the letter's purpose.

Middle paragraph(s)
Give details of the problem(s) and consequences.

Final paragraph
Summarize the difficulties and request action.

Useful language

The first and most serious problem is …
A further problem is …   I am also concerned about …
In addition, …   Finally, …

REMEMBER TO …

- state the purpose of your letter in the first paragraph.
- use language from the unit to list problems and give details of consequences.
- use a range of formal words and expressions from the unit.
- summarize the problem and request action in the final paragraph.
- check your letter for correct article use.
- start and finish your letter with an appropriate salutation and ending.

6 | Writing An essay

SPEAKING

1 Which of the activities below have you done recently? Did you enjoy them? Which have you never done? Why?

- go to the ballet
- visit an art exhibition
- watch street theatre
- see a musical
- go to a concert
- visit a sculpture park
- attend a poetry reading
- go to the opera

2 Which of the activities can be classed as 'the arts'? What other activities could be included?

READING

1 Read the essay about public funding of the arts. Which of these statements, 1, 2 or 3, is closest to the writer's opinion?

1 Public money should be spent on social needs, not on the arts.
2 The arts are a minority interest, so should be paid for by the people who use them.
3 Public money should be used to fund the arts because art is an important human activity.

2 Make notes to complete the writer's essay plan, as in the example.

> **Paragraph 1**
>
> Introductory statement   <u>Value of arts in civilized society</u>
>
> Supporting statement   _____
>
> Controversial question   _____
>
> **Paragraph 2**
>
> Main opinion   _____
>
> Arguments   a) _____
>
>   b) _____
>
>   c) _____
>
>   d) _____
>
> **Paragraph 3**
>
> Counter-argument   _____
>
> Refuting counter-argument   a) _____
>
>   b) _____
>
> **Paragraph 4**
>
> Conclusion   _____
>
> Supporting statement   _____

Few people would contest the value of the arts in a civilized society. Great art enriches people's lives by providing
5 pleasure, stimulation and an escape from the pressures of everyday life. However, it is also true that many of the arts, such as classical music,
10 the ballet, and the visual arts have always attracted a minority audience. The question is whether the arts should be publicly funded, or
15 whether it is the consumers who should pay.

It is my view that the government should subsidize the arts, for a
20 number of reasons. First of all, without subsidies, many artists would undoubtedly be unable to survive financially. Government grants can enable them to work with artistic freedom and
25 integrity, whereas if they worked independently or relied on private subsidies, they might be subject to market pressures and the need to make a profit. Secondly, the arts contribute to a nation's cultural heritage and can create a sense of social cohesion and identity. They can
30 also play an important role in education, community regeneration and even crime prevention. However, the main argument for public funding of the arts is not social usefulness, but rather because they are important for their own sake.

35 Of course, there are those who argue that public money would be better spent on meeting the needs of the poorer members of society, and on healthcare, education, and social welfare schemes rather than catering for the interests of an elite. However, I believe
40 that a healthy society is one in which art and creativity are valued alongside these basic needs. Indeed, a civilized society ought to make the arts accessible to everyone, regardless of their background or income.

In conclusion, the arts should be funded across a
45 broad spectrum of activities, for example; by supporting community or school theatre projects, or bringing sculptures and art installations to public places. This is not for purely social reasons, but because enjoyment of art is part of what it means to be human.

3 Which discourse markers or expressions are used to introduce each point?

4 Do you agree or disagree with the writer's opinion? Why?

LANGUAGE FOCUS

Expressing a viewpoint

1 Complete the expressions in the table with the words in the box.

> widely   whether   evidence   say   personally   dispute
> would   case   doubt   agreed   view   ~~claimed~~

A commonly-held view	A personal opinion	A strong claim
It is often (1) _claimed_ that …	It is my (5) _____ that …	All the (9) _____ suggests that …
It is (2) _____ believed that …	I (6) _____ believe that …	It is simply not the (10) _____ that …
It is probably true to (3) _____ that …	I (7) _____ argue that …	There can be no (11) _____ that …
It is generally (4) _____ that …	I personally would question (8) _____ …	No one would (12) _____ the fact that …

Choose one of the expressions from the box to modify the statements below.

> Television is dumbing down our culture.
> Children should not be made to study literature at school.
> It is not worth going to the cinema when you can watch a DVD.
> Education systems often stifle creativity.
> Museums and art galleries should not charge an entrance fee.
> Censorship should not interfere with freedom of expression in the arts.

Arguing against a viewpoint

2 Complete the statements to argue against the view expressed.

1 <u>There are those who argue that</u> anyone can learn to play a musical instrument. However, _____.

2 <u>Of course</u>, not everyone has an innate talent for art. But surely _____?

3 <u>It is true that</u> pop music has a wider popular appeal than classical music. But _____.

4 <u>Opponents of</u> modern art argue that it has no aesthetic value. But surely _____?

5 Advocates of free speech <u>claim that</u> censorship stifles debate. However, _____.

3 Choose two of the opinions in exercise 2 and write similar pairs of statements using the underlined expressions.

WRITING

1 Work in pairs. Prepare to write an essay expressing an opinion.

1 Choose one of the statements in Language focus exercise 1 that you would like to write about.

2 Make a list of the arguments for and against the statement. Decide whether you agree or disagree with the statement.

3 Write statements a) saying why the topic is controversial and b) expressing your opinion.

4 Make a plan for the essay following the structure used by the writer on the previous page.

5 Write your essays individually following the plan, and using the advice in the *Remember to …* box.

2 Exchange your essay with someone who chose a different topic. Were his or her arguments convincing?

Useful language

In conclusion, …	*On balance, …*
To conclude, …	*In short, …*
To sum up, …	

REMEMBER TO …

- state the importance or relevance of the topic, and why it is controversial, in the introduction.
- contain a clear statement of your opinion, supported with clear reasons.
- mention the counter-arguments using language from the unit.
- use a range of discourse markers and expressions to introduce new points and express your opinion.

Communication activities

10C Reading exercise 2   page 100

Student B

Part 2

'At first there was no sensation of falling, only of zooming through the air,' said William Rankin of the moments after he ejected from his stricken jet. 'I felt as though I were a chunk of beef being tossed into a cavernous deep freeze,' he remembered. 'Almost instantly all exposed parts of my body – around the face, neck, wrists, hands and ankles – began to sting from the cold.' Even more uncomfortable was the decompression caused by the low pressure at the top of the troposphere as he began the free fall until his parachute would automatically open. He was bleeding from his eyes, ears, nose and mouth as a result of the expansion of his insides, and his body became distended. 'Once I caught a horrified glimpse of my stomach, swollen as though I were in well-advanced pregnancy. I had never known such savage pain.' The one benefit of the extreme cold was that it began to numb his body.

In spite of the spinning, flailing nature of his free fall, Rankin managed to secure the emergency oxygen supply to his mouth. It was essential to remain conscious if he was to have any chance of surviving the descent. He was within the upper reaches of the storm cloud, with deteriorating visibility, when he saw on his watch that five minutes had passed since he had ejected. He should have passed the 10,000 feet* point by now – the height at which the barometric trigger in his parachute would cause it automatically to open. But there was no sign of the parachute. It was beginning to look like he was hurtling through the air strapped to a parachute that didn't work.

Deep within the ice-particle upper region of the cumulonimbus it was dark with zero visibility. This made Rankin totally disorientated, with no idea of his altitude. For all he knew, without his parachute opening he might hit the ground at any moment. It was therefore with great relief that he felt the violent jolt as his parachute finally deployed.

He was also relieved to find that, though his emergency oxygen supply had run out, the air at this level was now dense enough for him to be able to breathe without it. In the gloom of the enormous cloud, things appeared to be looking up: 'Under the circumstances, overjoyed to be alive and going down safely, consciously, even the increasing turbulence of the air meant nothing. It was all over now, I thought, the ordeal had ended.' But the turbulence he was beginning to feel and the freezing hailstones starting to hit him meant that he was only now reaching the heart of the storm.

*10,000 feet = 3,048 metres

3A Grammar exercise 3   page 27

Student A

Take turns with your partner to read out your sentences. You should contradict what your partner says, using a stressed auxiliary verb, then add an extra comment.

A: *You've forgotten my birthday again.*
B: *I **haven't** forgotten it – your present is parked outside in the street!*

1 You're not going to the party, and that's final!
2 You didn't tell me you had a brother.
3 That man looks like Matt Damon.
4 There's no way she'll get the job.
5 You haven't combed your hair!
6 You don't love me any more!

1D Listening exercise 2   page 12

The Quarterlife Crisis

Like the midlife crisis, the quarterlife crisis occurs when there is a major change in our lives – the transition from childhood to adulthood, from the academic world to the 'real' world of work. Those affected can experience feelings of confusion, anxiety and helplessness arising from the overwhelming range of choices available, decisions to make and responsibilities to assume. Young people are faced with many important questions such as 'Which career should I choose?', 'When should I think about starting a family?' or, more immediately, 'Should I continue to live with my parents or become more independent and move out into rented accommodation?' The answers to these questions are not always easy to find.

This period of uncertainty and instability may also be accompanied by a sense of disillusionment with adult life, which, for some twentysomethings, fails to live up to expectations. Those hoping to earn enough money to buy their own home, for example, are often disappointed to discover that this is not possible until they are well into their thirties.

11D Grammar exercise 3   page 113

Student A

Work in pairs. Roleplay the situation. Use *I wish*, *I'd rather you* and *It's (about/high) time ...* when voicing your complaints.

You live in a flat and your upstairs neighbour is a composer of experimental music. He/She has a great deal of technological equipment in his/her flat and often spends more than twelve hours a day composing, producing unusual electronic sounds with no clear melody. You find the noise unbearable, and your cats and dogs are showing clear signs of distress. You go upstairs to complain.

1D Speaking exercise 1   page 13

STARTING WORK

You are eighteen years old and have just finished school. You had intended to study philosophy at university, but now feel that a philosophy degree would probably not help you find a good job. Your parents are disappointed to hear that you have decided to turn your back on university in favour of learning a trade. You have heard that plumbers are in short supply in your country.

LEAVING HOME

You are 23 years old and live with your mother, fourteen-year-old sister and elderly grandmother. You all get on very well, but you feel you would now like to move into a place on your own. You have decided to rent the small but attractive one-bedroomed flat you recently went to see. It is in the next town, 45 minutes by public transport from where you currently live, but just two minutes' walk from the office where you started work last year.

GETTING MARRIED

You are 22 years old, living in a village with your parents, who still refer to you as their 'little one', and still looking for work after graduating last year. Your 32-year-old partner, who has a house in the town centre, has asked you to marry him/her and you have decided to accept. You have been going out together for just six months, but it has been a very exciting six months and you have never had a single row. Your partner has spoken about wanting children, an idea which appeals to you.

GOING ABROAD

You are 28 years old and working for an insurance company. Your job as a sales representative is well-paid and has enabled you to take out a mortgage on a small house, where you now live with your two dogs. Your partner is proud of your success, but you have begun to feel dissatisfied with the very routine life you lead. Languages have always been your passion and you have applied and been accepted for work as a language teacher in China.

RETIRING EARLY

You are 49 years old, divorced and living on your own – your two children have both left home. You have calculated that you can stop work next year and live on your savings until you are entitled to draw your pension. In addition, you are looking at properties in a number of Mediterranean resorts, where the cost of living is generally much cheaper than in your own country. You do not speak any foreign languages but you are sure you will be able to get by.

9A Speaking exercise 1   page 86

Two nearby cities, Bentham and Hillborough, are suffering from overcrowding and a new town is required to house the growing number of inhabitants. The only available site is the area around Greenvale, a village of 380 inhabitants set in a beautiful valley of the River Eden.

Working in small groups, use the map to discuss how you would plan the new town, which is expected to provide housing for 15,000 residents in the next five years. You should consider the following:

- Type and approximate location of housing and health, education, shopping and leisure facilities.
- New transport requirements, eg road and rail links.
- Location of sewage treatment plant.
- Changes required, eg Will the buildings be left or demolished? Will the marshland need to be drained?

Note that:

- Most houses in Greenvale are built of local stone and are over 100 years old. They are scattered over a wide area. The church is a protected building.
- The marshland is a nesting site for a number of rare birds.
- Most of the new residents will be young middle-class families.
- You will need to build 70 six-storey blocks of flats to house one third of the population.
- You will need to build on at least 75 per cent of the area contained within the dotted line on the map.

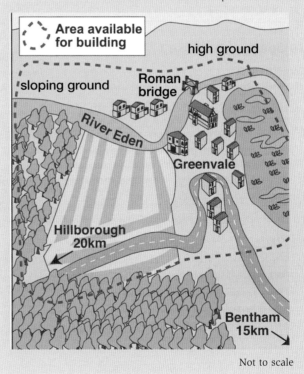

Not to scale

4D Listening exercise 6   page 42

Choose one of the following options and write a brief speech. Include at least one of the techniques included in the Speech Writing Tips on page 42.

1 A 40th birthday speech. You may either be the person whose birthday it is, a friend of that person or a relative.
  Note: The birthday is being celebrated in a restaurant.

2 A retirement speech. You may either be the person retiring, that person's boss or another employee.
  Note: The person retiring has been presented with a clock.

3 A best man speech at a wedding. You may either be a friend or a relative of the groom.
  Note: You have known the groom since you were at school together.

4 An acceptance speech for a major film award. You may either be the recipient of the award or a person collecting it on that person's behalf.
  Note: After 26 years in the business this is the person's first major award.

5 A speech at the inauguration of a new shopping centre. You may either be the architect, the local mayor or a famous person.
  Note: The shopping centre contains a cinema complex, several restaurants and its own train station.

2D Speaking exercise 1   page 23

Committee A

A plot of land has become available in your area for the siting of a new national museum. The authorities have invited suggestions for the exact nature of the museum and your committee will put forward a proposal at a forthcoming planning meeting. Either choose one of the following options or come up with your own suggestion, then prepare for the meeting using the questions to help you.

| clothes | sport | traditional music | other |

- Who would your museum appeal to (eg age groups, interest groups, personality types)?
- What permanent exhibitions would it house?
- What temporary exhibitions could it host (three possibilities)?
- Will there be interactive displays?
- What extra events and activities could be organized?
- What extra facilities could be provided?
- What would the museum shop sell?
- Why would your museum be successful?

2B Speaking exercise 1   page 19

Group A

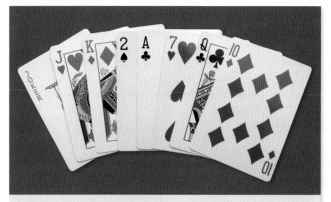

You are going to use Dominic O'Brien's journey method to memorize the above cards in the order in which they are shown. Work together and do the following.

- Agree on a journey you could all make together, visiting eight different places. It might, for example, be a journey in your local area, a bus route or a tour of different towns in your country.
- As you come to the first place, make up a scene or story to associate it with the first card in your sequence. Do the same for the second place and the second card, and so on until you have matched each of the eight cards with each of the eight places on your route.
  Let's start in the park and imagine eight people, each digging a hole with a spade (the eight of spades). Then we can go to the railway station, where James Bond, 007, (the seven of hearts) is ...
- Practise telling your story to another member of your group.

11D Speech feature exercise 2   page 113

Group A

Use the words below to write six sentences like those in exercise 1 on page 113. You should:
- include an example of dislocation in each sentence.
- put a gap where the noun in bold should be.
- write a second sentence containing clues to enable another student to guess the word in the gap.

*eg be poor/**turnout***
It was very poor, the _____ for the election. Only 25 per cent of people bothered to vote.

1 vary/**diet**
2 shuffle/**cards**
3 be **overrated**/film
4 **book**/have (someone) laughing out loud
5 be man-made/**lake**
6 be rotten/**teeth**

5C Speaking exercise 1   page 50

Student A

Read the list of household duties and observations, then discuss in broad terms who will do which duties. Individual duties may be shared between two or all three of you. Make brief notes of your decisions.

HOUSEHOLD DUTIES

Cleaning: once a week: bathroom, kitchen, living room, three bedrooms.
Washing: two loads of washing each week (excellent washing machine with tumble dryer in flat).
Ironing: two hours' worth of ironing in total each week (good steam iron available).
Cooking: you want to eat a cooked meal together every weekday evening.
Washing up: no dishwasher in flat.
Shopping: nearest supermarket over two kilometres away.

OBSERVATIONS

1 You like cooking, even though your dishes don't always turn out as planned.
2 Your shirts/blouses have to be ironed for work. Someone else has always done this for you in the past.
3 You recently broke your left wrist, and it will be in a plaster cast for the next six weeks. You are right-handed.
4 Your favourite TV soap is on Wednesday and Friday evenings from 7.30 to 8.30. You haven't missed an episode for nearly two years.
5 There is only one television in the flat and you cannot afford another.

11C Speaking exercise 1   page 110

Student A

3C Speaking exercise 2   page 30

Student A

You are a magazine journalist who has been sent to interview Sonya Thomas. Prepare eight to ten questions you could ask her about her involvement in competitive eating contests. You could consider the following:

• The types of records she holds
• Her training programme
• Her reasons for competing
• Any special techniques she adopts
• Other

4A Vocabulary exercise 4   page 36

Student A

Work in pairs. Take turns to say your sentences in the manner of the verbs in brackets. You must each try to guess which verbs your partner is illustrating.

1 'Oh, it's not fair. You never let me stay up late.' (*whine*)
2 'What's the matter? What do you want?' (*snap*)
3 'I don't think much of the food in this restaurant.' (*mutter*)
4 'I just wanted to say how much I like you.' (*stutter*)
5 'Come here this minute!' (*bellow*)

10D Grammar exercise 3   page 103

Student A: Imagine that you have been having a lot of problems recently. For each of the areas below tell your partner about something which went wrong and the consequences it had for you.

    car   holiday   cooking   school   parents

Student B: Tell your partner what he or she should or shouldn't have done in order to prevent each of the problems occurring.

Now change roles and talk about things that have gone wrong in the following areas:

    house   health   sport   work   partner

5B Speaking exercise 1　page 49

Group A

Choose one of the following and prepare your pitch. Consider the points below, as well as any others that you think may be relevant.

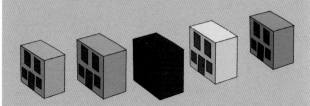

plastic houses

luxury hotel conversion

The idea or product
- How will you describe your idea or product?
- What is its purpose?
- Are any special materials required for its production?

The target market
- What type of consumers is it aimed at?
- Why would they be interested in it? What benefits will it bring them?

The competition
- What makes it different from or better than similar ideas or products already on the market?
- How will you convince consumers of these advantages?

Sales and marketing
- What media will you use to advertise your product?
- In which type of outlets will it be sold?

The brand identity
- What is the name of your business and the product or service?
- What business logo will you have?

6B Listening exercise 3　page 58

Student A

Summarize the following text to your partner, but include three major factual errors. Your partner will try to spot all three.

The History of Glasses

The Roman Emperor Nero is said to have watched gladiator fights through precious stones – emeralds, to be precise – but the first time glass lenses were used to aid or correct vision was almost certainly in the 1280s in Florence, Italy. It is not clear who actually invented these spectacles, but it is known that they consisted of two convex lenses which corrected long-sightedness. It was not until the beginning of the 16th century that the first use of concave lenses to correct short-sightedness was recorded in a painting of Pope Leo X by Raphael. Initially, spectacles were a luxury item, worn only by rich, well-educated members of the nobility or influential and well-read priests. However, with Gutenberg's invention of the printing press in 1456 and the greater availability of books, the use of reading glasses became more widespread. Early versions had to be held up to the face or else balanced on the nose, until at the beginning of the 18th century, English optician Edward Scarlett produced the first spectacle frames with side arms extending to the ears. Later that same century Benjamin Franklin is believed to have invented bifocal glasses by combining convex and concave lenses in the same frame.

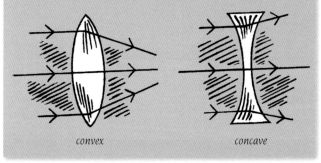

convex　　　　*concave*

9A Grammar exercise 4　page 86

Student B

> greengrocer's　cinema　park　restaurant
> bookshop　railway station　university
> tourist information office

Choose **five** of the places in the box and for each one write a sentence which makes reference to or is said in that particular place, but without actually mentioning it. Your sentences should each contain a different use of *will*, *would* or *shall*.

Read your sentences to your partner, who will try to identify the five places.

6c Reading exercise 4   page 60

Student A

EXTRACT 4

(*Nicholson and Natasha arrive at the airport of departure.*)
The first ordeal was the police security examination. They searched my bags, I offered my passport, they hardly looked at it, so I went to move on.

They held up their hands. 'Girl passport,' they demanded.

'No, no! She's on mine … look, it's here … in England we put our children on our passports.' My heart thumped as they flicked the pages. How often had they seen a child's entry before? Had they ever? Did they believe it? They did, and we walked on to the next and final examination.

In front of us now, behind her glass partition, was a young girl with a single gold band on her epaulette, a beginner. She hardly looked at me or my passport, but stamped it with a bang and pushed it back across her counter. I held Natasha's hand tight and we walked on, hardly believing we had done it so easily.

'One moment! Stop!' someone shouted behind us. I turned and froze. Another woman, another immigration officer, older, with two rings on her grubby grey uniform, came hurrying towards me. 'Passport,' she said, stony-faced, holding out her hand, 'and boarding cards.' I handed them to her, suddenly, horribly nauseous with the sensation of déjà vu, remembering scenes like this in so many films … caught at the final barrier, turned back at the last fence, found out, here, now, helpless, losing control, a grey uniform, my passport and tickets in her hands. This is how it would end. Natasha stood a few yards behind me, waiting.

'Stamps … no stamps,' the woman spat out.

'Stamps?' I repeated, bewildered.

'No stamps, no airport tax. You pay for stamps.'

'Do you take dollars?' I asked sweetly. I would happily have given her gold!

7B Speaking exercise 1   page 69

Group A (home)

Here are the first drafts of five posters representing the main areas of concern of the tourist board regarding the behaviour of its citizens in their own country. Discuss the relative importance of each area, and say how effective you think each poster might be. Then select **three** which you think should be included in the campaign. You may suggest changes to the illustrations and/or slogans, or you may design one or more of the posters completely from scratch.

7C Reading exercise 3   page 70

Student A

> **Grace's mother, Veronica, talks to Alex about Will and Grace.**
>
> 'I appreciate that these questions might seem irrelevant at this stage, but without much to go on, we have to consider ...'
>
> 'Nothing to go on? Rubbish! [Will]'s just playing innocent. Trying to make you think he doesn't know anything about what's happened to Grace! Trying to make the *world* think he doesn't know!'
>
> Nothing Will had said had prepared me for the strength of Veronica Bailey's prejudices, nor the malevolence of her delivery. She was burning with contempt and unshakeable righteousness. Even allowing for her anxiety over her daughter, her animosity was without the slightest moderation or self-restraint.
>
> 'You're making some extremely serious allegations,' I said.
>
> 'Indeed I am!' she retorted. 'It's been deceit all the way along the line, so why should he change now? He tricked her into marrying him, he ...' Watching my face, her eyes lit up avidly. 'You didn't know that? Oh, *yes*, totally tricked her. Pretended he owned all that land, pretended he was the lord of the manor,' she recounted with bitter relish. 'So grand, so full of himself. And all the time he hadn't got a penny, not a penny! He was a cheat! Leading her on! Never saying a word until after the wedding. Just wanted her money, you see! Just waiting to get his hands on it!'
>
> ....
>
> 'Did you know Grace wanted to leave him?' she demanded.
>
> 'No.'
>
> 'Soon after they were married. When she discovered the truth about the farm. Rented. *Rented*.' For all the disgust in her face she might have been talking about a hanging offence. 'She felt totally betrayed – and who could blame her? I encouraged her to leave. God only knows, she had reason to, if anyone did! But she was too good, of course. Too *forgiving*, too *generous*. That was Grace – *generous* and *loving*. She felt she should stick it out.'

12B Reading exercise 4   page 118

Group B

Write a brief dialogue between a human being and one of the smart objects from the box. You should not mention the object in your dialogue, but rather give clues as to its possible identity.

shoes	cooker	bed	computer
glasses	rubbish bin	other	

Your dialogue might include one or more of the following functions.

criticizing	complaining	praising
apologizing	requesting	inviting
offering	advising	other

8D Speaking exercise 1   page 82

Group A

Look at the photos of four people and discuss what you imagine each one might be like. Consider the following:

- Name and age
- Studies and work
- Daily routine
- Personality – both positive and negative aspects
- Interests
- Likes and dislikes
- Habits
- Other

12B Reading exercise 2   page 118

> 'Mind if I sit down?' I say, and collapse onto a large boulder before the suit can reply.
>
> 'What hurts?' it asks.
>
> 'Everything. Mostly my legs and my feet.'
>
> 'It'll take a few days for your feet to harden and your muscles to tone up. Rest when you feel like it. There's no sense in pushing yourself too hard.'
>
> My suit. I've had the thing for over a century and I've hardly used it. The brain's spent most of its time plugged into the main house unit back home. Even on holidays, I've spent most of my time on board ship, rather than venture out into hostile environments.

6D Vocabulary & speaking exercise 2   page 62

Discuss the following situations you might encounter as a babysitter and try to agree on the best alternative. Give reasons for your decisions.

1 After feeding a four-month-old baby girl, you have to **burp** her to get rid of swallowed air. You sit her on your lap, supporting her chest and head with one hand, and then ...

a squeeze or rub her stomach gently until she burps.
b rub or pat her back gently until she burps.
c simply wait until she burps.

2 A fifteen-month-old boy refuses to eat more than a few spoonfuls of the food his parents have left for him. After trying unsuccessfully for several minutes, you decide the best thing to do is ...

a turn the television on to distract him.
b remove the plate, wipe his face and hands and take him out of the **high chair**.
c force him to eat it, squeezing both cheeks firmly to open his mouth.

3 A two-and-a-half-year-old **toddler** wants a sweet before going to bed. When you refuse, she **throws a temper tantrum**, dropping to the floor, **yelling** and screaming uncontrollably, and kicking her legs. After a minute or so, the next-door neighbours bang on the dividing wall. What do you do?

a Walk away calmly and do something else until the tantrum has run its course.
b Give her a sweet.
c Shout at her to stop screaming and get up from the floor. **Smack** her if she ignores you.

4 Three-year-old Sam **bursts into tears** as his parents walk out of the door. He is inconsolable and won't let you **cuddle** him. Neither does he respond when you ask him to play with you. You ...

a go out of the door and ask the parents to come back.
b sit on the floor and start playing with one of his toys.
c tell him not to be a **crybaby** and threaten to send him to bed if he doesn't stop.

5 You hear five-year-old Susie **squabbling** with her eight-year-old brother, Luke, over a toy. You go to investigate and find them hitting each other. What do you do once you have separated them?

a Give the toy to Susie and tell Luke not to be a **bully**.
b Try to establish who hit who first, then punish the guilty child in some way.
c Tell them to play separately until they have calmed down.

6 A six-year-old girl has been **picking her nose** and now has a **nosebleed**. You ask her to open her mouth, then pinch her **nostrils** shut with your thumb and forefinger and get her to ...

a sit or stand with her head leaning back for five minutes.
b sit upright with her head bent forward for ten minutes.
c lie down for fifteen minutes.

7 It is 8.30pm and ten-year-old Paul's normal **bedtime**. When you remind him of this he says 'I'm ten. You can't tell me what to do', and goes on playing on the computer. How do you react?

a You let him carry on playing but resolve to try again in fifteen minutes' time.
b You switch off the computer and threaten to tell his parents if he doesn't go to bed now.
c You agree that he can **stay up** until 9 o'clock if he gets ready for bed first.

5B Speaking exercise 1   page 49

Group B

Choose one of the following and prepare your pitch.
Consider the points below, as well as any others that
you think may be relevant.

double-decker car

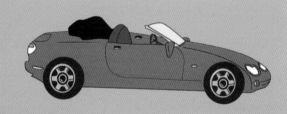

one-seater sports car

The idea or product
- How will you describe your idea or product?
- What is its purpose?
- Are any special materials required for its production?

The target market
- What type of consumers is it aimed at?
- Why would they be interested in it? What benefits will it
  bring them?

The competition
- What makes it different from or better than similar ideas
  or products already on the market?
- How will you convince consumers of these advantages?

Sales and marketing
- What media will you use to advertise your product?
- In which type of outlets will it be sold?

The brand identity
- What is the name of your business and the product
  or service?
- What business logo will you have?

3A Grammar exercise 3   page 27

Student B

Take turns with your partner to read out your
sentences. You should contradict what your partner
says, using a stressed auxiliary verb, then add an
extra comment.

A: *You've forgotten my birthday again.*
B: *I **haven't** forgotten it – your present is parked
outside in the street!*

1 You can't tell me what to do – I'm not a child
  any more!
2 You don't care about the future of the planet.
3 Be careful! Peter's got a contagious disease.
4 You didn't know she was a spy, did you?
5 I don't think Sally's working at the moment.
6 It never snows here in winter.

11C Vocabulary exercise 4   page 110

Group B

Include at least six of these sounds in your story. You may
change the form of the words. If the sound is given as a
verb, you may use it as a noun (and vice versa).
- the wind rustles (leaves) in the trees
- thunder rumbles
- an alarm clock beeps
- a light aircraft/helicopter/fly/bee buzzes past/overhead
- an owl screeches
- coins/bracelets jingle
- a camera clicks
- a door creaks open
- someone bangs on a door
- something plops into the water
- a balloon pops
- the clatter of horses' hoofs

11C Speaking exercise 1   page 110

Student D

2B Speaking exercise 1   page 19

Group B

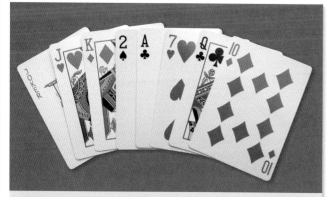

You are going to use Dominic O'Brien's journey method to memorize the above cards in the order in which they are shown. Work together and do the following.

- Agree on a journey you could all make together, visiting eight different places. It might, for example, be a journey in your local area, a bus route or a tour of different towns in your country.
- As you come to the first place, make up a scene or story to associate it with the first card in your sequence. Do the same for the second place and the second card, and so on until you have matched each of the eight cards with each of the eight places on your route.

Let's start in the department store and imagine a young, newly married couple (the two of hearts) buying curtains or something for their new house. Then we can go to the main square, where Bill Gates (the ten of diamonds) is ...

- Practise telling your story to another member of your group.

2C Vocabulary exercise 5   page 20

Student A

Take it in turns with your partner to talk about your topics. Your partner will try to guess what your topics are, but you must not use any of the adjectives, nouns or verbs given in 1–5 below. Your partner's topics begin with the same expressions in bold as in your own topics, but not in the same order.

1 **the quickest way** to make a lot of money
2 **the cheapest way** to get from your school to the nearest airport
3 **the safest way** to dispose of batteries once they have run out
4 **the most effective way** to deal with terrorism
5 **the most common way** for people in your country to travel to work

2D Speaking exercise 1   page 23

Committee B

A plot of land has become available in your area for the siting of a new national museum. The authorities have invited suggestions for the exact nature of the museum and your committee will put forward a proposal at a forthcoming planning meeting. Either choose one of the following options, or come up with your own suggestion, then prepare for the meeting using the questions to help you.

    toys   food   domestic life   other

- Who would your museum appeal to (eg age groups, interest groups, personality types)?
- What permanent exhibitions would it house?
- What temporary exhibitions could it host (three possibilities)?
- Will there be interactive displays?
- What extra events and activities could be organized?
- What extra facilities could be provided?
- What would the museum shop sell?
- Why would your museum be successful?

5C Speaking exercise 1   page 50

Student B

Read the list of household duties and observations, then discuss in broad terms who will do which duties. Individual duties may be shared between two or all three of you. Make brief notes of your decisions.

HOUSEHOLD DUTIES

Cleaning: once a week: bathroom, kitchen, living room, three bedrooms.
Washing: two loads of washing each week (excellent washing machine with tumble dryer in flat).
Ironing: two hours' worth of ironing in total each week (good steam iron available).
Cooking: you want to eat a cooked meal together every weekday evening.
Washing up: no dishwasher in flat.
Shopping: nearest supermarket over two kilometres away.

OBSERVATIONS

1 You hate ironing and would rather someone else ironed your shirts/blouses for you.
2 You have never cooked so much as a boiled egg in your life.
3 You have a bad back: you cannot carry heavy weights and bending over is painful.
4 You don't want to do any housework on Wednesday evenings – your favourite music programme is on television from 8.30 to 9.30.
5 There is only one television in the flat and you cannot afford another.

5D Vocabulary exercise 4   page 52

Student A

Talk to your partner for a maximum of five minutes about one of the jobs in Vocabulary exercises 1 & 2 on page 52. You can mention the name of the job, but you must not use the words *man, woman, he, she, his* or *her*.

If you use one of these words, your turn has finished and you should stop speaking.

You could talk about some or all of the following:

- What the job involves
- Personal qualities required
- Rewarding aspects of the job
- Unpleasant aspects of the job
- Reasons why people choose to do this work
- Reasons why you would (not) or could (not) do the job

5D Vocabulary exercise 4   page 52

Student B

Your partner is going to talk for a maximum of five minutes about one of the jobs in Vocabulary exercises 1 & 2 on page 52. He/She can mention the name of the job, but must not use the words *man, woman, he, she, his* or *her*. As your partner speaks, ask questions with the aim of forcing him/her to use these words. As soon as he/she uses one of these words, your partner's turn has finished and he/she must stop speaking.

11C Speaking exercise 1   page 110

Student B

6B Listening exercise 3   page 58

Student B

Summarize the following text to your partner, but include three major factual errors. Your partner will try to spot all three.

The History of the Ambulance

The Spanish word 'ambulancia' first appeared in the late 15th century, when it referred to the tents in which physicians treated soldiers wounded in the campaign to drive out the Moors from Spain. But the history of the ambulance as a means of transporting the sick and wounded goes back further. The first organized ambulance service was started by the Knights of the Order of Saint John. During the Crusades of the 11th century, they gave first aid to the wounded from both Muslim and Christian armies, and carried them for further treatment to nearby tents on 'litters'. These were a type of stretcher made from strong canvas* hung between two poles and carried by two men. The idea was developed in Europe by the Normans who invented the horse litter, a similar device carried by two horses. A major development occurred in 1792 during France's war with Austria and Prussia, when Dominique Jean Larrey created a fleet of 'flying ambulances' – lightweight two-wheeled vehicles pulled by medics on horseback. The first civilian ambulances did not go into service until 1869 in New York and the first motorized ambulance was manufactured in Chicago in 1899. Its top speed was about 25 kilometres an hour.

litter

horse litter

Glossary
*canvas n a strong heavy cloth used for making items such as tents, bags and sails

6c Reading exercise 4   page 60

Student B

EXTRACT 5

(Nicholson and Natasha arrive at London Heathrow airport.)

Natasha and I went happily towards the British Immigration officer's desk, walking, as the song goes, on air. We shuffled forward in the short queue until it was my turn to hand him my passport. As he opened it, I turned, pointed to my companion and said, 'I think you should know that I have a little problem.'

We were ushered into a British Immigration interview room by a polite man with a big smile. I had expected British Immigration officers to be hostile, cussed and uncooperative, and I was wrong three times over. To begin with, we had tea. Then a man who spoke Serbo-Croat sat with Natasha and told her, translating for me, that she had to have a proper piece of paper to say she could stay in England. She agreed with him, not that anything he said really interested her. There were now so many other things to investigate. The interview room was filling with people of more shapes, colours and tongues than Natasha could ever have imagined the world contained. Much encouraged, she went from one bewildered foreign person to another, introducing herself and her story.

I told my story to three Immigration officers in turn, the last, a pleasant young lady, promising that once it had all been digested by the Home Office computer, I would be allowed to take Natasha home on a temporary visitor's permit. Within the hour we had it, authorization IS 96, giving her access with one restriction only ... that she did not 'enter employment, paid or unpaid, or engage in any business or profession'. As we left, the young lady said, 'All of this has been rather fascinating ... my father will be delighted when I tell him.' I asked why her father especially? 'He's in your business,' she replied. 'He's Mark Tully, the BBC's correspondent in India and a bit of an authority on refugees.'

7b Speaking exercise 1   page 69

Group B (abroad)

Here are the first drafts of five posters representing the main areas of concern of the tourist board regarding the behaviour of its citizens on holiday abroad. Discuss the relative importance of each area, and say how effective you think each poster might be. Then select **three** which you think should be included in the campaign. You may suggest changes to the illustrations and/or slogans, or you may design one or more of the posters completely from scratch.

7c Reading exercise 3   page 70

Student B

Will's Italian mother, Maggie, talks to Alex about Grace and her 11-year-old son, Charlie.

'But, Alex, always she was so cruel to him, from the time he was a baby! Nothing [Charlie] did was good enough. Nothing! A painting, a model ... [Grace] would say, "What is that?"' She mimicked a caustic tone. '"What do you call that?" Always she would make him feel he was no good. Always she would make him feel he had failed. She would say, "You're no good at anything, you're stupid, you'll never make anything of your life, you must go to this special school!" Oh, he was so desperate to please her! But he could not go to this school. This was the one thing he could not do. All he wanted was to stay at home, to be on the farm with Will. No, in this one thing he could not give in to her. And she never forgave him – no! She was angry, and she wasn't going to let him escape ... She was planning it all, to get Charlie to this school, because she could not bear to be opposed.'

....

'She says, "I'm leaving anyway. I'm finished with [Will]. I'm going tomorrow! ... I've had enough, and I'm taking what I'm owed." "Owed!" I say. "What can you be owed?" "Money," she says. ... I said to her, "You don't get money if you cheat on your husband." And she laughed. She *laughed*, Alex. She said, "It's all different now. I get half the house, half the cash. I checked it out. I went to a lawyer." "But it will ruin Will," I said. But she didn't care, Alex. She didn't care. For her, this was a fine punishment to him for not giving her what she wanted ... And then it comes to me – oh, it was like a knife in my heart, Alex – it comes to me: *Charlie*. "But not Charlie," I said. "After this, you will not take Charlie." She turned to me, and she said, very cool, "I will take Charlie. Of course I will take Charlie. He's mine." '

4A Vocabulary exercise 4   page 36

Student B

Work in pairs. Take turns to say your sentences in the manner of the verbs in brackets. You must each try to guess which verbs your partner is illustrating.

1 'Keep quiet. I think he's coming.' (*whisper*)
2 'Oh, I wish I'd listened to your advice.' (*sigh*)
3 'What rubbish!' (*grunt*)
4 'It's very hot and it hasn't rained for weeks.' (*moan*)
5 'Look, there's a mouse!' (*shriek*)

8D Speaking exercise 1   page 82

Group B

Look at the photos of four people and discuss what you imagine each one might be like. Consider the following:

- Name and age
- Studies and work
- Daily routine
- Personality – both positive and negative aspects
- Interests
- Likes and dislikes
- Habits
- Other

11D Grammar exercise 3   page 113
Student B

Work in pairs. Roleplay the situation. Use *I wish*, *I'd rather you* and *It's (about/high) time* … when voicing your complaints.

> You live in a flat and your downstairs neighbour has a large number of cats and dogs which rarely leave the building. Not only does the smell of the animals permeate into your flat but they often spend much of the day miaowing and barking. You find the smell unbearable and the noise affects your concentration when composing experimental music. You are considering going downstairs to complain when your pet-loving neighbour knocks at the door.

11C Vocabulary exercise 4   page 110
Group A

> Include at least six of these sounds in your story. You may change the form of the words. If the sound is given as a verb, you may use it as a noun (and vice versa).
> - the wind whistles (eg *through the trees*, *down the chimney*)
> - thunder cracks
> - (church) bells chime
> - a bus/lorry/train rattles along/past
> - tyres screech
> - coins/bottles/ice cubes clink
> - someone clicks their fingers
> - a floorboard/bed/chair creaks
> - someone bangs a drum
> - something crashes to the floor
> - a computer/fridge/machine hums
> - the clatter of footsteps

11C Speaking exercise 1   page 110
Student C

5B Speaking exercise 1   page 49
Group C

> Choose one of the following and prepare your pitch. Consider the points below, as well as any others that you think may be relevant.

head light

shoe light

The idea or product
- How will you describe your idea or product?
- What is its purpose?
- Are any special materials required for its production?

The target market
- What type of consumers is it aimed at?
- Why would they be interested in it? What benefits will it bring them?

The competition
- What makes it different from or better than similar ideas or products already on the market?
- How will you convince consumers of these advantages?

Sales and marketing
- What media will you use to advertise your product?
- In which type of outlets will it be sold?

The brand identity
- What is the name of your business and the product or service?
- What business logo will you have?

9c Speaking exercise 1   page 90

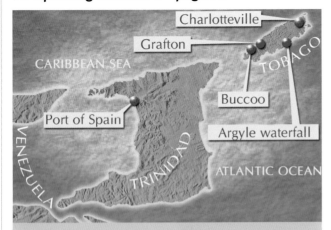

Argyle waterfall – a tiered climb with cool pools of water to swim in as you go. Worth hiring a guide.

Buccoo beach – meet the locals at the open-air dance and music fest, including steelpan bands – starts at 9pm.

Buccoo reef – snorkelling and diving in a coral reef.

Charlotteville – lovely fishing village in the north of the island with good swimming beaches.

Fort King George – historic site with stunning views of the coast. Includes Tobago museum – military relics and colonial documents.

Play golf – on one of the island's two championship golf courses. Views of the sea between bamboo and palm trees.

Helicopter flight – see the island from the air.

Jeep hire – travel the length of the island and see the breathtaking views on the coast road. The roads are winding, so take your time!

Mountain bike hire – a great way to see Tobago's lush and hilly terrain. The island boasts one of the oldest rainforests in the world.

Grafton beach resort – cabaret-style event every night. Great for tourists.

Grafton wildlife sanctuary – spectacular birdwatching. Hand-feed the colourful blue-crowned motmots.

3c Speaking exercise 2   page 30

Student B

You are Sonya Thomas and you are going to be interviewed about your involvement in competitive eating contests. Predict the type of questions you might be asked and prepare your answers. You could consider the following:

- Examples of records you hold
- Your training programme
- Your reasons for competing
- Any special techniques you adopt
- Other

2d Speaking exercise 1   page 23

Committee C

A plot of land has become available in your area for the siting of a new national museum. The authorities have invited suggestions for the exact nature of the museum and your committee will put forward a proposal at a forthcoming planning meeting. Either choose one of the following options, or come up with your own suggestion, then prepare for the meeting using the questions to help you.

television	women	public transport	other

- Who would your museum appeal to (eg age groups, interest groups, personality types)?
- What permanent exhibitions would it house?
- What temporary exhibitions could it host (three possibilities)?
- Will there be interactive displays?
- What extra events and activities could be organized?
- What extra facilities could be provided?
- What would the museum shop sell?
- Why would your museum be successful?

10d Listening & speaking exercise 2   page 102

CULTURE   OPERA

FLORENTINE OPERA

A CUT ABOVE THE REST

The stabbing scene in Leoncavallo's masterpiece *I Pagliacci* is always guaranteed to grip the audience, but never more so than during last night's performance at the Milwaukee Opera Theater.

5B Speaking exercise 1   page 49
Group D

Choose one of the following and prepare your pitch. Consider the points below, as well as any others that you think may be relevant.

bread delivery service

ironing service

The idea or product
- How will you describe your idea or product?
- What is its purpose?
- Are any special materials required for its production?

The target market
- What type of consumers is it aimed at?
- Why would they be interested in it? What benefits will it bring them?

The competition
- What makes it different from or better than similar ideas or products already on the market?
- How will you convince consumers of these advantages?

Sales and marketing
- What media will you use to advertise your product?
- In which type of outlets will it be sold?

The brand identity
- What is the name of your business and the product or service?
- What business logo will you have?

5C Speaking exercise 1   page 50
Student C

Read the list of household duties and observations, then discuss in broad terms who will do which duties. Individual duties may be shared between two or all three of you. Make brief notes of your decisions.

HOUSEHOLD DUTIES

Cleaning: once a week: bathroom, kitchen, living room, three bedrooms.

Washing: two loads of washing each week (excellent washing machine with tumble dryer in flat).

Ironing: two hours' worth of ironing in total each week (good steam iron available).

Cooking: you want to eat a cooked meal together every weekday evening.

Washing up: no dishwasher in flat.

Shopping: nearest supermarket over two kilometres away.

OBSERVATIONS

1 You don't mind ironing – as long as you can watch your favourite documentary series on Wednesday evenings from 8.00 to 9.00 while you do it.
2 You can cook but don't enjoy it and you have a very limited repertoire.
3 You are allergic to cleaning products.
4 You are the only person in the flat who can drive. You have your own car.
5 There is only one television in the flat and you cannot afford another.

11D Speech feature exercise 2   page 113
Group B

Use the words below to write six sentences like those in exercise 1 on page 113. You should:

- include an example of dislocation in each sentence.
- put a gap where the noun in bold should be.
- write a second sentence containing clues to enable another student to guess the word in the gap.

eg *be poor/***turnout**
It was very poor, the _____ for the election. Only 25 per cent of people bothered to vote.

1   change/**nappy**
2   **smell**/bring back memories of (something)
3   put out **rubbish**
4   **flying**/frighten the life out of (someone)
5   be understaffed/**school**
6   be swollen/**feet**

12B Reading exercise 4   page 118

Group A

Write a brief dialogue between a human being and one of the smart objects from the box. You should not mention the object in your dialogue, but rather give clues as to its possible identity.

> hat   fridge   car   TV   handbag
> armchair   other

Your dialogue might include one or more of the following functions.

> criticizing   complaining   praising
> apologizing   requesting   inviting
> offering   advising   other

7C Reading exercise 3   page 70

Student C

> **Edward talks to his sister, Alex, about his affair with Grace.**
>
> 'Oh, *she* wanted to talk about the future – she always wanted to talk about the future. When we'd be together, all that sort of stuff. Wanting me to name the day when she'd move in. Laying on the pressure, boxing me into a corner. Virtually had us married off, for God's sake! Oh, don't get me wrong, Lex. I mean, it wasn't that ... that ...' Unable to articulate the thought, he circled a hand in frustration. 'I mean, I was fond of her, Lex. *Very fond.* We had good times together and all that. Seeing her in London, away from everyone – that suited me fine. Just fine. Couldn't see why we couldn't leave it at that – you know? Just go on the same way. Not doing anyone any *harm*.' The mention of harm made him wince with some expression I had never seen in him before, something like remorse or regret. He hung his head.
>
> 'To be honest,' he said, in the tone of the confessional, 'she was too much for me, Lex. You know what I mean? A bit *overpowering*. In fact ... well ... she frightened me, the way she had everything worked out. I could see her taking over my life. Trying to change me, trying to make me into this other regular sort of chap. You know what I'm like, Lex – a bit of a slob,' he said disarmingly. 'Like my fry-ups and my fags and my home comforts. Nothing too fancy. Don't want to change. Don't want to be brought up to scratch, have the house all tarted up. Don't want to – you know – have to behave all the time. Just not *me*, Lex.'
>
> ....
>
> 'Well, I finally plucked up courage that afternoon. Finally came out with it straight, no interruptions. Actually said, "I don't think it's such a good idea, us getting together." She was angry.'

2C Vocabulary exercise 5   page 20

Student B

> Take it in turns with your partner to talk about your topics. Your partner will try to guess what your topics are, but you must not use any of the adjectives, nouns or verbs given in 1–5 below. Your partner's topics begin with the same expressions in bold as in your own topics, but not in the same order.
>
> 1 the most common way for students in your country to earn some extra money
> 2 the quickest way to learn a foreign language
> 3 the safest way to carry money when you travel abroad
> 4 the cheapest way to travel to the UK from your country
> 5 the most effective way to ease traffic congestion in towns and cities

7C Reading exercise 2   page 70

Blurb from *A Dark Devotion*

> Grace Dearden is beautiful, clever and admired. The last person to disappear into the lonely Norfolk marshes in the black depths of winter.
>
> Seven days ... and still no trace.
>
> With police investigations stalled, Grace's husband, Will, calls upon old family friend and criminal solicitor Alex O'Neill to help out. Returning to the village where she grew up, Alex immediately begins to uncover disturbing new clues ...
>
> Each one drawing her closer to a family's tragic secret ...

9A Grammar exercise 4   page 86

Student A

> petrol station   butcher's   hospital   town hall
> football stadium   beach   circus   airport

Choose **five** of the places in the box and for each one write a sentence which makes reference to or is said in that particular place, but without actually mentioning it. Your sentences should each contain a different use of *will*, *would* or *shall*.

Read your sentences to your partner, who will try to identify the five places.

9B Vocabulary & speaking exercise 5   page 88

Student A

You want to rent a furnished room. You saw an advertisement for the room in the illustration and have come to see it. Express your doubts to the landlord/landlady.

Student B

You are the landlord/landlady of the room in the illustration and are showing it to a prospective tenant. Respond to his/her doubts, highlighting its positive aspects.

8A Reading exercise 5   page 76

Work in pairs, A and B. You are going to describe someone.

A: Describe a person you know well to your partner, using the categories in the box in exercise 4, as well as any other details you consider relevant. Do not describe personality.

B: Give your impression of the personality of the person whose description you have just heard. Your partner will tell you how accurate your impression is.

When you have finished, change roles.

10C Reading exercise 2   page 100

Student A

Part 3

Ten minutes into his descent, Rankin should have been reaching the ground, but the enormous draughts of air that surged up the core of the cloud were retarding his fall. Soon the turbulence became much more severe. He had no visual point of reference in the gloomy depths but he sensed that, rather than falling, he was being shot upwards with successive violent gusts of rising air – blasts that were becoming increasingly violent. And then for the first time he felt the full force of the cloud.

'It came with incredible suddenness – and fury. It hit me like a tidal wave of air, a massive blast fired at me with the savagery of a cannon … I went soaring up and up and up as though there would be no end to its force.' Rankin wasn't the only one being hurled up and down. In the darkness around him, hundreds of thousands of hailstones were suffering the same fate. One minute they were falling downwards, dragging air down with them; the next minute they were swept back up by the enormous convection currents within the cloud.

With this falling and rising, the hailstones picked up freezing water and grew in size, hardening layer by layer. These rocks of ice pelted Rankin with bruising force. He was now vomiting from the violent spinning and pounding and he shut his eyes, unable to watch the nightmare unfolding.

The lightning appeared as huge, blue blades, several feet thick, which felt as though they were slicing him in two. The booming claps of thunder, caused by the explosive expansion of the air as the enormous electrical charge passed through, were so overpowering up close that they were more like physical impacts than noises. 'I didn't hear the thunder,' he said, 'I felt it.' Sometimes he had to hold his breath to avoid drowning from the dense torrents of freezing rain. At one point he looked up just as a bolt of lightning passed behind his parachute. It lit up the canvas, which appeared to the exhausted pilot as an enormous, white-domed cathedral.

After his vision of the parachute billowing as a cathedral above him, he began to notice the air becoming less turbulent, the rain and hail losing intensity. He was finally emerging from the underside of the cloud. In spite of his ordeal, Rankin managed to land successfully in a forest of pine trees. He had been buffeted up and down by the violent turbulence of the cumulonimbus for a full forty minutes.

When he was later examined in the hospital at Ahoskie, North Carolina, the doctors reported that his body was discoloured from frostbite and covered in welts and bruises from the impact of the hailstones. The doctors were as amazed as Rankin was that he'd survived.

Audioscripts

2B Pronunciation exercise 3 1.11

I'll, I'll just give you a brief example let's say er in playing cards let's say you have three cards the ten of diamonds erm the queen of clubs and the seven of hearts now the ten of diamonds to me is Bill Gates the richest man in the world and the queen of clubs is Kylie Minogue if you know her erm the singer and the seven of hearts would be er an international heart throb like erm James Bond double 0 seven so that's the association now to get the three in sequence I would have a journey round my house take taking the bedroom bathroom staircase et cetera

3B Speech feature exercise 3

1 1.14

Four years old it is, and it's only got 7,000 miles on the clock. Apparently, he had an operation on his leg not long after he bought it, so it's been sitting in the garage these last few years. Why he didn't ask more for it, though, I really don't know. Maybe he didn't realize its true value. £4,000 we paid for it, and its book price is well over twice that – a real bargain, don't you think? And the boot's enormous – with three young children we need lots of space to put their things in when we go away anywhere. So of course, we're absolutely delighted.

2 🔘 1.15

What a ridiculous present this is! Why on Earth he thought I'd want one of these I cannot imagine. I mean, I don't *like* travelling. I've never been one for hotels – like my own bed too much. And look at it – it's not even very good quality. Made of cheap plastic it is. Five quid that must have cost him. And he chose the smallest one he could find, of course – there's just about enough room in that for a pair of pyjamas and a toothbrush. How you're supposed to get anything else in there, I just don't know. What a cheapskate he is. Always has been, always will be.

4B Listening exercise 3 🔘 1.19

P = presenter   EW = Ellen Wainwright

P: ... that report there on complaining from Julie Somersdale. Now, we move on from the subject of voicing complaints to ... well, the whole area of voice complaints, that is, medical problems with our voice. According to a recent report, one in three workers in the world's modern economies rely on their voice to carry out their job and around one in four experiences voice problems on a regular basis. Now, I'd certainly include myself in those figures – in the last year or so I've been decidedly hoarse on more than a couple of occasions. But why do so many of us suffer in this way? With me to help answer that question is voice expert, Ellen Wainwright. Ellen, why is the voice taking such a beating?

EW: Well, as you mentioned, the most important tool for many of us now is our voice, particularly as we shift to more service-based economies. Broadcasters like yourself are at risk of course, but so too are people like shopworkers, receptionists, politicians, performers, fitness instructors and teachers. In fact, the report singles out teachers and call centre workers as the most regularly affected types of worker. Too much talking in the wrong environment can lead to voice loss, and in some cases, more serious damage.

P: What kind of damage can people suffer to their voice?

EW: Well, there's a whole range of complaints, including 'odynophonia', which is soreness in the throat that makes speaking painful, and 'vocal cord paresis', which is partial paralysis of the vocal cords. There's also, of course, 'laryngitis' – inflammation of the larynx, that organ in our throat which actually *contains* the vocal cords. People like catchy names they can remember, though, and we've now got a new term that's come into the language to describe this phenomenon – 'repetitive voice injury', based of course on the more familiar RSI, or 'repetitive strain injury'. It covers all manner of ills, but basically means overuse of the voice.

P: And are these problems treatable?

EW: Well, unfortunately, in some cases permanent damage can be caused – chronic laryngitis, for example, can mean having to give up work. Generally, though, people with prolonged voice loss can recover some or all of their ability to speak with the help of a good speech therapist. Occasionally, an operation such as vocal cord surgery may be needed.

P: Not very pleasant. Though I saw recently that people are actually opting to have vocal cord surgery in order to make them sound younger. Apparently, they can turn old shaky voices into strong clear ones by injecting collagen into the vocal cords to bring them closer together.

EW: Yes, that's the so-called 'voice lift' – another kind of cosmetic surgery. Once you've had your face lift, you can have a voice lift to match. The vocal cords become stiffer with age and move further apart – and this helps put that right. This can occur in younger people too, when their vocal cords become damaged, and that's the original, more serious purpose of this kind of surgery. But of course, as with everything, prevention is ten times better than cure, and if we look after our voice, we can avoid the need for any intervention of this type.

P: And how do we go about that? I mean, a teacher has to speak if she wants to do her job, and she probably has to raise her voice to make herself heard. And the poor call centre worker inevitably has to talk all day on the phone.

EW: Well, there are two considerations here: what our employers can do for us, and what we can do for ourselves. The working environment is crucial in all of this, and the employer has a responsibility to make sure conditions are right. Centrally heated offices in winter with low humidity are bad for the vocal cords and can lead to throat infections. Erm, high levels of background noise in factories, for example, can cause voice strain if we're forced to shout above it – that's particularly true of people who have to give instructions. And teaching in overlarge classrooms with poor acoustics can have the same effect. In the case of the call centre workers – well, they often don't have enough breaks to enable them to drink an adequate amount of water. The employer should ensure that this is possible.

P: Yes, and I'll be talking to mine right after the programme. Now, Ellen, what can we do ourselves? How can we look after our voice?

EW: Well, I've mentioned water already. That's essential if we want to keep our vocal cords well lubricated. And try and avoid anything with caffeine – things like coffee, tea or soft drinks with caffeine in them, as these dry out the vocal cords. That's the first point. Also, if you feel you've been speaking too much, try asking a question or two – that puts the onus on the other speakers and gives you a bit of a rest. And *when you speak, don't push your voice from your throat* – instead, your navel, your tummy button should move towards your backbone. If not, you won't get the best from your voice and it may suffer damage.

P: And how about vocal exercises, the kind of thing actors or singers do before they go on stage? Do they help?

EW: Certainly. Vocal warm-ups are excellent for helping voice projection and ensuring you use your voice correctly. Proper breathing from the diaphragm and a good posture are important though. Make sure you keep your head up, your chin level and your shoulders sloping, not dropped or hunched. Oh, and relax – that's very important.

P: And not very easy! Can you give us a couple of examples of vocal warm-ups?

EW: Yes, alright. Well, the obvious one is: *Do re me fa so la te do.* Then there are those that combine the same vowel sounds with different consonants: *Ma me mi mo mu, Ba be bi bo bu, Ta te ti to tu.* And then you have sentences such as '*Bring back my bonny baby's beautiful blue bonnet'.*

P: Marvellous, Ellen. Unfortunately, on that note, we have to finish I'm afraid. But if you want to find out more about looking …

5D Grammar exercise 1

1 🔘 **2.9**

It quickly became clear when I was pregnant with Jamie that they were going to make life difficult for me. My boss said he felt 'let down' – can you believe it? – and he wouldn't give me time off work for antenatal appointments. And then when I got back from maternity leave I found I'd been demoted to a junior position. Five years I'd been with them and that was the thanks I got. They were very obviously trying to force me out of the company. The Equal Opportunities Commission were very supportive and gave me funding to bring my case before the Employment Tribunal. If it hadn't been for the EOC and the Sex Discrimination Act, my fight wouldn't have been possible. But isn't it just incredible that something like this can still happen in the 21st century?

2 🔘 **2.10**

When I was studying at university, I spent my summer holidays working as a temporary secretary. This was the late 70s and in those days male secretaries were even rarer than they are now. In one marketing firm I temped at, I was told by the personnel manager soon after I started that I wasn't needed anymore. He said it was better for the company's image to have women on the front desk. Blatantly sexist of course, and clearly against the law, but in those days I was very green and it never occurred to me that the Sex Discrimination Act might also apply to me. Had I made the connection, I would definitely have taken them to an employment tribunal. The SDA is such an important piece of legislation, and is obviously there for men as well as women. I just wish I'd realized that at the time.

3 🔘 **2.11**

When I found out that the male sales reps in my company were getting a higher basic salary than me I was furious. They were being paid 15% more for doing exactly the same job. I was even more upset when management refused to listen to my complaint. Part of me wishes I hadn't taken my case to the Employment Tribunal – the whole thing put a lot of pressure and strain on my family and myself, and it was both emotionally and financially very draining. OK, the result was positive and I received compensation, but I was fortunate – if I hadn't recently inherited some money, I might never have been able to take my claim to the Employment Tribunal. To my mind, the law doesn't go far enough to protect ordinary people – it depends too heavily on individuals to bring cases against offending employers. The Government could certainly do more to help.

4 🔘 **2.12**

I can safely say that I have *never* discriminated against any of my workers because of their sex. That's not to say of course that all employers are like me, and yes, of course, we need laws to protect individuals against more unscrupulous types – I'm all in favour of that. But there needs to be a balance, and I don't think they've got that quite right yet. I mean, I have to be so careful – if I give promotion to a man, you can be sure there'll be two or three women knocking on my door the next day claiming they've been treated unfairly. And you know, last year, there was a woman here who told me the day after I gave her the job that she was three months pregnant. Now if I'd known that at the interview, I'd never have taken her on.

5 🔘 **2.13**

We've come a long way since the 1970s. If the SDA hadn't been brought in, we almost certainly wouldn't have so many women in full-time employment now, and doing jobs they would never have dreamed of doing a generation or two before. I read the other day that nearly a quarter of all Britain's coastguards today are women – and before 1978 there wasn't a single one! Some things take a bit longer to change though. My sister works in the City and she tells me that although there's no active discrimination, there are certain differences in male and female culture which affect how you get on. She works extremely hard but she doesn't go to the pub after work, she doesn't like talking about football and she's not one for telling jokes. And she's convinced this has held her back. There are still a number of unspoken barriers in some male-dominated professions – the so-called 'glass ceiling'.

7D Vocabulary exercise 1

P = presenter   JS = Jenny Sanders   L = lawyer
SB = Sally Blofeld

1 🔘 **2.25**

P: A pensioner who stabbed a would-be burglar with a kitchen knife has been cleared of assault. Sixty-eight-year-old Peter Simpson had been charged with the offence following a failed burglary at his home in March. Having been knocked to the floor by James Boyle, an unemployed plumber who had climbed in through an open window in the kitchen, Mr Simpson grabbed a knife from a drawer and stabbed the intruder three times in the leg.
In his trial last Monday, Boyle, who had stolen from a number of neighbouring houses in the same morning, pleaded guilty to six counts of burglary and one of attempted burglary. He was given a six-year jail term.
Jenny Sanders was in court to hear Peter Simpson's acquittal.

JS: Former army officer Peter Simpson explained how on the morning of March 15th he had heard a noise in his kitchen and gone to investigate. When he ordered 22-year-old Boyle to leave his home, the younger man had shouted insults at him and pushed him to the floor. Simpson said he had used the nearest available knife and applied his army training to overcome his attacker, without at any moment attempting to cause him permanent harm.

Judge David Westwood expressed regret that charges had been brought against Mr Simpson, who, he said, had clearly acted with reasonable force to defend himself and his property. The incident has revived debate about exactly how far homeowners should be allowed to go when confronting intruders. Under current legislation, anyone can use what is described as 'reasonable force' to protect themselves against burglars who enter their homes. The government recently issued a set of guidelines explaining the law.

Speaking after the trial, Anna Coleby from the organization 'House Defence' insisted that householders should have the right to use any force they consider necessary to defend themselves and their homes, without having to worry whether it is reasonable or not. She said that burglars should lose all their rights when they trespass on other people's property and be prepared to face the consequences.

Members of James Boyle's family refused to comment.

2 💿 **2.26**

P: In the first case of its kind in the Radio Ambria area, a single mother has been jailed for allowing her daughter to play truant. Thirty-five-year-old Sheila Danbury was sentenced to 60 days' imprisonment by Brenton magistrates yesterday for failing to ensure that her eldest daughter attended school regularly. Parents can be fined a maximum of £2,500 for each child playing truant, or imprisoned for up to three months. Speaking after the trial, Educational Welfare Officer Paula Banes said that the local education authorities had been working closely with Ms Danbury for over 18 months and she had been warned repeatedly that she faced a prison sentence if she continued to allow her daughter to miss lessons. Sheila Danbury was said to be shocked and upset by the decision. Her four children, including 14-year-old Sandra, who attended only 25% of classes in the last academic year, are currently being cared for by their aunt.

Earlier, I spoke to Ms Danbury's lawyer, Ian Stride, and asked him for his reaction to the sentence.

L: Well, it's excessive. I think, I think the legislation is there, or should be there at least to persuade, to convince parents of the need to send their children to school, but I but I really don't think a jail term will help to get my client's daughter back into the classroom. The very person the girl needs won't be there to encourage her.

P: Does your client regret not doing enough?

L: Well, she did everything she could. She got the girl ready in the morning and drove her to the school gates, but even if she'd dragged her in screaming, she couldn't have forced her to stay. Clearly, the school has to accept some of the responsibility for that.

P: In a statement yesterday, the local education authority welcomed the decision, saying that it hoped it would send out a clear message to parents that truancy will not be tolerated. Ms Danbury's lawyer said his client would be appealing against the sentence.

3 💿 **2.27**

P: Fines imposed on companies convicted of polluting the environment are insufficient, according to environmental groups. The criticism comes after yesterday's decision by Redford Magistrates to fine the Ambrian Water Authority

£15,000 for allowing sewage to leak into Lake Carston last year. The leakage killed a large proportion of the lake's wildlife as well as making it unfit for water sports. Our environmental correspondent, Sally Blofeld reports.

SB: In yesterday's court hearing, the Ambrian Water Authority pleaded guilty to allowing raw sewage to enter Lake Carston last November. The sewage had overflowed from a blocked sewer, causing the death of the lake's entire fish population as well as frogs and other wildlife.

The penalty brings the total of the company's fines for environmental offences to nearly half a million pounds this year alone, drawing criticism from the region's environmental groups. Jerry Wexford of 'Action Now' called for tougher penalties for organizations found guilty of causing pollution. He said that £15,000 was just a 'drop in the ocean' for large companies and urged courts to increase fines and impose prison sentences on company officials who are shown to be negligent. Larger fines, he said, would pay for the costs of clean-up operations, and jail sentences would serve as an encouragement to businesses to prevent such incidents occurring again.

Daniel Roberts, a spokesman for the Water Authority, accused the environmentalists of exaggerating the extent of the problem. He maintained that sewage leaks were inevitable, but had been kept to a minimum in the region. He also pointed out that the Water Authority had paid the entire bill for Lake Carston to be cleaned and was investing over a million pounds in new treatment technology.

8D Grammar exercise 1

1 💿 **2.32**

You see, the fact is, I don't need a man to feel complete as a woman. And some people just find that difficult to accept. You know, they still have this image of the single woman as some kind of lonely spinster, on the shelf, with only her dogs or cats to turn to. But that's just so old fashioned. For me, being single is a lifestyle choice and I don't need to be pitied. You know, I hate it when people say 'Oh, you poor thing, it must be terrible.' Well, no, actually, it isn't. Anything but. I like my own company and my life is very full, thank you very much. In fact, I think as a rule, women are much better able to cope on their own than men. We're far more self-sufficient.

2 💿 **2.33**

Well, yeah, OK, living with your parents *does* have its advantages, I suppose. I mean, I don't have to do any housework, my mum does all my ironing and she won't even let me *near* the kitchen. Even so, I'd rather be in my own place and sharing it with someone – you know … a woman … as in, er, 'serious relationship'. No disrespect to my mum, of course, but her hugs and kisses just aren't … well, they're not the same, are they? Anyway, there's not much chance of a move in the near future, I'm sad to say. For one thing, I'll need to save up a lot more – property prices round here are sky-high at the moment and I just haven't got enough to pay a deposit. Plus, of course, I have to find someone to be in a serious relationship *with*. And I'm afraid I'm not having much luck in that department right now.

3 💿 **2.34**

When he walked out, I thought, 'Good riddance! I'm *glad* he's gone. I don't want him here and I don't need him here. I don't need *anyone*.' And if it was just me, if I only had myself to look after, I'd still feel the same way. But I've got my two boys to think of and they really need to have a man about the house. Darren, stop that this minute! Put it down. Now! You see – they're a bit of a handful. They need a dad and I need the extra pair of hands. Mind you, they're bone idle, most men, aren't they, so there's no guarantee the next one would be any better than the last. But of course, that's not the only reason for being in a relationship, is it?

4 **2.35**

On balance, I'd say I'm better out of a relationship than in at the moment. Of course, I do enjoy the companionship of a steady girlfriend – I split up with someone recently, and I think one of the things I miss most is the regular conversation – you know, politics, the planet, a film we've seen – whatever. But my job's taking up a lot of my time at the moment – my boss keeps sending me away on business – Eastern Europe mostly – so I'm hardly ever around during the week. And anyway, there's a lot to be said for being single. I get to see my chums more often, for one thing, and we all go out partying and clubbing together at the weekend – a whole group of us. We have a great time. And there's not that same pressure to be somewhere or do something at any specific time – I don't feel tied down like I used to.

5 **2.36**

To be perfectly honest I just couldn't imagine going out with another man, let alone being married to one. I mean, relationships are all about compromise, aren't they, and I'm just hopeless at that. Like, why should I have to spend the evening watching football on the telly or going out with his boring friends? I know, I know – I'm just selfish and inflexible, but at least I admit it. Let's be honest, though, men have some pretty unendearing qualities of their own. They leave their dirty handprints all over the walls, they spill coffee on the sofa and don't clean it off, and they go on and on about their problems as if everyone else was really interested. I should know, I've been married twice. No, it's not always easy being single, but that's how I want it. I'm much better off that way.

6 **2.37**

Nine years to go to my retirement, and I still haven't found that elusive 'woman of my dreams'. I've tried – believe me, I've tried – but she just hasn't shown her face yet. Perhaps she's hiding from me. Haven't given up hope yet, though. In fact, I've just started going to a singles club – every Friday down at the Beach Hotel. The Tropical Bar. I've already got my eye on somebody. Dorothy, her name is – she works in Gamidges in Brent Street. I might pop in there one day this week and surprise her. Nothing to lose.

9B Listening exercise 4 3.1

P = Presenter   A = Annie Taylor   G = Gerry Burnham

P: Messy, long-haired layabouts in dirty, scruffy clothes; rowdy parties that keep the neighbours awake, and crumbling run-down houses and flats that bring down property values in the local area. That, at least, is the traditional image of squatters and the buildings they inhabit. But according to a recent study that's all changing. The number of squatters in the UK has risen dramatically in the last ten years, from around 9,500 to almost 15,000 – that's an increase of 60% – and around 10,000 of those are to be found in the London area alone. With me is Annie Taylor from the SRA, the Squatters' Rights' Association, the group that carried out the study. Annie, why are so many people squatting?

A: Several reasons, really. Principally, though, it's a question of necessity. Most people squat simply because they have to. Property prices and rents are currently just too high for many people and there is a serious lack of social housing up and down the country.

P: That's homes provided at low cost by non-profit organizations, right?

A: That's right. Rented accommodation, mainly. There are over 100,000 families queuing up for this type of housing, so it's absurd – criminal, even – that there are so many empty homes in Britain – 750,000 at the last count. That's three quarters of a million unused flats and houses that are going to waste – in many cases because of property speculation.

P: Hardly surprising, then, that so many people decide to squat.

A: Indeed.

P: And what type of people are they? How would you describe this new generation of squatters?

A: Well, for one thing there are more students squatting than before. Erm … but we're also seeing large numbers of graduates, young people in career jobs who just cannot afford to get on the property ladder. Erm, and then increasingly we're offering advice to people who come here from the Continent … from other European countries.

P: Interesting. And do you find yourself having to speak their languages as a result?

A: We try. We do our best. But to be honest many of these people have a very good level of English, and all our technical, legal advice is printed out in a number of different languages, anyway. So … yeah … that means they're, they're clear on all aspects of squatting in Britain.

P: You mention there the legal aspects – because of course, what surprises many visitors to this country is that squatting here is a civil offence, not a criminal offence.

A: That's right. You can legally occupy a vacant building as long as there's no sign of a forced entry. In other words, you mustn't break any windows or locks to get inside. And once you're in, then you have to prove you have exclusive access to the property, which basically means changing all the locks.

P: Uh huh? The law is very clear on that, is it?

A: Yes, it is, but we also tell squatters to put up a copy of Section 6 on the outside of the building – on the doors and windows. Just in case.

P: And what is a Section 6?

A: It's a document, a legal warning, spelling out clearly to the owner – or even the police – exactly what your rights are.
It begins 'Take notice that we live in this property, it is our home and we intend to stay here'.

P: But the landlord can still evict you.

A: Yes, he can, or she can. But they have to go through the courts and that can take time – usually up to four weeks, sometimes months. Even years, in some cases.

P: My goodness me. Thank you, Annie. Very enlightening. It's time now, I think, to bring in our other guest today – Gerry Burnham, who is a squatter. Good morning, Gerry.

G: Morning.

P: Gerry lives in a squat – a semi-detached house – with three other people in Chiswick, West London. Gerry, how did you get into the property? Or rather, before that, how did you know it was empty in the first place?

G: Well, firstly, er, it's er, it's a detached house, actually, not a semi. Only the best.

P: Sorry, yes, of course. I do beg your pardon.

G: Anyway, er, my mates and I, we, er, we were about to be evicted from our last place so we went looking for somewhere else to live – house-hunting, like – and, er, we saw this place looking a bit run-down. The, er, garden was overgrown and the whole place needed a coat of paint. It was, er, well it looked pretty abandoned really.

P: So you moved in.

G: Not straightaway, no. You have to make sure it really *is* empty first. We gave it a couple of weeks. We, er, we looked in the dustbin every day to make sure no one was throwing any rubbish out, like, and, er, we watched the postman to see if he brought any letters or not.

P: Which he didn't, presumably?

G: No, nothing.

P: So what did you do next?

G: We got in through the kitchen window – it was in such a bad state, like, that it more less just fell open. Then we did what Annie was just talking about – changed the locks and all that.

P: And how do you feel about squatting? Because you're a computer programmer, aren't you? Can't you afford to rent?

G: Well, I could, yeah, but in London all I'd get for my money'd be a tiny flat, with nothing left over to save. At least this way I'm putting money in the bank. Should be able to get a mortgage soon, with a bit of luck. Hope so, anyway.

P: So you can't wait to get out.

G: Well, no, I wouldn't say that. I suppose I've got mixed feelings about it all, really. I mean, it's pretty depressing when you first move in to a place – no running water, no gas, no electricity. Sometimes you never do get connected – especially electricity – they can be really difficult, they can, when it comes to squatters. Some refuse point blank. But then, you know, you're with your mates and little by little you get settled in, and before you know it you've made a little home for yourself.

P: And then you get evicted.

G: Yeah, that's a bit of a hassle, but, er, it makes it all interesting as well, though. I mean, you're always on the move. Always busy, too - I've got quite good at DIY and all that, since I've been squatting, like. Fact, I think landlords benefit quite a bit from people like us. We do their houses up for them, keep them maintained and so on.

P: Yes, I'd like to come back to you, Annie, on that, if I may. I understand there are now squatting co-operatives, who move into places and actually restore them. Is that right?

A: Yes, it is, particularly in the Manchester area. There are several groups of people, students …

9D Speech feature exercise 2

 3.3 Extract 1

I = Ian   S = Sally   A = Alison   J = John

S: That's what they say and you know, I think wearing it really did kind of sharpen my other senses. I put it on when I was on the train to get used to it and I sort of became aware of every sound – every little knock or scrape – and I could smell every coffee or sandwich or whatever.

I: And what about when you got to York, Sally? What was it like?

S: Well, we did all the sights and everything – the cathedral, the city walls, the historic buildings and so on – except of course they weren't really 'sights' because I couldn't actually see them. Paul, though, did a marvellous job of describing everything to me and by the end of our day there I felt as if I knew the city *really* well.

A: What about things like eating and washing and all that – how did you get on with that?

S: Yeah, all those little things that form part of our daily routine – they were a real challenge. I had to sort of learn to sit down again or eat with a knife and fork. In this restaurant we went to, they had these tall kind of tube-shaped glasses and every time I reached out to pick mine up I knocked it over and spilt everything all over the place. Disastrous!

A: That's awful!

J: Did you do anything else when you were there? Did you like go into any museums or anything?

S: Yeah, we did actually. Paul took me into an exhibition by some local sculptor – Anna Kirby, or something, I think her name was. It was all modern stuff, from local stone – lots of curves and holes and that sort of thing.

I: And he described everything to you.

S: Well, yeah, some things. But luckily for me, many of the works there were hands-on exhibits – which is great if you're visually handicapped.

J: Or a child.

A: Or an adult! It must be brilliant feeling your way around an exhibition.

S: Yeah, it really was something else. Paul had to describe the rest to me but it was the tactile experience I most enjoyed.

J: Obviously.

 3.4 Extract 2

I = Ian   D = Dave   T = Tom   A = Alison

I: Dave, you went a bit further than Sally, didn't you?

D: Yeah, not as far as the place I had on my sign, though.

A: What was that?

D: Tokyo

All: Tokyo!

D: Yeah, that was my 'faraway place'. It was a good conversation starter, helped break the ice and all that. But apart from that it's just like the normal version. Well, I *imagine* it is, anyway – I was a complete novice, you see – a real rookie.

A: Really? So what did you think of it?

D: Well, pretty dull really – not my cup of tea. I mean, I met some nice people and practised my languages and everything, but the bits in between, all that waiting next to busy roads, it's not my idea of fun. And it was really hard to get lifts, especially in France.

T: Maybe they just thought you were a bit crazy or something – standing on a French roadside trying to get to 'Tokyo'.

D: Yeah, maybe. Mind you, the ones who did pick me up were often madder than me. There was this one guy who kept swerving onto the wrong side of the road – I couldn't work out if he was doing it for fun or he was just a lousy driver, but we very nearly had a head-on collision at one point with this oncoming lorry.

A: Ooh, sounds hairy.

D: Yeah, it was. And then after that bit of excitement – if you can call it that – I had to wait for about four hours outside this town called Bar-le-Duc, or something. Great laugh – I got really cheesed off, I can tell you.

I: So how far did you get eventually?

D: Munich.

I: And then what? You gave up?

D: Well, some guy who gave me a lift there put me up for a couple of nights – he gave me a key and I could sort of come and go as I pleased – just like a hotel.

A: That was good of him.

D: Yeah, and it meant I could do a bit of good old, non-experimental, conventional sightseeing …

All: Aha

D: … before I got the overnight train back to London.

All: Cheat!

3.5 Extract 3

T = Tom   H = Helen

T: Helen, you actually *flew* to Lithuania, didn't you?

H: Yeah, I managed to get a cheap flight. And I also took in the main sights as well – like Dave.

All: Aah? Oh yeah?

H: Yeah, I wanted to compare the two types – as in 'experimental', you know.

T: Hm hm. So what did you discover?

H: Well, the first day I did all the left-right business, and I have to say I was very pleasantly surprised. I had a lovely time, it was fascinating.

T: In what way?

H: Well I saw all those parts of Vilnius that I wouldn't otherwise have seen if I'd just done the typical tourist thing – you know, all the bits of the city that are kind of off the main tourist routes. I saw some lovely old buildings with these really pretty courtyards and everywhere there was loads of greenery, you know, trees and grass and stuff like that.

T: Sounds lovely

H: Yeah, it was. But I think what I enjoyed most about the whole thing was not knowing what I was going to discover every time I turned a corner. When I went sightseeing the next day, I knew what I was going to find because I'd already seen it in the brochures and things. This was different.

T: But presumably it wasn't *all* quite so pretty – I mean, you must have seen some unattractive places as well.

H: Oh yeah, of course. I mean I walked through some really ugly run-down housing estates – some of the buildings were in a terrible condition. But I mean you expect that in a city, don't you, wherever you are. And anyway, it all helped to give me a true flavour of the place, to see both sides of the coin. And as the day went on, I got to realize that there was always a park or a river or something close to every built-up area, so I never got down or fed up or anything.

T: And when did you decide to stop?

H: When I came to a brick wall.
No, seriously, the book says something about carrying on until something blocks your path, and for me it was a brick wall in a dead-end street – I couldn't go left or right. I can't say I was sorry, mind – I was worn out. I'd been walking for something like six hours.

All: Oh!

3.6 Extract 4

I = Ian   S = Steve   E = Emma   A = Alison   T = Tom

S: I mean, the thing is, it's like, do you go where you *want* to go, or do you go where you think *your partner* will go, or do you go where you think your partner will think *you* will go?

A: Ooh, tricky.

T: Very.

E: Yes, and if I'd gone where I thought Steve would go, I'd have headed straight for the district with all the bars.

S: She knows me too well.

A: Got some good bars in Madrid.

E: Hmm. Quite. But that's not my idea of a good time.

S: No, and I figured that was what she'd think. So I went to all the main tourist sights instead.

A: You as well!

T: Looks like everyone did.

S: Yeah, I did the lot – the Puerta del Sol, Plaza Mayor, the Royal Palace …

E: And I was following in his footsteps, would you believe? Though I didn't know it at the time, of course.

I: What, everywhere?

S: Yep. About ten minutes behind me, she was.

I: Wow! What a coincidence.

E: Not really – I mean, it's the tourist thing, isn't it? Everyone does what the guidebook tells you to. Understandable, really, I suppose. And anyway, I had a marvellous time. It's a lovely city, Madrid.

S: Better if you can see it with someone, though.

A: Oh, did you miss her?

S: Well, yeah, you know, I mean, it's a bit boring walking all day round a city on your own.

T: So you didn't bump into each other? You didn't meet up at all?

S: Well, yeah, but only because we cheated.

A: How come?

E: We had a plan B in case we didn't find each other. We didn't want to go to Madrid and not have a romantic meal together, did we? Lovely, it was.

S: Yeah, lovely and expensive.

E: Ooh, you old misery guts.

10B Grammar exercise 1

1 3.7

What is success? That's easy – you just have to look at my sales figures to know the answer to that. Best in the whole southern region, they are. I've sold more policies this quarter than anyone else on the sales team did for the whole of last year. Mick the Machine, they call me. They all say to me 'What's the secret, Mick – how do you do it?' Of course, personality's important – you've got to have a bit of spark, you've got to know how to win people over. But most of all I put my success down to self-discipline and perseverance. You've got to get up in the morning, get out there and do the business – it doesn't matter what the weather's like, how you're feeling, how unsure you are of pulling off a deal – you've just got to keep going.

2 3.8

A successful person for me is not someone who makes pots of money. Success is not about accumulating *wealth*, it's about achieving *happiness*. It means enjoying whatever you do. Life is so short, we have to make sure our stay on this planet is a pleasant one. Have a good time, let your hair down, that's what I say – as long as you treat others with respect. And if you want to enjoy life, you've got to adopt a positive outlook on everything. If things don't turn out well, don't let it get you down. We all come up against problems – we just have to face up to them, try and solve them. And we all make mistakes at some time – in all areas of our lives. The important thing is to try and learn from them, not let them destroy you.

3 🔘 **3.9**

I'll be 83 next month – and I've just signed up for a computer course. How about that, then? It starts next Monday. I told my son about it – I said 'I'm going to learn to use the computer,' and he said 'What? At your age? Never.' He seems sure I won't be able to do it but I know I will. You see, all through my life I've been successful – I've always got what I wanted. And the key to that success has always been the same – confidence. Being sure of yourself and knowing you can achieve anything if you really want to. And you know, success for me here won't only be learning to use the computer – in a sense, that's the least of it all. No, I'll get most satisfaction out of proving that son of mine wrong.

4 🔘 **3.10**

Success is all about achieving goals – accomplishing what you set out to do. But it's not so much *what* you achieve as *how* you achieve it that counts. You have to earn your success. For instance, people tell me I'm an excellent cook – now, whether that's true or not is not for me to say, but it's always a great source of satisfaction to me when my dinner guests express their appreciation of one of my meals. I feel valued – and that, for me, is success, but particularly because I know that I have invested an enormous amount of time and effort in preparing the meal and organizing the whole evening. If I just threw something together in half an hour, they'd probably still enjoy it, but it wouldn't be quite the same, would it?

5 🔘 **3.11**

When, or rather, *if* I get to old age, I hope I'll have had a useful life. That for me is a true measure of success – doing something positive with your life and at the same time making the world a better place. My dad always said you should aim to leave a legacy when you've gone, something useful for people to remember you by. He wrote several books – very good ones too – but he wasn't suggesting that everyone has to do that. It could be something more simple, like planting trees, doing up a house or even having children. I expect I'll have my own kids one day, but for now I'm happy just to keep it to planting trees. In fact, I'm driving up into the mountains with some friends of mine next week to do just that.

6 🔘 **3.12**

You often hear people say it's not the winning, it's the taking part that's important. That's fair enough, particularly if, like me, you're an amateur, rather than a professional. Though I reckon it's more the doing your best that's important – after all, there's no point taking part if you don't at least *try* to win. Round about this time next week I'll be setting off for Stockholm to take part in a European club competition. Success for me in Sweden will be knowing I've gone out there and given it my best shot, both for me and for my club – even if I don't win any medals – which is more than likely given the strength of the other runners! Anyway, to give ourselves the best chance of doing well, we've been training hard all season. Preparation is obviously an essential factor in achieving success.

12c Vocabulary exercise 1

P = Presenter   GW = Geoff Winning   SP = Sally Plumtree

Part 1 🔘 **3.41**

P: Hello and welcome to *For and Against*, where this week we'll be discussing the following statement: *There is too much technology in sport*. And by 'technology' we mean any human-made means, any method, machine, device or piece of clothing or equipment which is developed using scientific knowledge for practical purposes. Exactly what those purposes are in sporting terms, I'll leave for our guests to say, but it's clear that in recent times technology has revolutionized the world of sport.

In athletics, for example, marathon runners are now electronically tagged and their progress during a race can be followed online; materials technologists are constantly working on improving footwear and clothing for the different athletics events; and their work extends to equipment, such as the pole in the pole vault – we've seen there a progression from hard wood to bamboo in the early 1900s, followed by steel in the 1950s and the more flexible fibreglass in the 60s. Tennis rackets – both their material and their design – now bear little resemblance to those used in the 1970s when personalities like Bjorn Borg or John McEnroe graced the tennis courts. It would be strange, unthinkable even, for players of the calibre of Rafa Nadal to appear on court now with a racket made of wood.

And then in football of course there is the use of microphones and earphones by referees, who are now able to communicate more easily with their linesmen and the fourth official. And the controversial issue of goal-line technology to determine whether a goal has been scored or not.

Now, our two studio guests today will be debating the extent to which these developments and others like them are beneficial to sport; whether technology should continue in the same way to help us achieve our sport-related goals or whether it is having too much influence and should be kept out of sport, or at least be subject to more restrictions. A fairly recent example of this was the full-length swimsuit. This reduced friction in the water and gave swimmers more buoyancy and speed, leading to nearly 200 world records in under two years. FINA, the world governing body of swimming, felt they gave wearers an unfair advantage and banned their use by professional swimmers in 2010.

Part 2 🔘 **3.42**

P: Now let me introduce our guests. Firstly, we have Geoff Winning, who's a sports scientist and regular columnist for the magazine *Technosport*. Good morning, Geoff.

G: Good morning.

P: And we also have with us Sally Plumtree, the successful former athlete and now an equally successful freelance sports journalist. Good morning, Sally.

S: Hello, Peter.

P: Right, let's begin. For listeners who are new to our programme, both Geoff and Sally now have approximately one minute each to put forward their main arguments. Geoff, let's begin with you – you're very much pro-technology. Tell us why.

G: Well, the effects of technology in sport cannot be understated. And there are basically three areas where its application is of tremendous benefit. The first of these, of course, is the fact that it enables athletes to improve their performance, to surpass their own limits. Some of the examples of developments you mentioned just now have led to humans running faster, jumping higher or in the case of tennis, hitting harder. Technology helps us to push out the boundaries of human achievement, to see just what the human body is capable of. Secondly, it helps to maximize safety in sport. Helmet design in cycling and hockey is an example of this, and so is the headgear used in amateur boxing, those heavily padded hats that protect boxers from soft tissue damage. And then finally, technology ensures a greater degree of fairness in sport. You mentioned microphones and goal-line technology in football, and in tennis there is the Hawkeye system which creates virtual 3D images to help the umpire in disputed line calls. Performance, safety and justice – the three reasons why technology should continue to be used in sport.

P: Thank you, Geoff. Now, Sally, over to you. Why are you in favour of more restrictions in the use of technology?

S: Well, like Geoff I, too, have three main arguments to support my case. Firstly, technology has come to dominate sport, so much so that I believe it overshadows human achievement and we are losing the raw physical challenge that is central to sporting competitions. When I was competing we depended much more on ourselves, on our own abilities and efforts, not on the work of scientists and engineers. It really was *human* achievement and not *technological* achievement that was on show. Secondly, I think that spectators realize this and their enjoyment of sporting events is diminished as a result. This is particularly true with the computer technology used in the control of tennis matches, for example. It reduces the human aspect of sport, makes it more mechanical, less entertaining. Human error when making decisions has always added that extra excitement to sport, particularly when there are fiery characters around like John McEnroe, who you mentioned earlier. And finally, the prevailing climate of using technology to run that extra thousandth of a second faster encourages sportsmen and women to bend the rules, or to put it another way, to *cheat*. We see them using technologies which endanger health, such as blood doping, gene doping and all manner of drugs. So …

P: Thank you, Sally, have to stop you there. Time's up, but I think you made your points.

Part 3 💿 3.43

P: Now, let's pick up on one or two of those points you made there. Interestingly, you both mentioned the role of technology in decision-making during football and tennis matches. Sally said it reduces the spectator's enjoyment. Would you agree with that, Geoff?

G: Not at all, no. I'm absolutely certain that the technology only serves to *heighten* interest, to intensify the drama and the tension. And we still see the same displays of passion and anger from players – but they're directed more at themselves rather than at the referee or the umpire.

S: Hmm, it's certainly good for match officials, but I really cannot see that it makes a game more exciting. Anyway, I think there are other reasons why tennis in particular no longer captivates spectators like it used to. And it's all down to technology.

P: In what way?

S: Well, it was always such an exciting sport before, with long rallies that had everyone on the edge of their seats. Then in the late 1970s, early 80s, players began using the oversize racket – the one with the very large head. And sure, tennis became a much faster sport, but there aren't so many of those rallies now, and there's a lot more dead time without any action, time when nothing's happening. And as a spectator, I find that dull.

G: Maybe, but the oversize racket makes it easier to hit the ball, and that can only be a good thing for amateur players – let's not forget *them*.

P: OK. Some interesting points there. Geoff, let's go back to what you said about technology helping us to push out the boundaries of human achievement. Are all forms of technology acceptable in your book?

G: Yes, I think if everyone has access to the same equipment, then virtually *any* technological innovation is acceptable.

S: Oh right. So presumably then, doping is acceptable, as long as everyone has access to it. That's brilliant.

G: I'm not suggesting that at all. That should be obvious. There is no way we can justify the use of performance-enhancing drugs or any kind of interference with our blood or genetic make-up. These practices are not permitted by sporting authorities, and for good reason. There are moral issues involved here, quite apart from the legal aspects and the potential dangers to our health.

P: Yes, you did use the word *equipment*, perhaps we should emphasize that.

G: That's right. And its use *has* to be standardized by the relevant sporting authority. Earlier you mentioned the case of full-length swimsuits. Another example is in the sport of cycling. Radical new designs in the 1980s and 90s meant that previous records were being smashed beyond recognition. The International Cycling Federation felt these so-called 'superbikes' were having too much influence on the sport and their huge cost gave richer countries an unfair advantage. So consequently they were banned from certain competitions such as the Olympics or the world hour record. It just shows that there *are* controls on the use of technology and we should feel safe in that knowledge.

P: Anything to say on that, Sally?

S: Well, I'm pleased the Federation saw sense in the end, but I just think the whole episode highlights the uneasy relationship that exists between sport and technology …

1 | Review

1 Complete the sentences with the correct noun form of the words in the box. You may need to use a negative or plural form of the noun.

> accurate   aware   responsible   urgent   achieve
> adapt   offend   please   satisfy   survive

1 It was a **remarkable** _____, and the record stood for many years.
2 Rainforest destruction is **threatening** the _____ of many endangered species.
3 **It gives me great** _____ **to** announce the winner of this prestigious award.
4 The campaign is intended to **raise** _____ of a number of environmental issues.
5 The law **makes it a criminal** _____ to publish insulting remarks about the President.
6 Food and medical aid are to be sent to the affected area **as a matter of** _____.
7 I am writing to **express my** _____ with the poor service I received recently at your bank.
8 The successful applicant will be required to **carry out** a wide range of _____.
9 Gregory Peck starred in the **film** _____ of Harper Lee's novel *To Kill a Mockingbird*.
10 Part of the editor's job is to **correct** any **factual** _____ which appear in the manuscript.

2 Choose the correct alternative, A, B, or C, to complete the sentences.

1 In her thirties? No, she _____ 40 ages ago.
   A turned   B moved   C came
2 In fact, she must be _____ on for 50 now.
   A reaching   B approaching   C getting
3 I had the jacket _____: the sleeves were too long.
   A adapted   B altered   C amended
4 The money will be _____ to your account at the end of the month.
   A converted   B transformed   C transferred
5 Smith _____ sides and voted against his former party.
   A switched   B adjusted   C varied
6 The painting is expected to fetch _____ of $3 million at auction.
   A more   B over   C upwards
7 _____ two thousand people turned out to demonstrate.
   A Many   B Some   C Any
8 It'll cost you somewhere in the _____ of 50 euros.
   A zone   B region   C district

3 Complete sentences a and b with the same form of the same verb.

   a) I *'m getting* my ears pierced next week.
   b) I think I'll put my jumper on – I *'m getting* a bit cold.

1 a) He _____ horrible to me. Can you tell him to stop it?
   b) Our house _____ renovated, so we've rented a flat for the next two months.
2 a) That _____ to three pounds sixty.
   b) Jeanne's French – she _____ from Lille.
3 a) It _____ up to 6.30 and time for the news.
   b) My sister _____ to stay next weekend.
4 a) I _____ my homework – hope to finish it after the match.
   b) I _____ this job for as long as I can remember.
5 a) I _____ the beds – what shall I do now?
   b) So far this year I _____ five business trips.
6 a) I'll _____ lunch with John tomorrow. We've booked at Marcello's.
   b) This time next week I'll _____ a massage!
7 a) I _____ piano lessons for over a year.
   b) We always _____ fish on Fridays back then.

4 In the following extract from a letter there are ten mistakes in the use of reference and substitution. Correct the mistakes.

> My youngest boy, David, starts school next week. He's a bit nervous about it all, and to tell you the truth, so do I. My other two never seem to worry about anything, and never does their father. David obviously takes after I do in that respect. We know, though, that he's got the same class teacher as a one Paul had two years ago, so there's good. Its name's Miss Appleby. She's a caring person and a very good teacher – at least I think it and I know most of the other parents think too. There's a two-week period of adaptation at the beginning, and it may be that David will come home at midday during then time. If yes, I've arranged for my mum to pick him up and look after him until I finish work.

2 | Review

1 Complete the texts with the words in the boxes. There are more words than you need.

> the same   far   quite   as
> like   a lot   so   such

The town is quite (1) _____ bigger and busier than I remember it. The centre looks much (2) _____ as it always did but there seem to be twice (3) _____ many people walking around and (4) _____ more cars on the roads than when I was last here. It doesn't have (5) _____ a cosy atmosphere and the people don't seem (6) _____ as friendly as they used to be.

> like   near   by far   more
> most   each   every   so

Sarah was (7) _____ the cleverest in our class and, (8) _____ her older sister, went on to study law at university. I was nowhere (9) _____ as intelligent as her but we were quite close during our school years. When I saw her recently, she was (10) _____ bit as friendly as she was then, but she didn't seem quite (11) _____ bubbly or content with her life. She said the (12) _____ she earned, the less time she had for herself and this affected her happiness.

2 Choose the correct alternative to complete the sentences.

1 He's so annoying. I think he *tries / goes / makes* out of his way to irritate me.
2 She's lived there for several years so she knows her way *around / aside / away*.
3 You can't expect to *win / get / do* your own way every time. In fact, sometimes it's wiser to *give / lend / lose* way to the wishes of others.
4 He *earned / promoted / worked* his way up from office clerk to general manager in eight years.
5 I think the photo on page 67 has been printed the *bad / wrong / reverse* way round.
6 Our friendship goes back a *far / big / long* way, to the time when we both worked at Green's.

3 Complete the texts with the missing words.

1 For this game you need an ordinary pack _____ cards. Put the four kings face _____ in the middle so that everyone can see them, but put the rest of the pack face _____.
2 I have a very poor memory _____ facts and figures but I know loads of songs _____ heart, especially those by Abba – they bring _____ memories of my teenage years.
3 The worst thing _____ this government is that it's full of lying politicians. What they promised _____ do before the elections bears very little resemblance _____ what they've actually done since they've been in power.

4 Complete the second sentence so that it has a similar meaning to the first. Use the word given in bold, without changing it in any way.

They made him resign.
forced
He *was forced to resign*.

1 Don't worry about it – it's not worth it.
use
It's _____.
2 I got the impression she didn't believe me.
seemed
She _____.
3 I can't wait to see Sally next week!
forward
I'm really _____.
4 He was a top-class player first, then he became a successful coach.
on
After a top-class playing career, he went _____
_____.
5 It amazes me that you can keep so calm.
ability
I'm amazed at _____.
6 She finds it difficult to pronounce my name.
difficulty
She _____.
7 I ought to get ready – she'll be here soon.
better
I _____
– she'll be here soon.

3 | Review

1 Complete the sentences with appropriate adjectives formed from the words in capitals and the suffixes in the box. You may need to add a negative prefix.

-ory	-ary	-ful	-less	-able
-ial	-ing	-ed	-ious	-ive

1 As a child I had an _____ **friend** called Eric – he was invisible to everyone except me.   IMAGINE
2 The parachute jump was an _____ **experience**, but I don't think I'd do it again.   FORGET
3 A perfectly safe drug? I've heard that all drugs have **potentially** _____ **side-effects**.   HARM
4 We understand the problem but **feel** _____ **to do anything about it**.   POWER
5 The opposition leader **found a** _____ **audience among** students, angered by the government's education policies. RECEIVE
6 It was a **totally** _____ **outcome**: who could have predicted such a result?   EXPECT
7 Her _____ **laugh** had us all in fits of giggles.   INFECT
8 Don't forget to write an _____ **paragraph** and a conclusion.   INTRODUCE
9 _____ **expressions** are a form of non-verbal communication.   FACE
10 Pensioners were hardest hit by the _____ **cost** of energy.   RISE

2 Complete the sentence beginnings 1–7 with the endings a–g.

1 Every year the average family **throws**
2 If you get chest pains or feel **short**
3 In this town we're not so **well-off**
4 He rushed down the stairs, **wolfed**
5 I was always very shy and **lacking**
6 Just lately we've been **bombarded**
7 Wear a plain suit and don't **go**

a **for** parking spaces so you should go by bus.
b **in** confidence, and hated going to parties.
c **of** breath, sit down and rest for a while.
d **with** calls from mobile phone companies.
e **away** one tonne of rubbish.
f **over** the top with the tie – nothing too showy.
g **down** his breakfast and raced out of the house.

3 Work in pairs. Study the sentence endings in exercise 2 for two minutes, then cover them up. Read out the sentence beginnings and try to remember the corresponding ending.

4 Complete the gaps with a word from the box which is commonly used with all three words in the group.

binge	bank	dust	litter	rubbish

1 _____   man   bin   cart
2 _____   tip   skip   collection
3 drop   pick up   take home   _____
4 eating   shopping   drinking   _____
5 bottle   memory   savings   _____

5 Complete the sentences with a word formed with *over*.

1 I've gone _____ at the bank – I have no idea how I'm going to pay it back.
2 The alarm didn't go off so I _____.
3 I thought the film was _____ – too much hype.
4 Of course he's _____: half that salary would still be too much for the job he does.
5 The hotels are _____: renting an apartment offers better value for money.

6 Choose the correct alternatives to complete the text.

… and Simon was there, as well. You know, (1) *it / what / something* annoys me most about that man is his obsession with sport. What (2) *a bore / boring / bored* he is! (3) *Only / All / What* he ever talks about is football, or rugby, or basketball or whatever. And if you (4) *will / do / might* manage to get the conversation on to another topic, he soon brings it back round to sport. Mention a year, like 1968, and he'll say: 'Did you know it was in 1968 (5) *when / who / that* Bob Beamon (6) *broke / did break / could break* the world long jump record?' (7) *What / How / Something* very interesting, Simon – (8) *do / can / not* tell us more …

Anyway, apparently Jenny went on holiday with him for a fortnight. Why anyone (9) *would they / would he / would* want to spend two weeks in the company of Simon, I really don't know. Anyway, what they did was (10) *spending / have spent / spend* the time travelling round Spain watching – you guessed it – major sporting events. They saw football, basketball, athletics …

4 | Review

1 Choose the best alternative, A, B, C or D, to complete the text.

Nellie was (1) _____ to tears. The news that her ex-boyfriend, Barry, had moved in to the village had come (2) _____ a shock and, as she had told her sister, Alice, the thought of him living nearby 'frightened the (3) _____ out of her'. At two metres and 105 kilos, Barry cut an imposing figure and his deep, (4) _____ voice caused many weaker spirits to (5) _____ at the knees. Alice was doing her level best to (6) _____ her sister up, trying to convince her that Barry was not a violent man. 'He's a gentle giant,' she (7) _____, 'he wouldn't hurt a fly.' But Alice had not seen Barry storm out of the room in anger when Nellie had told him she wanted to end their relationship. 'You'll (8) _____ doing this!' he had (9) _____ at her, (10) _____ her of ruining his life.

The phone rang and Nellie jumped. Could this be Barry? She answered it, her voice (11) _____ and barely above a whisper. 'Hello?' Silence. 'Hello, is that you Barry?' 'No, dear, it's me,' squeaked her mother. 'Do I sound (12) _____ Barry?' It was a mixture of tension and relief that caused Nellie first to (13) _____ with laughter then cry her eyes (14) _____.

1	A nearly	B crying	C close	D sad
2	A as	B like	C to	D for
3	A living	B life	C death	D dead
4	A high-pitched	B squeaky	C whining	D booming
5	A moan	B croak	C tremble	D move
6	A animate	B encourage	C light	D cheer
7	A insisted	B persuaded	C agreed	D demanded
8	A forgive	B regret	C apologize	D be sorry
9	A warned	B threatened	C bellowed	D promised
10	A blaming	B criticizing	C telling off	D accusing
11	A movie	B sweetie	C softy	D shaky
12	A as	B so	C like	D of
13	A roar	B snap	C stutter	D blubber
14	A out	B away	C off	D from

2 Complete the second sentence so that it has a similar meaning to the first. Use the word given in bold, without changing it.

1 Perhaps she didn't understand you.
   have
   She _____.

2 I'm sure I wasn't speeding – my car's too old for that.
   been
   I _____
   – my car's too old for that.

3 Why didn't you save a piece of cake for me?
   could
   You _____!

4 It can't be repaired so let's throw it away.
   well
   It can't be repaired so we _____.

5 I was full of energy; I felt like dancing all night.
   could
   I was full of energy; I _____.

6 Unlike you, I don't want to live in a flat.
   might
   You _____.

3 Correct the mistake in each sentence.

1 They complained that the heater was not working and asked for be moved to another room.

2 He apologized for losing my old raincoat and insisted in buying me a new one.

3 The tour company representative advised us against going out on our own at night and suggested us to leave all our valuables in the hotel safe.

4 John's parents refused him to buy a mobile phone, claiming it would damage his health.

5 When my son admitted to steal the computer he had mysteriously 'acquired', I insisted he tell the police.

6 Sykes denied of having any connection with the robbery and demanded to speak to his lawyer.

4 Work in pairs. Discuss with your partner what the original direct speech might have been for each of the sentences in exercise 3.

'Our heater isn't working. Would you please move us to another room?'

5 | Review

1 Complete each business collocation with an appropriate word from the box.

> backing   prototype   business plan
> deal   supplier   idea   logo   return

1 build a _____
2 design a _____
3 obtain a good _____
4 pitch an _____
5 put together a _____
6 secure financial _____
7 source a _____
8 strike a _____

2 Complete the sentences with an appropriate adverb + adjective collocation. More than one adverb may be possible with a particular adjective.

> acutely   fiercely   fully   perfectly
> pitifully   practically   sorely   vehemently

> aware   capable   competitive   disappointed
> embarrassed   impossible   inadequate   opposed

1 Paul was _____ when he heard he hadn't been accepted for the job.
2 It's _____ to find this make of camera now – I know of only one retailer in the whole country that sells it.
3 The opposition leader said the measures were '_____', falling far short of what was needed to address the problem.
4 He gets furious if he loses – he's _____.
5 We have always been _____ to the idea of privatizing the railway system.
6 I don't need your help – I'm _____ of doing it myself, thank you.
7 The transport minister was said to be _____ by revelations that he had committed five traffic offences in the last three years.
8 Many consumers are not _____ of their rights and fail to complain.

3 Correct the mistakes in the sentences.

1 If he'd have said that to me, I don't know what I would have done.
2 If only you would come to the party – you'd have had such a good time. It was great fun.
3 If it hadn't been with that hold-up on the motorway, we'd have been here ages ago.
4 Had he been given that information earlier to her, she might have been able to do something about it.
5 Imagining we'd had to do this without a computer. It would have taken us years!
6 I wish we'd had our camera with us – we'd been able to take some lovely photos.

4 Complete the article with one word in each gap.

Career Woman

THE MAGAZINE FOR
women moving up

Your questions to business entrepreneur, Anne Shears.

Q Can you tell us the reasons (1) _____ you sold your share in (2) _____ was a very successful clothing manufacturing company?

A Basically, I wasn't happy with the way in (3) _____ my business partner, (4) _____ shall remain nameless, was running his side of things. He thought nothing of sourcing suppliers in countries (5) _____ record on human rights is questionable and (6) _____, for textile workers, unhealthy working conditions are the order of the day. Our materials were being produced by an exploited workforce, (7) _____ was both unethical and damaging for the company image. There were one or two occasions (8) _____ my partner deliberately ignored my requests not to do business with certain companies, (9) _____ clearly had an effect on our working relationship. In fact, it got to the point (10) _____ we were barely on speaking terms, something (11) _____ didn't go unnoticed among the rest of the office staff. Then one day he swore at me in front of everyone, at (12) _____ point I decided it was time to leave.

5 Complete the sentence beginnings 1–8 with an appropriate question tag a–h.

1 You'd have told me if he'd phoned,
2 Don't tell Joe what you've just told me,
3 You managed to speak to her then,
4 You couldn't wait to leave school,
5 So you wish you'd never met me,
6 You'd better look for it straight away,
7 You will iron that shirt before we go out,
8 Got a lot of work to do tonight then,

a hadn't you?   e do you?
b have you?   f wouldn't you?
c could you?   g won't you?
d did you?   h will you?

6 Work in pairs. Take turns to read out the sentences with their question tags in exercise 5, paying particular attention to intonation. Respond appropriately to each others' questions.

6 | Review

1 Complete the sentences with the words in the box.

good   well   less   longer

1 My gran's in a home for the elderly – she's very _____ cared for.
2 To be honest I couldn't care _____ who wins the cup.
3 He's been married for _____ than he cares to remember.
4 She takes very _____ care of her fingernails.

2 Complete the phrases with an appropriate part of the body.

1 wisdom _____   5 _____ strain
2 a _____ bleed   6 _____ plugs
3 in bare _____   7 a hooked _____
4 an upset _____   8 help is at _____

3 Form nouns using a verb and a particle from the boxes to complete the collocations.

look   break   turn   burst   pour

out   out   out   through   down

1 a scientific _____
2 a poor _____ for an election
3 a heavy _____ of rain
4 a bleak _____ for the economy
5 a violent _____ of anger

4 Complete the second sentence so that it has a similar meaning to the first.

1 Police think she's living in Argentina.
   She _____.
2 There are allegations that Dee bribed Smith.
   Smith is _____
3 The newspaper claimed Ryan had been dating the supermodel for over a year.
   Ryan _____
4 They believed the gang was planning to kidnap the heiress.
   The gang _____
5 The police raided our flat at the weekend.
   We _____
6 You need to get your hair cut.
   Your hair _____
7 The teacher made me rewrite the essay.
   I was _____

5 Choose the correct alternatives to complete the emails at the bottom of the page.

6 Work in pairs. Discuss how you might reply to each of the emails.

7 Look again at the last of the three emails and mark the intrusive sounds /j/, /r/ and /w/.

   ... up to our tenth wedding anniversary ...
        /w/

8 Work in pairs. Take turns to read the last email aloud.

Our 13-year-old son had his tongue (1) *piercing / pierced / pierces* last month without consulting us first. I (2) *burst / fell / poured* into tears when he showed us – I just don't understand what's wrong with my little boy lately. He seems to enjoy doing rude things just to annoy us: he swears a lot, (3) *fingers / picks / blocks* his nose in public and the other day he let out an enormous (4) *bleep / burp / bump* at the supermarket (5) *checkout / buyout / payout* – it was so embarrassing, but he just burst out (6) *laughs / laughter / laughing*. Now we've been called into school because he's been (7) *bullying / squabbling / rattling* other children. We've always (8) *given / taken / had* great care to give him everything he wanted and this is how he repays us. Can anyone give us any advice? I think I'm heading for a nervous (9) *outbreak / breakout / breakdown*.

Our three-year-old won't go anywhere unless we put her in her (10) *pram / cot / pushchair*. If we tell her she has to walk, she (11) *gives / throws / makes* a huge tantrum. My disciplinarian husband resorts to (12) *smacking / stroking / cuddling* her, but that just makes her scream and (13) *bellow / yell / sigh* more. What can we do?

My wife, Heather, and I are (14) *coming / getting / nearing* up to our tenth wedding anniversary and we plan to go out for a meal in a posh restaurant to (15) *note / mark / place* the occasion. Heather wants our two children, Sophie and Joe, aged four and six, to go as well. How can I get her to understand that this is clearly a bad idea?

7 | Review

1 Rewrite the underlined parts of the text using participle clauses.

A popular television actor convicted of dangerous driving ...

EX-SOAP STAR JAILED

(1) A popular television actor who was convicted of dangerous driving and damage to property was jailed for two years at Carston Crown Court yesterday.

The court heard how (2) John Hope, who is known to television viewers as 'Pricey' in the popular soap Westenders, drove at speeds of over 90mph through Redford town centre last April, (3) and left a trail of destruction. In just ten minutes, (4) Hope, who was said to be depressed at being dropped recently from the long-running television programme, crashed into five parked cars, a bus shelter and a bottle bank. The spree ended when his SUV careered into a butcher's shop window, (5) and caused extensive damage to the property. Hope was taken to hospital (6) because he was suffering from multiple fractures to both his legs. (7) When he was arrested by police, he was alleged to have become aggressive (8) and shouted, 'Don't you idiots know who I am?'

(9) When he was passing sentence, Judge Michael Latham said, 'You put your own life and that of others in serious danger. (10) I have heard the evidence and I have no choice but to send you to prison, where you can reflect on the foolishness of your actions'. (11) Hope's lawyer spoke to journalists after the trial and announced he would be appealing against the sentence.

2 Complete the sentences with the adjectives in the box.

| best   disruptive   foul   lenient   orderly   rowdy   serious |

1 'Right, children, before we go in, I'd like you to **form** a nice, straight, _____ **line**.'
2 The students living next door to us are always **throwing** _____ **parties**. We've had to call the police three times.
3 There's no discipline at my son's school – his class is full of rowdy and _____ **pupils** and the **teachers** are far too _____.
4 'I want you two to be **on your** _____ **behaviour** tonight – no fighting and no _____ **language**, otherwise you'll both be in _____ **trouble**.'

3 Choose the correct alternative, A, B, C or D.

1 After a week-long trial, Hodge was _____ of arson.
   A dropped   B charged   C cleared   D sentenced
2 She was _____ guilty of murder and sentenced to life imprisonment.
   A pleaded   B convicted   C fined   D found
3 The former chief executive is being held on _____ of fraud.
   A arrest   B charge   C suspicion   D trial
4 Henson pleaded guilty to three _____ of burglary.
   A verdicts   B counts   C examples   D convictions
5 He _____ a plea of 'not guilty' to assault.
   A entered   B imposed   C put   D said

4 In the dialogue, cross out any words which can be omitted from the beginning of sentences.

A: Would you like an orange juice?
B: I can't drink it, unfortunately.
A: Why's that? Is there anything the matter?
B: I've got a bad stomach. It hurts when I eat or drink certain things.
A: Have you been to the doctor about it?
B: I'm going next week.
A: It might be an ulcer.
B: I hope not.
A: Is there anything else I can offer you?
B: Have you got any whisky?
A: Are you serious?
B: No, I was just joking!

5 Put the lines in the correct order to make a paragraph.

☐1 I haven't seen the new Harry Burdock film, but I'd certainly like

☐ should about her boss's illegal activities. She decides to go to the police but before she

☐ can to try and find her. Sounds simple, but, of course, nothing ever

☐ will when they've finished. Anyway, if Anne says it's alright then it must

☐ to. She says it's about a secretary who finds out more than she

☐ to. My friend Anne has and she loved it. She asked me to go with her but I

☐ can her boss has her kidnapped. Then Burdock is called in to do all he

☐ couldn't. I've got exams, so I can't see it for a while, but I definitely

☐ be – she thinks Burdock's films are too slow, but apparently this one

☐ is in a Harry Burdock film, is it?

☐ isn't. According to Anne, it's very pacy and nothing ever happens as you expect it

8 | Review

1 Choose the correct alternative and complete the sentences with the words in the box.

easy	hard	high	late
light	loud	short	wide

1 In keeping with his frugal *type / nature*, he has few possessions and always **travels** _____.
2 She has an ambitious *streak / lack*, and tends to **aim** _____ in everything she does.
3 I admire his relaxed *tendency / attitude* to life, and his ability to **take things** _____.
4 She has a real *sense / nature* of fun and you'll often hear her **laughing out** _____.
5 Indignant at the presenter's *attitude / lack* of sensitivity, she abruptly **cut** _____ the interview and stormed out of the studio.
6 She was a conscientious *streak / type*, always at her desk, always **working** _____.
7 He has a *tendency / sense* to leave things to the last minute, and he always **turns up** _____ for appointments and meetings.
8 I'll never forget her bubbly, outgoing *livelihood / nature* and those large _____-**awake** eyes.

2 Complete the headlines with the words in the box.

breakups	family	links
rapport	relations	terms

1 **FORMER COMEDY DUO BACK ON FRIENDLY** _____

2 **WARNING: EXTENDED** _____ **CAN DAMAGE YOUR HEALTH!**

3 **Republic to break off diplomatic** _____ **with neighbour**

4 **MARRIAGE** _____ **AND SEPARATIONS ON THE DECLINE**

5 **DOCTORS TO GET LESSONS ON** _____ **BUILDING WITH PATIENTS**

6 **Region's schools to foster closer** _____ **with local businesses**

3 Complete the sentences using noun phrases formed from the words in brackets. There may be more than one possible answer.

1 Apart from _____ (*five days; holiday*) at the _____ (*end; March*), I've been working flat out this year.
2 We had always considered the _____ (*company; chief executive*) to be a _____ (*great integrity; man*), so his involvement in the _____ (*scandal; corruption*) was a _____ (*shock; source*) to us.
3 The _____ (*referee; decision*) to send off Sedan in _____ (*final; cup; last night*) led to a serious _____ (*violence; outbreak*) between rival supporters.
4 She found her _____ (*ring; wedding; diamond*) in an upturned _____ (*mug; coffee*) in one of the _____ (*cupboards; kitchen*).
5 You should have seen the _____ (*surprise; look*) on _____ (*people; faces*) when he turned up wearing _____ (*women; clothes*) – he'd been told it was a _____ (*party; fancy dress*), but of course, it wasn't.

4 Choose the correct words to complete the blog.

I've just read an article that claims the average American has only two close friends. The writer gives a number of explanations: (1) *actually / for one thing*, he says, people are working longer hours, so they have little time to socialize. And (2) *on top of / above* that there's a growing tendency for people to hide themselves away and go and live in secure, gated communities. (3) *Mind you / After all*, that's probably only if you're rich – I can't imagine that applies to the average American. (4) *Clearly / Actually* though, maybe it does, I'm not sure. And how would I know? (5) *As a rule / After all*, I've never been to America!

(6) *Anyway / By the way*, (7) *sarcastically / ironically* enough, it seems that the growth in communication technology is the biggest culprit. (8) *At least / At last* that's what the article says – all about people communicating through mobile phones, emails and the internet, and friendships lacking depth. (9) *To put it another way / To be honest*, I have my doubts. (10) *Certainly / Surely* it's got more to do with TV? I (11) *mean / want to say*, isn't the reason people don't go out much because they just want to flop in front of the box all evening? (12) *To start with / Besides*, people share some of their deepest thoughts in emails, with people they might not otherwise be able to talk to. In (13) *fact / all honesty*, I regularly write to an old school friend who lives in Australia now and we discuss things I'd find it difficult to talk about face-to-face with my best friend here. (14) *Ultimately / Lastly*, I think the number of friends you have depends on your personality – whether you're outgoing or shy – not on things like working hours or technology.

5 Work in pairs and discuss the views expressed in the blog in exercise 4. Do you agree more with the writer of the blog or the article he read?

9 | Review

1 Choose the correct alternative, A, B, C or D, to complete the advert and the email.

TO RENT: fully (1) _____ one-bedroomed apartment on fifth floor of modern block of flats, conveniently (2) _____ near the town's main shopping centre. All rooms are (3) _____ decorated and the accommodation is in excellent (4) _____. To (5) _____ a viewing, telephone 020 786 50991.

I went to look at that flat we saw (6) _____. It's fairly central and very near the shopping centre, but it's in a really (7) _____, neglected part of town – not sure I could live there. The flat itself wasn't very impressive – nicely decorated but a bit (8) _____ and the (9) _____ were more than a little threadbare. And the building as a whole looked in really urgent (10) _____ of repair – crumbling brickwork, broken drainpipes, patches of damp … I guess I'll just have to keep looking, won't I?

1	A sized	B filled	C reformed	D furnished
2	A put	B stationed	C located	D approached
3	A previously	B formerly	C lately	D newly
4	A way	B condition	C form	D circumstance
5	A arrange	B see	C set	D place
6	A announced	B marketed	C advertised	D rented
7	A well off	B run-down	C out-of-town	D faraway
8	A cosy	B cramped	C tasteful	D brand new
9	A carpets	B tables	C floors	D walls
10	A desire	B state	C necessity	D need

2 Complete the collocations with the nouns in the box.

> activities   collision   critic   exhibits   meal
> place   struggle   suit   superstore   traffic

1 an uphill _____
2 hands-on _____
3 a sit-down _____
4 oncoming _____
5 a head-on _____
6 an outspoken _____
7 an out-of-the-way _____
8 an out-of-town _____
9 an off-the-peg _____
10 indoor and outdoor _____

3 Complete the sentence beginnings 1–8 with the endings a–h, and write one word in each gap to complete the phrasal verbs.

1 I think the new motorway will **bring**
2 Book online and you won't have to **queue**
3 It took us quite a while to **settle**
4 I pity first-time buyers trying to **get**
5 It's much cheaper to buy and **do**
6 The council has promised to **carry**
7 The new property law clearly **spells**
8 The tenant wouldn't leave so we had to **go**

a _____ **our new home** – it was all so different.
b _____ **the courts** to get him out.
c _____ **a study into** homelessness in the city.
d _____ **property values** in the area.
e _____ **an old property** than get something new.
f _____ **the property ladder** – prices are sky high.
g _____ **the rights** of tenants and housebuyers.
h _____ **for tickets**.

4 Complete the sentences with a suitable phrase.

1 It was a marvellous holiday – not since their honeymoon _____ such a good time away together.
2 Never again _____ any money – she still hasn't paid me back what she owes me!
3 Only _____ home did he start to notice any pain.
4 No sooner _____ the house than my two children make it dirty again.
5 On no account _____ your bags unattended in the airport.
6 The spitting image of Brad Pitt. And not only _____ him, he sounds like him, too!
7 At no time _____ for helping her last month – she's so ungrateful!
8 Hardly ever _____ the chance to speak English in my job.

5 Work in pairs. Discuss how you would complete each sentence.

1 When I was in my teens, I would often _____.
2 _____ is so irritating. He/She will keep _____.
3 In the next general election I think the government will _____.
4 I used to think I would one day _____.
5 I wouldn't _____ if I were you.
6 I wouldn't care if I never _____.

10 | Review

1 Complete the sentences with one word in each gap.

1. John's hard work paid _____ and he did very well: mine came _____ nothing and I'll have to resit **it**.
2. Jackson stood a real _____ of winning **it**, but then _____ to grief at the sixteenth hole, where he _____ a mess of his first shot.
3. Things didn't work _____ as well as expected: the plans to expand in Asia fell _____, investors pulled out and **it** eventually _____ bankrupt.
4. It's a bit of a _____ cause, I'm afraid. I've washed **it** several times but it just doesn't do _____ good – the stain won't come out.
5. **It** is currently riding _____ in the charts and looks set to make _____ to number one.
6. Far from being the overnight _____ critics had predicted, **it** flopped at the _____ office and lost millions.
7. When **it** came out I felt an enormous _____ of achievement: I had finally _____ my ambition of getting something published and at last things were turning _____ well for me.
8. If you're an _____ -and-coming singer who wants to get _____ in the music business, here **it** is – the chance of a lifetime!

2 Work in pairs. Discuss what **it** might refer to in each sentence in exercise 1.

3 Complete the sentence beginnings 1–8 with the endings a–h.

1. Not surprisingly, the government has **come in**
2. No more tinned food – I'm going to **sign up**
3. When I was about eleven or twelve I **went in**
4. Their plans to build a house in Spain **came up**
5. The new legislation is designed to **crack down**
6. They had to move – they just couldn't **put up**
7. It really is so expensive – they're **getting away**
8. A self-made man, Relf **puts his success down**

a. **for a competition** and won a trip to Paris.
b. **with daylight robbery!**
c. **on juvenile crime** and delinquency.
d. **for criticism** over its handling of the crisis.
e. **to** hard work and persistence.
f. **with the constant noise** of the motorway.
g. **for a cookery course**!
h. **against a few problems** and they had to abandon the idea.

4 Work in pairs. Cover up the endings a–h in exercise 3 and see how many you can remember.

5 Choose the correct alternative to complete the sentences. Either one or two alternatives are possible.

1. I *mustn't / didn't have to / couldn't* get my nose pierced until I was eighteen – my dad wouldn't let me.
2. I was always told I *mustn't / shouldn't / needn't* speak with my mouth full. They said it was bad manners.
3. It was very kind of you, but you really *mustn't / shouldn't / needn't* have gone to all that trouble.
4. She *must / need / should* have finished by now – she started over two hours ago.
5. The lesson *must / had to / should have* started at six o'clock, but the previous class overran by fifteen minutes.
6. It's alright, you *oughtn't to / didn't need to / needn't have* come – we managed perfectly well without you.
7. Sorry I'm late – I *needed to go / had to go / must have gone* to the bank.
8. I said she *must be / must have been / should have been* mad to go out with a man like that.
9. What do I *need / have / ought* to do to convince her I love her?
10. It's Elisa's birthday on Saturday – I really *must / need / should* buy something for her.

6 Find ten mistakes in the email and correct them.

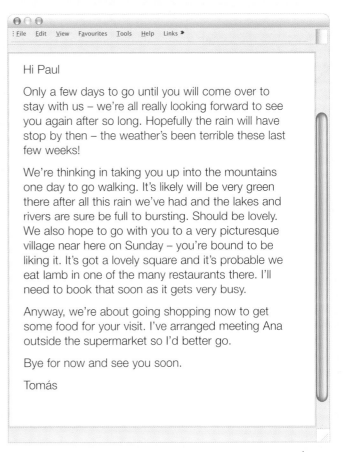

File   Edit   View   Favourites   Tools   Help   Links »

Hi Paul

Only a few days to go until you will come over to stay with us – we're all really looking forward to see you again after so long. Hopefully the rain will have stop by then – the weather's been terrible these last few weeks!

We're thinking in taking you up into the mountains one day to go walking. It's likely will be very green there after all this rain we've had and the lakes and rivers are sure be full to bursting. Should be lovely. We also hope to go with you to a very picturesque village near here on Sunday – you're bound to be liking it. It's got a lovely square and it's probable we eat lamb in one of the many restaurants there. I'll need to book that soon as it gets very busy.

Anyway, we're about going shopping now to get some food for your visit. I've arranged meeting Ana outside the supermarket so I'd better go.

Bye for now and see you soon.

Tomás

11 | Review

1 Correct the two mistakes in each sentence.

1 I'm sure all of we would like to wish you every successes in your new career, John.

2 Neither my parents has any brothers or sisters so, of course, I have no any cousins either.

3 The campsite is plenty of space for children to run and play in, and each of the caravans are equipped with a number of toys and games.

4 Let's wait another few minutes – most of trains are running a little late today and he's bound to get here some times soon.

5 I still write to several of the people I studied with at university, but quite few of us live abroad now so we don't get to see each another on a regular basis.

6 For all that his attention to detail, Jackson's biography contains more than a few factual inaccuracies, many of the which might have been spotted by a more alert editor.

7 We used to have quite a lot of brandy glasses, but we seem to have just a couple of now. I found one in the kitchen and there's other in the sideboard – have you seen any more?

8 When asked for the secret of her long life she said she drank a very little alcohol, smoked one cigarette every other days, ate plenty of vegetables and as much fruit as possible.

2 Complete the sentences with a suitable word or phrase.

1 I wish _____ tapping your foot – it's really irritating.

2 If only I _____ the piano like her.

3 I _____ for their sake they get here soon – it'd be a shame if _____ the firework display.

4 It is not clear who would succeed him, _____ he to resign.

5 Phone me at home if you have to – although I _____ didn't.

6 It's high _____ how to cook – you can't keep eating tinned food all the time!

7 I do all the cleaning – if _____ for me, this house _____ a complete mess.

8 Imagine _____ no cars on the roads. Difficult, I know, but _____ be wonderful?

3 Choose the best alternative, A, B or C, to complete the text.

Billy sat at the back of the class and (1) _____ into space. His mind was (2) _____. He imagined he was (3) _____ admiringly into Sharon Whiting's (4) _____ blue eyes. She (5) _____ her hair back and (6) _____ her eyelids. 'Come here, Billy,' she whispered. Billy (7) _____ softly to himself. As if to echo this, his stomach gave a faint (8) _____. He was hungry. He (9) _____ quickly at his watch: another half an hour to go until lunchtime. Then he remembered his crisps. He dug into his jacket pocket and felt for them. The bag (10) _____ so loudly he might just as well have (11) _____ a drum and shouted his intention to eat them. Then the bell (12) _____, signalling the end of the lesson – and the beginning of lunch. His watch had obviously stopped. 'Come here, Billy,' he heard his teacher say.

1	A browsed	B viewed	C stared
2	A wandering	B wounding	C winding
3	A gazing	B glancing	C glimpsing
4	A jingling	B clinking	C sparkling
5	A blushed	B tossed	C trussed
6	A fluttered	B muttered	C stuttered
7	A bellowed	B sighed	C shrieked
8	A rumble	B sizzle	C clatter
9	A searched	B gazed	C glanced
10	A rustled	B hummed	C creaked
11	A popped	B banged	C crashed
12	A timed	B went	C clicked

4 Complete the sentences with the prepositions in the box. You need to use each preposition more than once.

at in on off by out of

1 The earthquake had left the town _____ ruins: many of the buildings still standing were _____ fire and _____ danger of collapse.

2 He is _____ nature a very relaxed person with an ability to make people feel _____ ease in his company.

3 PC Jacobs had just come _____ duty when he and his girlfriend, Pat Stones, were robbed _____ knifepoint. Stones has since been _____ work suffering from anxiety and panic attacks.

4 She appeared at my house _____ breath and _____ tears. Apparently, she had closed her front door _____ mistake and locked herself out.

5 'The machinery is _____ date and workers' lives are constantly _____ risk,' said one defiant employee. 'That is why we are _____ strike.'

6 Her boat was blown _____ course towards the island, which is _____ limits to all but military personnel.

12 | Review

1 Complete the sentences with the correct form of the verbs in the box.

> come   do   get   let   run   tell

1 'Does your brother speak French?' 'He can hardly speak English, _____ **alone** a foreign language!'
2 'My stomach hurts.' 'I'm not surprised. **That's what** _____ **of** eating too much too quickly.'
3 'Is that Amy or Emily?' '**It's difficult to** _____: they both look so much alike.'
4 'Who won the election?' 'Brown, by a handful of votes. It was **a** very **close** _____ **thing**.'
5 'You went cycling in Italy this summer, didn't you? How far south did you _____?' 'Not very far – we only _____ about forty kilometres a day.'

2 Complete the text with the correct form of the words in brackets. The answer to numbers 5 and 6 is the same.

The Red List

The International Union for Conservation of Nature (IUCN) Red List provides objective, scientifically-based information on those animals, birds and plants that have been (1) _____ (*identity*) as being (2) _____ (*threat*) with extinction, with the aim of promoting their conservation. The list (3) _____ (*category*) species according to the degree of risk they face, (4) _____ (*difference*) between those which are Critically (5) _____ (*danger*), (6) _____ (*danger*) and Vulnerable. Those species which do not qualify for any of these categories and have been (7) _____ (*value*) to have a low risk of extinction are (8) _____ (*class*) as Least Concern. The IUCN's website contains tables (9) _____ (*summary*) the information on their database, and the search engine (10) _____ (*able*) anyone to find out the current status of any species which is on the list.

3 Complete the gaps with verbs formed from a particle in box A and a verb in box B. Use each particle twice.

A

> down   out   over   under

B

> charge   come   go   load   number
> play   take   weigh

1 I don't often buy CDs – I usually _____ my music from the internet.
2 He had to _____ an operation on his right knee.
3 They managed to _____ these problems and now the marriage is a huge success.
4 There are 43 men in a staff of 51, so they far _____ the women.
5 New consultants tend to _____ for their services, in the mistaken belief that a low fee will attract more business.
6 Common sense tells you that you shouldn't _____ another car on a zebra crossing.
7 Critics of the scheme claim that the costs _____ the benefits.
8 The government has pressured scientists to _____ the threat of global warming, to deny what we all know to be true.

4 Each sentence contains two incorrect plural forms. Find the mistakes and correct them.

1 I bought half a kilo of kiwis and three kiloes of tomatos.
2 And the two young ladys in these photos are my daughters-in-law: one works in a supermarket filling shelves and the other buys and sells work of arts.
3 Put your hats, coats and scarfs over there then come in and make yourselfs comfortable – I'll just go and get some knifes for the cheese.
4 The royal wedding was attended by heads of state from nineteen different country's together with their husbands, wives and in some casies, children.
5 You'll find all the different chemical formula in one of the appendices at the back of the book on pages two hundreds and fifty to sixty nine inclusive.

5 Complete the sentences with one word in each gap.

1 The people of this country _____ growing tired of the police and _____ aggressive tactics.
2 My pyjama trousers _____ a little too long. Could you shorten _____ for me, please?
3 The news _____ not good, and I don't think _____ will get any better.
4 I see the unemployed _____ moaning about the minimum benefit again, but 190 euros _____ a lot of money not so long ago.
5 The government _____ not doing what _____ promised to do.

Macmillan Education
4 Crinan Street, London N1 9XW
A division of Macmillan Publishers Limited

Companies and representatives throughout the world

ISBN 978-0-230-42344-2 Student's Book
ISBN 978-0-230-42449-4 Student's Book & website access

This edition designed by eMC Design Limited
Original design by Oliver Design
Illustrated by Carlos Araujo (The Organisation) p108tr; Rowan Barnes-Murphy
(illustrationOnLine.com), pp76, 134, 155; Fred Blunt (Beehive Illustration) pp48, 63,
88; Annie Boberg (The Organisation) pp143, 149; Ray & Corinne Burrows pp142r,
148; Anne Cakebread (The Art Market) pp102, 139, 142l, 146, 151, 152r, 153; John
Dillow (Beehive Illustration) p108tl; Mark Duffin pp108cl, 152l; Graham Evernden
(The Organisation) p108tc; Joanna Kerr (Meiklejohn Illustration) p98; David
McConochie p132; Sarah Nayler (NB Illustration) pp39, 62, 78; Mark Ruffle p167
Cover design by eMC Design Limited
Cover photograph by Alamy/Images & Stories (main); Getty Images/Doug
Chinnery; Alamy/Robert Harding Picture Library Ltd; Corbis/Roger Tidman;
Corbis/Lois Ellen Frank; Corbis/Gerolf Kalt
Picture research by Sally Cole

Author's acknowledgements
I would particularly like to thank Amanda Jefferies for her work on the writing
sections, by brother, Graham Norris, for his help with research, Mike Curtis for
his scientific advice, Paco Barba and Eli Ortiz for their technological expertise,
my wife, Azucena, and daughters, Lara and Elisa, for their continued support and
understanding.

A big thank you, too, to all the students at International House, Madrid, who
tried out the material and gave invaluable feedback, especially Beatriz Almodóvar
González, Alejandro Arnáez Barrio, Marta Elvira Muñoz, Jesús Estrada Royo,
Laura Gómez Alonso, Luis Jurado Jiménez, José Antonio Leiva Izquierdo, Maria
Ángeles Mañas Lázaro, Anna Matinyan, Cristina Moreno de Barreda, Fernando
Moreno Velasco, Rubén Naranjo Izquierdo, Daniel Pablo Barbero, Rufi Pena
Carreiras, Carlos Pérez Roca, Javier Rodríquez de los Santos, Esther Sánchez
Gómez, Ana Segura Romero, Sonia del Val González and Miguel Wert Ortega.

I would also like to thank everyone at Macmillan who was involved in the project,
and the freelance editors, Nicola Gardner, Jo Kent and Louise Fonceca.

The publishers would like to thank all the teachers from around the world who
provided invaluable comments, suggestions and feedback on the second edition.

The author(s) and publishers are grateful for permission to reprint the following
copyright material:
Page 21: Extract from 'The Rise of the Bicycle' copyright © Dennis Publishing 2005,
first published in *The Week* on 21.05.05, reprinted by permission of the publisher;
Page 17: Extract from 'Never forget facts and figures', by Dominic O'Brien
copyright © Dominic O'Brien 2003, reprinted by permission of the publisher; Page
111: Material from 'If these walls could talk, they would whisper' by Oli Usher
copyright © Oli Usher 2005, first published in *The Guardian* 11.08.05, reprinted by
permission of the publisher; Page 27: Material from 'Enough: Breaking free from
the world of excess' by John Naish, copyright © John Naish 2008; Page 101 and
138: Material from 'The Cloudspotter's Guide' by Gavin Pretor-Pinney, copyright ©
Gavin Pretor-Pinney 2006; Page 17: Material from 'Drugs to boost brain power
will become 'common as coffee'' by Steve Connor copyright © Steve Connor
2005, first published in *The Independent* on 14.07.05, reprinted by permission of
the publisher; Page 17: Material from 'Food for Thought' by Kate Watson
Smythe © Kate Watson Smythe 2005, first published in *The Independent*
31.05.05, reprinted by permission of the publisher; Page 31: Material from 'Me
and my big mouth' by Andrew Buncombe copyright © Andrew Buncombe 2006,
first published in *The Independent* 17.06.06, reprinted by permission of the
publisher; Page 47: Material from 'Ingvar' by Christian Sylt copyright © Christian
Sylt 2005, first published in *The Independent* 13.02.05, reprinted by permission
of the publisher; Page 51: Material from 'A woman's work is never done' by Lena
Corner copyright © Lena Corner 2002, first published in *The Independent* 14.01.02,

reprinted by permission of the publisher; Page 91: Material from 'Want to save the
planet? Pick up your towels' by Helen Truszowski copyright © Helen Truszowski
2005, first published in *The Independent* 16.01.05, reprinted by permission of the
publisher; Page 67: Extract from 'Ahead of the Class' by Marie Stubbs copyright ©
Marie Stubbs 2003; Page 119: Extracts from 'The State of the Art' by Iain M Banks,
copyright © Iain M Banks 1993, reprinted by permission of Mic Cheetham Literary
Agency; London; Page 81: Material from 'End of the friendship' by Jane Munro
copyright © Jane Munro 2006, first published in *The Times* on 04.03.06; Page
102: Material from 'Best of Times Worst of Times' by David Rendall, copyright
© David Rendell 2006, first published in *The Sunday Times* 24.07.05, reprinted
by permission of the publisher; Page 71: Extracts from 'A Dark Devotion' by
Claire Francis copyright © Claire Francis 1997, reprinted by permission of Pan
Macmillan and Johnson & Alcock Limited; Page 61: 143 and 149: Extracts from
'Welcome to Sarajevo/Natasha's Story' by Michael Nicholson copyright © Michael
Nicholson 1997, reprinted by permission of Pan Macmillan; Page 61: Extracts from
'Natasha's Story' by Michael Nicholson, copyright © Michael Nicholson, reprinted
by permission of Peters Fraser & Dunlop (www.petersfraserdunlop.com) on
behalf of Michael Nicholson; Page 77: Extract from 'Felicia's Journey', by William
Trevor copyright © William Trevor 1995, reprinted by permission of Penguin
Books and Johnson & Alcock Limited; Page 87: Extracts from 'The Architecture
of Happiness' pp 139–145 by Alain de Botton copyright © Alain de Botton 2006,
reprinted by permission of Penguin Books and United Agents; Page 7: Unadapted
material from 'The Rough Guide to Climate Change' by Robert Henson, copyright
© Robert Henson 2011, reprinted by permission of the publisher; Page 7: Material
from 'Career change: Adman-househusband-entrepreneur' by Sally Williams
copyright © Sally Williams 2008, first published in The Daily Telegraph 30.12.08,
reprinted by permission of the publisher; Page 32 and Audioscript: Material from
'The Tiny Pacific Island that went from riches to rags' by Rob Crossan copyright
© Rob Crossan 2005, first published in *The Daily Telegraph* 19.11.05, reprinted
by permission of the publisher; Page 41: Material from 'Nicholas Mosley: "The
King's Speech therapist gave me hope, too"' by Elizabeth Grice, copyright ©
Elizabeth Grice 2011, first published in *The Daily Telegraph* 03.02.11, reprinted
by permission of the publisher; Page 97: Material from 'Man on Wire: the poet of
the sky' by Murphy Williams, copyright Murphy Williams 2008, first published in
The Daily Telegraph 23.07.08, reprinted by permission of the publisher; Page 77:
Extract from 'A Spanish Lover' by Joanna Trollope copyright © Joanna Trollope
1993, reprinted by permission of the publisher; Page 108: Will Ramsey Interview;
Nick Sheard/Paddy Radcliffe Interview used with permission; Interview with
Dominic O'Brien used with kind permission.

The authors and publishers would like to thank the following for permission to
reproduce their photographs:
AFP pp29(tl), 32-33, 96(tr), 120(tr), 120(tcl), 123(trophy); **Age UK**/Frederic
Courbet/HelpAge International 2012 p13(cl); **Alamy**/R.Abboud p73, Alamy/BL
Images Ltd p106(b), Alamy/Bubbles Photolibrary p72(c), Alamy/Catchlight Visual
Services p150(cr), Alamy/Alamy Celebrity p43, Alamy/A.Cooper p106(tr), Alamy/
Cultura Creative p8(b), Alamy/C.Elia p89(br), Alamy/Enrem Images p144(tl),
Alamy/E.Ereza p11(B), Alamy/Fancy p144(cl), Alamy/Corbis Flirt p72(A), Alamy/
Beyond Fotomedia GmbH p72(B),Alamy/Foodfolio p90, Alamy/J.Fox p29(cr),
Alamy/Gallo Images p12(tl), Alamy/S.Grant p52(tr), Alamy/D.Grossman p150(cl),
Alamy/Hemis p22(D), Alamy/D.Houghton p88(c), Alamy/Kuttig-Travel-2 p22(E),
Alamy/Images of Africa Photobank p28(tr), Alamy/Imagebroker pp42(bl),
144(tr), Alamy/Image Pix p116(c), Alamy/Itanistock p150(tl), Alamy/Itar-Tass
Photo Agency p60(tr), Alamy/M.Kemp p136, Alamy/P.Lane p165, Alamy/I.
Masterton p47(t), Alamy/D.Matthews p123(puzzle), Alamy/Moodboard p72(E),
Alamy/C.Pancewicz p71, Alamy/Photoedit p13(cr), Alamy/Phototake Inc p38(bl),
Alamy/Radius Images p37(b), Alamy/Real Image p92(inset l), Alamy/Margaret S.
p144(cr), Alamy/A.Segre p47(tr), Alamy/SFL Travel p68(bl), Alamy/P.Solloway
p42, Alamy/Stock4B GmbH p150(tr), Alamy/C.Strover p22(B), Alamy/J.Sullivan
p28(tl), Alamy/M.Taylor p91(tcr), Alamy/Tetra Images p116(tl), Alamy/Transtock
Inc p20(tr), Alamy/Armand-Photo Travel p91(tl), Alamy/Art Directors & Trip
p91(tc), Alamy/K.Olga Underwater p91, Alamy/Westend61 GmbH p56, Alamy/D.
White p68(bc), **Apic** p7(tr); **Archive Photos** pp50, 87; **Bananastock** p11(A);
Beehive Illustrations/J.Dillow p108(tl); **Bettmann Archive** p79(cr); **Corbis**
p21(tr), Corbis/U.Ryd/Ansa p47(cl), Corbis/Atlantide Phototravel p93(inset),
Corbis/W.Burgess p22(c), Corbis/C.Cazalis p29(cl), Corbis/T.Chang p148, Corbis/
L&J. Jacobs/Cultura p12(br), Corbis/Duomo p123(winner), Corbis/M.Haegele
p11(E), Corbis/P.Frilet/Hemis p91(tr), Corbis/ G.Irving p123(end), Corbis/Jetta
Productions/Blend Images p128, Corbis/F.Krahmer p123(sunset), Corbis/D.Linder
p123(plane), Corbis/C.Lovell p21(bl), Corbis/R.DeMartin p116(main b), Corbis/
M.Moellenberg p57(tl), Corbis/Ocean pp108(cl), 118, Corbis/A.Chederros/Onoky
p36, Corbis/ T.Pannell p113, Corbis/A.Peisl p123(wave), Corbis/J.L Pelaez/
Blend Images p123(graduate), Corbis/J.Reed Photography p101(c), Corbis/
Reuters p28(cl), Corbis/M.Riley p30, Corbis/P.Simcock/ Blend Images p11(D),
Corbis/P.Souders p6(tr), Corbis/S.Westmorland p146(br); **Corbis RF** pp12(tr),
52(br); **Duncan Baird Publishers**.Used by permission. Never Forget Facts and
Figures by Dominic O'Brien(Duncan Baird Publishers,London 2003) p17(cl);